McGRAW-HILL SERIES IN FINANCE

Professor Charles A. D'Ambrosio
University of Washington
Consulting Editor

Christy and Clendenin Introduction to Investments
Committe Managerial Finance for the Seventies
Curran Principles of Financial Management
Dobrovolsky The Economics of Corporation Finance
Francis Investments: Analysis and Management
Haley and Schall The Theory of Financial Decisions
Hastings and Mietus Personal Finance
Robinson and Wrightsman Financial Markets: The Accumulation and Allocation of Wealth
Sharpe Portfolio Theory and Capital Markets
Troelstrup The Consumer in American Society: Personal and Family Finance

Financial Markets:
The Accumulation and
Allocation of Wealth

Financial Markets: The Accumulation and Allocation of Wealth

Roland I. Robinson
Michigan State University

Dwayne Wrightsman
University of New Hampshire

McGraw-Hill Book Company

New York
St. Louis
San Francisco
Düsseldorf
Johannesburg
Kuala Lumpur
London
Mexico
Montreal
New Delhi
Panama
Paris
São Paulo
Singapore
Sydney
Tokyo
Toronto

Library of Congress Cataloging in Publication Data

Robinson, Roland I
    Financial markets.

    (McGraw-Hill series in finance)
    Bibliography: p.
    1. Finance—United States. I. Wrightsman,
Dwayne, joint author. II. Title.
HG181.R589   332.4   73-17218
ISBN 0-07-053273-7

Financial Markets: The Accumulation and Allocation of Wealth

Copyright © 1974 by McGraw-Hill, Inc.
All rights reserved.
Formerly published under the title of MONEY AND CAPITAL MARKETS
copyright © 1964 by McGraw-Hill, Inc. All rights reserved.
Printed in the United States of America.
No part of this publication may be reproduced, stored in a retrieval system,
or transmitted, in any form or by any means, electronic, mechanical, photocopying,
recording, or otherwise, without the prior written permission of the publisher.

    34567890KPKP798765

This book was set in Times Roman by Black Dot, Inc.
The editors were Jack R. Crutchfield, Renée E. Beach,
and Richard S. Laufer;
the designer was Anne Canevari Green;
and the production supervisor was Sam Ratkewitch.
The drawings were done by ANCO Technical Services.
Kingsport Press, Inc., was printer and binder.

Contents

Preface   vii

PART I   THE ECONOMIC LOGIC OF FINANCIAL MARKETS

1. Markets in General; Financial Markets in Particular   3
2. Economic Determinants of Saving and Investment   20
3. Financial Institutions: Intermediaries between Savers and Investors   37
4. Flow of Funds in Financial Markets   58
5. Portfolio Selection and Security Pricing   80
6. Structure and Behavior of Interest Rates   101

PART II   MONEY MARKETS

7. Money Markets: A General Introduction   127
8. Money-Market Instruments, Intermediaries, and Rates   146
9. Commercial Banks in the Money Markets   162
10. The Federal Reserve: Evolution of Economic Goals, Monetary Instruments, and Operating Criteria   181
11. Federal Reserve Operations   196
12. The International Monetary System in Turmoil and Transition   210

PART III   CAPITAL MARKETS

13. A Capital Market Overview   225
14. The Market for U.S. Government Securities   240
15. The Market for State and Local Government Securities   259
16. The Mortgage Market   277
17. The Market for Corporate Debt   306
18. Markets for Corporate Equities   328

PART IV   EVALUATION OF FINANCIAL MARKET PERFORMANCE

19. Financial Markets and Economic Stability   367
20. Financial Markets and Economic Progress   381
21. Efficiency, Equity, and Safety   398

Bibliography   419
Index   431

Preface

This book began as an ordinary revision of the senior author's *Money and Capital Markets* (1964). With the long passage of time between editions, however, and the rapid development of new ideas, information, and institutions, a great deal of new and original work was required. Two differences between this and the earlier work are reflected in the changing of the title to *Financial Markets: The Accumulation and Allocation of Wealth*. The new main title recognizes that the similarities between money markets and capital markets are more important than their differences. The subtitle emphasizes the twin functions of financial markets: to provide a link between saving and investment for the creation of new wealth and to permit portfolio adjustments in the composition of existing wealth. This latter function is treated much more extensively and analytically in this book than in the earlier version thanks to the recent development of modern portfolio theory. Chapter 5 on portfolio selection and security pricing is completely new.

Another feature of this book is a greatly expanded section (six chapters, most of which are new) on money markets. The liquidity adjustment function of these markets is explained relative to the needs of the different sectors in the economy. Relatively new methods of liquidity management by commercial banks, including such sources of funds as negotiable certificates of deposit (NCDs) and Eurodollars, are described and analyzed. Also included in this section is a discussion of new dimensions in the guidance of open money-market operations by the central bank. Reserves to support private deposits (RPDs) are given special attention as the newest and apparently leading guide to open-market policy.

Another change is a greater integration throughout the book of the much improved flow-of-funds data provided by the Federal Reserve. The data are explained early in the book and used in later sections to provide some quantitative dimensions of the markets. Finally, the book concludes with an almost wholly new section evaluating the performance of financial markets in the economy. This section considers the performance criteria of efficiency, equity, stability, and progress.

Expositionally, the book follows the same mold as its predecessor. It is written for upper-level undergraduates who have had some exposure to economics. It strives for a balance of description and analysis. The analysis is intended to convey a maximum of understanding with a mimimum of technical or formal apparatus. An effort has been made to be as consistent as possible in the usage of language. It was not possible, however, to be invariate in practice. Words such as "investment," "capital," and "money" are used in different places of the book with different meanings. Such words will have to be interpreted according to the context within which they are used. This is an ancient problem, and we do not expect to solve it; the most we can hope to do is reduce the uncertainty. We hope to minimize this problem with an unusually comprehensive index, enriched with many definitions of terms and acronyms. The chapters can now be assigned in any order with assurance that the student will have ready access to the necessary support materials.

In the earlier edition, teachers were encouraged to use many outside materials to supplement the teaching of money markets. As a result, the money-market section of the prior edition was incomplete. In this edition, the section can be considered complete and can be used without supplements. However, all conscientious teachers are urged to continue to use as much outside material as possible. Many sources are listed in the bibliography. The *Federal Reserve Bulletin* and the monthly bulletins of the Federal Reserve banks, particularly that of New York, are excellent sources of current analyses of financial markets. Teachers will constantly encounter the problem of dealing with text citations or magnitudes that are out of date. Student projects which not only update the text data but also require short-term forecasts can help to overcome this gap and provide students with the useful exercise of working with source materials.

A textbook with so many factual references cannot possibly appear without a few errors. No matter how diligent the search, some mistakes will inevitably elude the critics, editors, and others who deal with this material in the publication process. Readers are urged to call any detected errors to the attention of the authors; we shall be grateful for this service to us and other users of the book. An early reprinting of the first edition benefited from a number of comments, and we will welcome similar help this time.

Roland I. Robinson
Dwayne Wrightsman

Part One

The Economic Logic of Financial Markets

Chapter 1

Markets in General; Financial Markets in Particular

Economic freedom leads to the development of markets. Consumers are free to buy the goods they want; they seek the product they want in the market of their choice. Workers can sell their services in the most advantageous market. Producers are free to buy their raw materials where they will and, though possibly not as free as consumers, are relatively free to hire the needed workers in the most advantageous markets.

Indeed, the price agreed upon by buyers and sellers—the crucial point to most market transactions—performs an economic service of great significance. Market prices and market popularity (or lack of it) guide production. By guiding production, market prices determine the use made of economic resources. Market prices also have an important bearing on the way in which income is distributed. Those who win a majority of the ballots of the market get high rewards; those who do not, feel an income pinch.

Financial markets are the result of financial freedom and can survive only when freedom prevails. Individuals are free to save or spend their incomes as they choose. If they spend their incomes, the proceeds flow through commodity markets. If they save, they may put the funds to work directly in some form of real productive capital. Most savers, however, do not have the means for doing so. As a result, a large fraction of individual saving is channeled through the financial markets. The parallel aspect is that individuals and groups formed into business corporations are free to operate productive economic enterprises from which they hope to realize a profit. Both business and individuals frequently need to find outside sources of financial capital to aid them in their enterprises.

The price in financial markets is rather special: It is a money price on the use of money (a ratio) which is quoted as an interest rate. In reality, many types of interest rates exist, and many thousands of individual interest rates are embodied in debt contracts. This price is a cost to the borrower and income to the lender.

Stated in these terms, financial markets perform simple and fully understandable functions. In practice, however, the significant economic contributions of these markets have not always been fully appreciated. Possibly because of the intangible nature of their operations, they are mistrusted by people who feel quite at home in commodity market dealings; yet it can be argued that almost every characteristic of financial market operations has a close parallel in some commodity market characteristic. Perhaps it would be instructive to start with commodity markets and move from them into a closer examination of financial markets.

The role of markets is easily observed and understood when dealing with a simple commodity such as potatoes. The ease with which housewives can prepare potatoes and the gusto with which potatoes are eaten have great influence on the market. A moment's thought also shows that speaking of "the market for potatoes" in the singular is far too simple. Various kinds of potatoes are grown; some sell much better than others, and preferences vary from place to place. Red-skinned potatoes sell well in one section of the country but are disdained in other areas. For this reason separate markets exist for various kinds of potatoes.

Since potatoes are a rather bulky commodity and cost a fair amount to ship, the markets are more local than national. But potatoes can be shipped nationally, so it can be said that a national market exists. The national market handles enough traffic to keep prices in various areas from getting too far out of line with national averages. Indeed, there is a modest international market in potatoes.

Still one more point is worth observing. Although potatoes will store reasonably well for one season, unprocessed ones will not last any longer than that. The supply of potatoes varies according to the amount produced in any given year. For this reason, supplies and prices fluctuate greatly from year to year depending on acreage and growing conditions. However, new technology by which potatoes may be flaked and stored may change this circumstance in some measure. Prices of storable commodities are not as unstable as those of perishable goods.

A full investigation of the potato market would require a look into demand characteristics. Is potato consumption quite sensitive to price (an elastic demand), or is price a weak deterrent to someone about to take a second helping of mashed potatoes (an inelastic demand)? The second presumption is commonly accepted; but some uses of potatoes (as for making starch) do depend very much on price.

Other markets have quite different characteristics. The market for real estate includes many kinds of properties: homes, stores, office buildings, factories, farmlands, lake frontage, and plain unimproved land. Buildings can be erected and land can be modified (lake fronts) and improved (farm lands), but the basic supply of land is very nearly fixed. The amount of land that can be "produced" is negligible. Thus the study of the market for unimproved land depends on a close study of demand characteristics: What is unimproved land used for, and what income does each use yield? What proportion of unimproved land is adaptable to various uses? What is the income cost of carrying such unused land until a demand for its active use emerges?

By now the point should have become reasonably clear: ==The characteristics of markets vary greatly. Some markets are interesting largely because of special supply conditions and some have special demand characteristics that explain their behavior; some markets are national, some are local; some markets have characteristics that lead to price stability, some do not.==

The automobile market has many interesting facets. A limited number of national producers establish list prices. These prices, however, are greatly modified by local bargaining, including trade-in practices. A dealer is influenced by his inventory, his quotas, and in the end the individual salesman may have some final influence on the price by negotiation of his own commission on each deal. New and used cars each have separate markets, though the prices in one area react on prices in the other. Used-car prices are not nationally set but reflect a complex of demand factors.

The market for rare art goods presents many fascinating aspects. The price of French impressionist paintings has increased very rapidly. Some stock market speculators bought these paintings not for aesthetic considerations but solely in anticipation of price appreciation. The boom even extended to other schools of painting, such as abstract expressionism. Untutored investors were touring art galleries trying to find unnoticed bargains. It is worth noting that an outside influence—the conviction that secular inflation was inevitable—spurred a great deal of this unusual but still very significant rush.

Markets are sometimes subject to irrational whims or at least to whims that prove in retrospect to have been irrational. However, the rationality of investors should be questioned rather hesitantly. People who have accumulated money generally have done so by virtue of a considerable degree of prudent rationality. One should not presume without evidence that money is irrationally employed; although investors, like everyone else, are often guilty of unexplainable actions.

What does this account of potatoes, real estate, automobiles, or art markets have to do with financial markets? They have been brought in as illustrations of several principles of market organization. The first and most important is that, for the most purposeful analysis, a large market area must be broken down into many smaller ones. In the detailed study of financial markets, we shall identify a great many divisions (Chapter 4). Another point is that the student of a market must look into the special conditions of supply and demand that prevail there. Supply conditions are often complex, but they generally can be analyzed objectively, in terms of factors that can be quantified with statistics and described in graphic terms. Demand can also be studied in quantitative terms, but many aspects of demand lead back to questions of human tastes and preferences, points about which economists have less useful things to say.

Financial markets present several interesting parallels with other markets. The price system in the financial markets clearly allocates the scarce resource of funds. Financial markets also are interrelated in many ways, just as commodity markets are. For example, the corporate bond market and the market for Treasury bonds are closely related, just as the markets for potatoes and cereal grains are. Many interesting examples of price elasticity may be found in the money and capital markets. Price elasticity is particularly great in the market for corporate bonds: The price at which a new offering fails to sell may be just fractionally above one at which it would sell quickly. Price elasticity also influences supply: The quantity of tax-exempt securities supplied is clearly sensitive to market rates of interest, at least for short periods of time. Examples of fixed supply may also be found. The supply of corporate equities is not exactly fixed, but it is so nearly so that analysis of the market for corporate stocks is similar to analysis of the market for land. It must also be admitted that financial markets are not free of the fads and myths found in other markets. At one time a given type of security may enjoy a preference that, in retrospect, is hard to explain. Railroad securities were once the most highly regarded obligations in the capital markets, and industrial securities were accorded much less esteem. Those positions have been reversed. More recently "growth" stocks and "conglomerates" came to have a kind of zealous support that far exceeded rational explanation. What one knows about other markets can be used to understand financial markets.

ECONOMIC CHARACTERISTICS OF FINANCIAL MARKETS

Financial markets are bound together by one characteristic: They all involve the lending of "funds" in some form or other. Some of these loan contracts are simple and informal and may run for only one day; others are detailed and complex and run for many years. Corporate stock issues also have a place in the financial markets; they involve the acquisition of "equity funds" and run for an indefinite period of time. Short-term credit contracts are generally included in what is known as the money market; the longer-term debt contracts and equities are capital market instruments. The maturity limit of one year is sometimes used as a device for distinguishing between the two markets, but this line of division is artificial at best. A later section of this chapter will explain why we have elected to include these segments in a single analytical account.

The price involved in the debt segment of the money and capital markets is usually expressed as an interest rate. The price at which a corporate stock sells implies both a current dividend yield and an expected growth rate of future dividends. Although a great deal of economic discussion proceeds as if there were one leading interest rate, this is not so; there are many interest rates. One of the complex but fascinating parts of the study of capital markets is the identification not only of the forces affecting the overall level of interest rates but also of those forces determining interest-rate relationships. Chapters 5 and 6 will deal with such relationships in detail, but the problem will be encountered in various forms in other sections. This pricing problem enters into almost every aspect of financial market operations.

As is true of other markets, the most fruitful way of penetrating the financial markets analytically is to break the subject down into the supply and demand aspects. The problem of doing so in this case is that the same institutions may be supply elements at one time and in one circumstance but demand elements at other times and under differing circumstances. For example, business corporations are important elements in these markets and are usually on the borrowing side of both the money and capital markets. Nevertheless, most large corporations are also important lenders in the money markets. Foreign participants appear on both sides of our money and capital markets. Perhaps the most confusing case of all is that of the federal government. Although it is more often than not a borrower in these markets, for short periods of time it may be a large supplier of funds.

Supply and demand analysis is further complicated, particularly in the money markets, by the fact that the Federal Reserve, which is the central banking system of the United States, plays a very special role in these markets. As manager of the monetary system, it varies the base of reserves on which the commercial banking system operates. The Federal Reserve aims to influence general economic conditions, but its effects on short-term money markets are of great importance, and its influence spreads out into other parts of these markets and at times seems to influence prices in the equity market.[1]

Another complexity in the study of financial markets is the number of institutional layers that may intervene between the basic economic functions of saving and investment. The number of institutional layers varies both in number and character. For example, the market for "Fed" funds (which will be explained in some detail in Part Two) is a highly specialized one almost wholly limited to commercial banks but with some participation by U.S. government security dealers. The steps between this market and the economic ultimates of saving and investment are complex; it will tax our analytical powers to make these steps clear. Other markets are less complex. The conventional mortgage market, for example, typically involves only one institutional layer between saving and investment. Individuals deposit their savings at savings institutions, which in turn lend to people investing in homes.

The analytical effort to strip away the institutional coatings of the financial markets is not done because these coatings are unimportant. Quite the contrary: The habits, customs, traditions, and business logic of these institutions are very much at the heart of financial market analysis. Nevertheless, an excessive preoccupation with describing these many interesting and fascinating characteristics of market institutions can obscure the economic fundamentals at work in them.

FOUNDATIONS AND FUNCTIONS OF FINANCIAL MARKETS

The ultimate foundations of supply and demand in the capital markets are saving and investment. Nevertheless, the channel between the economic ultimates of saving and investment and the debt and equity obliga-

---

[1] See Sprinkel (209). (Numbers in parentheses refer to the bibliography at the end of the book.)

tions found in money and capital markets is a rather long and sometimes devious one. Careful analysis is needed to make these channels clear.

The equality of saving and investment ($S = I$), explained in most beginning economics textbooks, is really a kind of identity. Everything produced is either saved or consumed. The things not consumed are the cumulation of wealth, or "investment." Thus saving and investment are necessarily equal.[2] This equality is not disturbed by the fact that saving is frequently held in the form of money or some other credit instrument. (It should be recognized immediately that most forms of money are non-interest-bearing credit obligations of the banking system.) Every debt is one side of a contract with a lender on the other side. Some people save and become lenders either directly to ultimate investors or through some financial intermediary. Other people may borrow to finance an investment act—again, either directly from savers or indirectly through financial intermediaries. Thus real saving and real investment can be separated by these financial transactions in debt and credit instruments. Indeed, it can be said that the primary purpose of financial market organization is to make it possible for saving to be done by some members of society while real investment operations are managed by others.

The separation of the acts of saving and investment serves to increase both saving and investment and hence the growth of the economy. Individuals who want to save but not invest (in a real sense) can do so only if there are financial markets in which to lend. Others who want to invest but lack the saving can do so only if there is recourse to borrowing or external financing via the financial markets. If the only way capital goods could be financed were for each investor to save in advance, economic growth would be slow indeed. Financial markets increase the availability of financial capital by tapping the savings potential of noninvesting individuals. Thus a major function of financial markets is to provide a link between saving and investment, thereby facilitating the creation of new wealth.

The concept of ultimate equality of aggregate saving and investment—even though individual sectors may be far from such a balance—can be demonstrated by some very simple equations. The starting point is that of the balance sheet equation:

Assets = liabilities + net worth

which can be expanded slightly to the form

---

[2] While actual saving is always equal to actual investment, desired saving and desired investment are equal only when the economy is in equilibrium (see Chap. 2).

Real assets (RA) + *financial assets* (FA) = liabilities (L; all financial) + net worth (NW)

Net worth can be viewed as a cumulation of all past saving. The balance sheet, which is a statement of a point of time, can be converted into a statement of changes over time:

$$\Delta RA + \Delta FA = \Delta L + \Delta NW$$

That is, investment + lending = borrowing + saving.

For a closed economic system, financial assets must equal total liabilities, since they are two ways of looking at the same magnitudes and can therefore be cancelled in the equation above. This leads to the wholly sensible result that current saving (ΔNW) is measured by the net increase in real assets (ΔRA). Financial froth cannot and should not obscure the basic fact that we are not richer except as is expressed in some form of real wealth. "Real" wealth does not exclude intangibles such as greater human skills, but it does exclude the paper claims created by financial transactions.

Again, the equality of the aggregate figures does not apply to given sectors of the economy (but only because financial markets make it possible for a sector to save more than it invests or to invest more than it saves). Some sectors (the household sector is a good example) have far larger financial assets than liabilities; they save more than they invest. On the other hand, the government sectors have larger liabilities than financial assets; they spend more than they tax. Similarly, the business sector has larger liabilities[3] than financial assets; this sector invests (through capital expenditures) more than it saves (through retained earnings.) Since on balance some sectors save and lend while others borrow and expend, financial activity tends to parallel real activity: Lending and borrowing tend to move with saving and investment. This is not always the case, however. We have already mentioned the fact that some individuals and sectors "save up" to finance investment. In this case, real investment takes place without the proliferation of debt contracts or financial obligations in any formal sense. The householder who builds an addition to his home, the farmer who improves the fertility of his land, the corporation that adds to plant and equipment from retained earnings have all saved and directly invested their savings. The net worth of each is increased in the process, and no increase in debt obligations takes place.

[3] Common-stock equity claims are here included as liabilities. Technically they are not liabilities, but analytically they are more like liabilities than they are a part of savings.

The opposite case is also true: Financial claims can be created and are in fact often proliferated by the financial system, and no net saving takes place. If Mr. Profligate borrows to indulge his taste for luxurious living and Mr. Pinchpenny is willing to save and lend him the wherewithal for this fling, a debt contract will have been created without any net saving. Mr. Pinchpenny has saved, but Mr. Profligate has done quite the opposite: he has "dissaved." This situation illustrates still one more point to be considered. Just as Mr. Pinchpenny had to save to acquire this receivable (unless he disposed of some other asset or himself borrowed the money with which to make the loan), the net acquisition of financial assets requires saving just as the acquisition of real assets does.

The somewhat trivial illustration of the Messrs. Profligate and Pinchpenny has a profound parallel in the finance of war. When a nation is fighting a war which cannot be paid for by taxation, its borrowings are likely to build up a complex of financial assets in the economy. The nation as a whole probably grows poorer as the war proceeds (even if it does not suffer physical damage of its homeland), but the increase in financial assets may produce an artificial feeling of prosperity on the part of a great majority of its citizens.

In spite of these qualifications that debt contracts can increase without any parallel net saving and investment and, conversely, that saving and investment can take place without creation of any new financial obligations, a real foundation in saving and investment exists for most of the new debt and equity contracts that are handled in financial markets. The economic factors that influence the rate of both saving and investment will be dealt with in some detail in Chapter 2.

As incredible as it may seem, a giant proportion of financial market transactions have no effect on either the creation of new real wealth or the creation of new financial assets. The stock markets (the New York Stock Exchange, for example) are a good case in point. Millions of individuals and institutions play these markets, switching back and forth among issues of different corporations. When John Doe buys Xerox stock, he does not get new securities from Xerox but instead gets Xerox stock already outstanding and in the hands of some willing seller. Similarly, Xerox does not get any funds with which to finance capital outlays; the money goes to the seller. He, in turn, will likely reinvest in some other stock already outstanding. The stock, bond, and other security exchanges are the "used car lots" of the financial markets; they are "secondary" markets. Trading in them adds no new wealth, real or financial.

The trading and switching is not without significance, however. It enables individuals and institutions to adjust the composition of existing assets. This is an extremely important function, not only from the individual's point of view but from society's as well. An individual naturally does not want to be trapped into any given holding of securities, neither does he want to be stopped from buying a security which is not presently being issued. With secondary markets, he can buy and sell what he wants when he wants. He is free to adjust his portfolio to suit his tastes, to maximize his utility. This portfolio-selection function of financial markets will be discussed in considerable detail in Chapter 5.

Society at large likewise benefits from secondary markets. The actions of the numerous individual buyers and sellers in the secondary markets produce signals in the form of prices which indicate a market consensus of relative values. These values, or prices, feed back into the "primary" market, or market for new issues. Unlike new and used cars, new and used securities are nearly perfect substitutes. Prices determined in the secondary market have a powerful influence as to prices which can be expected from the purchase and sale of new issues. Secondary markets provide valuable pricing information to society. Without these markets, ultimate savers and investors would have to make lending and borrowing decisions in the dark.

The ultimate economic function of financial markets, both new-issue and secondary markets, is to allocate resources efficiently as between consumption and investment and as between different kinds of investment. An economy's preferred mix of consumption and investment usually requires more saving than that which can be generated without financial markets. Underinvestment is a chronic ailment of financially underdeveloped countries. The level of investment is constrained by the level of saving. Financial markets not only increase saving but channel it to the best investment opportunities. Saving flows to those who are willing to pay the highest prices (interest rates) and able to earn the highest real returns on investment (the ultimate employment of saving). Allocative efficiency is further enhanced by the existence of the secondary financial markets. These markets add to the number of available choices in the formulation of the level, composition, and timing of saving and investment. In general, greater choice means greater allocative efficiency. The ultimate purpose of financial markets is to allocate resources efficiently by making more choices available. In this sense, financial markets are really no different from other markets.

THE MONETARY ROLE IN FINANCIAL MARKETS

Financial market transactions can be distinguished from transactions in the markets for goods and services by looking at the substance being exchanged. In markets for goods and services, real assets (or services derived from real assets) are exchanged for money, and vice versa. In financial markets, the exchange is between financial assets and money. Money is traded in both markets; it is a link between the real and financial sides of the economy. Moreover, since money itself is a financial asset, financial market transactions involve pure exchanges of financial assets, one of which is money.

The market for the financial asset, money, should not be confused with the so-called "money market." Financial assets in this latter market are not really money, but they do have such short maturities that they are close substitutes for money.

Money is at the heart of financial market analysis. It gets traded in all market transactions. It is itself a financial asset and a uniquely important one. It is thought to bear such a strong relation to other markets that its supply is a matter of public policy. A whole field of economic thought called "monetary theory and policy" is devoted to the study of money.

What is money? A functional definition of money would be any object that does money's work. What is the work of money? Mainly it is to act as a medium of exchange and as a standard of value. As a result of performing these two functions, money becomes the unit in which debt contracts are written and is used as a store of value. In the United States at present, what objects perform these functions? Metallic coins and currency in paper form clearly do so, but commercial bank demand deposits are the principal money asset. Some other financial assets are good substitutes for money, but none performs all the functions of money.

As is true in most modern countries, the money system of the United States is a blend of public and private elements. The public part of the money system includes such rather simple elements as manufacturing and distributing the metallic coins and paper money we use in hand-to-hand money transactions. But the more important monetary functions in the public sphere are of a policy sort: the management of money (or monetary policy) both in the international sphere and in the domestic sphere. The exercise of monetary policy by public agencies, however, has direct and significant influence on private monetary institutions—in the main, the commercial banks.

The functions of the commercial banks are varied, and many of them are not directly related to their monetary role. The principal business of commercial banks, however, is extending credit. Banks prefer to extend credit in the form of loans to customers, but they also extend credit by the purchase of securities. The individual commercial bank gets funds with which to make loans or buy securities mainly from the deposits left with it by customers. Banks cannot lend all the funds left with them as deposits; they must keep some cash reserves. This is basically a matter of prudence, but in the United States it has become more a matter of formal legal requirements. Banks are "required" to keep reserves. These reserves can either be cash in a vault or a deposit in some other bank. For the commercial banking system in the United States, this "other" bank is in most cases a Federal Reserve bank.

An individual bank is a financial intermediary just as most other financial institutions are. But commercial banks differ from other financial institutions in one important way. Most depositing customers of commercial banks treat their checking accounts as their basic reservoir of money. When these customers receive payments, the money will be deposited in their bank accounts. As a result of this national habit or custom, any payment made out of one bank is very likely to be restored to some other bank. As a result, what one bank loses, another bank is likely to gain. This habit seems like a trivial circumstance, but it is of vast importance in monetary management.

When banks have reserves in excess of those legally and practically required, they can extend credit. But what is the origin of these reserves? The Federal Reserve System, a public agency but one which has considerable independence of the hurly-burly of politics, supplies them through its own banking actions. The volume of currency and deposits in Federal Reserve banks—in other words, the claims that can be used as reserves by commercial banks—can be and are controlled by the Federal Reserve. The principal expression of domestic monetary policy by the government of the United States is the policy of the Federal Reserve in making these reserves available.

When the Federal Reserve makes reserves available, some banks find themselves with "excess" reserves. They can now extend credit by lending or investing. The power of this action, however, results from the fact that the portion of the reserves that are excess, and therefore the basis of credit extended, will almost certainly return to other banks within the commercial banking system. This permits still another cycle of credit expansion to take place. Each level of banks retains the amounts of reserves required by the added deposits which first brought the new reserves to it, and it then extends credit on the remainder. The end result is *multiple expansion*. The theoretic maximum multiple of expansion is the geometric reciprocal of the reserve ratio, as is explained in all good elementary economics texts. What this amounts to is that domestic money management is accomplished by the Federal Reserve through its control of bank reserves. But since multiple expansion is at work, the Federal Reserve has to provide less than $1 of reserves for every $1 of total monetary expansion.

Of what concern is this process to financial markets? As will be shown in Chapter 2, the basic supply factor in these markets is saving. An analyst of financial markets should constantly be looking to saving as an economic ultimate. But for a variety of reasons, management of the supply of money has become a rather actively exercised instrument of public policy. The way in which it is exercised is determined by a number of public policy goals discussed in Part Two. When money is managed as a matter of public policy, this management has sharp and immediate effects on the financial markets.

THE JOINT ANALYSIS OF MONEY AND CAPITAL MARKETS

Frequently money and capital markets are analyzed separately. Part of the reason is that many of the financial institutions involved are specialized and do not often cross over from one side of the market to the other. Furthermore, there is a general feeling that the money markets have an economic foundation different from that of capital markets; capital markets are thought to involve "real" saving while money markets deal with artificial magnitudes.

Modern economics, however, recognizes that although some money market institutions, particularly commercial and central banks, have special characteristics for the reasons outlined just above, the markets are logically joined together. Flow-of-funds analysis, introduced in Chapter 4, takes this view. Furthermore, financial institutions are no longer so clearly specialized; many cross the lines between markets more freely than was formerly true. In economic terms, the interest rate cross-elasticities between money markets and capital markets are sufficiently high that one market cannot be meaningfully analyzed without the other. For all these reasons it seems better that they should be joined together in any analysis that is undertaken.

The economic reason for joining the analysis of money and capital markets is supplemented by a good practical reason: Their operations are interrelated and many times depend on one another. Several of the most important financial institutions operate in both sectors; the commercial banking system is a good illustration. We shall also find ties between the markets created by speculation and its financing. Speculation takes place in the capital markets; it is ordinarily thought of as an effort to capture and realize capital gains. The financing of it, however, usually requires money-market funds. A pinch on money market supplies of funds has often cooled off capital market speculation.

Successful speculation depends on a correct forecast of price changes. While speculative gains are technically possible from either a fall or a rise in prices, speculation on price falls requires selling what the speculator does not own, borrowing the security for delivery, and later buying an identical block for return to the security lender. "Short" sales are technically possible in all markets, but the practical difficulties and costs of being bearish are enough to limit this action in most markets and to make it prohibitive in some. Most speculation is long or bullish. Credit can increase the speculator's leverage. It can permit the magnification of gains and, unfortunately, also of losses. So the availability and cost of credit, which is a money-market matter, becomes a vital consideration and sometimes an imperative condition in capital market speculation.

CLASSIFICATION OF MARKETS, PARTICIPANTS, AND MARKET CHARACTERISTICS

As has already been indicated, financial markets break down into a number of subcategories: the market for Treasury securities (which straddles both the money and capital markets), the market for corporate bonds, the mortgage market, the commercial paper market, etc. Markets are usually classified according to the sector classification of the debtor (for example, corporations are the debtors of the corporate bond market).

Classification of market participation is more diverse, but one line of demarcation should be kept in mind. Some participants are ultimate economic entities in their own right. Individuals, businesses, and governments procure funds from financial markets in order to finance expenditures on goods and services. Others, however, are financial intermediaries. Commercial banks, savings banks, savings and loan associations, credit unions, insurance companies, finance companies, pension funds, and mutual funds borrow from savers (and from each other) in order to make loans to the ultimate economic entities. These intermediaries comprise the institutional layers that intervene between the functions of saving and investment. Serving the intermediaries and the ultimate lenders and borrowers are various marketing institutions. These institutions promote the sale of securities (not necessarily their own). Investment bankers and security dealers are such institutions. More attention will be given to the degree of institutional differentiation in Chapters 3 and 4.

Open money markets are national in their scope; at any given moment prices in the U.S. government security market are uniform throughout the nation. Short-term interest rates on other open money-market obligations are also almost precisely uniform throughout the nation. Money is so easily transferred that disparities could hardly exist for more than a few moments. Negotiated borrower-lender money-market transactions are strongly influenced by national money markets, but moderate regional differences exist. Negotiated loans may be "tighter" in one section of the country than another for the same quality of credit, and rates vary slightly. The uniformity, however, is more impressive than the differences.

Capital markets also tend toward uniformity. The open-market capital instruments trade at almost identical prices at any one moment. Negotiated capital market transactions, however, do vary appreciably, and these differences seem to persist for longer periods than, for example, differences in negotiated money-market loans. Clear differences mark the regional markets for conventional mortgages (mortgages without a government guarantee or insurance). The market for mortgage money in the Far West can differ considerably from the market for mortgage money in New England. A significant rate differential does prevail, and New England rates are below those in the Far West by one-half to a full percentage point.

Another important point in the classification of financial markets which bears repeating is the difference between the "primary" market for newly issued securities as opposed to the "secondary" market for outstanding securities. Organized stock exchanges are almost wholly secondary markets: They deal in securities that have already been issued.[4] Trading takes place between owners. The exchanges seldom handle sales of securities by issuers to investors. A market for newly issued equities exists; it is one conducted by investment bankers. For corporate bonds, the principal market is the new-issue market and secondary market transactions are less important. Most investors, once they buy corporate bonds, keep them until they mature or are otherwise retired. An interesting fact is that the principal secondary market in corporate bonds is for rather low-grade issues. Secondary markets are of less significance in the money market than in the capital market, since the variety of maturities available tends to minimize the extent to which investors sell money-market obligations before maturity. One exception should be noted: one of the biggest secondary markets in terms of dollar volume is the market for Treasury bills, which are very short-term obligations. On the other hand the market for bankers' acceptances is largely a new-issue market.

One more kind of classification must be kept in mind in observing money and capital markets: the distinction between open markets and negotiated markets. The rules of the New York Stock Exchange (NYSE) require that bids and offers must be made audibly. This means that the NYSE is a kind of open double auction market. While actual mem-

---

[4] "Rights" financing is one important exception to this generalization.

bership in the exchange is restricted, anyone of minimum financial respectability can engage a broker to act for him in that market. It is effectively an "open market." At the other extreme a loan arranged between a farmer and his banker is clearly a negotiated transaction. Many transactions fall between these two limits. The open-market system implies interest rates and prices that are freely available to anyone who meets the minimum tests of market participation—which means, in effect, anyone who can pay the cash or deliver the securities involved. Furthermore, the operating rules of open markets are usually standardized. The negotiated market often results in a price or interest rate that applies to that one transaction with side conditions tailored to fit the special circumstances of the case.

An interesting parallel can be drawn in corporation finance. The sale of corporate bonds by competitive bidding to investment bankers and their reoffer of these obligations on the markets would clearly fall within the accepted idea of an open-market operation. On the other hand, a private placement of corporate bonds with some investor such as a life insurance company or a group of companies involves negotiation of both the interest rate as well as many important contractual requirements that are a part of such a lending operation.

The terms prevailing in related open and negotiated markets tend to be similar. The rates that are negotiated will be strongly influenced by those that prevail in open markets. At the same time, open-market rates would not and could not get far out of line with rates and terms known to be available in the negotiated market.

PURPOSE AND PERSPECTIVE OF THIS BOOK

The primary purpose of this book is to deepen the reader's understanding of the system of financial markets. These markets play an important role in the workings of the overall economy. One cannot really understand how the economy works without an understanding of the financial side of the economy. Most elementary economics books stress the real side of the economy and give short shrift to the financial side. One purpose of this book, therefore, is to fill a knowledge gap in the reader's understanding of the economy in general.

An equally important reason for understanding the financial market system is to prepare one for the study of specialized subjects in finance such as monetary theory and policy, investments, business finance, public finance, international finance, consumer finance, real estate finance, and insurance. These specialized aspects of finance do not exist in a vacuum. Each is a subset of the larger financial system. Understanding the whole system of financial markets is a logical first step to the in-depth study of any one of its parts.

What is the best way to gain an understanding of financial markets? The answer depends on the kind of understanding sought. On the one hand, a descriptive approach is appropriate for those who want to understand *what* financial markets are and *how* they operate. On the other hand, an analytical approach is useful if one wants to understand *why* financial markets and their participants behave the way they do.

The approach of this book is to strike a balance between description and analysis. The purpose is to impart a *general* understanding of financial markets. The book is written from the perspective that the whats, hows, and whys of finance go together inextricably. In the chapters to follow, analysis is interwoven with description as much as possible. As such, most of the analysis is informal and nontechnical, but it is nevertheless there.

The basic formula of this book is that a general understanding of financial markets can be derived from describing and analyzing their operations. It would not be appropriate, however, to let the matter drop at that point. Possibly because their operations involve many elements of mystery, some critics of our economic system have felt that these markets furnished the means by which powerful moneyed interests gained a stranglehold on economic power and wealth.

This sort of critical view has by no means been confined to our external critics. Wall Street has never had much of a hold on the affections of the country, and it is still possible to make political capital out of attacks on the "money interests." Very little is gained by getting into the middle of that debate. It will be relevent, however, to ascertain the social utility of financial markets. Do these markets promote the best possible use of capital? Do they facilitate full employment without inflation, or do they add to our economic ups and downs? Do they make a contribution to economic progress, or are they stumbling blocks in the road of change? Do their end results serve social justice? These questions cannot be confined to any one chapter or section of this survey but are dealt with in greater concentration in the concluding chapters.

Chapter 2

Economic Determinants of Saving and Investment

Even the most pragmatic of financial market practitioners reverts to economic fundamentals rather quickly in accounting for current developments in these markets. Bankers explain the levels of their deposits in terms of the saving done by and the cash holdings of their customers. When accounting for movements of bank loans, they tend to look behind their customers' affairs into such matters as inventory accumulation, other working capital needs, capital expenditure plans, and the state of their cash flow.

Investment bankers often base forecasts of the state of capital markets partly on the volume of new issues scheduled for sale in the market —the so-called "visible supply." Even so, they quickly look behind visible supply to more fundamental factors such as the level of expected capital expenditures, the volume of capital expenditures now being made on an unfunded basis which will later require funding, and similar factors. When looking at the demand for securities in the capital markets, they examine the rate at which various institutional investors will be accumulating funds. But, back of that, they are aware of the basic importance of ultimate saving.

ECONOMIC DETERMINANTS OF SAVING AND INVESTMENT

Behind saving lies the whole complex of factors that determine the level of saving. How much do interest rates, as against income, determine how much people save? Behind investment lies a similar complex of causal circumstances. Is the chief stimulant profit expectation or is it the need to maintain competitive position? To what extent do interest-rate costs offset these gains and therefore act as a deterrent to investment? In the process of reaching a balance between saving and investment, where are the adjustments made? This chapter is concerned mainly with these issues. Its purpose is to examine those features needed to understand the direction of movements in money and capital markets.

THE DETERMINANTS OF SAVING

The factors that account for saving by individuals form a complex of many elements. While considerable research has been devoted to assessing the various incentives for saving, the results are inconclusive. The traditional view that people save for their old age has some validity, but it is not the whole story. People also save for large-unit or "lumpy" expenditures. Other incentives also seem to be at work. It is clear that some cultural backgrounds encourage saving and others do not. The puritan tradition that encouraged thrift may have had something to do with the early rapid development of this country, particularly those parts of it most under that influence. A low saving rate hampers many underdeveloped nations.

Saving for large-unit expenditures explains an interesting point about the saving process. The gross volume of saving is constantly being offset by a varying amount of spending from saved funds, or dissaving. Studies suggest that fluctuations in dissaving account for more of the irregularity in net saving than changes in gross saving.

Whatever the reasons for saving, the level of saving is influenced by economic conditions. This section examines a number of leading theories of saving. A flow diagram of some of the major determinants of saving (discussed below) is shown in Figure 2-1.

The assumption of classical economists was that interest rates had a significant influence on the volume of saving. Low interest rates—the market force which was thought to balance saving and investment—were supposed to curb saving as well as encourage investment. Modern economists have come to question the direction of influence of interest rates on aggregate saving. This is because there are different offsetting effects of interest rates on saving. One effect is the substitution effect. When interest rates drop, the return or utility from saving decreases relative to the utility of present consumption. Rational individuals can be expected to

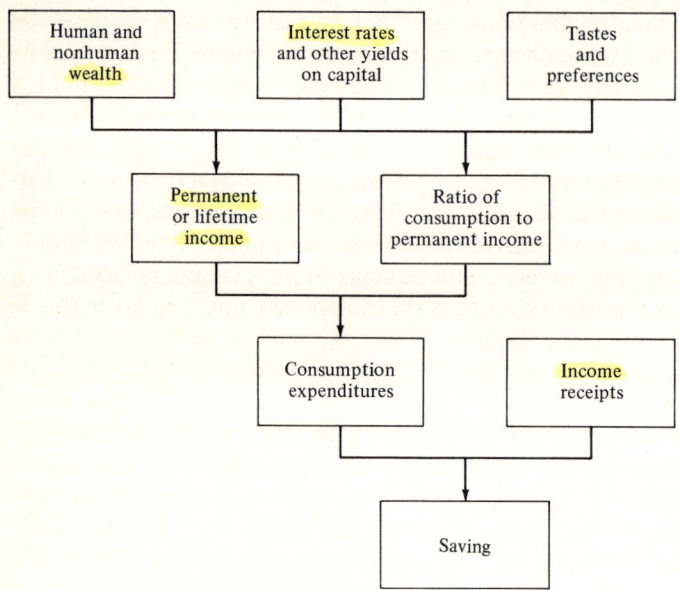

Figure 2-1 Some determinants of saving.

devote a larger proportion of their given incomes to consumption and less to saving. Thus the substitution effect implies a direct relation between saving and interest rates. A second effect, the income effect, implies an inverse relation. With lower interest rates, future interest income declines. Less optimistic prospects of future income can be expected to bring cuts in current consumption. For given current incomes, this means higher saving. A third effect, the wealth effect, can go in either direction, depending on the wealth status of the individual. If an individual has more financial assets than liabilities, a drop in interest rates increases the capital value of his net financial worth. Being wealthier, he does not need to save as much as before out of given current income. In this case, saving varies in the same direction as interest rates. On the other hand, if an individual owes more than he owns, he feels his debt more keenly as market interest rates drop relative to the rates he must continue to pay. Feeling less wealthy, he can be expected to save more out of given income. In this case, saving varies inversely with interest rates. Thus the substitution effect works in one direction, the income effect in the other direction, and the wealth effect in either direction. No wonder economists are unsure as to the net effect of interest rates on saving.[1]

---

[1] A study by Weber (224) suggests a negative net effect, while one by Wright (235) indicates a strong positive substitution effect. Both cannot be right unless there is an even stronger negative income effect. Most empirical studies of saving have simply ignored interest rates as a determinant.

The influential ideas of Keynes (124) and the monumental study of saving by Goldsmith (86) were instrumental in convincing economists that income, not interest rates, is the principal determinant of saving. Keynes hypothesized that both saving and the ratio of saving to income vary directly with income. Budget studies of individual and individual-household saving behavior have tended to support this hypothesis. Low-income families and individuals save proportionately less of their incomes than high-income individuals and families do. A large portion of saving is done by a relatively small number of upper-income families.

While the concentration of saving in upper-income groups seems to be well established empirically, one logical problem still has not been answered with complete satisfaction. For many years the United States (along with other countries) has enjoyed a considerable increase in income. If higher-income groups save more than lower-income groups, an increase in average income shifts people up the income scale. If they save the proportion of income characteristic of this new income level, aggregate saving should increase not only absolutely but proportionately. Aggregate statistics, however, indicate that this has not proved to be the case. As near as can be estimated, the proportion of income now saved is about the same as it was a generation ago or two generations ago.

Long-term estimates made by Goldsmith and published in his study of saving suggested that the saving rate has increased slightly when equity in consumer durables is counted as saving; but that if these durables are excluded, the saving rate appears to have actually dwindled slightly. Since this definitional issue could be decided either way with almost equal logic, a rough generalization of "no change" is probably not too far from the truth.

This absence of secular increase in the saving ratio has stimulated a great deal of speculation. Some interesting and plausible hypotheses have been developed in an effort to reconcile the facts. One such hypothesis is the "relative income" hypothesis developed independently in the late 1940s by several different economists. This hypothesis, which gained wide attention in a book by Duesenberry (49), maintains that the difference in saving by income levels is a relative matter: At any one time a given stratum of society saves about the same proportion of its income as the same relative stratum did in other periods.

Another hypothesis relies on the wealth effect. Here the position is taken that the aggregate saving-income ratio *does* increase over time with increases in current aggregate income, *all other things held constant*. But all other things are not constant. Wealth, for example, grows with income, and the effect of increases in wealth is to decrease the saving ratio: Growing wealth decreases the need to save out of current income. Thus, with the wealth effect working in the opposite direction from the income effect, the two effects may cancel out, leaving the saving ratio intact as both income and wealth increase.

While saving bears a close relation to income over the long run, it is quite erratic in the short run. Goldsmith found the ratio of aggregate annual saving to annual income to be about one-eighth on the average, with no upward or downward trend but with considerable cyclical fluctuations around the average. Others have found that the fluctuations are even more severe when the saving ratio is computed from quarterly data.

A widely accepted explanation for an unstable ratio of current saving to current income is provided by the "permanent income" hypothesis. This hypothesis has several forms, but the best known is one developed by Friedman (77). The basic argument is that spending and saving decisions are guided by a long-run view of income rather than income of the moment. What one family spends and saves on, say, Tuesday has little or no bearing to income received on Tuesday. (Payday might be Friday.) The same applies to weekly, monthly, quarterly, and even annual flows of receipts and expenditures, though with diminishing force. Accordingly, the permanent income hypothesis contends that consumption, and therefore saving, depends on a more permanent notion of income, that is, income normalized from past experiences or future expectations or both. Friedman has found that the ratio of consumption, or saving, to permanent income is more stable than it is to current measured income. What instability remains is attributed to interest rates, wealth ratios, and other nonincome variables.

A closely related hypothesis is the "life cycle" hypothesis advanced by Modigliani, Brumberg, and Ando (7). Their contention is that saving is proportional to lifetime income as measured by the present value of that income. As expected, the ratio of saving to lifetime income is more stable than it is to current income. But it is not perfectly stable. Variations in the ratio are attributed to differences in savers' ages.

Economic factors do not tell the whole saving story, but they go a long way. The relation between saving, or consumption, and income is one of the tightest in economic theory. Nevertheless, there are times when economists are hard pressed to explain spending and saving behavior on purely economic grounds. Behavior which economists cannot explain is frequently attributed to the whims of consumer psychology.

DETERMINANTS OF INVESTMENT

Investment that affects capital markets is of several sorts. The most important segment, if measured in gross volume of expenditures, is business investment. Residential construction, however, usually uses more credit than business investment. State and local governments have also come to play a fairly large role in capital expenditures. In one sense the federal government should also be treated as "investing" a part of its outlays; a great many of its expenditures are economically similar to private investment expenditures. The reasons for not treating any part of these expenditures as capital outlays are twofold: First, adequate estimates of the appropriate part of such expenditures on a capital basis have never been prepared; second, expected profit does not determine federal government expenditures, as is true of private expenditures. It is hard to count an expenditure as capital unless we can see a stream of future benefits flowing from it.

Business Investment

Approximately one-tenth of expenditures on the gross national product (GNP) are made by the private business sector for plant, equipment, and inventories. Most of this gross investment is for capital to replace old capital which has depreciated; the rest is for net additions to capital, or net investment. Replacement expenditures, though large, are relatively stable because they are closely aligned to depreciation schedules. Net investment, on the other hand, is more volatile; it responds to changing economic conditions. Our concern in this section will be to examine the economic determinants of net business investment. These determinants are identified in Figure 2-2.

The direct determinants of investment are the desired stock of capital goods, the actual stock of capital goods, and the speed by which the actual stock is adjusted to the desired stock. For example, if the desired stock of capital is eighteen machines and the actual stock is twelve, total net additions to machines will be six in order to adjust supply to demand. If it takes a year to make a full adjustment, annual net investment will be six machines. If a year is required to make half the desired adjustment, investment will be three machines; if the adjustment is one-third, investment will be two; and so on. The more that desired capital exceeds actual capital, the greater the rate of investment. On the other hand, the longer the adjustment process, the lower the rate of investment. The adjustment period stretches out over time because it takes time to produce business structures and complicated equipment.

The indirect determinants of business investment are those factors that determine the desired stock of capital, the actual stock of capital, and the time structure of the investment process. The latter is largely determined by technological conditions, but it is not completely time-

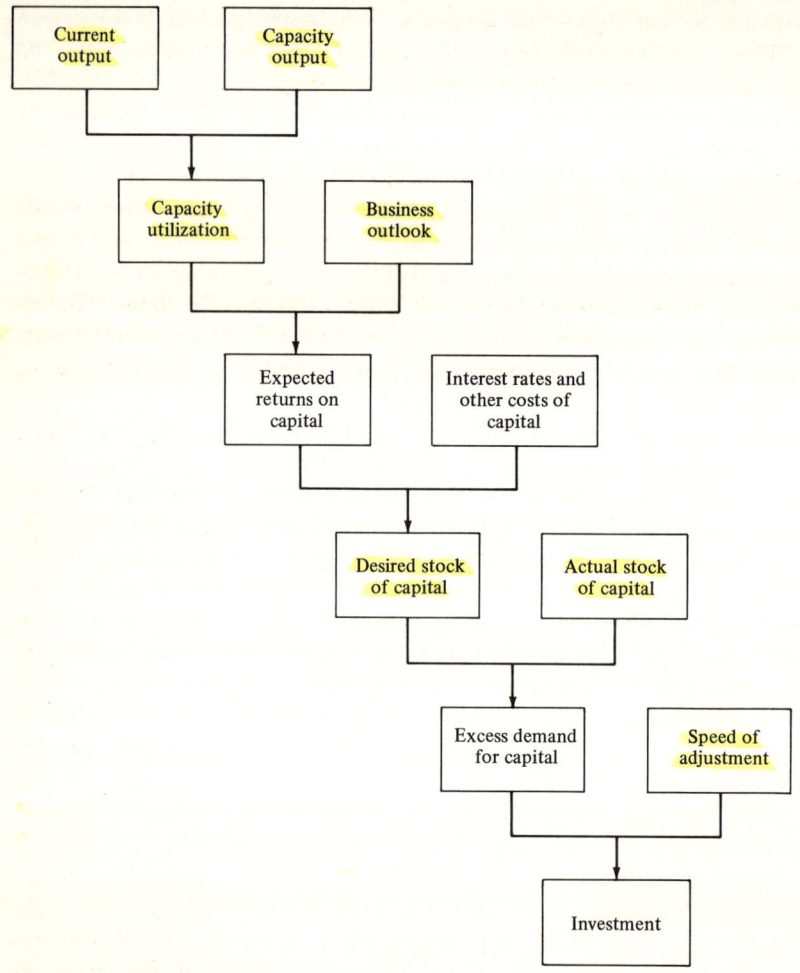

Figure 2-2 Determinants of investment.

inelastic. Business decision makers have some discretion over how fast they adjust actual to desired capital. It may be technologically possible to build a plant in six months, but the parties involved may decide to stretch it over a couple of years. Actual capital is, of course, predetermined; it is already in existence. The desired stock of capital is very sensitive to economic variables. This sensitivity carries over to investment, which is sensitive for the same reasons. What, then, are these economic variables which determine the desired stock of capital and, therefore, the rate of investment?

An important determinant is the extent to which current business activity presses against existing productive capacity or fails to use it fully. When existing capacity is fully used, there is a strong incentive to add to capacity. On the other hand, operations at a level considerably below capacity discourage further capital expenditures. Even the appearance of technological improvement, discussed below, may not be a motive strong enough to induce such expenditures.

The existence of some unused capacity does not necessarily mean that actual capital is greater than desired. Most operations can always squeeze out more output with given capital, but they may do so at extremely high marginal costs. When this happens, it may be cheaper in the long run to add to existing capital facilities. In short, desired capital may exceed actual capital even though the actual capital is not operating at "full" capacity.

Surprising as it might seem, the concept of industrial capacity is not a settled statistical question. This is more true of total capacity concepts than of those for individual industries, but it is really true of both. For the purpose of relating capacity to expected business investment, the principal point to bear in mind is that of costs. As long as variable costs do not increase faster than fixed costs are reduced by increased output, capacity has not been reached. Even after marginal costs start rising gently, it is not clear that plant capacity is being approached. But at some point optimum plant usage is reached and pressure for more plant is felt.

Despite measurement problems, capacity utilization is a pretty good indication of excess demand for capital. The demand for capital can be taken as a derived demand for output. (According to the "accelerator principle," the capital-output ratio is a constant.) Similarly, the supply of capital can be viewed as fixing the supply of output, or at least a least-cost supply of output. When the demand for output exceeds this least-cost supply of output, it implies that the demand for capital exceeds the supply of capital. But it also shows up as high capacity utilization.

There are other reasons why capacity utilization indicates demand for capital and, therefore, investment. Profit-maximizing businesses add to capital to produce more output only if they expect to earn a rate of return on capital greater than the cost of capital funds. Operations near capacity usually imply profits adequate to justify sizable capital expenditures. Lenders view high capacity utilization as a favorable sign, and financing is usually easily arranged by those using existing capacity fully. However, changed technology does not fall within the same category. If a concern has been suffering low profits and faces further trouble from competition based on new technology, it may have great problems in arranging financing. The threat of changing technology hurts some as much as it helps others.

Improved technology has a rather mixed bearing on capital expenditures. When technology is static, very little can induce capital expenditures except pressure on existing capacity. However, when technology improves products or reduces costs, capital expenditures may be forced on businesses even though they are operating considerably below capacity. This action, however, has great risks. Changed technology has sometimes moved so fast that it produced second-generation changes and made plant and newly designed equipment obsolete before they were fully completed. If such expenditures were needed because of pressure on existing capacity, then the business managers, though regretting the misfortune, could defend their policies. But few decisions would seem more absurd in retrospect, if the new plants and productive capacity subsequently become technologically obsolete, than the addition of capacity which was not currently needed simply on the grounds of capital expenditures regularity and "keeping up to date."

The influence of interest rates and other capital costs has been subject to dispute and speculation. Neoclassical economists have long theorized that the cost of capital funds is a crucial determinant of the demand for capital and investment. The cost of capital funds is the discount rate used by a firm to capitalize expected outlays and returns associated with investment. The capitalized value is called "net present value." The larger net present value is, the more profitable the investment. Since net present value varies inversely with the cost of capital, so should investment.

The firm calculates its percentage cost of capital as a weighted average of the costs of the debt and equity funds in its capital structure. The cost of debt is the interest rate which the firm must pay its creditors. The cost of equity is the rate of return required by the firm's owner. Since owners assume more risk than creditors, the cost of equity exceeds the cost of debt by a risk premium.

The firm cannot treat its cost of capital as a constant. When money and credit tighten, interest rates rise and stock prices fall. This increases the cost of debt, the cost of equity, and the overall cost of capital funds. Theoretically, this should have a depressing effect on capital expenditures. However, for many years inductive research on investment behavior failed to find any significant role for the cost of capital. Not until recently has there been any apparent merging of theory, practice, and evidence. Postwar experience seems to suggest that financial management spends much time evaluating the profitability of capital proposals and the cost of their financing. Some managers take their capital expenditures as given and follow a policy of timing their financing so as to achieve minimum financing costs. Others take the cost of capital as given and concentrate on discovering lucrative investment opportunities. In either case, the cost of capital has an influence on investment. Even those who try to outguess the financial markets with a timing policy are not immune to setbacks of planned capital expenditures. The ability to anticipate capital expenditures or to delay the financing of them is limited.

The determination of investment has been the subject of hundreds of different empirical studies. The different studies have sought empirical support for different theories of investment or different versions of the same theory. Conclusions have been diverse. It is not appropriate to our survey to examine the specifics of these studies, but we can offer some general observations found in recent reviews. In 1971, Jorgenson (119) reviewed twelve recent econometric studies of investment in fixed capital. Comparing their results, he found output or capacity utilization to be the most important single determinant of fixed investment. The second most important determinant of fixed investment turned out to be the cost of capital funds. The latter finding is significant because earlier reviews, including the massive 1963 review by Eisner and Strotz (53), found only mixed empirical support for the cost of capital as a determinant of investment. Before the 1960s, many observers clung to the notion that companies finance investment out of "costless" retained earnings. It is true that retained earnings have been used to finance much of investment, but such funds are not costless. Sophisticated financial managers recognize that the cost of internal funds is an opportunity cost approximately equal to the cost of external equity funds.

Inventory investment, like fixed investment, is guided by output and sales anticipations. However, unlike fixed investment, the cost of capital funds appears to play a minor role. Neither in the Eisner and Strotz review nor in the 1964 review by Lovell (137) of the empirical determinants of inventory investment were interest rates and other capital costs mentioned as significant determinants. This flies in the face of economic theory because inventory is capital and capital has a cost. Either the art of inventory control has not conformed to theoretical norms or the econometric studies reviewed failed to detect a true cost-of-capital effect. A few recent studies, including one by P. W. Kuznets (129), suggest that financial factors are significant determinants of inventory investment. However, the evidence is still not conclusive.

Residential Construction

Investment in new housing is determined by a complex of demand factors and supply factors. The demand for housing in general (as distinct from new housing) is shaped by such factors as population, household size, and family formation. People must have shelter. However, they do have choices. They can choose between new houses and old, between single- and multifamily dwellings, between mansions and shacks, between owning and renting. Prices, rents, incomes, and tastes help to determine these choices. When new houses are selling at prices which compare favorably to prices of existing structures and to rents, the demand for new houses is strong. Such is often the case in a growing community which has a housing shortage. When prices are high relative to incomes, demand weakens for new single-family dwellings, but it may increase for multi-family units. In recent years, incomes have not kept up with prices of new houses. The result has been that a large proportion (44 percent in 1970) of new housing starts has been in multifamily dwellings. More people are living in apartments and condominiums. Trailers, too, are becoming a way of life for millions, and this raises an interesting question: Should trailer manufacturing be counted in housing starts? If not, are we making a social judgment that trailers are inferior to houses constructed from the ground up? What about prefabs? Are they better than trailers but worse than "regular" houses?

The cost and availability of credit are important determinants of new housing demand. Residential construction makes somewhat greater demands on the capital markets than does business plant and equipment investment, even though the latter accounts for a much greater dollar volume of expenditures. In 1971, fixed business investment accounted for expenditures of $108.7 billion, whereas residential construction in the same year was only $40.6 billion. On the other hand, the net increase in residential mortgages was $34.9 billion, whereas corporate stocks and bonds showed a net increase of $33.8 billion. This disparity reflects the fact that business corporations make greater use of retained earnings, depreciation, and other internal sources of funds.

Credit factors that determine new housing demand include the mortgage rate of interest, the size of downpayment required, and the amortization period of the mortgage. Ordinarily, the mortgage rate is the device for rationing credit to finance new homes; its economic function is to clear the market for mortgage funds. High rates tend to stifle the demand for mortgages and, therefore, for housing; while low rates do just the opposite. The reason why home buyers are sensitive to mortgage rates is that an increase in the mortgage rate by a single percentage point can easily raise total interest payments by several thousand dollars over the life of the mortgage.

Sometimes, the mortgage rate fails to clear the market for mortgages. In the late 1960s, many prospective homeowners were prevented from buying houses because they could not get credit. They were willing to pay the going mortgage rates of 7½ to 9 percent, but the credit was not there. (In terms of clearing the market, the rates were not high enough.) The suppliers of mortgage credit, chiefly savings and loan associations, mutual savings banks, life insurance companies, and commercial banks, were forced to ration the limited supply of mortgage funds on nonprice bases. This usually took the form of increasing the amount of the downpayment and shortening the mortgage credit period. Some prospective buyers could not meet the required downpayments, others had insufficient incomes to make the larger monthly installments caused by shortening the credit period. Still others who could meet all the financial requirements were refused credit because of no previous credit record or economic standing in the community. Limited credit was rationed by lenders to the wealthy and the lucky.

Now that we are into the 1970s, mortgage money is more abundant. New housing appears not to be constrained so much by credit factors as by real factors. While incomes have had difficulty in keeping up with prices of real estate, prices have had difficulty in keeping up with construction costs. Thus, both demand and supply of new housing have tended to be depressed below the rate which many politicians and social scientists regard as socially necessary.

Construction costs are important determinants of the supply of new housing. The costs of labor and materials have risen dramatically in recent years. Contractors are caught in a squeeze. If they pass these costs on in the form of higher prices, demand falls and they lose some of their market. If they do not raise prices, they cannot cover their costs and are forced to curtail operations. Either way, investment in residential construction suffers.

Other determinants of new housing supply include inventories of new homes and vacancies in existing structures. When these go up, new housing starts to go down. Credit also influences supply. Contractors have to finance their in-process inventories of houses. However, this factor is not a crucial determinant of housing starts except when credit is extremely tight. For a contractor, the cost of credit is minor compared to the costs of labor and materials.

Unlike business investment, technology is not a significant determinant of the supply of new housing. In residential construction, there have been few technological breakthroughs. Houses are built by the same methods with the same materials for the same designs now as they were years ago. The shift to multifamily dwellings has an economic basis, not a technological one.

Numerous empirical studies have attempted to explain the level and cyclical movements of new housing starts and expenditures on residential construction. These studies have covered all the determinants discussed above plus others. Early studies were reviewed by Grebler and Maisel (91). More recently, Guttentag (93), Alberts (2), and Sparks (208) have studied the effects of mortgage credit and other financial market conditions on new housing; Muth (157) has examined the role of income and price; Maisel (141) has emphasized household formation, demolitions, vacancies, and inventories; Brady (23) has disaggregated housing investment by type of mortgage used to finance the investment; and Fair (54) has taken a disequilibrium approach as well as reviewing a number of other recent studies. The different studies do not agree on the specifics, but there is consensus that both real and financial market variables determine investment in new housing.

One final point: investment in residential construction is quite volatile. Housing starts are subject to sizable cyclical fluctuations. Moreover, the short cycle in housing tends to be counter-cyclical to the rest of the economy. When production in general is up, housing starts are often down. This is largely a function of the financial markets. As we shall discover later in this book, market forces combined with certain institutional arrangements cause dramatic cyclical shifts in the flow of funds between the mortgage market and other financial markets.

Government Investment

Government investment does not fit into the pattern of analysis used in dealing with private investment. As already indicated, measurement of federal government investment is subject to difficult conceptual problems. Useful estimates of the proportion of federal government expenditures that can be treated as capital expenditures do not exist. The capital-current distinction is not observed in federal government accounting. As a result little can be said about this subject.

In any event, the availability of figures would not make federal capital expenditures analytically parallel to such private expenditures. The economic bases on which federal expenditures are determined are quite different, as the government is committed to use its powers to satisfy collective wants and to promote a high employment level. The government can use cost-benefit analysis in making investment decisions, but the benefits cannot usually be reduced to dollar values as in the case of private investment. Military hardware, for example, does not provide benefits which can be perceived or measured in purely economic terms. More importantly, the federal government does not have to attune its expenditures to financial market conditions. The federal government cannot discharge its job of promoting employment if it reduces investment whenever its borrowing costs increase.

State and local government capital expenditures, however, do have a quality that lends them to some measure of economic analysis. School construction and road building, the two largest items of state and local investment, have more clearly definable benefits, and they are postponable. Another difference is that state and local investment is financed by borrowing to a much larger extent than federal expenditures are. Thus the impact of financial markets on state and local investment is clearly discernible.

State and local investment and its timing are sensitive to interest rates and their movements. In a model of public capital outlays developed by Gramlich (88), the interest rate appeared as a determinant of the level of capital outlays. Gramlich assumed that governments operate on a relatively fixed budget; thus if interest rates increase, the cost of capital increases and debt service absorbs a larger portion of a given budget. The increased cost of capital induces a substitution effect from capital outlays to current expenditures.

Gramlich's reasoning is sound assuming a budget constraint. But what if the budget is flexible? A 1961 study by Phelps (165) found that higher interest rates did not cause significant cutbacks in capital outlays but instead caused a substitution of tax revenues for bond sales. In other words, officials increased their budgets by increasing taxes. On the other hand, a 1971 study by Peterson (167) found very little evidence that officials relied on tax revenues to finance setbacks in capital outlays.

While interest rates may have an uncertain or weak effect on the level of state and local capital outlays, they certainly affect their timing. A 1969 paper by Phelps (166) argued that outlays are delayed when officials expect future interest rates to be less than current rates. The reasoning is that officials hope to lower interest costs by delaying bond sales and, therefore, capital outlays. McGouldrick and Peterson (146) found that bond sales are indeed delayed when interest rates are high, but that this does not necessarily involve a delay in outlays. Large state and local governments often have recourse to short-term borrowing and to liquid asset holdings. Thus capital expenditures can sometimes be made on schedule by turning to alternative sources of funds.

Different studies [Phelps (164, 166), McGouldrick and Peterson (146), Peterson and McGouldrick (168), and Peterson (167)] agree that tight money and high interest rates lead to setbacks and, to a lesser extent, cutbacks in bond sales and in capital outlays, and that the setbacks and cutbacks in capital outlays are less pronounced than they are for bond sales.

Peterson's study of fiscal year 1970 bears this out most dramatically. The first half of fiscal 1970 was one of severe monetary restraint and historically high interest rates. The second half began a period of easier credit. During the year, planned capital expenditures by state and local government were about $33 billion, while planned long-term borrowing was about $26 billion. Of the planned expenditures, about $3 billion was temporarily set back and another $3 billion was more permanently cut back. This was small compared to setbacks and cutbacks in borrowing. Over $7 billion of borrowing was set back and over $5 billion was cut back. One reason why capital expenditures were not as sensitive as long-term financing to the tight money conditions was the recourse to short-term borrowing and liquid asset disinvestment mentioned above. Another reason is that not all capital outlays are financed out of long-term borrowing, even normally. Highway construction, for example, receives only 18 percent of its financing from borrowing; the rest comes from current revenues such as gasoline taxes. However, these reasons do not apply with much force to school districts. School construction, more than any other element of state and local outlays, feels the pinch of credit restriction.

Finally, the fiscal 1970 setbacks and cutbacks might have been worse than they actually were had it not been for some easing in credit conditions later in the year. On the other hand, they would not have been as bad as they were had a number of states and municipalities not been subject to legal interest rate limits (ceilings). For many governments, market rates were above the legal limit. A few governments raised or eliminated the limits in order to market their bonds. Nevertheless, Peterson estimated that cutbacks in capital outlays were double what they otherwise would have been without the legal limits.

LINE OF CAUSATION BETWEEN SAVING AND INVESTMENT

Actual investment in the economy is always equal to actual saving. This confuses some people, since the group in society which does most of the saving (households) is different from the group which carries on most of the investment (business corporations). Moreover, the two groups save and invest for different reasons.

The equality is not really difficult to understand. If investors want to invest more than savers want to save, investors will actually invest less than intended and savers will save more than intended. Actual saving must equal actual investment because saving is unconsumed income and investment is unconsumed production. Since total income and total production constitute an identity, so do saving and investment. But again, this does not necessarily mean that desired investment equals desired saving.

ECONOMIC DETERMINANTS OF SAVING AND INVESTMENT

The amount savers wish to save has an effect on investment; likewise, the amount investors wish to invest affects saving. Suppose desired investment is greater than desired saving. What happens? In this case, producers underestimate consumption expenditures in their production planning. The producers will divide production between what they want to invest and what they expect consumers to consume. However, as consumers attempt to consume more than producers planned for, the producers will find their inventories falling to levels below what is desired. This unexpected decrease in inventory constitutes unintended disinvestment. Thus actual investment is less than intended investment. From the consumers' point of view, they find they cannot consume as much as they would like because consumer goods production and inventory carryovers of consumer goods are deficient. With actual consumption less than intended, actual saving is more than intended. Putting the two together, the unintended disinvestment and the unintended saving make actual investment equal to actual saving, even though desired investment is greater than desired saving (see Figure 2-3, panel A).

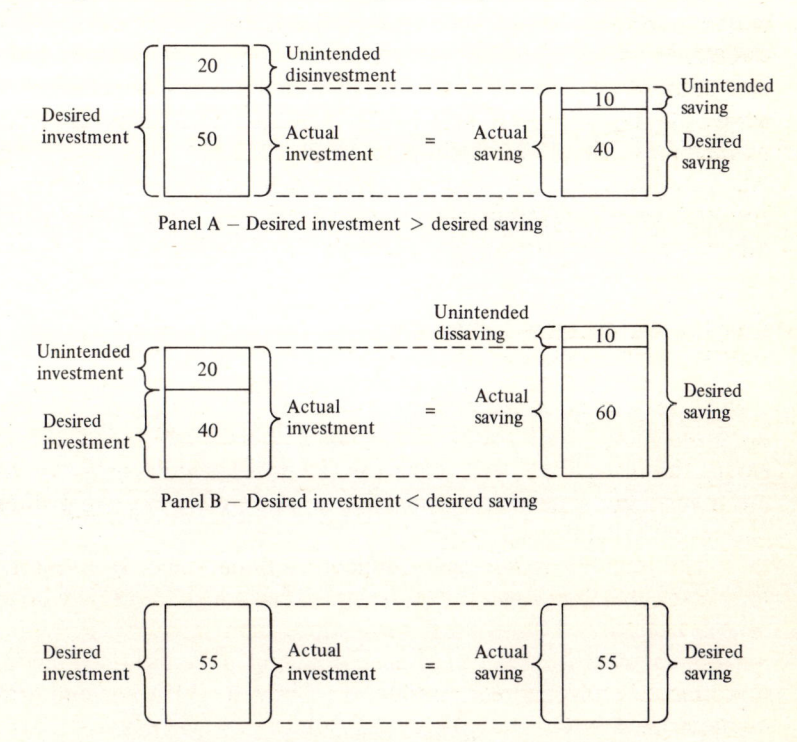

Panel A — Desired investment > desired saving

Panel B — Desired investment < desired saving

Panel C — Desired investment = desired saving (equilibrium)

Figure 2-3 Relations between saving and investment.

The above situation is not lasting because economic forces tend to bring desired investment and desired saving into equality. While actual saving and investment are always equal, equality of desired saving and investment constitutes equilibrium. The mechanics of the equilibrating process are quite simple. Producers will respond to the unintended drop in inventories by producing more. This creates more income out of which more saving is desired. Desired saving thus increases over its previous position. At the same time, the short supply of desired saving (relative to investment demand) will bring pressure to bear on the financial markets. Interest rates and other capital costs will tend to rise, which, in turn, will cut the amount of desired investment. Desired investment thus decreases from its previous position. Putting the two together, desired saving increases and desired investment decreases until equality is reached. At this point, the real side of the economy is in equilibrium (see Figure 2-3, panel C).

Summing up, if desired saving and investment are unequal, market forces will bring appropriate changes in income and the rate of interest, thereby changing desired saving and investment to a position of equality. But all the while actual saving and investment will have been equal. The line of causation between desired saving and investment is in both directions: Saving influences investment through an interest-rate effect; investment affects saving through an income effect.

Chapter 3

Financial Institutions: Intermediaries between Savers and Investors

The economic determinants of saving discussed in the previous chapter have general relevance. They describe the aggregate economic factors that influence the saving process. In reality, however, savers comprise many types of persons of much more specific desires and circumstances. This great variety of circumstances has led to specialization among financial organizations.

Legal regulation has also tended to specialize according to type of financial institution; each operates under somewhat different rules and regulations. While basic economic needs often explain the variations in legal regulation, historical accident has not been without its influence. This chapter cannot undertake the task of reviewing economic financial institutions in detail, but it will attempt to summarize some of the factors that account for the proliferation of institutions.[1]

Detailed attention to the investment policies of various financial institutions at this point runs the risk of duplication. They will be dis-

---

[1] A more detailed account of the system of institutions may be found in Ludtke (138), Goldsmith (84), Dougall (48), Polakoff and others (171), Smith (206), and Jacobs, Farwell, and Neave (108).

cussed again later, in the chapters dealing with the participants in the various segments of the capital markets. The same subject will thus come up for discussion at two different places. It seems preferable, however, to risk the duplication, since the early chapters of this text will have more realistic meaning for most students if they have clearly in mind the leading differences in basic financial policy between the major institutions in the financial system.

Individuals save for a wide variety of specific purposes: to buy an automobile, to make a downpayment on a home, to provide for a young and growing family, to assure independence in old age, to amass wealth of substantial proportions. The savings put aside for buying an automobile are stored temporarily in quite different forms from those whose purpose it is to give family security or to build an estate. Individuals combine these goals so that, except for those at the very lowest level of saving, they generally do not concentrate their savings in a single form. Portfolio diversification is usual for those with any great amount of wealth.[2]

Since the direct employment of savings in the markets demands a certain amount of self-confidence and financial sophistication, most individuals do not perform this function for themselves. Most persons use one of the financial intermediaries to perform these functions for them on a more expert basis. Some forms of saving for special purposes such as insurance protection can be done only by financial institutions, since the process requires the pooling of a large number of individual risks. Thus an examination of the financial investment policies that govern the employment of savings requires looking beyond the policies followed by individuals and into the sphere of institutional policy.

HOW INDIVIDUALS EMPLOY THEIR SAVINGS

A basic factor in determining how individuals employ their savings is the relationship between individuals' needs and the services which the different forms of saving provide. When individuals want convenience and liquidity above all other considerations, they hold money. Mistrustful of banks (or of the tax collector), some use paper currency for this purpose. The commonly used form of money, however, is demand deposits. Individuals who want some interest return and who, while willing to forego complete assurance of liquidity, wish to enjoy a high degree of it may choose a savings account in a commercial bank, a savings and loan association, or a mutual savings bank. In recent periods credit union accounts have also come to serve this purpose increasingly.

[2] Diversification not only reflects multiple needs but also the single need to reduce risk. See Chap. 5 for a discussion of the risk-reducing benefits of diversification.

FINANCIAL INSTITUTIONS

Insurance either of life or against risks of fire and accident does not, strictly speaking, require savings. The pooling of risk could be covered by current payments. This is, in fact, very much just what takes place in fire and accident insurance. In practice, however, insurance companies do not choose to work without reserves, and so some "prepayment" of insurance with an element of saving is present in most life insurance. In the case of fire and casualty insurance, it is the proprietors who supply this reserve, not the insured.

Life insurance is also involved with another type of saving: that of retirement incomes. Annuities and insured pension plans involve a large volume of saving. The distribution of benefits is subject to a risk-pooling element in that these plans undertake to pay a regular income to participants no matter how long they live. Thus the amount collected varies with length of life and fits into the insurance category logically.

Noninsured pension plans (funds administered by banks and other trustees) are also a very popular way of providing for retirement needs. Some of these plans are in the form of fixed annuities and are thus like insurance plans. Some, however, are variable annuities: The income payments received at retirement are determined by the financial investment performance of the funds. Since these funds are heavily invested in common stocks over a long period of time, large realized capital gains can provide for handsome retirement incomes.

Mutual funds represent another outlet for savings. By buying into a mutual fund, the saver is indirectly buying into a portfolio of corporate stocks. Mutual funds offer returns tied to the performance of the stock market plus built-in, risk-reducing diversification for individuals who lack the financial resources for do-it-yourself diversification. In short, they provide a relatively safe although indirect way of playing the stock market.

All the above forms of saving are done through financial intermediaries: commercial banks, savings banks, savings and loan associations, insurance companies, pension funds, and mutual funds. Aside from this, the principal way in which individuals employ their savings is in the purchase of corporate equities (stocks) or in the purchase of homes. Owned homes provide housing as well as being a direct means for channeling saving into investment. The purchase of corporate stocks does not directly affect real investment, but it does bypass financial intermediation. Moreover, corporate equities represent the one financial market area in which holdings of individuals exceed holdings by institutions. For some individuals, buying stock offers the hope of large and quick returns. Others diversify and hold, wanting nothing more than long-run returns which grow with the economy and keep pace with inflation.

One form of saving usually performs more than one service, while a given service usually is provided by more than one form of saving. The latter point is important because it means that savers have a choice of outlets through which to employ their savings. The allocation of savings among competing outlets is partly determined by relative interest rates. A good example is substitution between the different kinds of savings accounts. During the 1950s, a number of individuals withdrew savings from accounts at commercial banks and placed them with savings and loan associations in order to take advantage of higher interest rates. Then, during the 1960s, a reverse flow took place as commercial banks closed the interest-rate gap. Also, in the late 1960s there was a general shift of savings out of money, savings accounts, and other liquid assets into open-market securities where rates were much higher. Individuals do not automatically shift their savings from one form to another, but when movements in interest-rate differentials are sizable, as they were in the late 1960s, many do not hesitate to move their savings around.

The basic consideration is that of weighing risk versus expected return. Ordinarily, most individual savers stick to savings accounts rather than open-market securities because the greater expected return on securities is not worth the extra risk of holding them. However, if the return differential becomes large enough, as it did in the late 1960s, some savers will shift into securities because the extra return more than compensates for the extra risk.[3]

Another factor that determines the employment of savings is the income or wealth of the saver. Individuals of low income and wealth tend to allocate a relatively large share of savings to homeownership, while high-earning and wealthy individuals keep a relatively large proportion of savings in stocks, bonds, and other capital market securities. Liquid assets, insurance, and retirement plans lie somewhere between homes and securities. They are more "luxurious" than homes, but more "necessary" than stocks and bonds. Evidence of the influence of income and wealth on the demand for various forms of saving has been reported in a study by Crockett and Friend (42). Finally, while income and wealth are related, they do not necessarily go together: Some older people are quite wealthy but have low incomes; some young people have high incomes but little wealth. Age, too, is a factor in how individuals employ their savings.

THE INTERMEDIATING ROLE OF FINANCIAL INSTITUTIONS

Individuals have made increasing use of financial intermediaries as out-

---

[3] The trade-off between risk and expected return is a crucial element in the process of choosing assets, as we shall see in Chap. 5.

lets for personal saving. The proportion of saving channeled through financial intermediaries has grown steadily since 1900.[4] Currently, approximately 80 cents out of every dollar saved finds its way to some intermediary.

Financial intermediaries, whether they seek profits or not, must cover their costs of operation. The method for covering these costs is to borrow from savers at one rate of interest and then to lend to ultimate investors (businesses, governments, etc.) at a higher rate of interest. But why should savers go along with this? Why do they not forget the middleman and lend directly to ultimate investors? What can the intermediary do for the saver that the saver cannot do for himself?

Financial intermediaries have several operative characteristics which most individuals lack: financial expertise, economies of scale, and the ability to diversify and pool. It takes trained personnel to analyze securities, deal with Wall Street and corporate financial officers, and manage portfolios. The typical saver does not have this expertise, but he is expert enough to go to a financial intermediary which does. In addition to expertise, financial intermediaries enable the saver to share the costs of security analysis, market transactions, and portfolio management with other savers. One intermediary, acting in behalf of many savers, can perform these functions at a much lower cost than that which would accrue to many savers acting independently. By saving at a financial institution, the individual is indirectly able to lend in the capital markets with expertise and economy.

Another important facet is diversification. As we shall discover in Chapter 5, diversification of financial assets makes it possible to reduce risk with little impairment of expected return. Diversification is not available to the average individual because it takes a large sum of money to diversify successfully. But diversification is available to financial intermediaries because each invests the combined savings of many individuals.

The principal reason for financial intermediation has to do with the pooling effect, that is, taking advantage of the law of large numbers. An individual saver cannot accurately predict future contingencies. He therefore prefers to place his savings in liquid assets. On the other hand, corporate investors often prefer to borrow on a long-term basis in order to finance fixed plant and equipment expenditures. Financial intermediaries help satisfy both the liquidity needs of savers and the long-term financing requirements of ultimate investors by borrowing "short term" from savers and lending "long term" to investors. On the face of it, this appears to put intermediaries in a very risky position. It leaves them with illiquid assets on one side of the balance sheet and demand or early conversion liabilities on the other. Fortunately, contingencies which are un-

[4]Goldsmith (85).

predictable on an individual basis are quite predictable for large numbers. A given individual may withdraw his savings from a financial intermediary when a contingency arises. This may be a dramatic event for the individual but not for the intermediary. The law of large numbers secures the intermediary with the knowledge that there is a high probability of some other individual making a deposit at the same time the withdrawal is made. In other words, the aggregate savings of many individuals are more stable and more predictable than the savings of a single individual. It is this quality which enables financial intermediaries to meet the liquidity needs of savers. However, as extra measures of precaution, intermediaries keep cash reserves and space the maturities of their security holdings.

The emergence of financial intermediaries has been a key factor in the growth of the economy. Most savers prefer to keep their savings liquid and therefore find claims against financial intermediaries to be more attractive than stocks, bonds, and other capital market securities. Savers thus save more than they would without financial intermediation. At the same time, investors borrow more and expend more than they would without intermediation. Financial intermediaries are visible, centralized, and offer credit in sufficient quantity and on favorable terms. In short, the lending needs of savers are different from the borrowing needs of investors, so intermediaries come between them and meet the needs of both. The result is more saving, more investment, and a faster rate of economic growth.[5]

FINANCIAL INVESTMENT POLICIES OF DIFFERENT FINANCIAL INSTITUTIONS

Specialized institutions tend to have specialized policies for financial investment in the capital markets. The specialization itself constrains the intermediary's available investment alternatives. A commercial bank, for example, specializes in providing fixed-amount demand obligations to individuals. A person with a $100 checking account (demand deposit) can get exactly $100 in legal tender currency whenever he demands it. For the commercial bank, this limits the kinds of financial assets appropriate for investment. The bank must assure itself of adequate liquidity and security of principal by keeping cash reserves plus secondary reserves of high-grade, short-term, fixed-obligation securities. A variable-annuity pension plan, on the other hand, specializes in providing late-conversion liabilities of unfixed amounts. It is hoped that the amounts will be large

---

[5] See Gurley and Shaw (92) for an analytical account of the economic growth and stability aspects of financial intermediaries. We shall examine the stability aspects in Chap. 19.

and at least keep pace with inflation. The pension fund must assure itself of capital growth by investing heavily in common stocks. The assets of a commercial bank are inappropriate for a pension fund, and vice versa. Specialized institutions are therefore constrained in their financial investments by the general principle of employing assets that are appropriately geared to the kind of liabilities to be protected or discharged.

Laws and regulations also serve to constrain the various intermediaries. Each type of institution is highly regulated. Commercial banks, for one, are regulated by state and federal authorities. Commercial banks with federal charters (national banks) fall under the jurisdiction of three federal authorities: the Federal Reserve, the Treasury Department, and the Federal Deposit Insurance Corporation. Other types of financial institutions are perhaps not so heavily regulated, but all are subject to tighter financial regulation than are organizations in the nonfinancial sector. One aspect of financial regulation is the drawing up of authorized investments or legal lists. Another aspect circumscribes the percentages or proportions of the asset mix: Some institutions are subject to minimum constraints on certain assets and maximum constraints on others. Often, the laws and regulations governing financial policy merely enforce or reinforce the general principle of gearing assets to liabilities. Some laws and regulations, however, seem to serve little useful purpose.

Another constraint on financial policy is size and location. For example, a small savings and loan association located in a rural area has neither the financial resources nor contacts to finance an office building in the city. On the other hand, a large insurance company may choose not to service a large number of small mortgages if large-denomination mortgages are available.

Subject to self-imposed, legal, and practical constraints, financial investment policy is determined by striking a balance between the two opposing forces of expected return on assets and the risk of asset loss. Financial intermediaries, like most lenders, seek high expected returns and low risk. An intermediary can maximize its expected rate of return on assets by holding nothing but the highest yielding loans and securities, but this also tends to maximize risk. On the other hand, it can minimize risk by holding nothing but cash and short-term liquid assets, but this tends to minimize return. Because risk and expected return go together, it is impossible to maximize expected return and to minimize risk simultaneously. The optimal allocation between different financial assets is therefore a consideration of weighing risk versus return. The theoretical relation between risk and expected return and the general principles governing asset choices under conditions of risk are explored in much greater detail in Chapter 5. One lesson of that chapter is that different financial investors hold different mixes of financial assets due to differences in risk tolerance. This lesson certainly applies to financial intermediaries. Different intermediaries have different asset structures because of differences in risk tolerance and exposure. These differences are described in the sections below.

Commercial Banks[6]

The commercial banking *system,* subject to special control by the Federal Reserve System because of its monetary nature, creates its own funds on the basis of the reserves created for it by the Federal Reserve. Since the amount of money is believed to be important in determining price levels and economic activity, this governmental control is accepted as a part of our financial system.

Individual commercial banks do not have any special way of creating their own holdings of funds. They must compete with other commercial banks for them; something that amounts to competing for the scarce and limited supply of reserve funds created by the Federal Reserve. The customers of a commercial bank bring to it the funds it needs for its operations. This fact accounts for one principle that governs the employment of commercial bank funds: They must meet the basic service needs of customers to continue to enjoy their patronage. The basic thing customers want is ready access to their deposits without question and without delay. Banks must use some portion of the funds that they acquire for liquidity purposes. These funds are not the *required* reserves (which tend to be a frozen and quite illiquid asset because they are required) but rather excess reserves and secondary reserves which give banks liquidity. Two ways in which secondary reserves are invested are U.S. government securities and loans to securities dealers. Since we shall have a great deal more to say about commercial bank liquidity in Chapter 9, we shall not do more than mention the forms of secondary reserve investment at this stage.

Another principle is that banks be prepared to lend to good customers when the customers want loan accommodation. A "good" customer is naturally a creditworthy one with enough net worth, liquidity, and earning power to make his business attractive. Yet another attribute of

---

[6]The danger of duplication mentioned early in this chapter is particularly acute with respect to commercial banks. Many of the points made in this section will be alluded to once more when we describe the money market. It is probably better, however, to duplicate discussion than to risk an air of unreality in these early chapters. While economic factors do unify the markets, institutional factors differentiate them and sometimes even seem to fragment them. Commercial banks are a particularly important part of the institutional scene, and a quick overview of their institutional policies should be helpful in attaining the desired tone of realism.

a good customer is that he ordinarily keeps good deposit balances with his bank during times when he is both in and out of debt. The satisfaction of customers' credit needs is a two-way street. The customer receives a necessary service, but the bank earns its bread and butter in the process. Interest on loans is the primary source of income and profit for commercial banks.

Commercial banks have to be both liquid and profitable. Unfortunately, assets which are liquid (reserves) are not profitable, while those which are profitable (loans) are not liquid. The task of bank asset management is to strike a balance between the two. Modern portfolio theory views this balancing as a problem of maximizing utility. According to this theory, a bank will allocate assets in such a way that the marginal utility of return from investing an additional dollar in earning assets is equal to the marginal utility of risk avoidance from investing an additional dollar in nonearning cash reserves. Such an approach was implicit in Goldfeld's study of commercial bank behavior (81).

A simpler solution to the problem was provided by Robinson (182). He suggested that the liquidity objective may take priority over the interest income objective. Accordingly, the first job of bank asset management would be to ensure adequate liquidity by building up sufficient reserves. After this priority is met, the bank's next job would be to accommodate customers' loan demands. Still another view was taken by Hodgman (103). He felt it was wrong to view the problem as a matter of allocating given total assets. He argued that total assets can be increased if a bank concentrates on making loans to depositor customers who will leave part of the money at the bank (either voluntarily or through the imposition of a compensating balance requirement). Accordingly, a bank may be able to increase income with little sacrifice in liquidity if it specializes in loaning to its depositor customers. There is a problem, however, with this approach. If all banks try to keep their reserves intact, one bank may not lose reserves to other banks, but neither will it gain reserves from other banks. However, the approach is merited in that it tends to reduce uncertainty and strengthen bank-customer relations.

Loans, like reserves, can assume different forms. At one time, short-term business loans were the dominant use of bank funds. These loans continue to occupy a special place in banking, but this type of credit fails to exhaust available funds in most banks; most are extended into wider lending activities (see Table 3-1). One extension takes the form of greater maturity. Business "term loans," a form of intermediate maturity credit, accommodate businesses in a way not available through short-term credit. In addition, banks now lend to consumers in a substantial way. This has always been done indirectly through lending to consumer financing con-

Table 3-1 Commercial Banking Statement of Financial Assets

	Year-end outstandings (billions of dollars)		
	1950	1960	1970
Cash reserves	20.2	21.2	40.2
Open market paper	.7	2.4	8.4
U.S. government securities	64.3	64.9	76.9
State and local obligations	8.2	17.7	70.2
Corporate bonds	2.2	1.1	2.7
Mortgages	13.7	28.8	73.3
Bank loans	27.5	62.5	162.9
Consumer credit	7.4	20.6	50.1
Security credit	3.0	6.0	13.0
Miscellaneous assets	2.7	5.7	19.2
Total financial assets	149.9	230.9	516.9

Source: Adapted from *Flow of Funds Accounts: Financial Assets and Liabilities Outstanding, 1945–1971,* Board of Governors of the Federal Reserve System, June 1972.

cerns such as small loan companies and sales finance companies, but more is now done directly. Banks also lend to farmers and to many others, including even churches, universities, and other nonprofit enterprises.

Aside from liquid assets and loans, commercial banks purchase mainly tax-exempt state and local government securities. These securities are favored by commercial banks because they are one of the few financial intermediaries fully exposed to the corporate income tax. This point will be discussed later at much greater length. Commercial banks buy corporate bonds only when after-tax yields on them are particularly attractive. Usually, the term loan has seemed a better deal than the corporate bond, partly because it could be used to attract or hold deposits.

Commercial bank asset management of the funds secured from time deposits deserves separate mention. The competition for these funds is primarily with savings and loan associations and mutual savings banks, and it might be expected that the policies followed would be familiar—investment in real estate mortgages.

To some extent this is true. The legal regulation of national bank investment in real estate mortgages is indeed tied to the amounts of time deposits they hold. Nevertheless, commercial banks have not been as active in this form of investment as the other savings institutions have. Commercial banks originate many mortgages and keep some in their own portfolios, but they also pass such mortgages along to trust department funds and in some cases even to other institutional investors.

The basic consideration is one of taxes. Under most circumstances a commercial bank can secure a better after-tax return from a tax-exempt security than from a mortgage. Although tax-exempt securities do not have exceptional qualities of liquidity, they are undoubtedly better than mortgages in this regard. In addition, they are more economical to purchase and to service.

Mutual Savings Banks[7]

Mutual savings banks are much more specialized than commercial banks. Their original purpose was to encourage thrift among working-class people, that is, to provide an easy and safe way for the "average" person to save. The savings banks, in turn, were to invest these savings in the capital markets in such a way as to guarantee security of principal and interest. Savings banks experimented with several forms of financial investment, but they have settled on mortgages as their primary investment medium (see Table 3-2).

The turnover of deposits at mutual savings banks is rather slow, and balance sheet totals in most individual mutual savings banks are usually sufficiently stable that liquidity requirements are low. However, because of conservatism, mutual savings banks have tended to maintain more than adequate liquidity reserves. Part of these reserves are a holdover from World War II, when loan demand was so weak that they could find an outlet for funds only in U.S. government securities.

In recent times, mutual savings banks have been putting almost all added funds into mortgages. Mortgages now constitute 75 percent or more of savings bank assets. Since the areas in which savings banks operate, mainly the slower-growing Eastern and New England states, have not generated enough mortgages, the banks have had to devise new methods for acquiring mortgages or to use the service of mortgage bankers located in states of higher loan demand. Mutual savings banks acquire all classes of mortgages—Federal Housing Administration (FHA), Veterans Administration (VA), and conventional—and their rates are usually competitive. Their terms (downpayments and loan periods) tend to be slightly more conservative than those of savings and loan associations, about equal to those of insurance companies, and a bit more liberal than those of commercial banks. Mutual savings banks make commercial and multifamily mortgage loans as well as mortgage loans on single-family homes.

Mutual savings banks formerly were important buyers of corporate bonds, but they have not revived that practice in the postwar period. Even

---

[7] See Welfling (225) for an account of the history and lending policies of mutual savings banks.

Table 3-2 Mutual Savings Banks' Statement of Financial Assets

	Year-end outstandings (billions of dollars)		
	1950	1960	1970
Cash	.6	.7	1.0
U.S. government securities	10.9	6.7	4.9
Corporate bonds	2.1	3.8	8.3
Home mortgages	4.3	18.4	37.3
Other mortgages	3.9	8.6	20.6
Consumer credit	.1	.2	1.2
Corporate equities	.2	.8	2.5
Miscellaneous assets	.4	1.4	3.2
Total financial assets	22.5	40.6	79.0

Source: Adapted from *Flow of Funds Accounts: Financial Assets and Liabilities Outstanding, 1945–1971*, Board of Governors of the Federal Reserve System, June 1972.

after servicing costs or charges, mortgage yields were rather higher. Recently, mutual savings banks have shown some interest in corporate equities as some states (the New England states more so than the Middle Atlantic states) have liberalized regulations limiting stock acquisitions. The proportion of assets in corporate stocks, however, is still very small—below 5 percent.

Savings and Loan Associations[8]

Savings and loan associations were originally introduced for the purpose of making mortgage credit available to persons who sought homeownership but who lacked access to banks and other sources of credit. Loans were made to members from savings of other members. The associations grew up with the westward expansion of the country. Many towns in the Middle and Far West were built with building and loan money. Today there is little functional difference between savings and loan associations and mutual savings banks. Both these institutions secure funds by issuing savings accounts and both use funds by acquiring mortgages.

The investment policies of savings and loan associations are simple: They maintain required liquidity reserves and use all remaining funds to acquire mortgages (see Table 3-3). Liquidity is supplied by intermediate-term and longer-term U.S. government securities. Membership in the Federal Home Loan Bank System and in the Federal Savings and Loan Insurance Corporation reinforces this liquidity. Turnover in their savings

---

[8] A host of studies of the savings and loan industry appear in the four-volume study prepared for the Federal Home Loan Bank Board (59).

Table 3-3 Savings and Loan Associations' Statement of Financial Assets

	Year-end outstandings (billions of dollars)		
	1950	1960	1970
Cash	.7	1.7	1.6
U.S. government securities	1.5	5.2	12.3
Home mortgages	13.1	55.4	125.0
Other mortgages	.5	4.7	25.4
Consumer credit	.2	1.0	1.5
Miscellaneous assets	.9	3.5	10.4
Total financial assets	16.9	71.5	176.2

Source: Adapted from *Flow of Funds Accounts: Financial Assets and Liabilities Outstanding, 1945–1971*, Board of Governors of the Federal Reserve System, June 1972.

accounts tends to be relatively low, less than 30 percent a year. New funds have almost always been far more than were needed for the withdrawal of funds.

The savings and loan associations tend to prefer conventional mortgages on in-state, single-family homes, but many of them have acquired VA mortgages as a matter of service to the veterans in their local areas. Because of early opposition to the federal government program of mortgage insurance, these associations seldom acquire FHA mortgages. The downpayments and loan periods on conventional mortgages granted by savings and loan associations are typically rather more liberal than those granted by either commercial banks or life insurance companies on similar mortgage loans. On the other hand, mortgage rates charged by savings and loan associations are usually higher than rates charged by other institutions. This is partly a function of acquiring riskier mortgages, but it is also linked to the fact that the associations have tended to pay higher rates of interest on savings accounts. Higher rates on savings, location in fast-growing areas, and effective advertising and promotion help to explain the rapid growth in assets of savings and loan associations.

Life Insurance Companies[9]

The primary mission of life insurance companies is to sell protection. The element of saving and investment associated with life insurance is incidental to this primary mission. The actuarial liabilities of life insurance companies are very long-term and highly predictable—in large numbers, human life expectancy can be quite accurately calculated. Life insurance

---
[9] See Jones (116) for a recent analysis of investment policies of life insurance companies.

policies give their holders cash surrender values that equal or approach the holders' equity share of policy reserves. Experience shows that this right of surrender is exercised mostly in predictable degrees. Since policyholder equity is stable, predictable, and slow to turn over, liquidity needs for life insurance companies are modest. Most investment is in long-term assets.

Life insurance companies must act prudently, and this carries over to their financial investment policies (see Table 3-4). The need to safeguard principal restrains life insurance companies from investing in high-risk, high-return securities. Within the safety-of-principal constraint, life insurance companies seek good returns on their investments. High-grade corporate bonds and mortgages offer both good returns and capital stability. The life insurance companies' distaste for defaults rules out low-grade corporate bonds. Ninety percent of life insurance company holdings of corporate bonds are in bonds of Baa quality or better. The companies' taste for returns rules out U.S. government bonds. High-grade corporates outyield Treasury bonds without imposing excess extra risk. Coming out of World War II, life insurance companies held large amounts of Treasury bonds, but these holdings have been gradually liquidated.

Mortgages and long-term loans to business are about equally important in life insurance investment. Together they constitute about 80 percent of life insurance company assets. At one time, life insurance companies were important buyers of corporate bonds in the open markets,

Table 3-4 Life Insurance Companies' Statement of Financial Assets

	Year-end outstandings (billions of dollars)		
	1950	1960	1970
Cash	1.0	1.3	1.8
U.S. government securities	13.5	6.5	4.2
State and local obligations	1.2	3.6	3.3
Corporate equities	2.1	5.0	15.4
Corporate bonds	24.7	48.2	74.1
Home mortgages	8.5	24.9	26.7
Other mortgages	7.6	16.9	47.7
Other loans	2.4	5.5	18.2
Miscellaneous assets	1.6	4.0	9.1
Total financial assets	62.6	115.9	200.5

Source: Adapted from *Flow of Funds Accounts: Financial Assets and Liabilities Outstanding, 1945–1971*, Board of Governors of the Federal Reserve System, June 1972.

and small life insurance companies still make such purchases; but the companies learned to make direct placement loans and found they could get better loans at higher rates in this way. Private placements have also been instrumental in enabling life insurance companies to make forward commitments of funds. In this way, life insurance companies make investment decisions prior to the actual employment of funds.

Mortgages are also an important life insurance investment outlet. Because most life insurance companies are rather large, they are not in a good position to acquire mortgages directly; most of them use the services of mortgage bankers to do this. Exceptions exist; one very big life insurance company has developed an extensive system of regional offices for the granting of mortgage loans. Life insurance mortgage acquisitions include all the major types: FHA and VA as well as conventional. Their downpayments and loan periods on conventional mortgages are fairly conservative, but their rates are competitive. They also buy or make commercial and rental property mortgage loans.

The investment policies of life insurance companies have been rather closely regulated by law. These regulations have sometimes limited access to investment outlets that some life insurance companies would have otherwise used. In some cases, however, the limits have been extended with the result that few companies take advantage of them. Statutory limits have restricted life insurance company investment in corporate stocks below what it otherwise would be. On the other hand, life insurance companies have not fully exercised the authority they have to invest in real estate.

To some extent the legal regulation is more qualitative than quantitative; life insurance companies are required to buy securities on "approved" lists or to observe the "prudent man" rule in making such purchases. Few life insurance companies in modern times have had any desire to breach the reasonable elements in such standards, but it cannot be said that the standards have always been wholly reasonable. The preference for direct placements may have been induced by the fact that life insurance companies were more confident of their ability to judge investment quality and to write protective features into their loan agreements than they were of the standards of rating used by the supervisory authorities.

Because the federal income tax rule applying to life insurance companies is complicated and has been frequently amended, these companies have had a varying role in buying tax-exempt securities. In some periods they have bought them, but the practice varies from company to company. On the average, investment in tax-exempt bonds has been only about one-tenth of the investment in corporate bonds.

Fire and Casualty Insurance Companies

Fire and casualty insurance companies are not typical financial intermediaries. Payments to fire and casualty insurance companies are not saving in the usual sense of the word. This business, however, requires reserves even more than does life insurance. Casualty underwriting risks are less subject to forecast than life risks, so that reserves are needed. In stock companies, stockholders supply these reserves, and such funds were built up from payments by early policyholders in mutual fire and casualty insurance companies. These reserves are not exactly in the equity province of either stockholders or policyholders, but funds do accrue and they require investment. The growth of reserve funds in casualty insurance has averaged more than $2 billion a year for more than a decade.

The assets of fire and casualty insurance companies consist mainly of tax-exempt bonds and corporate stocks (see Table 3-5). Tax-exempts are attractive because fire and casualty companies, like commercial banks but unlike other financial intermediaries, are subject to the corporate income tax. Equities are attractive assets, particularly to automobile insurance companies, because of the potential for stock prices to grow with auto repair and other settlement costs for which these companies are liable. Aside from tax-exempts and equities, corporate bonds are important investments for fire and casualty companies, but usually only at times when corporate bond yields are high.

The total asset holdings of fire and casualty companies do not reveal the degree of churning about or turnover of these holdings. Those companies that suffer underwriting losses (as many do in a surprising number of

Table 3-5 Nonlife Insurance Companies' Statement of Financial Assets

	Year-end outstandings (billions of dollars)		
	1950	1960	1970
Cash	1.2	1.3	1.4
U.S. government securities	5.3	5.6	4.3
State and local obligations	1.1	8.1	17.8
Corporate equities	2.6	7.5	13.2
Corporate bonds	.7	1.7	8.6
Miscellaneous assets	.8	2.1	4.6
Total financial assets	11.7	26.3	49.9

Source: Adapted from *Flow of Funds Accounts: Financial Assets and Liabilities Outstanding, 1945–1971*, Board of Governors of the Federal Reserve System, June 1972.

years) tend to reduce holdings of tax-exempt securities and acquire equities. Those that have profits are likely to switch in the opposite direction. Thus these institutions make more use of *secondary* securities markets than most other institutional investors do.

Private Pension Funds[10]

The growth of private pension funds has been one of the striking financial developments of recent years. Pension plans were not at all common before World War II (although a number of excellent plans were in operation long before that). Since then almost all companies have established such plans. In the attraction and retention of able officers and employees, they have become a virtual necessity. The establishment of social security and the general demand for personal financial security that grew out of adverse experience of many individuals in the Great Depression also added to this popular demand. Tax exemption also has stimulated the growth of these funds. Employer contributions to the funds, as well as income earned on the funds, are exempt from the federal income tax.

Pension plans have proved to be very costly. As time has gone on, employers have borne a larger share of the total cost. High earnings are therefore demanded of the investors of these funds. Since pension benefits are often tied to salary levels near the date of retirement, the potential liabilities of these funds are very much a function of price level. Higher price levels would increase the liability of these funds greatly. Those paying the bill have thus put another demand on the investment process: price level protection. Only one demand is really absent: liquidity. The dating of liabilities is so easily forecast that no liquidity is needed in the operation of these funds.

Faced with these demands, private pension funds have invested heavily in corporate stocks and to a lesser extent in corporate bonds (see Table 3-6). Equities are used for price level protection and bonds for their regularity of income.

So far there has been very little specific legal regulation except as the common law of trusteeship applies to them. Trustees of pension funds have wide investment latitude. Whether or not the pension funds and their trustees should be subjected to statutory regulation of investment is a question currently being debated. Full disclosure of pension fund investments would shed considerable light on this question.[11]

---

[10] See Gardner (79) for an inside view of the world of pension fund investment.
[11] See Wrightsman (238).

Table 3-6 Private Pension Funds' Statement of Financial Assets

	Year-end outstandings (billions of dollars)		
	1950	1960	1970
Cash	.3	.6	1.8
U.S. government securities	2.0	2.7	3.0
Corporate equities	1.1	16.5	67.2
Corporate bonds	2.8	15.7	29.7
Mortgages	.1	1.3	4.3
Miscellaneous assets	.4	1.4	4.8
Total financial assets	6.7	38.2	110.8

Source: Adapted from *Flow of Funds Accounts: Financial Assets and Liabilities Outstanding, 1945–1971*, Board of Governors of the Federal Reserve System, June 1972.

Governmental Pension Funds

Unlike the private pension funds, public pension systems have often been subject to detailed regulations and rules for the investment of their funds. Some have been relieved from the less rational and more inhibiting rules, but many are still rather restricted. As is true of private pension funds, they have no need for liquidity. Public pension plans tend to require somewhat larger relative contributions from employees and relatively less from the employing governments; even so, the larger part of the burden is still on the employing governmental units. The social security and civil service plans of the federal government are, without material exception, invested in the securities of that government. With fixed benefits (not dependent on fund earnings), this only means that part of the federal share of contributions is concealed.

In the past pension funds of state and local governments were often limited to investment in the securities of those bodies or in U.S. government securities. The numerous small funds and lack of financial experience of the trustees were often cited as the reason for this severe limitation. But a more compelling reason might have been to enlarge the market for state and local government securities. In recent years these rules have been much liberalized. Pension funds of public authorities now are investing mainly in corporate bonds and stocks (see Table 3-7). Bonds are all acquired in the public open market; direct placements are quite rare. At present state and local government pension funds are among the leading buyers of newly offered corporate bonds.

Investment in stocks is a relatively recent phenomenon. It is an attempt to remedy a former inconsistency between public pension prom-

FINANCIAL INSTITUTIONS

Table 3-7 Governmental Pension Funds' Statement of Financial Assets

	Year-end outstandings (billions of dollars)		
	1950	1960	1970
Cash	.1	.2	.6
U.S. government securities	2.5	5.9	6.9
State and local obligations	1.6	4.4	2.0
Corporate equities	.0	.4	8.0
Corporate bonds	.6	6.7	31.8
Mortgages	.1	1.5	6.8
Miscellaneous assets	.1	.4	1.9
Total financial assets	5.0	19.5	58.0

Source: Adapted from *Flow of Funds Accounts: Financial Assets and Liabilities Outstanding, 1945–1971*, Board of Governors of the Federal Reserve System, June 1972.

ises and public pension laws. The laws prohibited investment in stocks, but stocks were the only securities which could have delivered the promised benefits: retirement incomes tied indirectly to increases in productivity and the cost of living. While stockholdings are now being increased, they are still far below those for private pension funds. In 1971, the private funds held 70 percent of their $130-billion assets in the form of corporate equities. Equities held by state and local funds, on the other hand, were still less than 20 percent of the $65-billion assets of these funds.

Mutual Funds[12]

Mutual funds come closest to following the policy of gearing assets to liabilities. Mutual funds secure savings by selling their own stocks or shares to individuals, and they utilize savings by acquiring corporate stocks (see Table 3-8). When an individual buys into a mutual fund, he is indirectly buying a portfolio of stocks of many business corporations.

Mutual funds have a greater impact on the allocation of existing financial wealth than on the level and growth of real wealth. There are two reasons why. First, mutual fund stockholdings have a greater than 50 percent annual turnover rate, which means gross purchases of stocks by mutual funds are far greater than net purchases. Second, these purchases are made in the secondary stock markets. The sellers on the other side of these markets are other institutions and individuals who unload

[12] A recent and thorough account of mutual fund investment can be found in Friend, Blume, and Crockett (73).

Table 3-8 Mutual Funds' Statement of Financial Assets

	Year-end outstandings (billions of dollars)		
	1950	1960	1970
Cash	.1	.3	.7
Corporate equities	2.9	14.8	39.7
Corporate bonds	.2	1.2	4.3
Miscellaneous assets	.1	.7	2.9
Total financial assets	3.3	17.0	47.6

Source: Adapted from *Flow of Funds Accounts: Financial Assets and Liabilities Outstanding, 1945–1971,* Board of Governors of the Federal Reserve System, June 1972.

stocks already outstanding. These sellers, in turn, may channel the proceeds into either real investment or consumption. If the latter, the real wealth of the economy is unaffected.

The intermediating role of mutual funds is premised on two considerations. One is the ability to diversify. The small investor cannot sufficiently diversify on his own, but he can spread his risks by buying a mutual fund, which is essentially a diversified portfolio in a single package. The second consideration is management expertise. There is a presumption that professional mutual fund managers have the skill and financial acumen to select the highest-yielding stocks for a given level of risk. Recent studies have shown, however, that mutual funds do not consistently perform any better than diversified portfolios whose stocks are selected at random. In short, mutual funds do offer the advantage of diversification, but it is doubtful that they have an advantage of *superior* diversification.

A FINAL NOTE

All financial intermediaries are similar in that they borrow funds from savers and put them to work by acquiring financial assets. The amount of assets which each intermediary can acquire is determined by the amount of savings placed with it. When new saving is placed, the intermediary has more funds for financial investment. When savings are withdrawn, its assets shrink.

This holds not only for the individual intermediary but for intermediaries in the aggregate except for one group: the banking system. When banks trade with savers, they take away and give back to the saver the same thing: money. Money is the debt of the banking system; it is a financial asset to everyone else. Holding money is one form of savings.

Spending money is an act of dissaving. But what one person spends, another receives. What one person dissaves, another saves. In the aggregate, savings *in the form of money* is pretty much beyond the control of savers. Instead, the money supply is primarily determined by the Federal Reserve through its management of bank reserves.

The point of all this is that banks are more than just an intermediary in the flow of funds from savers to investors. The funds they make available to business, government, and consumers are not tied in any simple way to the decisions of savers. Banks, as a system, create their own loanable funds. Sometimes this is at the expense of funds which would otherwise flow through nonbank intermediaries, but more often than not, it represents a net addition to loanable funds.

Chapter 4

Flow of Funds in Financial Markets

The first two chapters stressed the essential unity in financial markets. The third (and preceding) chapter, however, described a great variety of institutional arrangements which might have seemed to emphasize differences between segments of the financial system. These themes are not inconsistent. In ultimate purposes, the various parts of the financial market system are quite similar. In detail, they differ greatly. The point might be described in this way: in a modern, complex, and well-developed economy, the specific financial needs of individuals and businesses differ in many important details even if they have a general similarity.

The purpose of this chapter is to present the flow-of-funds system of social accounting in simplified form. This system stresses the unity of the financial system but allows for a great deal of institutional disparity in its framework.[1] This method of social accounting is closely related to the computation of gross national product (GNP) and national income. These product and income accounts depend on background capital accounts, but these capital accounts have never been much stressed or

---

[1] The intellectual logic of flow-of-funds accounting was developed by Professor M. A. Copeland (41). Current work on this system is centralized in the research division of the Federal Reserve Board.

used in published analyses of GNP. The flow-of-funds system not only establishes and uses capital accounts but also brings in a variety of gross financial transactions. These gross financial transactions are, in effect, what takes place in the financial markets.

The flow-of-funds system of social accounting starts out with the analysis of a single time period, in practice a year or a quarter. Within this period the financial economy is cross-classified by types of transactions and by sectors. Transactions of each sector are summed into statements of the sources of funds and the uses of funds. These sources and uses are classified according to type of financial transaction. The sources and uses for the various sectors are then summed for the economy as a whole. Since financial transactions tend to cancel each other (as explained in Chapter 1), the summary results, cleansed of such duplications, tend to stress the real investment and saving of the economy as a whole.

THE BREAKDOWN OF TRANSACTIONS IN FLOW-OF-FUNDS ACCOUNTING

The transactions within the flow-of-funds accounts are categorized by type of use or source of funds. They are first divided between uses and sources which relate to real investment and saving and those financial uses and sources which relate to lending and borrowing. Real investment and financial investment (lending) are the two broad categories of uses of funds; saving and borrowing the two broad categories of sources.

Since financial investment and borrowing take many forms, the financial investment and borrowing categories are further subdivided by type. For example, financial investment in corporate bonds is separated from financial investment in savings accounts. Similarly, borrowing in the form of issuing corporate bonds is separated from borrowing through real estate mortgages. There are about as many subdivisions as there are different financial markets. In fact, most of the transaction categories are named after financial markets. The use of a financial market classification of transaction categories allows for a balancing of the uses and sources of funds within each market. For every borrower in a given financial market there is a lender; a source of funds for one individual is a use of funds for another. Borrowing transactions (sources of funds) must equal lending transactions (uses of funds) for each transaction category.

Financial transactions within each transaction category appear as either uses of funds or as sources of funds. Financial investment is clearly a use of funds, borrowing is clearly a source. But what are transactions such as financial disinvestment and debt repayment? The uses and sources of funds figures that appear in the flow-of-funds accounts are usually netted. Financial disinvestment transactions are subtracted from financial investment transactions in arriving at financial uses of funds. Similarly, debt repayment transactions are subtracted from borrowing transactions in figuring sources of funds. The result of this netting is to conceal a great many financial transactions. It also has the effect of allowing for negative entries into the accounts. For example, if corporations retire more old bonds than they sell new bonds over a given period, the accounts will show a negative source of funds in the corporate bond transaction category. The accounts will also show a negative use of funds as corporate bondholders will have experienced net disinvestment.

SECTORING FLOW-OF-FUNDS TRANSACTIONS

The economy as a whole is a complex entity. The detail that might be included if many sectors were used is almost endless. The practical necessities of statistics and analysis, however, limit the number of these sectors. In practice the sectors usually shown separately are individuals, business, government, financial institutions themselves, and "the rest of the world." Some further subcategories are used in the Federal Reserve flow-of-funds system, such as, under business, corporate and noncorporate business, and, under government, the federal, state, and local levels.

The logic for appropriate sectoring is that of combining those segments that are similar in their motives, operations, legal constraints, and other behavior-explaining factors. If we have homogeneous categories, what is true of a category can be safely imputed to the individual units within a category. However, logic and practice cannot always be squared, and some odd companions are lumped together. For example, nonprofit units are included with individuals in the published flow-of-funds accounts. Availability of raw data sometimes accounts for such strange combinations. Sometimes a small sector is included with the least illogical larger sector to avoid cluttering up the accounts with too much detail.

**COMBINING TRANSACTIONS AND SECTORS
IN A USE-SOURCE MATRIX**

The uses and sources of funds by transaction categories can be combined with the uses and sources of funds by sectors to form a kind of matrix or a table. The Federal Reserve regularly publishes such flow-of-funds tables, listing sectors across the top and transaction categories down the left-hand side. Each number inside the table is a use or source of funds which, reading up, identifies the sector and, reading to the left, identifies the transaction category. Each sector column of uses and sources of funds gives a reading of the involvement of that sector in the different financial markets. Each transaction-category row of uses and sources of funds gives a reading of the involvement of the different sectors in that transaction category or financial market category.

The official Federal Reserve summary of flow-of-funds accounts for the first quarter of 1972 is shown in Table 4-1. The easiest way to learn how to read the table is to pose a couple of hypothetical questions and then seek the answers from the table. Suppose we want to know what percentage of commercial bank financial investment was in state and local government securities. A glance at the commercial banking column shows that the banks invested $42.9 billion (annual rate) in financial assets. Of this total, $17.3 billion, or 40 percent, went for state and local government obligations. Now let us frame the question differently. Suppose we want to know what percentage of state and local borrowing was from commercial banks. A look at the state and local obligations row reveals that $16.5 billion was raised in this market, with $17.3 billion (or more than 100 percent) coming from commercial banks. The fact that banks invested more in this market than state and local governments borrowed can only mean that other sectors, combined, disinvested. Glancing along the row again, we see that the household sector was indeed unloading its holdings of state and local obligations.

A given financial market may not dominate the financial activity of a given sector, but the sector may dominate the market. In our example, the state and local government securities market did not dominate the financial investment of commercial banks (bank loans did), but the banks definitely dominated the market for state and local obligations. Likewise, one market may dominate one sector's investment while the sector does not dominate the market. Here, an example is the relation between the monetary authority sector (the central bank) and the U.S. government securities market.

COMBINING TRANSACTIONS AND SECTORS IN AN ASSET-LIABILITY MATRIX

Uses and sources of funds are flows between two points in time. These flows are additions or subtractions (if negative) to financial assets and liabilities. Assets and liabilities, on the other hand, are amounts outstanding—stocks—that exist at a point in time. Stocks are essentially

Table 4-1 Summary of Flow-of-Funds Accounts for First Quarter, 1972

	Sector Transaction category	House-holds U	House-holds S	Busi-ness U	Busi-ness S	State and local govts. U	State and local govts. S	Total U	Total S	Rest of the world U	Rest of the world S
1	**Gross saving**		182.4		102.5		−2.7		282.2		10.0
2	Capital consumption		97.2		86.6				183.9		
3	Net saving (1-2)		85.2		15.9		−2.7		98.3		10.0
4	**Gross investment (5 + 10)** A+F	183.2		83.9		−5.5		261.7		11.4	
5	Private capital expenditures	144.0		128.9				272.9			
6	Consumer durables	107.6						107.6			
7	Residential construction	30.7		18.3				49.0			
8	Plant and equipment	5.7		110.0				115.7			
9	Inventory change			.6				.6			
10	**Net financial investment (11-12)**	39.2		−44.9		−5.5		−11.2		11.4	
11	**Financial uses**	98.3		27.2		11.7		137.2		18.9	
12	**Financial sources**		59.1		72.1		17.3		148.5		7.6
13	Gold SDRs, and official fgn. exchange							2.2		−.3	
14	Treasury currency and SDR certificates										
15	Demand deposits and currency										
16	Private domestic	20.2		6.3		2.7		29.2			
17	U.S. government										
18	Foreign									−1.6	
19	Time and savings accounts	84.6						86.8			
20	At commercial banks R↑	27.9		.8		1.4		30.2		1.4	
21	At savings institutions	56.7						56.7			
22	Life insurance reserves	7.2						7.2			
23	Pension fund reserves	14.9						14.9			
24	Interbank items										
25	Corporate shares	−10.0				11.0		−10.0	11.0	2.7	−.1
26	Credit market instruments	−19.1	49.4	6.7	56.7	7.2	16.8	−5.1	122.9	13.4	4.3
27	U.S. government securities R↓	−21.3		−4.5		7.7		−18.1		11.4	
28	State and local obligations	−2.2		1.0		−.1	16.5	−1.3	16.5		
29	Corporate and foreign bonds	13.9			14.2	−.4		13.5	14.2	−1.0	1.7
30	Home mortgages	.2	26.1		1.3			.2	27.5		
31	Other mortgages	2.8	1.5		20.1			2.8	21.6		
32	Consumer credit		13.9	3.0				3.0	13.9		
33	Bank loans		6.5		15.0				21.4		.4
34	Other loans	−12.4	1.3	7.2	6.1	.3	−5.2		7.7	3.0	2.3
35	Security credit	1.3	8.7					1.3	8.7		.1
36	To brokers and dealers	1.3						1.3			
37	To others		8.7						8.7		.1
38	Taxes payable				2.1	.5		.5	2.1		
39	Trade credit		.6	7.7	4.9		.5	7.7	5.9	.1	.2
40	Equity in noncorporate business	−3.2		−3.2				−3.2	−3.2		
41	Miscellaneous claims	2.4	.5	5.5	.6			8.0	1.1	.7	3.4
42	Sector discrepancies (1-4)	−.8		18.6		2.8		20.5		−1.4	

(Seasonally Adjusted Annual Rates—Billions of Dollars)

	U.S. govt.		Total		Sponsored credit agencies		Monetary auth.		Coml. banking		Pvt. nonbank finance		All sectors		Discrepancy		Natl. savings and investment	
	U	S	U	S	U	S	U	S	U	S	U	S	U	S	U		U	
	−14.7		6.8			.1			3.6		3.1		284.3				274.3	1
			2.8						1.1		1.7		186.6				186.6	2
	−14.7		4.0			.1			2.5		1.5		97.7				87.7	3
	−16.7		2.4		−1.3				2.4		1.3		258.8		25.5		264.5	4
			3.0						1.2		1.8		275.9		8.4		275.9	5
													107.6				107.6	6
													49.0				49.0	7
			3.0						1.2		1.8		118.7				118.7	8
																	.6	9
	−16.7		−.6		−1.3				1.2		−.5		−17.1		17.1		−11.4	10
	−13.4		139.1		7.0		2.1		42.9		87.0		281.9				7.6	11
		3.3		139.7		8.3		2.1		41.7		87.5		299.0				18.9	12
	−.2		−2.2				−2.2						−.3	−.3				13
		.7	1.0				1.0						1.0	.7	−.4			14
					18.5				4.0		14.5		· 14.6	18.5				15
			−.8	29.9	−.3		7.3		22.6		−.5		28.4	29.9	1.5			16
	−12.2			−9.8			−2.5		−7.4				−12.2	−9.8	2.4			17
				−1.6			−.8		−.7					−1.6				18
			.7	88.8							.7			88.8				19
	−.2			31.3							31.3			31.3				20
			.7	57.4									.7	57.4				21
		.1		7.2										7.2	7.2			22
		1.3		13.6										13.6	14.9			23
			−25.5	−25.5				−.6		−24.9	−22.9			−25.5	−25.5			24
			15.4	−2.8									15.4	−2.8	8.1			25
	3.0	3.6	129.3	9.7	7.2	6.6	3.9		57.9	4.2	60.4	−1.1	140.5	140.5				26
		3.7	16.6	6.3	5.6	6.3	4.3		−4.1		10.8			10.0				27
			17.8						17.3		.5			16.5				28
			10.6	7.2							3.4	10.6	3.8		23.1				29
	−.8	−.1	28.2	.2	4.8				6.7		16.7	.2		27.6				30
	.4		18.4		2.0			/	4.1		12.4			21.6				31
			10.9						5.6		5.3			13.9				32
			26.1	4.2					26.1				4.2	26.1				33
	3.4		.5	−8.2	−5.2		.3	−.5	2.2	.8	4.1	−9.4		1.7				34
			13.6	6.2					5.8		7.8	6.2		14.9				35
			4.9	6.2					4.9			6.2		6.2				36
			8.7						.9		7.8			8.7				37
	−1.6			−1.7				−.4		−.9			−.4	−1.1	.4	1.5		38
	−1.7	−1.5	.5								.5		6.7	4.6	−2.1			39
														−3.2				40
	−.3	−.9	6.9	25.8	.1	1.7		1.0	4.1	15.5	2.6	7.6	15.2	29.4	14.3			41
	2.0		4.4		1.4				1.1		1.9		25.5		25.5		9.8	42

63

Table 4-2 Financial Assets and Liabilities, December 31, 1971—All

                                      Private domestic nonfinancial sectors

Sector Transaction category	Households A	Households L	Business A	Business L	State and local govts. A	State and local govts. L	Total A	Total L	Rest of the world A	Rest of the world L
1 Total assets	2170.4		421.4		87.3		2679.1		151.4	
2 Total liabilities		525.8		749.8		178.4		1454.1		155.2
3 Gold							33.1			
4 Official foreign exchange										.3
5 IMF position										.6
6 Treasury currency										
7 Demand dep. and currency										
8 Private domestic	134.9		57.3		10.4		202.7			
9 U.S. government										
10 Foreign									6.4	
11 Time and savings accounts	496.0						540.5			
12 At commercial banks	221.8		14.1		30.4		266.3		7.2	
13 At savings institutions	274.2						274.2			
14 Life insurance reserves	137.0						137.0			
15 Pension fund reserves	268.1						268.1			
16 Interbank claims										
17 Corporate shares	878.7						878.7		21.4	
18 Other credit mkt. instr.	224.9	503.3	63.8	542.3	44.5	171.7	333.2	1217.2	52.1	57.4
19 U.S. govt. securities	77.1		10.1		34.4		121.5		46.0	
20 State & local govt. oblig.	52.3		3.2		2.1	166.5	57.5	166.5		
21 Corp. & foreign bonds	47.5			187.3	5.9		53.4	187.3	2.0	14.7
22 Home mortgages	13.4	296.1		5.2	2.2		15.6	301.3		
23 Other mortgages	31.5	21.9		170.2			31.5	192.1		
24 Consumer credit		137.2	33.0				33.0	137.2		
25 Bank loans		25.8		128.2				153.9		8.8
26 Other loans	3.1	22.2	17.6	51.4		5.2	20.7	78.9	4.1	33.8
27 Security credit	2.1	11.2					2.1	11.2	.3	.3
28 To brokers and dealers	2.1						2.1		.3	
29 To others		11.2						11.2		.3
30 Taxes payable				18.3	2.0		2.0	18.3		
31 Trade credit		5.8	180.5	129.3		6.8	180.5	141.9	5.7	6.9
32 Miscellaneous	28.8	5.6	105.7	59.9			134.5	65.5	25.1	89.8

cumulated flows. The relation between stocks and flows is encountered throughout economic analysis: "savings" is a stock, "saving" a flow; "real capital" is a stock, "real investment" a flow; "liabilities" is a stock, "borrowing" a flow; "financial assets" is a stock, "financial investment" a flow; and so forth.

The use-source matrix of Table 4-1 shows the funds flows that transpired between December 31, 1971, and March 31, 1972. However, it does not show the amounts outstanding, or stocks, that existed at the beginning or end of this period. For this we need an asset-liability matrix. Fortunately, the Federal Reserve publishes asset-liability tables which

Sectors (Amounts Outstanding—Billions of Dollars)

		Financial sectors					
U.S. govt.	Total	Federally sponsored credit agencies	Monetary authority	Commercial banks	Private nonbank finance	Total*	Discrepancies
A L	A L	A L	A L	A L	A L	A L	A

A	L	A	L	A	L	A	L	A	L	A	L	A	L	A	
103.4		1628.9		50.3		93.5		574.5		910.5		4562.8			1
	375.0		1538.6		49.3		93.5		541.3		854.5		3522.9		2
1.2		10.1				10.1						44.4			3
.3													.3		4
.7		−.1				−.1							.6		5
	6.4	8.0				8.0						8.0	6.4	−1.6	6
		255.2						56.4		198.8		238.9	255.2		7
		16.3	236.1	.2				53.4		182.6	16.1	219.0	236.1	17.1	8
13.5			12.7					2.5		10.2		13.5	12.7	−.8	9
			6.4					.5		6.0			6.4		10
		.5	548.7							.5			548.7		11
.5		.5	274.5						274.5	.5			274.5		12
			274.2								274.2		274.2		13
	7.4	129.5								129.5			137.0		14
	30.4	237.7									237.7		268.1		15
		49.8	49.8			4.4	35.3	45.4	14.5			49.8	49.8		16
		185.4	55.0					.5		184.9	55.0	1085.5	55.0		17
59.2	326.9	1280.2	123.3	48.2	43.2	71.0		494.2	4.9	666.7	75.2	1724.7	1724.7		18
	325.4	201.1	43.2	2.7	43.2	70.8		83.5		44.1			368.6		19
		109.0						82.9		26.1			166.5		20
		176.2	29.6					4.0	2.9	172.2	26.7		231.6		21
5.7	1.4	286.5	5.1	20.9				48.0		217.7	5.1		307.8		22
3.8		156.8		9.1				34.5		113.2			192.1		23
		104.3						54.9		49.4			137.2		24
		177.2	14.5					177.2			14.5		177.2		25
49.7		69.1	31.0	15.6		.3		9.2	2.0	44.1	29.0		143.7		26
		21.6	12.5					13.8		7.8	12.5		24.0		27
		10.1	12.5					10.1			12.5		12.5		28
		11.5						3.7		7.8			11.5		29
18.7			2.4					−.1		.9		1.5	20.7	20.7	30
4.9	3.5	4.9										4.9	195.9	152.3	−43.6	31
4.5	.3	52.1	124.5	1.8	6.1			1.9	20.6	47.8	29.7	68.7	216.2	280.1	63.9	32

complement its use-source tables. The asset-liability table has a structure similar to that of the use-source table: sectors are listed across the top; transaction categories are down the side. The numbers in the asset-liability table are what make the difference: assets and liabilities (stocks) replace uses and sources (flows).

The official Federal Reserve summary of financial assets and liabilities for December 31, 1971, is shown in Tables 4-2 and 4-3. Each sector column shows the various financial assets and liabilities of that sector. Each transaction category now reveals the amounts owned or owed by the various sectors.

65

RELATIONS BETWEEN THE USE-SOURCE MATRIX AND THE ASSET-LIABILITY MATRIX

Since stocks are cumulated flows, the numbers in the quarterly use-source table should resemble the differences in the numbers between the end-of-quarter and the beginning-of-quarter asset-liability tables. Alternatively, the numbers in the end-of-quarter asset-liability table should resemble the sums of the numbers in the beginning-of-quarter asset-liability table and the quarterly use-source table. One might attempt, therefore, to construct the asset-liability table for March 31, 1972, from Tables 4-1, 4-2, and 4-3. Such a construction would provide a valuable learning experience, but the result would probably differ from the official March 31, 1972, asset-liability table. Financial asset and liability accounts can change between two points in time without any financial investment and borrowing if there is a change in the prices at which financial instruments are valued. Corporate shares, for example, are measured in the Federal Reserve accounts at market value. A change in the price level of corporate shares effects a change in the value of shares outstanding even if the number of shares remains constant. In a rising market, the recorded change in corporate equities outstanding is larger than the recorded investment in equities. Similarly, the change in shares outstanding understates actual investment during a declining market. This valuation problem and other technical considerations complicate reconciliations between the Federal Reserve's use-source tables and its asset-liability tables.[2]

Aside from these problems, a stock-flow relation does exist between the asset-liability accounts and the use-source accounts. Financial assets and liabilities reflect cumulated uses and sources of funds, and current uses and sources of funds effect changes in financial assets and liabilities. Both types of accounts, asset-liability and use-source, are useful for discerning the behavior of individual transacting sectors and individual financial markets. Examination of one type alone can leave a distorted impression of financial behavior.

An instructive exercise is to compare the percentage composition of each sector's uses and sources of funds with the percentage composition of its financial assets and liabilities. Discrepancies between flow and stock compositions indicate divergences between short-run and long-run financial behavior. Such discrepancies and divergences do in fact appear in Tables 4-1 through 4-3. For example, Table 4-1 (the use-source table) shows that 40 percent of the financial uses of funds by commercial banks were for investment in state and local obligations. On the

[2] See (20) (March 20, 1970).

Table 4-3 Financial Assets and Liabilities, December 31, 1971—Private Nonbank Financial Institutions (Amounts Outstanding—Billions of Dollars)

	Sector	Total		Savings and loan assns.		Mutual savings banks		Credit unions		Life insurance cos.		Private pension funds		State and local govt. retirement funds		Other insurance cos.		Finance cos.		Open-end investment cos.		Security brokers and dealers	
Transaction category		A	L	A	L	A	L	A	L	A	L	A	L	A	L	A	L	A	L	A	L	A	L
1	Total assets	910.5		206.3		89.6		18.3		214.5		128.4		64.8		54.6		64.4		55.0		14.6		1
2	Total liabilities		854.5		193.1		83.3		18.3		199.6		128.4		64.8		37.9		61.4		55.0		12.7	2
3	Demand deposits and currency	16.1		2.2		.9		.9		1.8		1.6		.5		1.5		3.9		.8		2.0		3
4	Time and savings accounts	.5	274.2			.5																		4
5	At commercial banks	.5				.5																		5
6	At savings institutions		274.2		174.5		81.4		18.3															6
7	Life insurance reserves	129.5								129.5														7
8	Pension fund reserves	237.7									44.5		128.4		64.8									8
9	Corporate shares	184.9	55.0			3.0				20.5		86.6		11.2		15.5				47.1	55.0	1.0		9
10	Other credit mkt. instr.	666.7	75.2	193.6	14.1	82.9		17.4		182.2		35.4		51.1		32.7		60.4	61.1	7.1		3.8		10
11	U.S. govt. securities	44.1		17.5		5.2		2.4		4.0		2.7		6.0		3.9				.6		1.8		11
12	State & local govt. secs.	26.1				.4				3.5				1.9		19.3						1.0		12
13	Corp. and foreign bonds	172.2	26.7			12.6				79.3		29.0		36.2		9.3			26.7	4.9		1.0		13
14	Home mortgages	217.7	5.1	143.0	5.1	38.6		.9		24.6		3.7						7.0						14
15	Other mortgages	113.2		31.5		23.3				51.0				7.1		.3								15
16	Consumer credit	49.4		1.6		1.5		14.2										32.1						16
17	Bank loans		14.5		1.1														13.3					17
18	Other loans	44.1	29.0		7.9		1.3				19.8							21.3	21.1		1.6			18
19	Security credit	7.8	12.5																			7.8	12.5	19
20	To brokers and dealers		12.5																				12.5	20
21	Other	7.8																				7.8		21
22	Taxes payable		1.5		.2						.8						.2		.3				.1	22
23	Trade credit	4.9															4.9								23
24	Miscellaneous	29.7	68.7	10.6	4.4	2.3	1.8			10.0	24.8		4.8		2.0		37.8							24

67

other hand. Tables 4-2 and 4-3 (the asset-liability tables) show that only 15 percent of the financial assets of banks were holdings of state and local obligations. Table 4-1 overstates the banking sector's long-run position in state and local obligations. By the same token, Tables 4-2 and 4-3 understate the sector's short-run activity in these securities.

Another instructive exercise is to compare the dollar amounts of flows and stocks associated with each financial market or transaction category. Often the markets which are large in terms of amounts outstanding are also large in terms of funds flows. But there are exceptions. For example, new issues of corporate shares during a quarter or a year are usually a small fraction of the value of shares outstanding. Since outstanding issues swamp new issues, prices of corporate shares are largely determined by the supply of and demand for outstanding issues. An opposite case is the market for "Fed" funds, or one-day loan arrangements between commercial banks.[3] Gross funds flows in this market amount to several hundreds of billions of dollars per year. But at any moment in time, the amount of Fed funds outstanding is only about a single day's worth of loans. In this case, gross flow figures exaggerate the importance of the market.

DUPLICATION OF MAGNITUDES IN THE FLOW-OF-FUNDS ACCOUNTS

Flow-of-funds accounting can be used to provide some aggregate measures of the size of financial markets. Measurement of size in financial affairs is beset with difficulties. A major problem of measurement is that of duplication. Financial claims are the stock in trade of the financial markets. These claims take many forms: deposits, bonds, notes, stocks, and so on. These forms all have one element in common: Each of them is a credit item on the books of some member of the economy and a debit item on the books of some other member of the economy. For every credit there is a debit. If some master accountant of the economic universe were to put all balance sheets together—that is, consolidate them—financial claims would all be offset; they would disappear and the remaining assets would be real wealth in the form of land, buildings, equipment, and all other forms of real capital (possibly including the intangibles of personal skills which are a kind of capital equipment—the one that education seeks to develop). This is a sensible conclusion; paper claims are not real social wealth, they are just ways of redistributing legal title to real wealth. Consolidation brings us nearer the "real" truth.

[3] This market is described in considerable detail in Part Two. With respect to the flow-of-funds accounts, the market is subsumed under the "interbank claims" category.

The consolidation that would wipe out all financial claims, however, would obliterate the record of the very instruments that are bought and sold in money and capital markets. In other words, a study of financial markets requires the use of unconsolidated accounts. But the absence of consolidation opens the door to duplication. A very simple illustration will show this problem. One of the popular financial institutions at present is the open-end investment company (mutual fund) that sells its shares and invests these funds in basic corporate equities. If, in trying to measure the amount of corporate equities outstanding, the stocks of such open-end investment companies were added to those of the basic corporations, duplication would obviously result. Since financial organization has led to several layers of financial claims, some of them in places where they would be least expected, any sort of census of financial claims is likely to be inflated by such duplication. These layers, however, play an important functional role in the economy. Better we recognize them and study them than consolidate away their existence.

MONEY-MARKET MAGNITUDES

The principal participants in the money market are the commercial and central banking systems. One can take the view that these institutions together constitute the monetary system and are unified in most operational aspects. Other less central participants are the federal government, nonfinancial corporations which both supply funds to and demand funds from this market, nonmonetary financial institutions, and foreign interests. The latter group deserves a moment's attention. Because the United States dollar has become a reserve currency for so many foreign nations, the central banks or other monetary authorities of these nations keep a large volume of dollar claims, partly in the form of deposits and partly in short-term investment form. Thus foreigners are a large supply-of-funds element in our money markets, though not much of a demand element.

The monetary supply of funds in the form of currency and demand deposits has grown from $150 billion in 1962 to $250 billion in 1972. The annual growth rate, however, has varied widely depending on prevailing monetary conditions: that is, it has been much faster in years of monetary ease than in years of tightness.[4] More will be said about this point in Part Two, on money markets.

One can take the view that holders of currency and demand deposits "supply" these funds through the operation of the monetary system. The

---

[4]Critics believe that the rate of growth should at least be less erratic if it cannot be held constant.

principal holders of money are individuals and businesses. Individuals hold about one-half, businesses about one-third; the remainder is scattered among incidental groups.

Commercial banks also secure funds through time deposits. The household sector alone held about $225 billion of such deposits early in 1972. Funds from demand deposits and time deposits provide most of the financing for the nearly $600 billion of commercial banking assets. Just what part might be thought of as going into the money markets and what part into the capital markets is far from clear. About 30 percent of the total is in mortgages and state and local government securities which are clearly capital market instruments. About 50 percent is in the form of notes, loans, and credit to businesses, consumers, security dealers, finance companies, and others. A large proportion of this credit does not belong in the open-money-market category. Many loans to businesses and consumers are intermediate-term in length and negotiated in character. Such loans belong to neither the open money market nor to the open capital markets, although they are on the fringe of the open markets. About 20 percent of commercial banking assets is in short-term U.S. government securities and cash reserves. The government securities are clearly in the open-money-market category.

The central bank, the other half of the monetary system, is almost exclusively a participant in the open money market. About 75 percent of its nearly $100 billion of assets is in U.S. government securities, most of which are short-term.

The federal government enters the money markets almost wholly on the demand-for-funds side. In fact, it can be said that the federal government accounts for more demand than all other groups combined. Its short-term debt, in the form of Treasury bills and notes, is the principal instrument traded in the money markets.

Nonfinancial business corporations enter the money markets on both the supply and the demand side. Many of them are in the traditional position of covering working capital requirements by various kinds of borrowing. A few, like the sales finance concerns, sell commercial paper directly or through dealers; but the biggest share of the demand is directed toward bank loans. Nonfinancial corporations also supply funds to the money markets. They carry about $10 billion to $20 billion of Treasury securities (mainly short-term), about the same amount of time certificates of deposit, and about the same amount of commercial paper. They hold lesser amounts of bankers' acceptances and repurchase agreements. And, of course, they carry very sizable demand deposit balances at commercial banks to cover day-to-day transactions.

Nonmonetary financial institutions also enter on both sides of the money markets. Almost all the different kinds of institutions supply funds to these markets through their holdings of liquid assets. On the demand side, finance companies stand out: A large sum of short-term funds is acquired through the issuance of finance company paper.

Foreign participation in our money markets, as already indicated, is mainly on the supply-of-funds side of the market. Foreigners hold about $15 billion of deposits, much of it in time deposit form. But in addition, they also hold a large amount in Treasury securities, mainly short-term. While the loss of monetary gold as a result of our adverse balance of payments has been (or was) the publicized factor, the growth in the amount of foreign holdings of dollar assets in our money markets has been (and still is) the other expression of this imbalance.

The dealers in Treasury and other securities are not themselves appreciable net elements in the money markets. They carry substantial but fluctuating inventories of securities, but since they do this with funds borrowed mainly from banks and nonfinancial corporations, they take about as much funds out of the money market as they put in. Their influence in money markets, however, is vast and pervasive. This influence will be explored at length in Part Two of this book.

The money market is a strange and mysterious territory to many persons. Our discussion in this section has only scratched the surface of its magnitudes, functions, operations, and organization. A full description and analysis of money markets is presented in Part Two.

MAGNITUDES IN THE CAPITAL MARKETS

As we have used the term here, capital markets are those markets for longer-term debt and equity claims: stocks, bonds, mortgages, and other evidences of longer-term debt. The markets generally considered to be capital markets include (1) the market for longer-term U.S. government securities, (2) the market for corporate bonds, (3) the market for corporate stocks, (4) the market for state and local government obligations, and (5) the mortgage market. While the term "market" has been used in the singular, there are, in fact, both new-issue markets and secondary markets for most of these types of obligations. In some cases, as with corporate equities, the secondary market is very important but the new-issue market is small. In other cases, as for mortgages, the new-issue market is substantial but the secondary market is relatively underdeveloped.

The participants in the capital markets can be classified into a number of groups. On the demand-for-funds side are the issuers of the various financial claims enumerated above. The supply of funds that enters this market comes partly from individuals directly and partly from financial intermediaries. However, this second part comes ultimately from individuals who are the owners of claims on financial intermediaries. Many times these financial intermediaries seem to dominate the markets. The financial intermediaries include a long list of institutions: mutual savings banks, savings and loan associations, insurance companies (both life and nonlife), pension funds (both private and public), mutual funds, personal trusts, endowment funds, foundations, and, of course, commercial banks. Commercial banking is the one financial institution that supplies large amounts of funds to both the money and the capital markets. The other institutions listed are definitely capital market institutions.

The groups representing supply and demand in the market are served by a number of marketing institutions: the organized stock exchanges, the partly organized over-the-counter markets, investment banks and security dealers, mortgage bankers and brokers, and even such informal agents as business brokers (who sell grocery stores, motels, laundromats, and so forth).

How big are the capital markets? As of December 31, 1971, the aggregate amount of corporate stocks and bonds, mortgages, and government securities outstanding was $2,352 billion (see Table 4-2). Of this total, 77 percent were claims against the private sector; 23 percent was government debt. These percentages give a crude indication of our mixed capitalistic system. Another interesting percentage breakdown is by ownership. Roughly half of the $2,352-billion total was held by financial intermediaries, the other half by households. Excluding corporate stocks, intermediaries held roughly three-quarters of the capital market instruments, households one-quarter. Since households owned the claims against financial intermediaries, they indirectly owned the capital market holdings of the intermediaries. Thus the ownership of all capital market instruments can be traced directly or indirectly to the ultimate savers in the economy: households.

The biggest single capital market in terms of value of claims outstanding is the corporate stock market. As of the end of 1971, equity "claims" against corporations amounted to more than $1 trillion. However, this figure must be interpreted with care. Much of its size was not determined by sale of shares in the capital market. Rather, corporations have relied heavily on retained earnings to finance real capital growth. This growth, in turn, has reflected back on the prices of corporate shares. In fact, the growth rate of the average price of each share outstanding has tended to exceed the growth rate of the number of shares outstanding. While the sum of these two growth rates has determined the growth rate of the total value of all shares, only the growth in the number of shares has directly involved the capital markets.

The supply-of-funds side of the corporate stock market is dominated by households, pension funds, and mutual funds. Together they hold about 95 percent of all stocks outstanding. The pension funds and mutual funds currently hold a much smaller share than does the household sector, but the funds' share is increasing over time. By the year 2000, their share will probably be around 50 percent.

The mortgage market is the second-biggest capital market; $500 billion of mortgages were outstanding at the end of 1971. On the demand side of the mortgage credit market are households and businesses. Practically all the mortgages taken out by households are for the purpose of financing homes. Mortgages on business property are usually taken out by small unincorporated businesses. The supply of mortgage credit is mainly from financial intermediaries, with savings and loan associations, commercial banks, life insurance companies, and mutual savings banks doing most of the lending. Smaller but still important sources of mortgage credit are households and federal credit agencies. Many households hold second mortgages on the homes of other households. Mortgage credit from federal credit agencies is a postwar phenomenon. Federal participation in the mortgage market has been widely criticized for its practices, but in theory it serves the laudable purpose of smoothing and expanding the overall flow of mortgage credit.

The third-largest capital market is the market for U.S. government securities. At the end of 1971, the net federal debt approached $370 billion. Not all of this debt, however, was acquired through the open capital markets. A large portion was in the form of Treasury bills, which are short-term instruments traded in the money market. Another sizable portion was in savings bonds and other nonmarketable issues. The monetary system, the foreign sector, and the household sector own the largest shares of the federal debt. These sectors are not all that important, however, in the open market for long-term federal obligations. The monetary system and the foreign sector hold large amounts of short-term obligations, while the household sector is deep in nonmarketable holdings. Actually, no single sector dominates the supply-of-funds side of the open market for long-term federal securities. Holdings of these securities are spread rather evenly among all the different sectors.

The fourth-largest market is that for corporate bonds. Corporate bond issues outstanding total more than $200 billion. Most of this debt is owed by nonfinancial corporations; however, about $25 billion is owed by finance companies. Ownership of corporate bonds is concentrated in insurance companies (particularly life companies), pension funds (public and private), and households. Together, these sectors hold between 85 and 90 percent of all corporate bonds outstanding. A large portion of the bonds held by insurance companies and pension funds originated as nonmarketable private placements. This portion can be viewed as exempt from the open capital markets.

State and local government securities amount to just under $170 billion. Most of the credit to this important capital market comes from commercial banks, wealthy individuals, and property and casualty insurance companies. As a group they hold more than 90 percent of all state and local obligations. The tax-exempt status of interest earned on state and local obligations makes these securities particularly attractive to institutions and individuals in high tax brackets.

The capital markets are fairly familiar markets to most persons, at least compared to the money markets. Still, the capital markets are open to a multitude of complexities which most people do not understand. A detailed description and analysis of the different capital markets is presented in Part Three of this book.

LENDING, BORROWING, AND INTEREST RATES

Up to this point, the discussion of the flow-of-funds accounts has been purely descriptive and (perhaps) dry. It is time now to give the accounts some analytical substance. The task of this section is to relate flow-of-funds quantities to interest rates in a very general way. We shall find that these quantities not only affect interest rates but are affected by interest rates.

Unfortunately, the official flow-of-funds system of accounts presented in Table 4-1 is too complex and cumbersome to give us a good handle on the problem. It will be useful, therefore, to condense Table 4-1 into a simplified matrix. This is done in Table 4-4.

Abstracting from problems of statistical estimation, which give rise to the discrepancies in Table 4-4, it is clear that for each sector the following identities hold:

Saving + borrowing = investment + lending
Saving − investment = lending − borrowing
Saving − investment = surplus on current account
Lending − borrowing = net financial investment
Surplus on current account = net financial investment

Of the different domestic sectors, the household sector is the principal surplus sector. Its role in the financial markets is that it lends more than it borrows. The business and government sectors, on the other hand, are deficit sectors. They borrow more than they lend. The finance sector is pretty much in balance; it fulfills its intermediating role by lending what it borrows.

FLOW OF FUNDS IN FINANCIAL MARKETS

Table 4-4 Condensed Summary of Flow of Funds Accounts for First Quarter of 1972 (Seasonally Adjusted Annual Rates—Billions of Dollars)

Transaction category	Households	Business	Government	Finance	Rest of world	All sectors
A. Saving	182.4	102.5	−17.4	6.8	10.0	284.3
B. Investment	144.0*	128.9	0.0	3.0	0.0	275.9
C. Surplus on current account (A-B)	38.4	−26.4	−17.4	3.8	10.0	8.4
D. Lending	98.3	27.2	−1.7	139.1	18.9	281.8
E. Borrowing	59.1	72.1	20.6	139.7	7.6	299.1
F. Net financial investment (D-E)	39.2	−44.9	−22.3	−.6	11.3	−17.3
G. Statistical discrepancy (C-F)	−.8	18.5	4.9	4.4	−1.3	25.7

*Includes consumer durable goods.

When the sectors are combined (see the "all sectors" column in Table 4-4), surplus on current account and net financial investment vanish.[5] For the economy as a whole:

Saving = investment
Lending = borrowing

In other words, one sector's surplus is matched in the system by the other sectors' deficit, and one sector's net financial investment is the other sectors' excess of borrowing over lending.

Lending and borrowing are, of course, the transactions that take place in the financial markets. Lending represents the supply-of-funds side of the market, borrowing the demand side. The price of funds in the market is the rate of interest.[6]

The interest rate is the price factor that brings the supply and demand for funds into equilibrium. If supply exceeds demand—that is, if

---

[5] The nonzero values for these two accounts in Table 4-4 are due to statistical discrepancies in estimation procedures.

[6] The concept of "the" rate of interest only makes sense if we assume that it stands for the general level of interest rates or if we assume for the time being that there is a single homogeneous class of financial assets traded in the market.

desired lending is greater than desired borrowing—the interest rate is above its equilibrium and market forces will cause it to fall. On the other hand, if demand is greater than supply—that is, if intended borrowing exceeds intended lending—the interest rate is too low and will tend to rise. The relations between lending, borrowing, and the interest rate are depicted in Figure 4-1.

Movement from one equilibrium rate of interest to another requires a shift in either the supply schedule or the demand schedule for funds. Behind the supply schedule lies, of course, saving. Saving is the primary source of the funds which are loaned. Behind the demand schedule lies investment. It is the primary use of borrowed funds. Thus, if households have more income with which to save, they can be expected to lend more in the financial markets. The supply of funds is increased and the equilibrium rate of interest falls. Conversely, if businesses plan to make larger capital expenditures, they can be expected to seek more borrowing. The demand for funds is increased and the rate of interest rises.

In short, the interest rate is determined by the forces of lending and borrowing, which, in turn, are influenced by saving and investment. Financial activity reflects real factors. Simultaneously, saving and investment are influenced by lending and borrowing opportunities, which, in turn, are determined by the rate of interest. Real activity reflects financial factors. Cause and effect work in both directions.

A major shortcoming of this analysis is that it is at too high a level of abstraction. The flow-of-funds accounts, as we have seen, are quite complex and comprehensive. They reveal a multiplicity of financial markets. Rather than one market for loanable funds and one rate of interest

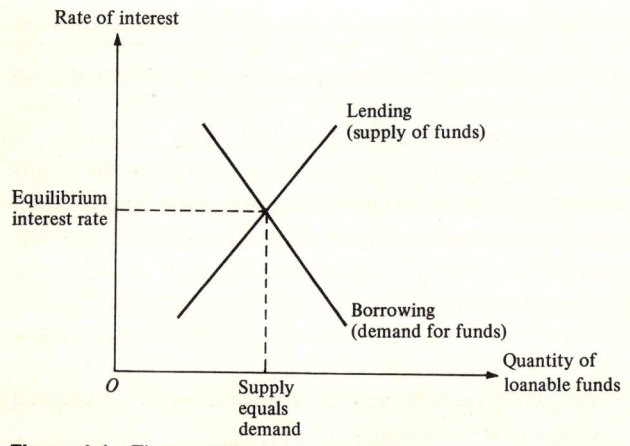

Figure 4-1 The market for loanable funds.

to be determined, there are really many markets and many rates (one for each market).

Fortunately, the analysis can be extended to handle any number of financial markets. For each and every market there is a supply schedule and a demand schedule for funds and an interest rate which brings supply and demand into equilibrium. The same principles apply in the many-markets case as in the single-market case. There is a problem, however, of market interrelations. Supply and demand in one market depend not only on the interest rate in that market but on interest rates in other markets. Moreover, the interest rate in one market depends not only on supply and demand in that market but on supply and demand in other markets. These complex interrelations make analysis of the flow-of-funds accounts difficult but not impossible.

ANALYTICAL USES OF THE FLOW-OF-FUNDS ACCOUNTS

One of the oldest paradoxes in economic analysis is that one cannot explain one phenomenon without "explaining everything else." In any equilibrium system this is true, whether it be the system of price markets for commodities, an electrical circuit, the solar system, or financial markets. The flow-of-funds system is also an equilibrium system. The actual uses and sources of funds figures which appear in the flow-of-funds accounts are not necessarily equilibrium quantities, but they are quantities which reflect a process of balancing supply and demand simultaneously in the various financial markets.

Practical analysts of various sectors of the financial markets recognize this truth intuitively. An investment banker in the state and local government security market would not dream of trying to analyze or forecast events in his market without bringing in the money markets and other capital markets. The flow-of-funds system allows this to be done formally with a minimum of sweat.

The two principal analytical uses of flow-of-funds are interest-rate forecasting and financial econometric model building. These two uses are not mutually exclusive. Some forecasters use econometric models and some econometricians use models for forecasting. Generally, however, interest-rate forecasting is done by practical analysts who feel there is more to forecasting than solving a constricted set of simultaneous equations. On the other hand, econometric model building is usually done by academically oriented economists who see their work in a broader context than that of mere forecasting; they are usually more interested in "explaining why" than in "forecasting what."

Practical analysts use the flow-of-funds framework in arriving at interest-rate forecasts. Some of the better-known forecasts are the ones prepared by the Bankers Trust Company, the Life Insurance Association of America, and Salomon Brothers. The basic procedure used in these forecasts is that of *iteration,* or successive approximation. The first step in the iterative procedure is to make a forecast of the GNP and its major components: consumer, business, and government expenditures. Expenditure forecasts are then translated into forecasts for the demand for funds. For example, the demand for residential construction is translated into a demand for residential mortgage funds. The same thing is done on the supply-of-funds side of the market. Forecasts of saving are converted into supply-of-funds estimates. Trends in the behavior of financial intermediaries also enter into the supply-of-funds estimates. After much thought and manipulation, a quantity of demand for funds and a quantity of supply of funds are estimated for each of the different capital markets. These first-round estimates are also based on some assumption of interest rates, since interest rates affect both the supply of and demand for funds.

After the first estimates of supply and demand have been made, the forecaster usually finds that supply and demand do not balance when put into flow-of-funds matrix form. The lack of balance itself then becomes evidence as to the nature of likely future developments. An excess of borrowing plans over lending plans suggests higher interest rates and a shortage of funds. A shortage of funds in one market and a surplus of funds in another suggest that relative interest rates may change even if the overall level remains unchanged.

The second round of successive approximations involves interest-rate revisions and hence supply of and demand for funds revisions. Even after the second round it is unlikely that the quantities will balance, because the quantities in each market are influenced by the whole spectrum of interest rates and each interest rate is affected by more than one financial market. Thus the iterative procedure is continued until all interest rates and all supply and demand quantities are consistent and reasonable. The final approximation of interest rates is the one which is expected to ensure equality of uses and sources of funds for each financial market or transaction category and for each transacting sector. Of course, different forecasters come up with different interest-rate forecasts. Very few forecasters are able to come close to the mark most of the time, and even the very best are way off target occasionally.

The iterative procedure used by practical analysts for forecasting interest rates involves working with behavioral relations. Quantities supplied and demanded are related to interest rates, and interest rates are related to supply and demand. The practical analyst usually has a feel for these interrelations based on his experiences in the capital markets; he may or may not take the step of formulating an explicit set of equations, and even if he does, he may or may not estimate the parameters of the equations statistically.

The mark of financial econometric model building is to specify the behavioral relations, market constraints, and market-clearing conditions in the form of a system of simultaneous equations. Observed flow-of-funds quantities and observed interest rates are used as data for estimating the parameters of the equations. These parameters provide a statistical measure of the response of demand and supply to interest rates and the response of interest rates to demand and supply.

The overall purpose of a financial econometric model is to explain financial market behavior—past, present, and future. Explaining the future is called prediction, but it is important to note that econometric models are capable of making any number of predictions, depending upon the assumed values of the exogenous variables fed into the model. For example, an assumption that the federal deficit will be $20 billion leads to one prediction of future interest rates and funds flows, while an assumption that the deficit will be $25 billion leads to another prediction. A good economist never states categorically that future variables will be such and such; rather, he is always careful to qualify his predictions with assumptions. This applies to all kinds of forecasting, real as well as financial.

In addition to interest-rate forecasting and financial econometric model building, the flow-of-funds accounts have been used as descriptive input for business cycle analysis, financial planning, international and interregional funds-flow analysis, analysis of economic growth and development, and so on.[7] Apart from the many analytical uses of the flow-of-funds, the accounts are interesting and valuable simply because they provide an excellent descriptive overview of the size and complexity of our financial market system.

[7] See Cohen (35) for a recent review of the many different applications of the flow-of-funds system.

Chapter 5

Portfolio Selection and Security Pricing

As was brought out in Chapters 1 and 2, the basic foundations of financial markets are saving and investment. The funds which get traded in financial markets come ultimately from saving and go ultimately into real investment. The path which funds travel as they flow from saving into investment is largely indirect. As Chapter 3 brought out, a system of financial intermediaries stands between savers and investors. Savers supply funds to these intermediaries, who, in turn, supply them to investors. This indirect flow of funds from saving into investment is also complex. Savers can choose from a wide variety of specialized intermediaries; likewise, the intermediaries can choose from a large variety of specialized money and capital market instruments. As Chapter 4 brought out, there are many different financial markets and many different participating sectors. Each market can have many different participants, and each participant can be into many different markets. The flow-of-funds matrix is ample proof of such complexity.

Every economic entity involved in the complex financial system must concern itself with two basic problems. One is deciding how much wealth to accumulate and the other is the form which it should take. Financial market conditions influence both these decisions. We have already seen in Chapter 2 how interest rates and other financial factors affect the level of saving and investment and therefore the level of wealth. And we have seen in Chapter 3 how financial customs serve to constrain the asset choices of intermediaries. The question of what determines the choice of assets after accounting for constraints on financial behavior thus remains. How does an individual person or organization choose from among alternative assets? What are the determinants of wealth composition? To solve the problem of asset choice or wealth composition, the present chapter turns to the theory of portfolio selection.[1]

The theory of portfolio selection is actually more than a theory of choosing securities. It is general enough to encompass the choosing of all kinds of assets, real as well as financial. But its introduction and early development were in the context of choosing securities, particularly equity securities, and so the theory continues to go by the name of portfolio selection. The present chapter follows tradition and focuses on the choosing of securities.

One of the determinants of choosing securities is the structure of security prices. In order to explain why who holds what and in what quantities, security prices must also be explained. The question of security pricing, however, turns back on the question of portfolio selection. Security prices are determined by, as well as determinants of, portfolio choices. This is similar to quantity and and price determination in any market. Demand depends on price, price depends on demand, and both are determined simultaneously. The same holds for financial markets. The choosing of securities and the pricing of securities are mutually interdependent. It will simplify matters, however, to take security prices as given when discussing the theory of portfolio selection and to take portfolio choices as given when discussing the theory of security pricing.[2]

But first, we must come to understand the key relationships, measurements, and principles which are instrumental to both theories.

RELATION BETWEEN MARKET PRICE AND RATE OF RETURN

There are three ways to perceive the value of a security. One way is to look at its current market price. Another way is to look at the future dollar

---

[1] Portfolio-selection theory was introduced by Markowitz (144) and refined by Tobin (217), Sharpe (200), and others.

[2] Security pricing theory is a logical extension of portfolio-style sheet and herein selection theory. It was developed by Sharpe (196), Lintner (135 and 136), Mossin (155), Stone (212), and others.

returns it will bring. Still another way is to calculate the future dollar returns on the current market price as a percentage rate of return. To illustrate, if a security has a current market price of $100 and a single future dollar return of $120 one year hence, the annual rate of return is 20 percent. If, instead, the current market price is $60 and the future dollar return is the same as before, then the rate of return is 100 percent. This example demonstrates a very important principle: Given future dollar returns, a security's rate of return is inversely related to its market price.

It is easy to compute the annual rate of return when there is but a single future dollar return one year hence. But for more complex patterns of future dollar returns, the calculation of rate of return is not intuitively obvious. Fortunately, there is an equation which is very general and will always provide a solution for the percentage rate of return:

$$\text{Current market price of a security} = \frac{\text{Dollar returns in first year}}{(1+r)^1} + \frac{\text{Dollar returns in second year}}{(1+r)^2} + \ldots + \frac{\text{Dollar returns in } n\text{th terminal year}}{(1+r)^n}$$

The r in the equation is the annual rate of return. It can be solved after plugging in the values for market price and future dollar returns. The equation confirms the principle that rate of return is inversely related to market price. The larger market price (the left-hand side of the equation), the smaller will be the rate of return. (Rate of return appears in the denominators in the right-hand side of the equation, and the smaller the denominators, the larger the sum of the terms on the right-hand side.)

The equation for determining rate of return is very general and can be applied to any kind of security in any situation. When applied to a common stock, the future dollar returns are dividends and the terminal value of the stock. When applied to a bond (or other debt instrument), the future dollar returns are interest payments and the terminal value of the bond. The terminal value of a stock is its market price when sold. The terminal value of a bond is its market price if sold, its call price if called, and its face or par value if held to maturity. The rate of return on a bond held to maturity is called "yield to maturity."

Whatever the situation, rate of return can be determined from future dollar returns and the current market price. For given future dollar returns, rate of return always varies inversely with current market price. In short, rate of return and market price are two sides of the same coin.

PORTFOLIO SELECTION AND SECURITY PRICING

RISK AND THE CALCULATION OF EXPECTED RATE OF RETURN

One might question how rate of return can be calculated given that no one knows the future with certainty nor the precise returns it will bring. Fortunately, there is a way around this problem. A person may not know the future but still be able to attach likelihood or probability coefficients to different possible outcomes. If so, he can calculate what statisticians call the "expected rate of return."

Expected rate of return is a weighted average of all possible rates of return. Each possible rate can be multiplied by its probability coefficient. The resulting products can then be totaled to get the expected rate of return. An example will illustrate how simple the procedure is. Consider a security which has a .3 probability of earning a 9 percent rate of return, a .4 probability of earning 10 percent, a .2 probability of earning 13 percent, and a .1 probability of earning 17 percent. In this case the expected rate of return is 11 percent. The calculations are shown below.

Possible rate of return		Probability of possible rate of return		
9%	×	.3	=	2.7%
10%	×	.4	=	4.0%
13%	×	.2	=	2.6%
17%	×	.1	=	1.7%
		1.0		11.0% (expected rate of return)

The 11 percent expected rate of return is a statistical expectation. It is not the most likely outcome. Nor in this case is it even considered a possible outcome. Rather, it is a weighted average of all possible outcomes.

Statistically, two securities can have different possible rates of return but the same expected rate of return. Consider a second security which has a .2 probability of earning 0 percent, a .5 probability of earning

Possible rate of return		Probability of possible rate of return		
0%	×	.2	=	0.0%
7%	×	.5	=	3.5%
25%	×	.3	=	7.5%
		1.0		11.0% (expected rate of return)

7 percent, and a .3 probability of earning 25 percent. In this case the expected rate of return is again 11 percent, as calculated above.

Although this second security has the same expected rate of return as the first, most persons would not be indifferent in choosing between the two. The second security is obviously more risky than the first. Persons who like taking risks would prefer the second security to the first. Those who dislike risk would choose the first security.

An important point emerges. Portfolio choices are governed not only by expected rate of return but by risk as well. People are indifferent neither toward risk nor toward expected return. A method has been demonstrated for calculating expected return. But how is risk calculated? How can a person tell how much more risky one security is than another?

CALCULATING RISK

There are two very closely related measures of risk. One is called "the variance of return," the other "the standard deviation of return." Both measures characterize the relative spread or dispersion of possible returns from the expected return. The variance is a weighted average of the squares of the deviations of all possible rates of return from the expected rate of return. The expected rate of return is subtracted from each possible rate of return. Each difference or deviation is squared and multiplied by its probability coefficient. The products are then totaled to get the variance of return. The standard deviation of return is then obtained by taking the square root of the variance.

This sounds a lot more complicated than it actually is. Variance and standard deviation are easily calculated for the two securities illustrated in the preceding section (see below).

Risk Calculations for First Security

Possible rate of return	Expected rate of return	Deviation of possible from expected	Deviation squared		Probability of possibility	
9%	11%	−2%	4%	×	.3	= 1.2%
10%	11%	−1%	1%	×	.4	= .4%
13%	11%	+2%	4%	×	.2	= .8%
17%	11%	+6%	36%	×	.1	= 3.6%
						6.0%
						(variance
Standard deviation = $\sqrt{6\%}$ = 2.45%						of return)

The standard deviation of return for the first security is 2.45 percent, while for the second, more risky, security it is 9.54 percent. The larger the standard deviation, the greater the risk. This is because the

PORTFOLIO SELECTION AND SECURITY PRICING 85

Risk Calculations for Second Security

Possible rate of return	Expected rate of return	Deviation of possible from expected	Deviation squared		Probability of possibility	
0%	11%	−11%	121%	×	.2	= 24.2%
7%	11%	−4%	16%	×	.5	= 8.0%
25%	11%	+14%	196%	×	.3	= 58.8%
						91.0%
						(variance of return)

Standard deviation = $\sqrt{91\%}$ = 9.54%

standard deviation measures the dispersion or spread of possible returns from the expected return. Standard deviation and its square, the variance, are not the only measures of risk, but they possess certain statistical and mathematical qualities which make them specially suited for portfolio analysis.

GREATER EXPECTED RETURN FOR GREATER RISK

The two securities examined thus far have the following characteristics:

	Security 1	Security 2
Expected rate of return	11%	11%
Standard deviation of return	2.45%	9.54%

Both have the same expected return, but the spread of possible returns is greater for the second security.

If this pattern of risk-return characteristics is generally perceived in the market and if the average investor in the market is averse to risk, market forces will cause the pattern to shift in the direction of greater expected return for greater risk. People who dislike risk but are willing to take risks if the returns are high enough will not want to hold the more risky security as long as the less risky security offers the same expected return. Such people will sell but not buy the more risky security, and they will buy but not sell the less risky one. As the more risky security is sold in the market, its market price falls and its expected rate of return rises. The opposite happens with the less risky security. Buying pressure causes its market price to rise and its expected rate of return to fall. Eventually, the expected rate of return on the more risky security will be so much greater than on the other that each investor still holding the more risky security will feel the risk is justified. At this point the market is in equilibrium.

The equilibrium pattern of greater expected return for greater risk assumes that investors are averse to risk. If, instead, investors liked risk for its own sake, they would trade return for risk. And if such behavior permeated the market, the equilibrium pattern of risk-return characteristics would be less expected return for greater risk. Some investors are known to like risk, but their influence on financial markets is overshadowed by the influence of the risk-averse majority of investors. Studies indicate that more risky securities are in fact associated with higher expected returns. The assumption of general risk aversion is thus consistent with observed market characteristics.

EFFECT OF DIVERSIFICATION ON RISK AND EXPECTED RETURN

Risk and expected return can be estimated for a portfolio of securities as well as for a single security. Most investors do diversify their holdings so that their portfolios contain more than one security. Diversification often has an interesting beneficial effect on risk and expected return. If separate returns on separate securities are not too highly and positively correlated, a combination of the securities will exhibit less risk than the risk of the securities taken separately. Thus diversification often makes it possible to reduce risk considerably with little impairment of expected return.

An example will show how this beneficial effect works. Suppose there are two securities, A and B, with the following characteristics:

Security A

Possible rate of return		Probability of possibility			Deviation of possible from expected	Deviation squared		Probability of possibility		
10%	x	.5	=	5%	−10%	100%	x	.5	=	50%
30%	x	.5	=	15%	+10%	100%	x	.5	=	50%
				20% (expected rate of return)						100% (variance of return)

Security B has the higher expected rate of return, but it also has the higher variance of return. This conforms to the principle of greater expected return for greater risk.

Now suppose that, instead of considering securities A and B separately, they are combined into a portfolio, with 80 percent of the port-

Security B

Possible rate of return		Probability of possibility		Deviation of possible from expected	Deviation squared		Probability of possibility	
0%	x	.5	= 0%	−25%	625%	x	.5	= 312.5%
50%	x	.5	= 25%	+25%	625%	x	.5	= 312.5%
			25% (expected rate of return)				625.0% (variance of return)	

folio invested in A and 20 percent in B. What then is the risk and expected return for the portfolio? It depends on the correlation of returns between A and B. The following contingency table illustrates three possible probability distributions.

		Probability of return when correlation of returns is:		
Possibility	Associated rate of return on portfolio	I Perfectly positive	II Zero	III Perfectly negative
High rate of return for both A and B	.8x.3 + .2x.5 = 34%	.50	.25	.00
Low rate of return for both A and B	.8x.1 + .2x.0 = 8%	.50	.25	.00
High rate of return for A but low for B	.8x.3 + .2x.0 = 24%	.00	.25	.50
Low rate of return for A but high for B	.8x.1 + .2x.5 = 18%	.00	.25	.50
		1.00	1.00	1.00

The probability coefficients in the above table require some explanation. Perfectly positive correlation means that security B's return is always high when security A's return is high, and that B's return is low when A's is low. Assuming A's return has an even chance of being high or low, perfectly positive correlation means that there is an even chance of both A and B having high returns or both having low returns. Perfectly negative correlation is just the opposite. In this case, B's return is always low when A's is high, and it is always high when A's is low. Assuming, again, an even chance of high or low returns for security A, perfectly negative correlation means that there is an even chance of a high return for A but low for B or of a low return for A but high for B. Finally, zero correlation means that returns on A and B are unrelated. If both have an even chance of being high or low, there is a 25 percent probability that (1) both will be high, (2) both will be low, (3) A's will be high but B's low, or that (4) A's will be low but B's high. In this case, there is an even chance for any one of *four* possible outcomes.

Given all these joint probabilities, risk and expected return can now be calculated for the portfolio of securities A and B for each of the three correlations.

I Risk and Expected Return on the Portfolio When the Return on Security A Is Perfectly and Positively Correlated with Return on Security B

Possible rate of return		Probability of possibility		Deviation of possible from expected	Deviation squared		Probability of possibility	
34%	×	.5	= 17%	+13%	169%	×	.5	= 84.5%
8%	×	.5	= 4%	−13%	169%	×	.5	= 84.5%
			21% (expected rate of return)					169.0% (variance of return)

II Risk and Expected Return on the Portfolio When Return on Security A Is Completely Uncorrelated with Return on Security B

Possible rate of return		Probability of possibility		Deviation of possible from expected	Deviation squared		Probability of possibility	
34%	×	.25	= 8.5%	+13%	169%	×	.25	= 42.25%
8%	×	.25	= 2.0%	−13%	169%	×	.25	= 42.25%
24%	×	.25	= 6.0%	+ 3%	9%	×	.25	= 2.25%
18%	×	.25	= 4.5%	− 3%	9%	×	.25	= 2.25%
			21% (expected rate of return)					89% (variance of return)

Calculations I, II, and III clearly demonstrate when diversification is beneficial and when it is not. It is most beneficial when returns are most negatively correlated. In case III, the variance of return for the 80 to 20 percent combination of A and B is 9 percent and the standard deviation is 3 percent. This is considerably less risk than the risk of the

PORTFOLIO SELECTION AND SECURITY PRICING

III Risk and Expected Return on the Portfolio When Return on Security A Is Perfectly but Negatively Correlated with Return on Security B

Possible rate of return		Probability of possibility		Deviation of possible from expected	Deviation squared		Probability of possibility	
24%	×	.5	= 12%	+3%	9%	×	.5	= 4.5%
18%	×	.5	= 9%	−3%	9%	×	.5	= 4.5%
			21% (expected rate of return)				9% (variance of return)	

least risky security, A, which by itself has a variance of 100 percent and a standard deviation of 10 percent. Diversification is also beneficial, though not as much, when returns are uncorrelated. In case II the variance of the combination of A and B is 89 percent and the standard deviation 9.4 percent, which is still less risk than the risk of the least risky security.

Diversification is least beneficial when returns are most positively correlated. In case I the variance and standard deviation of the securities combined are 169 percent and 13 percent respectively. In this case diversification does not reduce risk below the risk of security A taken by itself. In fact, when returns are perfectly and positively correlated, as they are in this case, the standard deviation for the portfolio is a weighted average of the standard deviations for the individual securities in the portfolio, the weights being determined by the proportions of each security in the portfolio.

Rate of return for a portfolio is similarly a weighted average of the rates of return for the individual securities in the portfolio, where again the weights are given by the proportions of each security in the portfolio. This result holds for all correlations and is not dependent on the special condition of perfectly positive correlation. Thus, unlike portfolio risk, portfolio return is completely independent of the correlation of returns between the securities in the portfolio. In all three of the cases considered above, the expected rate of return is 21 percent. This is because the portfolio contains 80 percent of security A, whose expected return is 20 percent, and 20 percent of security B, whose expected return is 25 percent.

In summary, it is beneficial to combine securities whose returns are not highly and positively correlated. Diversification reduces portfolio risk below the risk of the least risky security in the portfolio. At the same time it keeps portfolio return above the return on the least risky security. It thus enables the investor to reduce risk with little impairment of return.

EFFICIENT COMBINATIONS OF RISK AND EXPECTED RETURN

With the aid of a computer, one could calculate the expected rate of return and the standard deviation of return for each of a very large number of potential portfolios. (The number of potential portfolios is very large because there are many different securities in the market and many ways to combine them.) One could then ask the computer to plot the calculated risk-return combinations on a graph in the form of a scatter diagram. If the number of computed combinations were large enough, the diagram would not look very scattered but rather congested. In fact, the plotted points would merge into a dark or shaded area as illustrated in Figure 5-1.

Any point within or on the boundary of the area graphed in Figure 5-1 is a potential portfolio. An investor is free to select any point. A risk-averting investor would not choose just any point, however. Rather, he would select a portfolio where he gets the most expected return for a given amount of risk or the least risk for a given rate of return. Such a risk-return combination is termed "an efficient combination" or "an efficient portfolio." An inefficient combination, by default, is a combination of less than maximum return for given risk or more than minimum risk for given return.

All points within and on the boundary of the area in Figure 5-1 (except points on the extra dark boundary from K to L) are inefficient combinations. From such a point it is possible to move upward and increase expected return without increasing risk, or to move leftward and decrease risk without decreasing expected return, or to move both upward and leftward and simultaneously increase return and decrease risk. Only the extra dark boundary from K to L contains the efficient portfolios, that is, the efficient combinations of risk and expected return. Once on this segment of the boundary, it is not possible to change portfolios without either decreasing the expected return or increasing the risk.

The risk-averting investor can naturally rule out all the inefficient risk-return combinations in selecting a portfolio. Only the efficient combinations interest him. He knows that the best or optimal portfolio for him is one of the efficient portfolios lying on KL.

SELECTING THE PORTFOLIO WITH THE OPTIMUM COMBINATION OF RISK AND EXPECTED RETURN

The efficient portfolios of the preceding section are all portfolios of risky securities. It is time now to bring in two other sets of efficient portfolios.

PORTFOLIO SELECTION AND SECURITY PRICING

One is a portfolio of riskless securities, and the other includes combinations of risky and riskless securities.

A riskless security has certain returns. Its expected rate of return is the pure rate of interest and its standard deviation of return is zero. Short-term U.S. government securities are perhaps the best known kind of riskless securities. A portfolio of U.S. Treasury bills, for example, comes as close as anything to a riskless portfolio. Such a portfolio is itself efficient inasmuch as it offers the absolute minimum in risk.

In Figure 5-2, point P is the zero-risk, pure return combination for riskless securities. Points on the curve from K to L are efficient risk-return combinations of risky securities. Points on the straight line connecting P and Q are combinations of the riskless portfolio P and the risky (but efficient) portfolio Q. A point lying halfway between P and Q, for example, is a fifty-fifty combination of riskless securities and the risky securities which constitute portfolio Q. If P has a certain return of 4 percent (and zero standard deviation) and Q has an expected return of 10 percent and a standard deviation of 6 percent, an investor who puts half his money into P and half into Q can expect a combined return of 7 percent and a combined standard deviation of 3 percent on his overall portfolio. When a portfolio of risky securities is combined with a riskless portfolio, the standard deviation of return for the combined portfolio is a proportion of the standard deviation for the risky portfolio, the proportion being the same as the proportion of risky securities in the combined portfolio.

Combining riskless securities with an efficient portfolio of risky securities does not necessarily guarantee an efficient combination of risky and riskless securities. The combinations on the line from P to

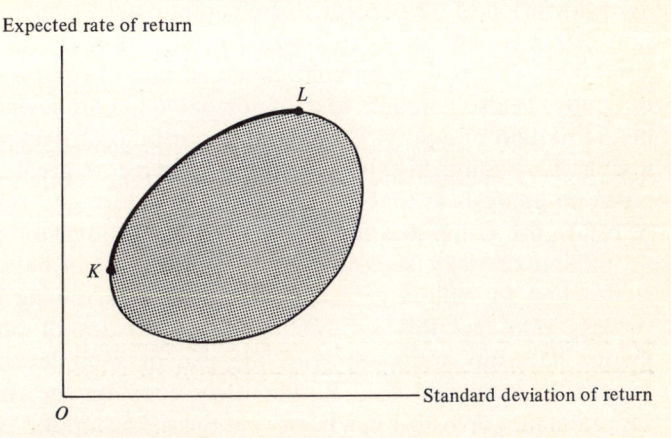

Figure 5-1 Possible combinations of risk and return.

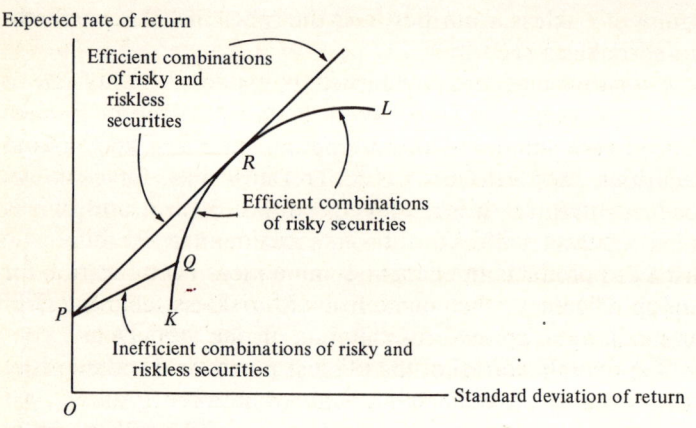

Figure 5-2 Efficient and inefficient combinations of riskless securities with efficient portfolios of risky securities.

Q in Figure 5-2, for example, are inefficient. The investor can get more return for the same risk, or less risk for the same return, by combining riskless securities with the efficient portfolio of risky securities represented by point R. Combinations of portfolio P and portfolio R lie on the line from P to R and beyond. These combinations are more efficient, since the line PR is positioned above (meaning more expected return) and to the left (meaning less risk) of the line PQ.

Before we can go any further, we must explain what it means to operate on the line beyond (to the right of) point R in Figure 5-2. Suppose an investor has an equity of $1 million to invest but that he would like to invest $2 million in R, which is expected to return 20 percent with a standard deviation of 12 percent. If he can borrow $1 million at the riskless rate of 4 percent, his net expected return from the $2 million of R is $360,000. This is a 36 percent expected rate of return on his $1 million of equity. It also amounts to a 24 percent standard deviation of return on his $1 million of equity. By holding a portfolio of risky securities that is double his equity, his risk on equity is twice as great. A key factor in portfolio analysis is that expected rate of return and standard deviation of return are computed for a given amount of investor's equity. Adding $1 million of risky securities to the portfolio can be accomplished by subtracting $1 million of riskless securities. Borrowing $1 million at the riskless rate has this subtracting effect. Critics of portfolio-selection theory have no argument with the use of such leverage to increase expected return and risk. Rather, they question the realism of the assumption that investors can borrow at the riskless rate.[3]

---

[3] See Friend and Blume (72).

Combinations of the riskless portfolio and portfolio R are efficient combinations. The line from P to R and beyond in Figure 5-2 is the line of efficient combinations of risky and riskless securities. This line is tangent to the curve from K to L. All other lines from P to or through points on KL are below and to the right of the tangent, PR. Combinations on these latter lines offer less than maximum return for given risk and less than minimum risk for given return. They are inefficient. Thus, except for R, no efficient portfolio of risky securities can combine with riskless securities to produce an efficient combination. Portfolio R alone is able to keep up efficiency when combined with riskless securities. For this reason it is called the optimal combination of risky securities.

The optimal overall portfolio of both risky and riskless securities depends on the investor's preferences toward risk and return. If he is strongly averse to risk and weakly motivated by return, he will maximize utility by investing a small part of his funds in the optimal combination of risky securities and a large part in riskless securities. If, on the other hand, he is only mildly averse to risk and strongly attracted to return, he may put all his funds into the optimal combination of risky securities. He may even go beyond this and borrow other people's funds (assuming he can get them at close to the riskless rate) to finance additional investment in the optimal combination of risky assets. Whatever amount the investor puts into or takes out of the market for riskless securities, there is only one best combination of risky securities in which to invest. The problem of selecting a portfolio of risky securities is thus separated from the problem of selecting a portfolio of both risky and riskless securities. The former is resolved somewhat objectively through calculation of risk and expected return. The latter is resolved more subjectively by the investor's attitudes toward risk and return.

LINEAR EQUILIBRIUM RELATIONS BETWEEN RISK AND EXPECTED RETURN

Up to now we have been looking at how an individual investor would theoretically select a portfolio given his estimations of and attitudes toward risk and return. We now turn to the larger issue of how security prices are determined, assuming each individual follows the rules of portfolio selection.

The theory of security pricing is a logical extension of the theory of portfolio selection. However, it operates at a higher level of abstraction. It assumes not only that each investor follows the rules of portfolio selection but that all investors have identical estimations of future prospects. This means that all investors seek the same optimal combination of risky securities.

What is in the optimal combination of risky securities that everyone seeks?

In equilibrium, the optimal combination consists of risky securities that actually exist in the market, and in proportions that actually exist. If, for example, 1 percent of the risky securities in the market are security X, each investor will (in equilibrium) want 1 percent of his own portfolio of risky assets to be security X. But suppose the market is not in equilibrium. Suppose each investor wants 2 percent of his risky securities to be security X. In such a case the desired amount of security X is twice its actual amount. Being in short supply, the price of security X must be bid up and its expected rate of return must fall. As expected return declines, each investor would decide that he does not want as much as 2 percent of his portfolio in X. At some lower expected rate of return, each investor would want only 1 percent in X. This would be an equilibrium expected rate of return, for it ensures that investors desire an amount actually in existence. The pricing mechanism thus brings demand into equilibrium with supply; it finds expected rates of return which induce investors to want what exists.

The same applies to the riskless rate of return. Recall that strongly risk-averse investors desire to invest (lend) part of their funds in riskless securities while mildly risk-averse investors prefer to borrow in this market. The equilibrium riskless rate equates desired lending with desired borrowing. If desired borrowing exceeds desired lending, there is a shortage of riskless funds. As a result, the risk-free rate rises, decreasing the desire to borrow and increasing the desire to lend, until eventually the risk-free rate is comfortably in equilibrium.

Thus in equilibrium, different investors will have different portfolios of risky and riskless securities. Conservative investors will hold relatively small proportions of risky securities in their portfolios; less conservative investors will hold relatively large proportions. Each investor, however, will hold the same combination of risky securities, a combination including all risky securities existing in the market. Moreover, each investor will hold each risky security in the same proportion as it exists in the market. The optimal combination of risky securities for every investor is, therefore, the market portfolio of risky securities.

In graphical terms, each investor selects a point from his line of efficient combinations of risky and riskless securities. Since each investor's line is identical to the lines of all other investors and since in equilibrium the optimal combination of risky securities is the market portfolio of risky securities, a simple linear equilibrium relation exists between risk and return on efficient portfolios of risky and riskless securities. This relation, as graphed in Figure 5-3, is called the capital market line

PORTFOLIO SELECTION AND SECURITY PRICING 95

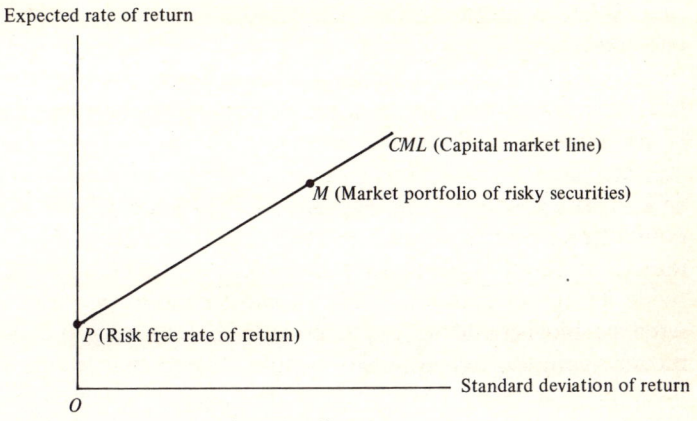

Figure 5-3 The capital market line.

(*CML*). Point *P* is again the risk-free rate of return associated with a zero standard deviation of return. Point *M* is the expected rate of return and the standard deviation of return for the market portfolio of risky securities. The *CML* is a straight line passing through points *P* and *M*. The *CML* shows that expected rate of return on an efficient portfolio of risky and riskless securities is a positive and linear function of risk as measured by the standard deviation of return. The *CML* stipulates (1) greater expected return for greater risk and (2) linear tradeoffs between risk and expected return.

The *CML* concept has implications for practical investment. It suggests that the investor should select a diversified portfolio of risky securities which has risk-return characteristics similar to those of the market portfolio. A dozen or so securities chosen at random should come close to the mark. (Obviously, no investor would find it feasible actually to assemble the complete market portfolio.) The *CML* also indicates the efficient equilibrium risk-return combinations of risky plus riskless securities from which the investor may choose in selecting his overall portfolio. It tells him how much return must be sacrificed in order to reduce risk or, alternatively, how much additional risk must be incurred to increase return.

The linear equilibrium relation between expected rate of return and standard deviation of return does not hold for inefficient portfolios or for individual securities. If it did, there would be no risk-reducing benefits derived from diversification. However, the relation between risk and return for individual securities is linear when certain measures other than standard deviation are used to specify risk. One such measure is the *covariance* between an individual security's (or individual portfolio's) rate of return and the market portfolio's rate of return. This measure is calculated as follows:

Covariance between security's rate of return and market portfolio's rate of return = correlation between security's rate of return and market portfolio's rate of return × standard deviation of security's rate of return × standard deviation of market portfolio's rate of return

Another measure is Sharpe's *beta coefficient*, which is simply a linear transformation of covariance:

Beta coefficient = correlation between security's rate of return and market portfolio's rate of return × standard deviation of security's rate of return × $\dfrac{1}{\text{standard deviation of market portfolio's rate of return}}$

Both measures indicate the "volatility" of the individual security's rate of return relative to the market portfolio's rate of return. Thus both measures indicate "systematic risk." Moreover, both measures provide a linear equilibrium relation between risk (so measured) and expected return for individual securities and for portfolios, efficient and inefficient.

Of the two measures, the beta coefficient is more easily applied to security analysis. When the security in question is a riskless security, the beta coefficient equals zero. When the security is the market portfolio or has the same characteristics as the market portfolio, the beta coefficient equals 1. Since the relation between expected return and the beta coefficient measure of volatility is linear, it graphs as a straight line passing through the risk-free rate of return and the expected rate of return on the market portfolio of risky securities. This line, as shown in Figure 5-4, is called the security market line (*SML*). As we shall see, the *SML* is a useful tool for analyzing security values and price movements.

IMPLICATIONS FOR SECURITY PRICES

The security market line graphed in Figure 5-4 is helpful in identifying overpriced and underpriced securities. It is a tool which the investor can use in making buy-sell decisions, and it offers a straightforward procedure

PORTFOLIO SELECTION AND SECURITY PRICING

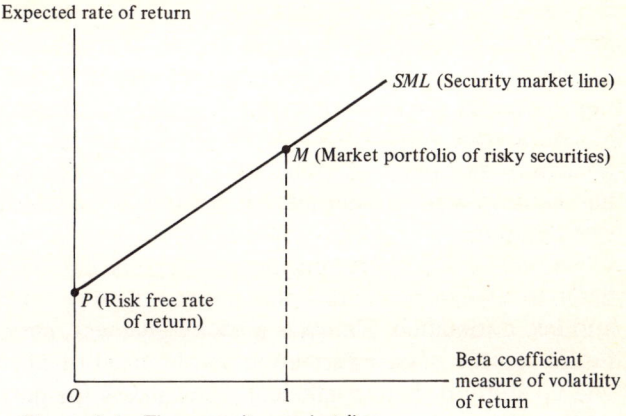

Figure 5-4 The security market line.

for analyzing securities. The first step is to estimate the risk-free rate of return. This can be done by using the Treasury bill rate as a proxy. The rate can be plotted on the vertical axis. The second step is to estimate the expected rate of return for the market. This can be tricky, but it essentially involves looking at recent overall market performance and adjusting for future expectations. Whether one makes an educated guess or avails himself of sophisticated computer programming, the estimated market return can be plotted against a beta coefficient of 1 or volatility of unity. The third step is to draw a straight line through the two plotted points. This is the *SML*, which shows the return-volatility combinations which should exist in equilibrium. The fourth step is to estimate return-volatility points for the various securities to be analyzed. These points should also be plotted and labeled. If security prices are in equilibrium, these latter points should lie on or near the *SML* because the *SML* is an equilibrium line.

Points which plot far above or far below the *SML* are the ones which interest the investor. These points represent securities whose prices appear to be out of equilibrium. Points above the *SML* represent securities which may be underpriced, while points below the line may indicate overpriced securities. The former have returns above their equilibrium returns for their volatility positions. Such securities should be in strong demand; their market prices should start advancing; their expected rates of return should fall toward equilibrium. The latter have unusually low returns for their risk. Their prices should drop and their returns increase until equilibrium is restored. The *SML* is thus a tool for identifying mispriced securities and for predicting the directions in which the prices should move to get into equilibrium.

It is far from a perfect tool, however. Remember, the *SML* is a theoretical construct. It is useful only insofar as it provides insights about the real world. We have seen that the theory is built on some artificial but necessary assumptions. This, however, does not render the theory invalid. If the implications of the theory are consistent with observed behavior, the theory is sufficiently robust to be acceptable. The theory has been gaining adherents, but adherents as well as critics recognize its limitations.

Even if the *SML* accurately depicts equilibrium, it may be difficult to estimate, as may the return-volatility points of individual securities. Estimation is always a tricky business, particularly estimates of future returns. Past information can be used to calculate rates of return and volatility or beta coefficients, but unless the past is a good indicator of the future, the calculations will not tell investors what they need to know. In this regard, studies indicate that beta coefficients are quite stable over time for efficient portfolios. However, for single securities and inefficient portfolios, beta coefficients are rather unstable.

Analysis of this kind is probably not suitable for the average investor. First, there is the practical consideration of the time and expense that it takes to perform such an analysis. Second, there is the risk of coming up with poor estimates of the return-volatility points which could lead to unprofitable decisions. It takes a lot of training in statistics to generate good statistics. Third, there is the possibility that the analysis will not reveal any significantly mispriced securities. If professional security analysts are doing their job well, security prices should always

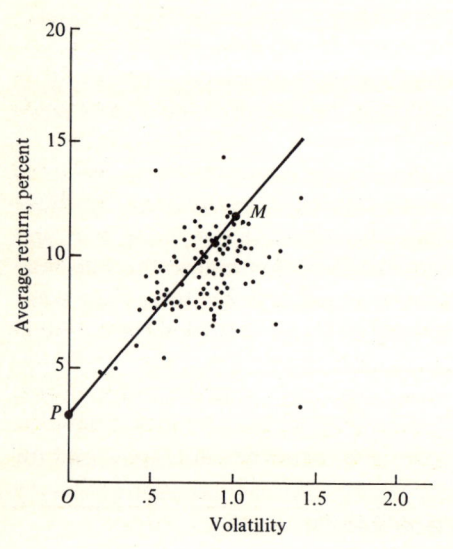

Figure 5-5 Volatility and return of 115 mutual funds studies by Jensen. *(Source:* W. F. Sharpe, Portfolio Theory and Capital Markets, *McGraw-Hill, New York, 1970, p. 166.)*

be at or close to equilibrium. The professionals should be able to detect and correct any mispricing of securities before the average investor can get into the act. Of course, one might ask: If security prices are always at or near equilibrium, why should there be so many professionals doing security analysis? Indeed, there is this curious paradox. The better the job done by security analysts, the worse the rewards of doing the job. The paradox is not difficult to resolve, however. Competition, the drive to outperform others, is what keeps the game alive. Fourth and finally, the *SML* model may not be able to predict the equilibrium structure of security prices if the model itself is incomplete or incorrect. As pointed out above, the validity of a model does not rest on the realism of its assumptions but rather on its predictive power. Unless the *SML* model can withstand the scrutiny of empirical evidence, it will be cast aside by all investors.

THE SECURITY MARKET LINE AND MUTUAL FUND PERFORMANCE

A look at realized risk-return characteristics of securities actually traded in the market lends modest empirical support to the theory of security pricing and the notion of a linear equilibrium relation between risk and expected return. Studies by Sharpe (197), Treynor (218), Jensen (114), and Friend, Blume, and Crockett (73) on the performance of mutual funds and by Roll (184) on federal government securities provide suggestive evidence that these markets behave fairly rationally and that the theory does a pretty good job of explaining actual behavior.

In this closing section we shall take a brief look at Jensen's study. His study is chosen because he actually plotted the *SML* over a scatter diagram of realized risk-return points for 115 mutual funds. The results are shown in Figure 5-5.

While many of the points in Figure 5-5 are not all that close to the *SML*, they do tend to form an upward-sloping pattern along the *SML*. This lends support to the assumption that the average investor is a risk-averter and the idea that the beta coefficient is a valid measure of risk. Still, one cannot help but notice that many points in Figure 5-5 are quite far off the *SML*. What does this mean? Are the points disequilibrium points which deviate from *SML* equilibrium?

In answer to this question, studies indicate that the stock market is highly efficient and that stock prices tend to move along their true equilibrium time paths.[4] The evidence is so overwhelming that it would

---

[4] See Fama (55) for a review of studies which support the efficient market hypothesis.

be difficult to attribute the deviations in Figure 5-5 to disequilibrium pricing.

Does this mean, therefore, that the *SML* is a deficient representation of the equilibrium structure of security prices?

We do not know. A large part of the problem derives from errors and omissions in the estimation of the return-volatility points. Jensen himself attached much weight to this problem. Subsequent analysis has demonstrated that some of the dispersion from the *SML* can be eliminated by improving the point estimates. Even so, the *SML* does not always provide the best statistical fit to the data. Better fits have been obtained from straight-line functions of the beta coefficient which are flatter than the *SML*. Some of these functions are refined versions of the *SML*.[5]

In sum, the development of the *SML* model has been a dramatic breakthrough in solving the problem of relating security prices and yields to risk. Although the model in its present form appears to do a less than fully adequate job of explaining the facts, it has become firmly established as the foundation for conducting current and future research.

[5] See Jenson (113).

Chapter 6

Structure and Behavior of Interest Rates

We have seen how rate of return varies with risk. Interest rates, the returns promised by debt instruments, are no exception. Different classifications of debt instruments are exposed to different kinds of risk, with the result that interest rates between the classifications are apt to be different. Within each classification, there are further interest-rate differentials owing to differences in the degree of risk exposure. The present chapter develops interest-rate structures by origin or type of risk. But risk does not tell the whole story. Market imperfections, tax effects, and other considerations also give rise to interest-rate differentials. We shall consider these, too.

The fact that interest rates are classified provides a clue to inherent differences among them. For every type of interest rate quoted, the name of the rate itself suggests its relative return. For example, financial market participants know without looking that the three-month Treasury bill yield is one of the lowest quoted rates. They know this because the maturity of a security and the creditworthiness of its issuer are two fundamental characteristics which determine risk. Nonetheless, financial market participants keep a constant eye on interest-rate quotations. They follow and study the quotes on a regular basis in order to better understand financial market movements. Interest rates are the prices in financial markets. Their behavior governs the interplay of the various markets and may even signal the course of the overall economy.

There are many different interest rates. A check of a 1972 issue of the *Federal Reserve Bulletin* showed that forty different types of open-market interest rates were quoted. Negotiated and discretionary rates were even larger in number. *The Wall Street Journal* carries daily quotations of nineteen different open-market rates—these exclusive of the interest rates mentioned specially in stories about the bond markets or the rates implied in the pricing of common stocks. Different rates are also quoted regularly in *The New York Times*. On top of this there are probably thousands of rates which are not quoted because they are arrived at informally (and sometimes illegally). The interest rates about which we have little or no information probably greatly outnumber those about which we do know, but the latter are more important because they are attached to the large and principal financial markets. Open-market rates, in particular, are the objects of our study.

VARIOUS WAYS OF CLASSIFYING INTEREST RATES

The large number of interest rates quoted are more understandable if they are grouped into classes or categories that emphasize common factors. In the sections below, a number of such classifications are suggested. Some are so self-evident that further comment is not necessary. Some of the classifications, however, involve economic considerations of such complexity that they will be taken up in more detail in later sections of this chapter.

One of the basic differences in classification of interest rates is in the maturity of the obligation. Maturities range as short as a single day—as, for example, in the case of "Fed" funds—to as long as thirty years or more in the case of long-term bonds. Original maturity is not as important, however, as term to maturity (or period to maturity). A twenty-year bond issued nineteen years ago is more short-term and more liquid than a five-year bond issued last year. The former has a period to maturity of just one year, while the latter's period to maturity is four years. Period to maturity has an important bearing on the interest-rate structure. Short-term interest rates have averaged considerably less than long-term rates over the present century. But this is an average relationship; it does not hold for all periods. During the downswing of a business cycle, short-term rates are often higher than long-term rates.

Interest rates can also be classified according to the general type of financial instrument involved. The yields on bonds of the highest-grade corporations are so closely bunched that one can legitimately speak of a "high-grade corporate bond yield." However, for many purposes, high-grade corporate bonds may be further classified according to the types of businesses that issue them—for example, public utilities, manufacturing and mining concerns, and railroads.

Strictly speaking, interest rates are associated only with debt obligations. Interest rates do not apply to corporate stocks because stocks do not technically pay interest. Instead, stocks pay dividends. The yield on a stock is therefore a dividend yield rather than an interest rate. Effective dividend yields are difficult to measure. Unlike interest, dividends are not paid regularly in fixed amounts but are instead declared out of profits if and when they are made. Also, unlike bonds, stocks have no contractual redemption values because they never come due.

Despite these differences, interest rates and stock yields are closely interrelated. Many investors look upon stocks and bonds as substitutes. When bond yields and other interest rates rise, investors are induced to shift their portfolio holdings away from stocks and into debt instruments. This behavior depresses the prices of stocks and thereby raises their prospective yields. The shifting continues until relative yields are restored to equilibrium. Interest rates are not the only elements determining stock prices, but they are a major factor. Many observers blamed high interest rates for the stock market doldrums of the late 1960s and early 1970s.

Theoretically, stocks should outyield bonds because of the extra risk involved. The claim of owners on corporate income and capital is residual to that of creditors. Among stocks, the highest yields are associated with those stocks where the residual claim is most tenuous. A major influence which shapes the strength of the residual claim and therefore the structure of stock prices and yields is the level and stability of corporate earnings relative to fixed charges, including interest. Firms with low margins and erratic earnings put their stockholders into a risky position. Stocks of such firms sell at depressed prices, producing high earnings-price ratios. The high yields are necessary to compensate the stockholders for the risks which they assume.

All credit instruments bear mute evidence to the fact that some creditor thought the likelihood of discharge of the contractual debt to have been reasonably good. But such hopes are sometimes disappointed. Some debt obligations have smaller protective margins than others from the beginning, but the biggest differences arise after such obligations have been issued. Interest rates often include an allowance for such risk differentials. They also include an allowance for difficulty of marketability. Many investors do not hold credit instruments to maturity but instead sell off in the market prior to maturity. If the market is thin, that is, if the spread between bid and ask is large, the investor may not be able to liquidate his holdings at a reasonable price within a reasonable period of time. Some corporate bonds go for days or even weeks without being traded.

Interest rates tend also to reflect the presence or absence of bond provisions such as callability and convertibility. Callability is a disadvantage to the investor, and thus callable bonds command higher yields than noncallable bonds. Convertibility (into common stocks) helps to sweeten a bond. An investor who places a high value on this feature will accept a lower interest rate than he would were the bond not convertible. Interest rates on convertibles are not always lower than rates on nonconvertibles. Some firms would have trouble finding a market for their bonds without adding the convertibility feature. Thus convertibility may compensate for default risk; it is not always a concession for lower interest.

Another basis on which interest rates may be classified is their tax status. The most dramatic difference appears between the yields on the securities of state and local government that are exempt from federal income taxes and those yields fully exposed to the federal income tax. A less dramatic but still important difference appears between yields on securities selling at par and above and those selling at a discount simply because the coupons on them are less than prevailing yields. Investors are required to report only the coupon interest as current income. The creeping disappearance of the discounts as these securities approach maturity is really accumulation of interest income, but the tax laws permit this to be treated as a long-term capital gain (if the security is held six months or more), so that it is taxed at a lower rate.

Differences in interest rates prevail between various geographic areas. Within the United States some rather material regional differences in interest rates exist. This is particularly true of essentially local markets such as those for conventional mortgage money. Some regional differences in the rates prevailing on short-term bank loans also remain. In general the East, and particularly New England, tends to experience lower rates than the West and Southwest. The differences that persist partly represent the fact that many borrowers and some lenders do not have effective access to markets outside the localities in which they live. Aside from such cases, however, most of our money-market interest rates and a majority of our capital-market interest rates tend toward national levels without discernible regional differences.

Interest rates set in open markets may also be contrasted with those arrived at by negotiations. Open markets imply good communications and public disclosure of prices. A publicly quoted open-market rate is likely to become a national rate. This is certainly true of the yields on securities of comparable quality. Public utilities operating in the Far West and Southwest probably borrow at rates that are just as good as those of comparable quality in the East or New England. The prime loan rate which governs the borrowing of the better and larger bank customers probably has increased uniformity in bank charges.

Rates on conventional mortgages and bank loan rates for customers that do not qualify for the prime loan rate, however, must be bargained. These bargains are essentially local. The borrowers have no access to the national markets. In such cases, the local supply of funds relative to the demands for them probably plays a part in setting rates. Regional differences can persist in such cases.

A negotiated rate, however, is not necessarily subject to such differentials. Large corporations which could, if they elected, go to public markets often elect to secure funds by direct sales to institutional investors ("direct placements"). The rates they pay are "negotiated" but are reasonably well in line with open-market rates. Nevertheless, life insurance companies appear to have been getting much higher yields from the aggregate of their direct placements than those prevailing in open markets. The quality of direct borrowers probably is not comparable to that of the open-market borrowers. This question remains: Are negotiated rates higher than open market rates? A study by Cohan (33) concludes that they are, except for smaller companies with lower-quality offerings.

One difference seems almost certain to be true: Open-market rates fluctuate more than negotiated rates. This is certainly true of bank loan rates when compared with open-market rates. It also appears to be true of direct placement rates compared with open-market rates. This raises an interesting question: Do open money and capital markets tend to increase interest-rate volatility? If they do, do borrowers pay a higher negotiated rate to escape this volatility? We do not know.

THE TERM STRUCTURE OF INTEREST RATES

"The term structure of interest rates" is the name given to the functional relation between yield to maturity and term to maturity (or period to maturity). This relation is easiest to examine when graphed in the form of a yield curve. Annual yield to maturity is measured on the vertical axis and years to maturity on the horizontal. The curve depicts yield as a function of maturity when all other factors are held constant. Since no two securities are identical in all respects other than maturity, yield curves constructed from empirical observations can only approximate the true relation. The best-known yield curves are those which were estimated by David Durand (50). More recently, this work has been carried on by Sidney Homer (105).

The slope and shape of a yield curve constantly change as market

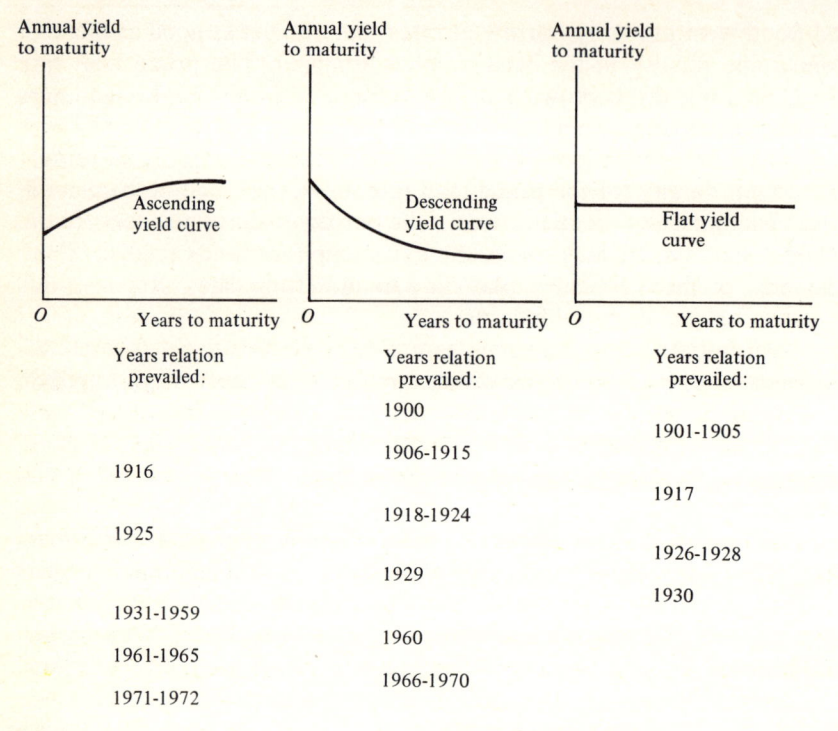

Ascending yield curve	Descending yield curve	Flat yield curve
Years relation prevailed:	Years relation prevailed:	Years relation prevailed:
	1900	
		1901-1905
	1906-1915	
1916		
		1917
	1918-1924	
1925		
		1926-1928
	1929	
		1930
1931-1959		
	1960	
1961-1965		
	1966-1970	
1971-1972		

Figure 6-1 Yield curves for high-grade corporate bonds, 1900–1972.

conditions change, but certain general forms always appear. In the market for high-grade corporate bonds, three forms appear. The most frequent is the ascending yield curve, where yield to maturity is a positive function of years to maturity. The next most frequent form is the descending curve. In this case yield is a negative function of maturity. The least frequent form is the flat curve; it exists when short-term and long-term yields are approximately the same. Figure 6-1 shows these three general forms and the years during which they prevailed.

Only two general forms of yield curves appear for the U.S. government securities market (at least since 1950). Again, the most frequent is the ascending curve, indicating higher yields for longer periods to maturity. The other form is the humped curve. In this case yields rise from short- to intermediate-term, reach a peak, and then decline from intermediate- to long-term. Figure 6-2 shows these two forms and the years during which they prevailed.

An examination of Figures 6-1 and 6-2 leads to three general observations. First, yield curves assume different forms at different times.

STRUCTURE AND BEHAVIOR OF INTEREST RATES   107

Second, the forms for U.S. government securities are apparently different from the forms for high-grade corporate bonds. And third, the ascending yield curve is the most common of all; on the average, long-term yields are higher than short-term yields. These three observations lead in turn to three questions. First, do the years in which nonascending yield curves prevail differ significantly in some important respect from the ascending years so as to explain the shifting forms? Second, does a humped yield curve really exist, or is it another form in disguise? And third, why is the yield curve ascending on the average?

The recent years of 1957, 1959 to 1960, and 1966 to 1970 stand out as years of generally high interest rates. In these years both short- and long-term rates were well above what might be considered the normal interest rate level. At the same time that all rates were high, short- and intermediate-term rates were even higher than long-term rates. Is there a connection? Different theories of the term structure say yes, but for different reasons.

One theory, the expectations theory, explains the term structure in terms of what investors expect future interest rates will be. When interest rates are unusually high, investors form expectations of lower future rates. Assuming investors are out to maximize expected return over their holding periods, the effect of expected lower future rates is to raise

Annual yield
to maturity

Ascending
yield curve

0   Years to maturity

Years relation prevailed:
1950-1956

1958

1960-1965

1971-1972

Annual yield
to maturity

Humped
yield curve

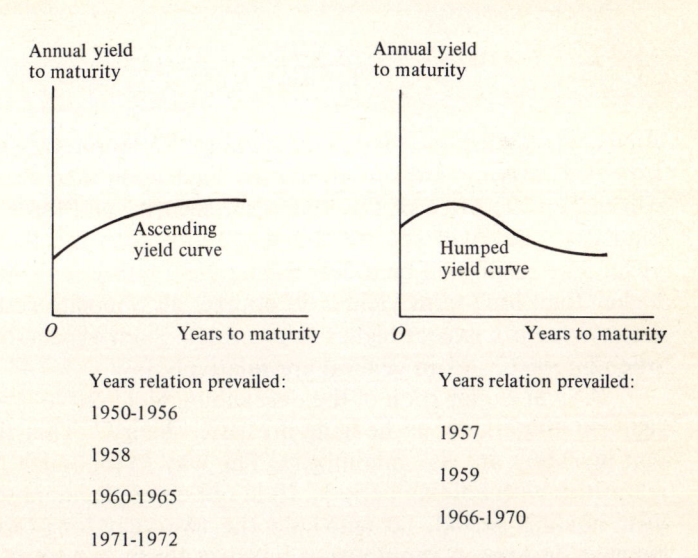

0   Years to maturity

Years relation prevailed:

1957

1959

1966-1970

Figure 6-2 Yield curves for U.S. government securities, 1950–1972. (In January 1970, a descending yield curve was almost but not quite reached as six-month to three-year Treasuries were still two or three basis points above three-month Treasuries.)

the current short-term rate above the long-term rate—hence the descending yield curve. An example will show why. Suppose there are two securities, a one-year short-term and a two-year long-term. Both pay a yearly coupon of $5, both have a face value of $100, and both currently yield 5 percent a year, so that the current price is $100 on both. Now suppose market rates are expected to fall to 4 percent next year. If an investor holds the two-year security and he has a two-year holding period, his net return is $10 in interest. If, instead, he holds the one-year security, he will get $5 interest the first year, reinvest his principal, and expect to get $4 the second year for a two-year total of $9 interest. Clearly, as an expected return maximizer, he is better off with the long-term two-year security. But what if his holding period is just one year? If he holds the one-year security, his net return is $5 interest. If instead he holds the two-year security, he will get $5 interest plus 97 cents in expected capital gains for a total return of $5.97. The capital gain is the difference between next year's price and this year's price of $100. Next year's price on a security which matures the following year is determined by the equation previously introduced in Chapter 5:

$$\text{Price (one year before maturity)} = \frac{\text{interest} + \text{principal}}{1 + \text{yield}}$$

$$\$100.97 = \frac{\$5 + \$100}{1 + 4\%}$$

Again, the investor is better off holding the long-term security because expected return is greater. If investors act upon their expectations, they will bid up the price of the long-term security and force down its yield. Similarly, they will sell off the short-term security, thereby raising its yield. The result will be a descending yield curve with short-term yields higher than long-term yields. Of course, an opposite result is predicted when investors expect higher future rates. Such expectations are formed when interest rates in general are relatively low.

A rival explanation of the descending yield curve is provided by the segmented-markets or hedging-pressure theory.[1] This theory assumes that investors are risk minimizers. The way to minimize risk is to match maturities with holding periods. If, in our example, an investor has a two-year holding period, he will hold the two-year long-term security not because he expects more return but because he is sure of getting his $10

[1] See Culbertson (44).

total return. If, instead, he has a one-year holding period, he will prefer the one-year short-term security and the sure return of $5. The two-year security has a $5.97 expected return, but if expectations fail to materialize, actual return might be less than the sure $5 return. The risk minimizer will forego possible capital gains in order to escape possible capital losses, and he will decline possible higher reinvestment rates in order to avoid possibly lower rates. The risk minimizer is interested only in those securities whose periods to maturity are equal to his holding period.

This behavior is assumed to operate on both sides of the market. Firms which need short-term funds will issue only short-term securities; those whose needs are long-term will issue only long-term securities. There is no substitution among securities of different lengths. As a consequence, the market for short-term securities is segmented from the long-term market and vice versa. Yields in the different markets are determined solely by supply and demand conditions which operate in the separate markets. An explanation of the descending yield curve thus becomes obvious. If short-term rates are higher than long-term rates, it is because short-term funds are scarce and long-term funds plentiful. Investors have plenty of long-term funds to invest in long-term securities, but firms need short-term securities. Equilibrium is reached, but the result is high short-term rates relative to long-term rates.

Which theory is correct? Empirical studies by Meiselman (148), Modigliani and Sutch (151), Malkiel (142), and Wallace (222) suggest that both expectations and hedging pressure are at work but that expectations strongly dominate quantitatively. The evidence is not altogether conclusive, however. In the authors' opinion, financial market participants are generally neither return maximizers nor risk minimizers but are rather risk-return traders.

We turn now to the question of the humped yield curve. According to the expectations theory, the hump results when investors expect rates to rise initially and then later to fall below their current level. This is a reasonable kind of expectation, but so, at times, is the reverse. Investors may expect rates to drop first and then to rise to much higher levels. In this case the expectations theory should predict an upside-down hump or saddlebacked yield curve. Such a curve has not been known to exist, however. This lack of symmetry casts some doubt on the expectations explanation of the humpbacked curve.

The hedging-pressure theory offers an alternative explanation. According to this theory, the hump is a result of a relatively weak demand for or a relatively strong supply of intermediate-term securities—or both. If intermediate-term securities are in excess supply relative to securities of shorter and longer maturities, their prices will tend to be relatively low and their yields relatively high. But the reverse might also be expected to hold. If and when there is a relatively strong demand for or weak supply of intermediate-term securities, the hedging-pressure theory should predict a saddlebacked yield curve; but again, such a curve has not been known to exist. It could be that asymmetry does exist in this case; perhaps there is a consistently weak market for intermediate-term government securities. Or it could be that the hedging-pressure theory is not particularly germane.

There is the possibility that the humpbacked yield curve does not truly exist. A true yield curve shows the relation between yield and term to maturity for a homogenous group of securities. But it is hard to find a homogenous group. Even government securities are differentiated. They are subject to differential estate and income tax treatment, differential redemption options, differential marketability, and differential coupon rates. Such differentials may distort the yield curve and give it its hump. Unfortunately, we do not know whether the hump is a genuine function of term to maturity or a distortion produced by nonmaturity differentials. Clearly, more work is needed in this area.

Finally, we turn to the question of why long-term rates are, on the average, higher than short-term rates. A generally ascending yield curve has been confirmed for high-grade corporate bonds by Durand (50) and for U.S. government securities by Kessel (122). Neither the pure expectations theory nor the pure segmented-markets theory can satisfactorily explain this phenomenon. Over the long pull, investors should expect interest rates to fall just as often as they expect them to rise. If anything, the pure expectations theory should predict a generally flat yield curve. As for the hedging-pressure theory, one would have to assume that maturity needs are generally short for lenders and generally long for borrowers. The whole point of the segmented markets theory, however, is that different lenders and different borrowers have different maturity needs. On the lending side, banks do have short-term needs, but the needs of life insurance companies, pension funds, and individuals saving for retirement are strictly long-term. On the borrowing side, government and firms do need long-term funds, but their short-term requirements are equally substantial.

The generally ascending yield curve is consistent with a term structure theory known as "liquidity preference." This theory does not assume that investors are return maximizers, as does the pure expectations theory, nor does it assume that they are risk minimizers, as does the pure segmented-markets theory. Rather, it assumes that investors are risk-return traders. As such, they seek more than minimum risk, because that entails too little return; and they pursue less than maximum return, because that implies too much risk. The liquidity preference theory thus contains elements from both the expectations theory and the hedging-pressure theory. Expectations certainly matter, but so do risk preferences.

According to the liquidity preference theory, long-term securities are more risky, on balance, than short-term securities. The variance of return of capital value is greater for long-term securities than for short-term. On the other hand, the variance of return of interest income is greater for short-term securities than for long-term. Assuming that stability of capital is valued more highly than stability of interest (a preference for liquidity), long-term securities have a net risk disadvantage. Investors will accept this additional risk when long-term securities are priced to yield more. Greater return for greater risk explains the generally ascending yield curve. This view is taken in the empirical studies of Kessel (122) and Cagan (27).

A shortcoming of the liquidity preference approach to the term structure of interest rates is its assumption that investors are more averse to the risk of instability of capital value than to the risk of instability of interest income. Are investors really biased in this way? Is this assumption really necessary in order to explain the generally ascending yield curve? Perhaps not. If we follow the logic of the theory of portfolio selection and security pricing developed in Chapter 5, long-term securities should have higher expected yields than short-term securities if the risk of return of capital gains *and* interest income, combined, increases with term to maturity. In other words, it may be that long-term securities have generally higher expected returns than short-term securities merely because long-term securities may have greater total risk (and not because one kind of risk is worse than another). Along these lines, Roll (184) has found that the risk of return on Treasury securities does increase with period to maturity. His evidence suggests, therefore, that the generally ascending yield curve can be alternatively explained by the theory of portfolio selection and security pricing. This theory, as we saw in Chapter 5, does assume that investors are averse to risk, but it does not assume that they are more averse to one kind of risk than to another.

Still another explanation of the generally ascending yield curve is worth noting, and that is the influence of transactions costs. It costs more to buy or sell a long-term security than a short-term security, so much so that the total transactions cost of a series of short-term purchases is about equal to a single purchase of long-term securities. An investor with a long holding period will show almost no concern between short- and long-term securities with respect to transactions costs. On the other hand, an investor with a short holding period can lower transactions costs by purchasing short-term securities. Long-term securities will interest him only if they hold the promise of greater yield. Thus, to the extent that investors have short holding periods, long-term yields will exceed short-term yields.

THE DEFAULT RISK STRUCTURE OF INTEREST RATES

The securities that appear in financial markets do not present equal certainty that the underlying contracts will be fulfilled. This is more true of capital than of money markets. Open money-market transactions are seldom conducted in any except a virtually riskless form.[2] Negotiated short-term loans contain some risk of default, but risk differentials tend to be merged with other factors and to be hard to identify. The task of this section is to examine the differentials in interest rates and yields that result from differential default risk elements.

"Default risk" refers to the possibility of not collecting interest and principal of the promised amount at the promised time. Virtually all capital market securities are subject to some degree of default risk except those issued by the federal government. The government always has the power to tax or to print money if it should get into financial difficulty. Private corporations, of course, do not have this power; they cannot guarantee that their promises will be kept. Why, then, should investors invest in privately issued securities? The answer is for the extra expected yield. A corporate bond may not be as good a promise as a Treasury bond, but it promises a higher yield—so much higher that the expected yield (after allowing for the probability that the promise will be broken) is sufficiently above the yield on the Treasury bond to compensate the investor for the extra risk.

The difference between the promised yield of a security subject to default risk and the yield of a risk-free security is called the "risk premium." The risk premium varies directly with the risk of default. When we see a corporate bond quoted at a relatively high yield (with a relatively large risk premium), we sense that it is subject to relatively high default risk. But why? Why are different issuers of securities associated with different degrees of risk? Basically, default risk can be attributed to three factors: (1) the internal risk position of the corporate issuer, (2) the external environment or economic climate within which the corporate issuer operates, and (3) the period to maturity of the security itself.

[2] For an attempt to measure default risk differentials in the money market, see Baxter (15). Baxter concludes that default risk is significant in the money market.

A firm's risk position is conditioned by several elements. One is the ability of the firm to generate enough cash to cover interest and principal payments. A measure of this ability is the coverage ratio:

$$\frac{\text{Expected cash flow before contractual interest and principal payments}}{\text{Contractual interest and principal payments}}$$

Natually, the higher the coverage ratio, the less the degree of credit risk. Default risk and risk premiums thus vary inversely with interest and principal coverage.

Another element determining the firm's risk position is the variability of the cash flow which provides the coverage. It is not enough for expected cash flow to more than cover interest and principal payments. If the cash flow is variable, a firm may not be able to meet its promises in a bad year, even though it easily covers them in good years. The more variable earnings are, the greater the degree of credit risk. Default risk and risk premiums thus vary directly with earnings or cash flow variability.

Still another element affecting the firm's risk position is the firm's past record in keeping its promises. A firm which has a long history of never defaulting builds up a reputation which carries into the future. Investors perceive such a firm as one which can weather any storm. Default risk and risk premiums tend to vary inversely with the firm's period of solvency. This factor, however, may not be completely independent of the level and variability of interest coverage.

The effect of capital structure (a proxy for coverage), earnings variability, and solvency period on risk premiums has been directly studied by Fisher (64). Using regression analysis, he found that these three variables plus a variable measuring marketability accounted for approximately 75 percent of the variation in the risk premium variable. Moreover, the effect of each determinant was significant and in the expected direction.

The ordinary investor does not have the resources to analyze the underlying risk elements or to determine the overall risk position of each firm whose bonds he is considering investing. Instead, he is apt to rely on bond ratings prepared by professional investment agencies. For many years a number of professional agencies for classification of securities have assigned ratings which express their judgment as to relative merit. The two agencies now operating independently in this field and the symbols they use are as follows.

		Moody's	Standard and Poor's
1.	Highest quality	Aaa	AAA
2.	High quality	Aa	AA
3.	Upper medium quality	A	A
4.	Medium to lower medium quality (marginal investment grade)	Baa	BBB-BB
5.	Speculative (not investment grade)	Ba-B	B
6.	In default or high probability of default	Caa and below	CCC and below

In general, the various agencies attach about the same absolute standards to each of the rating groups. It is significant, however, that a given security may be rated differently by various agencies. This only illustrates the fact that credit analysis cannot produce exact results and still depends partly on personal judgment.

Still, the ratings have been pretty good indicators of default risk. For the 1900 to 1943 period, Hickman (101) found a close relation between bond rating and defaults. He found that the higher the rating given a new issue of corporate bonds, the lower the incidence of subsequent

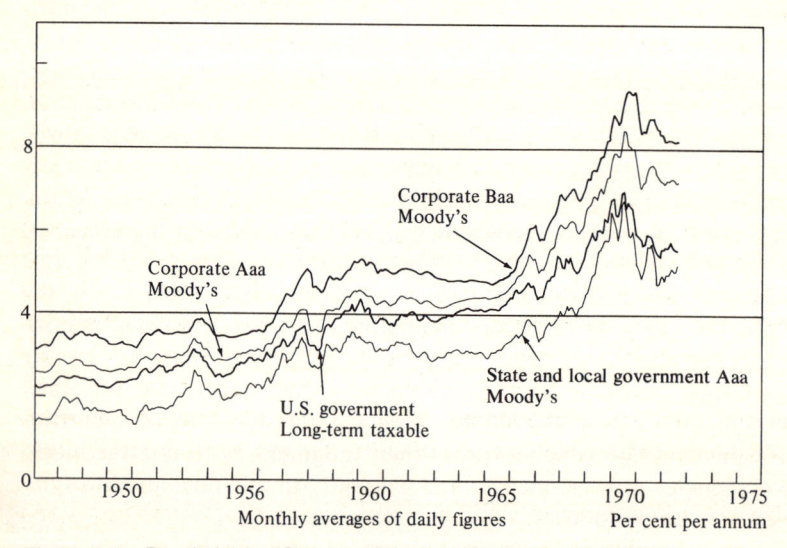

Figure 6-3 Bond yields. (*Source: Board of Governors of Federal Reserve System*, Historical Chart Book, *1972, p. 31.*)

default (*ibid.*, p. 176). In addition, risk premiums on lower-rated bonds have been consistently larger than those on higher-rated bonds, as shown in Figure 6-3.

In addition to the bond issuer's internal risk position as reflected by rating, default risk and the risk premium are determined by the firm's external environment, particularly the stage of the business cycle. Most defaults occur during severe depressions. A poorly rated bond may not be able to weather the storm of a depression, but it will keep from defaulting if there is no storm to weather. Some evidence on the average annual rate of default—measured for the last seven decades by the percentage of the par amount of corporate bonds not in default at the beginning of the year that went into default during the year—has been compiled by Atkinson (10) and is presented below:

Decade	Average annual default rate, percent
1900–1909	0.9
1910–1919	2.0
1920–1929	1.0
1930–1939	3.2
1940–1949	0.4
1950–1959	0.04
1960–1965	0.03

The above figures clearly indicate a greater incidence of default during the relatively unstable period before World War II than for the relatively stable period following the war. The decade of highest incidence was, of course, the 1930s, years of the Great Depression.

Risk premium patterns also bear the influence of the business cycle. Figure 6-3 shows some tendency for risk premiums to enlarge during contractions. The widening of the premium on Baa bonds is especially pronounced because Baa's are more vulnerable than Aaa's to default during adverse economic conditions. The widening of the premiums during the second half of the 1960s cannot be attributed to economic depression but can instead be traced to extremely tight credit conditions and general uncertainty prompted in large part by the Vietnam war.

The cyclical impact on risk premiums is probably tighter than one would surmise from viewing Figure 6-3, because that figure reflects both cyclical and noncyclical influences. Sloane (202) has studied and measured the cyclical influence on risk premiums for the 1954 to 1959 period using regression analysis. His results led him to conclude that the 1957 to 1958 recession explained much of the widening of risk premiums and that the widening effect was greater for lower-quality bonds.

The final determinant of default risk and risk premium of a bond is the bond's period to maturity. A bond which has twenty years to mature has more time and a greater chance to default than a ten-year bond. Theoretically, the yield and risk premium should vary directly with period to maturity. In other words, the term structure of yields should owe to default risk as well as to interest-rate effects discussed in the preceding section.

The evidence relating period to maturity to yield differentials is interesting. Robinson (183) found that in the case of the Aaa and Baa municipal bonds, yield differentials (measured at time of issue) were greater the longer the period to maturity, as theory predicts. On the other hand, Johnson (115) found that low-grade corporate bond yields increased over time as these bonds approached maturity. Johnson's explanation for this behavior is that there is a "crisis-at-maturity." An issuer of low-grade bonds may not have too much difficulty in meeting interest payments before the bonds come due, but refinancing and final redemption at maturity may be very difficult, particularly during recessionary periods. The two findings are not necessarily in conflict. It is possible that yield varies directly with maturity at time of issue and that it varies inversely with maturity as maturity is approached. We do not know if the "crisis-at-maturity" applies to municipal bonds. The secondary market for municipals is probably too thin to obtain reliable measurements.

A remaining question is whether or not risk premiums reflect the true risk of default. In his study, Hickman (101) concluded that risk premiums for lower-quality bonds were more than sufficient to compensate for the risks involved. In other words, lower-quality bonds were underpriced. Hickman attributed this to institutional investors being segmented from the market for subinvestment-grade securities. However, after adjusting Hickman's risk premium data for effects other than default risk, Fraine and Mills (66) found that lower-quality bonds were not nearly so underpriced nor was the bond market as imperfect as Hickman imagined.

THE CALL RISK STRUCTURE OF INTEREST RATES

Call risk is the opposite of default risk. Most corporate bond issues have a call option which permits the issuer to buy back the bonds at a specified call price before the bonds mature. Holders of callable bonds run the risk of having their bonds called and getting their money back before they voluntarily want it back. This is the reverse of default risk, where the holders run the risk of getting their money back later than they want it back, or, worse yet, never getting it back.

The call price of a bond usually bears a close relationship to the bond's offering price and coupon rate. For example, a bond sold at $100 par with an annual coupon of $5 will have a call price close to $105. The call price over the life of the bond declines toward par as the bond matures. At maturity, the call price is equal to par value.

The market price of a callable bond varies inversely with bond yields in the market except that the call price sets a ceiling on market price. As market yield falls, market price rises, but it stops rising once it reaches the call price or a price a point or two above call price. For example, investors will not pay more than a point or two above $105 for a bond which can be called at $105. No rational investor wants to invite a large and immediate capital loss.

Because call price sets a ceiling on market price, holders of callable bonds are limited in the amount of capital gains which, in the event of declining market yields, could be realized were the bonds not callable. Callability is thus a disadvantage to investors because it limits price appreciation. Moreover, there are other disadvantages. Bonds are usually called when market yields are low; issuers call when refinancing is attractive. Thus bondholders interested in long-term yields have to relinquish their bonds and reinvest at lower yields; further, they have to incur the transaction cost of reinvestment. Finally, there is the disadvantage of uncertainty. A bond may never be called, but the holder is never sure. Uncertainty as to the amount and continuity of future returns hangs over the head of every holder of a callable bond.

These disadvantages have to be offset in order for callable bonds to sell. The offset usually takes the form of a higher yield. The call risk structure of bond yields is higher yields for callable bonds than for noncallable bonds, all other things the same. There is some question, however, whether the higher yield of callable bonds fully compensates for the risk of call. In one study, Jen and Wert (112) suggest that it does not—that the extra yield on certain callable bonds during certain periods is a "yield illusion." More work needs to be done on this question.

The degree of call risk is determined largely by two factors: (1) the length of the call deferment and (2) the level of the coupon rate. The call deferment is the period of time after a bond is issued within which the option to call cannot be exercised. This period can be as short as zero in the case of immediately callable bonds, or as long as the period to maturity in the case of noncallable bonds. Call deferment periods have varied widely depending on market conditions.

Call risk is an inverse function of the length of the call deferment. A long deferment has a less limiting effect on price appreciation and reduces uncertainty in general. Bonds with the deferred call privilege do not require as high yields as immediately callable bonds. This is borne out in recent empirical studies by Jen and Wert (111), Pye (174), and Frankena (68).

The coupon rate is the contractual interest payment taken as a percentage of the face or par value of the bond. A $100 bond which pays $5 annual interest has an annual coupon rate of 5 percent.

Call risk is a positive function of the coupon rate. There are two reasons for this. First, the temptation for the issuing corporation to call and refinance is greater the higher the coupon rate the corporation is paying. For example, if the market rate of interest is 4 percent, a bond with a 5 percent coupon rate might be called whereas one with a 3 percent coupon rate would not. Second, high coupon bonds sell at higher market prices than low coupon bonds. Market rates do not have to fall much to push the price of a high coupon bond against the call price ceiling, but they have to fall considerably before the price of a low coupon bond reaches the ceiling. High coupon bonds thus have more limited capital gains potential than low coupon bonds.

Because high coupon bonds are more risky, they should sell at higher yields. The studies by Jen and Wert (112) and Frankena (68) find that this is in fact the case.

THE TAX STRUCTURE OF INTEREST RATES

Coupon rate differentials lead to yield differentials on noncallable bonds as well as on callable bonds. The differentials on noncallable bonds cannot be attributed to the call risk of high coupon rates because noncallables have no call risk. Instead, they can be explained in terms of tax effects. In this section we find that there is a tax structure of interest rates. According to one source, "In a random sample of bond yields, tax factors would probably account for almost as much of the variability as default risk or maturity."[3]

High coupon bonds tend to have higher before-tax yields than low coupon bonds. The reason for this, apart from call risk, is the fact that capital gains are taxed at a lower rate than interest income. The maximum effective tax rate on capital gains is 25 percent, while interest is taxed at rates which can go much higher, depending on the taxpayer's tax bracket. Investors in high tax brackets naturally prefer to receive capital gains over interest because it increases after-tax returns. If two bonds have the same before-tax yield, the bond with the lower coupon rate will provide proportionately less interest and proportionately more capital gains than the bond with the higher coupon rate. On an after-tax basis, the lower coupon bond outperforms the higher coupon bond. Investors who are in sufficiently high tax brackets tend therefore to bid up the prices (and bid down the before-tax yields) of low coupon bonds relative to high coupon bonds. Thus high coupon bonds have higher before-tax yields

[3] Pye (173).

than low coupon bonds owing to the differential tax system.

Economists are uncertain as to the significance of this tax effect. Frankena (68) has argued that the effect is negligible in determining yield differentials between corporate bonds with differential coupons. Pye (173), on the other hand, has maintained that the effect is considerable with respect to Treasury bonds. Clearly more empirical work is needed in this area.

Another and very significant tax effect on the yield structure is the tax-exempt status of state and municipal securities. Interest income on tax-exempt issues is not subject to federal income taxes. As a result, yields on tax-exempt securities are considerably lower than before-tax yields on nonexempt securities. In recent years, the yield on Aaa municipal bonds has varied in the range of 60 to 70 percent of the before-tax yield on Aaa corporate bonds. This means that municipals have the same after-tax yield as corporates for investors in the 30 to 40 percent tax-rate bracket. For investors in lower brackets, the tax advantage is insufficient to induce investment in the lower-yielding tax-exempts. But for investors in higher brackets, municipal bonds clearly outperform corporate bonds.

Because of tax exemption, the market for municipal securities is relatively segmented. Commercial banks, wealthy individuals, and casualty insurance companies dominate the market. These investors are in relatively high tax brackets and are therefore able to reap higher effective returns on municipal bonds than on corporate bonds. The corporate bond market, on the other hand, appeals to a group of institutional investors, investors who are not taxed or are taxed at very low rates. For this group, municipal bonds have no advantage.

Curiously, the low interest rates on tax-exempt securities may cost state and local governments more than would be the case if the securities were not tax-exempt. Ott and Meltzer (163) have studied the effects of eliminating the tax-exempt status. Their conclusion is that if this market were open to all bond investors, federal taxes on interest income would exceed the extra interest that state and local governments would have to pay. If such taxes were returned from the federal government to the local governments, the federal government would be no worse off, but the local governments would benefit. The latter, in effect, would receive income now going to the commercial banks, wealthy individuals, and casualty insurance companies.

Unlike interest, capital gains on municipal securities are not exempt from federal income taxes. Investors in municipals thus prefer interest to capital gains, which means they prefer high coupons to low coupons. The coupon rate effect is therefore reversed for tax-exempt securities. In this case, low coupon securities have higher yields than high coupon securities. The higher yields compensate for tax loss on capital gains.

The one general point still to be discussed is the differential tax treatment of equity securities as against debt securities. The traditional view that equity securities represent ownership has led to a tax status in which dividends paid are not deductible before computation of taxes. Interest on debt obligations, of course, is deductible. Preferred stock, admittedly, has the legal aspects of an equity interest but the practical role of outside financing or debt. Since preferred dividends are not tax-exempt, this form of financing has receded in use and importance. However, since only 15 percent of common and preferred dividends are treated as taxable income when such securities are held by corporate investors, preferred stocks still outstanding have found a good reception in this special market.

Another effect is that interest payments on debt, being made before taxes, tend to have far better protection than either the preferred or common dividends of the same company. With a corporate tax rate near 50 percent, interest coverage is automatically about twice as good as dividend coverage. By the same token, fears of changes in tax rates hurt equity prices more than debt security prices. Even though a corporate holder's taxes are less than 8 percent, the rate is enough to encourage consolidation of controlled subsidiaries so as to reduce the tax take (to the 2 percent joint-return surtax). This sometimes has led to the disappearance from the market of securities of large subsidiaries.

THE GEOGRAPHIC STRUCTURE OF INTEREST RATES

Most of the capital markets in the United States are truly national markets. Identical securities sell in these markets at identical prices. An investor from Michigan, for example, pays the same price for stocks and bonds traded in the national market as an investor from any other state. Interregional yield differentials do not exist in these national markets because funds are free to move about geographically. If a particular security were priced to yield more in Chicago than in New York, arbitragers would quickly sell in New York and buy in Chicago, thereby eliminating the differential. The absence of regional differentials is a test of the "perfectness" of our capital markets.

There is one important securities' market, however, in which interregional yield differentials persist. This is the mortgage market. In 1890, mortgage rates on the West Coast were about 9 percent, while on the East Coast they were around 5½ percent. By 1940, the differential had decreased to less than a percentage point. The narrowing of regional-mortgage-rate differentials during the 1890 to 1940 period is amply documented in a study by Grebler, Blank, and Winnick (90).

Since 1940, however, there has been no trend for these differentials to narrow. Studies by Davis and Banks (46) and Fredrikson (69) find short-term swings in the differentials but no long-term trend. Fredrikson's 1963 figures indicate that mortgage rates continue to be higher in the West and South than in the East and Midwest:

	Average effective mortgage rate, percent
East	5.71
Midwest	5.94
South	6.10
West	6.40

The largest differential is between East and West. At sixty-nine basis points it is about the same as it was in 1940.

An important question is this: Why do these differentials still exist? Do market imperfections prevent the establishment of identical yields for identical securities? Or are the securities not identical? Are West Coast mortgages more risky than East Coast mortgages?

Davis and Banks (46) have concluded that market imperfections are chiefly responsible for the differentials. It is their contention that customs and laws have prevented savings and loan associations, mutual savings banks, and commercial banks from allocating their funds geographically in order to obtain highest return. Greater legal uncertainties and service costs are additional barriers to out-of-state lending. Finally, many banks feel an obligation to lend locally to "friends and neighbors," even when "foreign" investment may be more lucrative.

Schaaf (186), on the other hand, has emphasized risk differentials as the explanation for mortgage-rate differentials. His contention is that West Coast mortgages are more risky than East Coast mortgages because West Coast borrowers put up less equity when financing homes, particularly new houses.

Both market imperfections and risk differentials are found by Fredrikson (69) to explain the mortgage-rate differentials. Among market imperfections, Fredrikson singles out the high cost of information, legal constraints, and varying costs of acquisition and servicing. Risk differentials are found to be a function of regional lender type. The concentration of savings and loan associations on the supply side of the mortgage credit market is much greater in the West than in the East. Savings and loan associations require smaller downpayments than do other lenders. Their loans are thus more risky, but their returns are higher.

THE GENERAL LEVEL OF INTEREST RATES

As important as it is to understand the relation of one interest rate to another, our understanding of the behavior of interest rates would be incomplete were we not to examine their overall level and movement over time. In fact, most people are more concerned about high interest rates or low than they are about how many basis points difference there is between one given interest rate and another. Of course, the student of financial markets needs to know about both the structure and the level of interest rates. We thus conclude this chapter with a discussion of the interest-rate level. This subject was introduced in the section entitled Lending, Borrowing, and Interest Rates in Chapter 4; it will carry over into Part Two entitled Money Markets; and it will be brought up again in Chapter 19 in the section entitled Cyclical Movements in Money, Interest Rates, and General Economic Activity. Our discussion here shall therefore be brief.

One of the most striking characteristics of interest rates is their extreme variability. The range of fluctuations for short-term rates is particularly great, but long-term rates also move through fairly wide ranges. This range of movement may be noted in Figure 6-4. A careful reading of this figure reveals that interest rates move in the same direction as the overall economy. Interest rates move up with increases in real out-

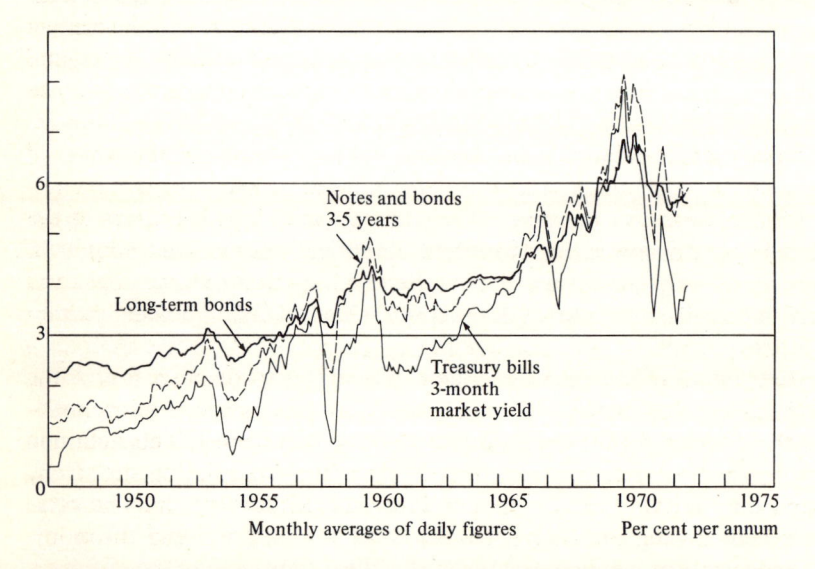

Figure 6-4 Yields on United States securities. *(Source: Board of Governors of Federal Reserve System,* Historical Chart Book, *1972, p. 25.)*

put and commodity prices and down when the economy is slackening. The interest-rate troughs in Figure 6-4 correspond almost exactly to the recessionary years of 1954, 1958, 1961, 1967, and 1971.

Interest theories attribute a cause-and-effect relation between fluctuations in overall economic activity and fluctuations in the interest-rate level. One important factor is the rate of inflation. When an economy is on the upswing, interest rates tend to rise with the rising rate of inflation. If the market rate is 6 percent, and prices are rising at an annual rate of 2 percent, $100 invested now will be worth $106 nominally one year hence; but the $106, in real terms, is worth only about $104 due to the 2 percent drop in real purchasing power. The real interest rate is thus about 4 percent. Investors are (or should be) interested in real rates. This means that if the rate of inflation increases from 2 to 3 percent, the market rate of interest must increase from 6 to 7 percent in order to maintain the same real rate of 4 percent. It is not surprising, then, that interest rates climbed dramatically during the late 1960s. This was a period of mounting inflation.

Another important factor is the demand for investment and the funds to finance investment. During economic boom, businesses plan large capital expenditures which require financing. Usually the supply of loanable funds out of saving cannot keep up with the demand for funds for investment, so that limited funds are allocated to the highest bidders—those firms and other borrowers willing and able to pay the highest rates. Thus a strong economy leads to an increased demand for capital goods and capital funds, which in turn leads to higher interest rates. The reverse happens during economic recession.

Still another factor is the demand for and supply of the stock of money. In an overheated economy, people need to keep larger cash balances for transactions purposes. The demand for money increases. If the central bank refuses in its monetary policy to increase the supply of money by as much as the increase in demand, money becomes tight and interest rates rise. Such was the case in 1966 and 1969. Holding back on the money supply is the correct policy if the central bank intends a counter-cyclical effect. Higher rates are required to dampen borrowing and spending. Sometimes, however, the monetary authority accommodates the demand for money, allowing the boom to persist. This action in itself does not pull interest rates up. But the persisting inflation and strong demand for capital expenditures and funds do. Either way, interest rates will be high during the boom. By the same token, they tend to be low during recessionary periods.

While high interest rates and inflation go together, it does not follow that interest rates should be fixed at low levels to check inflation. Some politicians think they should, but the truth is that any attempt by the central bank to fix interest rates at low levels is liable to make inflation worse, not better. A fixed-rate policy implies a perfectly elastic supply of money and credit by the central bank. In other words, the central bank would have to accommodate any level of loan demand at the fixed rate. In doing so, it would lose its power to apply the brakes to borrowing and spending during inflationary periods. This lesson was learned well in the 1940s, when the Federal Reserve was committed to pegging low interest rates on government securities. That policy had to be abandoned because it rendered monetary policy useless for the purpose of stabilizing the economy.

Part Two

Money Markets

Chapter 7

Money Markets: A General Introduction

Financial markets have a considerable degree of unity. They do not exist in isolation but are tied together by real economic forces. Within this embracing unity of financial markets, markets do differ with respect to the nature of the participants, the character of financial instruments employed, and the maturity of the instruments. This last characteristic is traditionally used to distinguish money from capital markets: Money market instruments are defined as those having an original maturity of less than one year. By negative exclusion, that defines capital market instruments as those having an original maturity of one year or more.

While maturity does furnish the characteristic by which money markets may be distinguished from capital markets, the one-year dividing line is not always controlling. Financial markets comprehend a continuum of maturities from one-day (or within the day or overnight) money to financial instruments of theoretically infinite life. Many lenders tailor maturities to the needs of their customers. For example, commercial banks lend money for a wide range of maturities. Corporate borrowers often canvass both markets before deciding where to borrow.

Maturity is relative, not absolute. In many ways it can be argued that a one-day maturity differs more from a one-year maturity than the latter does from a twenty-year maturity.

Figure 7-1 shows the principal money-market credit instruments with their range of original maturity and also an approximate average.

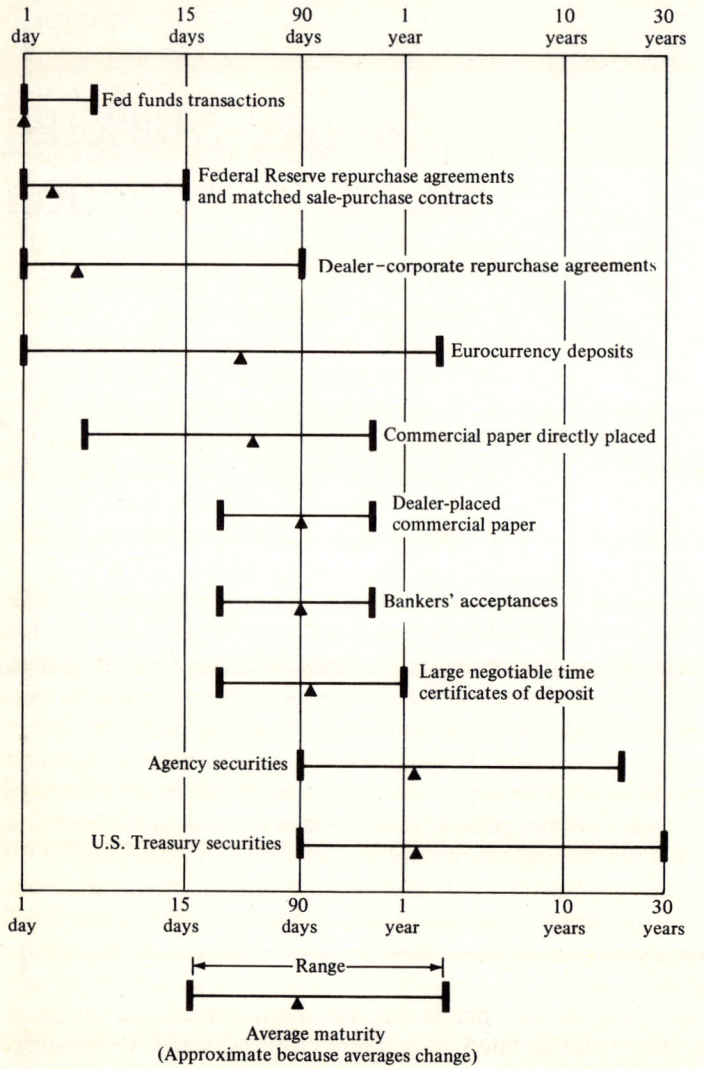

Figure 7-1 Original maturities of money-market credit instruments (time scale logarithmic).

This figure is logarithmic so as to show relative time relationships and demonstrate the wide range of averages in the money market.

CONTRASTS: MONEY AND CAPITAL MARKETS

Although maturity may be the controlling point of distinction, money and capital markets differ in other ways. As the first section of this text emphasized, real economic factors lie back of all financial markets: machinery, equipment, land, inventories, household appliances, homes, etc. But the real factors back of capital markets are more evident than those back of money markets. The Fed funds market (one-day loans among banks of qualifying reserve money) is influenced by real economic factors because banks offer or bid for these funds only because their customers, in turn, have or need money. But on a Wednesday afternoon (end of reserve computation period) when the Fed funds rate spurts because of a shortage of reserves or falls toward the floor because of a plethora of funds, it would be hard to call "real" economic factors the cause.

This introduces the nature of another distinction between money and capital markets. Supplying of money is one of the basic functions of a sovereign government. In modern practice this function is discharged by the central bank, which in the United States is the Federal Reserve System. It is inevitable that the central bank, in discharging its function as a supplier of money and controller of that supply, should have a powerful influence on the money market of its country. It does. And if the Treasury Department has a large public debt and finances much of that debt in the money markets, it also has a large stake in money markets and may try to nudge the central bank to accommodate it; but in any event it is also a powerful force in its money market. These arms of government have special roles in every national money market.

Both money markets and capital markets are international in scope. However, the dominant element in private movement of capital to another nation is direct investment. Direct investment does not get reflected in the open capital markets. Money markets, on the other hand, tend to be linked together. A necessary condition for such linking, of course, is free convertibility of currencies at reasonably stable exchange rates. When this condition is met, short-term money moves about in search of the highest yield.

The other side of the coin is that this condition of exchange-rate stability has often been violated. When this happens, shock waves move through money markets all over the developed world. Exchange-rate speculation then becomes a potential disturber of national money markets. A stock market break in one country is usually not transmitted to other countries, but a money market spasm almost always is.

Still another distinction may be advanced: Money markets are basically wholesale markets while capital markets are both retail and wholesale. In some capital markets the retail sector dominates. The wholesale-retail distinction, of course, is based on size of transaction. While commercial banks are the central private institutions of the money market, only a very few of the 14,000 commercial banks directly participate in these central money markets; the others delegate that function to their city correspondents. The central money market is characterized by big wholesale transactions. For this reason, romantic writers about the money market sometimes picture the market as physically located on the tip of Manhattan Island south of Fulton Street. It is true that a physical concentration of financial firms—banks and others—may be found in this area, but this image gives the wrong impression of the money market. Modern communications by phone, teletype, and (soon) computer are such that big banks all over the nation as well as some big corporations and others who can afford the rental of leased wires are participants in the central money markets.

MONEY MARKETS: WHERE LIQUIDITY IS ADJUSTED

Probably the most significant function of money markets is to provide major economic units with the facilities for adjusting their liquidity position. Almost every major economic unit—a corporation, a governmental body, or a financial institution—has a regular and recurring problem of liquidity management. The money market is where they solve this problem. If the problem is that of a cash outflow in excess of cash receipts, they go to the money market looking for funds. If the problem is that of an excess of cash inflow for which they are not yet prepared to make a long-term commitment, the money market is the place for short-term or temporary employment of these excess funds. But above all of this flux of liquidity adjustment stands the Federal Reserve, manager of the nation's money supply and guardian of the viability (if not stability) of the money markets.

To get a more explicit and detailed view of money market practices and relationships, we shall start with a broad examination of the methods by which various economic units typically manage liquidity. Table 7-1 lists these various major economic units in the heads along the top. The monetary and credit instruments are listed down the stub of the table, with an indication for when each is an asset or a liability. The description of liquidity management will consist of following the participation of each unit in the various credit instrument markets. For a reason that will later become evident, we will take the sectors in an order that departs from the order of listing in the heads.

Table 7-1 brings out an interesting division among the participants in the money markets. The U.S. Treasury Department is, as would be expected, a net debtor to the money markets. Commercial banks are net debtors to the open money markets; but if we extend our view to a broader concept of the money markets, they are about evenly balanced as debtors and creditors. Nonfinancial corporations are also on both sides of the debtor-creditor relationship, but in most periods they are more creditors than debtors. The leading creditors of the money market are the Federal Reserve, individuals, and foreign banks.

CORPORATE LIQUIDITY

A corporation typically receives it major regular cash inflow from the collection of the accounts receivable that have been generated by sales. If a corporation, operating at several locations, sells its product nationwide or over a wide area, it collects from many customers. To speed up the conversion of these incoming checks into collected bank balances, it may use a large number of banks as lockbox collection agents around the country. Thus cash flows into a considerable number of banks.

The outflow of cash takes a wider variety of forms. Payroll payments may be at many points. Typically these payments, by check will be from accounts at a number of banks. Indeed, the payroll checks may well have been prepared by the EDP department of the bank which also handles the payroll account. Accounts payable must be settled, and it is possible that the verification of invoices and physical receipt of goods may require that such payments be decentralized. In addition, other miscellaneous expense items—utility bills and the like—may be paid from a variety of accounts. Thus a major corporation is likely to have a large number of bank accounts, some of which typically disburse funds.

A corporation, however, is likely to have a "lead" bank or possibly major relationships with two or three major (money market) banks, which banks will handle such accounts as dividend and interest payments and manage its pension trust. These lead banks may also make credit advances to the corporation, in which several banks participate.

Even if the total current cash flows of a corporation were in balance, considerable transferring of funds would be required: money from some banks and into other banks. The assumption of a regular balance between inflow and outflow, however, is most unlikely. Even if a corporation should have such a balance over the course of a fiscal year, seasonal dif-

Table 7-1 Money-Market Matrix: Instruments and Sectors
Amounts (in billions of dollars) are rough estimates for the end of 1971

Instruments	Federal Reserve System A	Federal Reserve System L	Commercial banks A	Commercial banks L
High-power money: Reserve balance plus vault cash		36	32	
Public money: M_1†		55		180
Money-market credit instruments				
"Fed" funds plus Federal Reserve D&A	1		24	25
Broker and dealer loans and repurchase agreements	2		8	
Eurocurrencies (mainly dollars)				10
U.S. Treasury and agency short-term instruments	40		25	
State and local gov't short term			10	
Bankers' acceptances	1		1	
Commercial paper			8	2
Negotiable certificates of deposit				34
Short-term loans			150	

* This includes only items involving the United States money markets.
† M_1 = Adjusted demand deposits + currency in circulation.

ferences of "money in" and "money out" would be quite likely. If a corporation finds that more money is going out than coming in, it could allow the total of its bank balances to decline. However, the relationships with cash-accumulating lockbox banks, with funds-disbursing banks, and with lead banks are usually based on a rather clear and explicit understanding of what constitutes a "satisfactory" balance with each bank. This balance is a part of the price for the performance of banking services. This understanding about the appropriate balance is not so rigid and formal that each day's balance cannot depart from this level—it can and does—but the average balance is fairly clearly specified and understood. Thus the corporate treasurer can let his bank balances dwindle a bit on any one day, and even for a few days; but if he wants to stay on good terms with his bankers, sooner or later these balances must be restored. Sometimes corporate treasurers may keep balances somewhat in excess of these

	Financial			Nonfinancial				Government					
Dealers, brokers, and underwriters		Intermediaries		Corporations		Individuals		Federal and agencies		State and local		Rest of the world*	
A	L	A	L	A	L	A	L	A	L	A	L	A	L
								3				1	
3	16			38		150		5		17		6	
		17		5						2		2	
												10	
7		5		10		25		3	155			40	
1				3		6					19		
					2		2					6	4
1				16	29	3						3	
1		2		14		10						7	
8		2			100		50						10

minima, but if they do so persistently, they are wasting valuable income opportunities.

Thus a corporation can use its bank balances as a buffer for day-to-day unforecastable variations in net cash flows—but it needs other means for more persisting cash demands. This first line of recourse for cash is again the banks with which the corporation deals. Credit lines are maintained and can be used when needed. The use of these credit lines is also tied to the level of balances kept with these banks: so-called compensating balances. However, it must be admitted that the understandings between a corporation and its banks about which balances compensate for (used and unused) lines of credit and which compensate for services are not always as explicit and clear as indicated above.

Some corporations have found a cheaper source of short-term credit: the commercial paper market. They are expected to maintain unused lines of bank credit to cover such paper outstanding. The net cost of commercial paper borrowing to a corporation with high credit standing is usually less than that of direct bank borrowing. As we shall learn in more detail later, the commercial paper market has grown rapidly in recent years.

Some corporations have, at least for certain seasons of the year, an excess of funds flowing into their bank accounts. First, short-term debt should be retired. After the bank's reasonable balance expectations have been met, these funds can be employed or "invested" in the money market. The nature of the use depends on how long the funds are expected to be available. This, of course, requires corporations to forecast their cash flow. The credit instruments in which corporations typically invest are the commercial paper of other corporations, negotiable certificates of time deposit (perhaps issued by the banks with which they do business), and U.S. Treasury short-term securities. A few corporations invest in short-term tax-exempt obligations of state or local governmental units.

A corporation with a persistent deficit in its cash flows, as would be true of a corporation with large capital expenditures, will probably, sooner or later, fund its short-term debts in the capital markets. However, a calculating corporate treasurer may shift the timing of such capital market funding rather materially in order to avoid a high cost of long-term money, or sometimes he may even hasten capital financing when he believes the market to be favorable—and thus have an excess of temporarily unneeded funds to return to the money markets.

If the reader will look down the vertical column headed "non-financial corporations" in Table 7-1, he will find very rough indications of the various ways in which corporations invest in the money markets.

UNITED STATES TREASURY

The Treasury Department of our federal government also has a major cash management problem. Tax receipts tend to be concentrated around the scheduled tax payment dates. Federal government expenditures, however, are more evenly spaced out during the year—but not completely so. Furthermore, the annual totals of receipts and expenditures is seldom equal, and so the Treasury Department also has a problem of longer-term debt management.

The cash (mainly tax) receipts of the federal government are almost all first funneled into a commercial bank "tax and loan account." This system tends to limit the liquidity problem of commercial banks since it provides, so far as is possible, that a tax check will be redeposited in the same bank on which it is drawn. However, the Treasury Department makes disbursements only from its Federal Reserve bank accounts, and so there is a regular passage of funds from the tax and loan accounts of commercial banks into the Treasury accounts at the Federal Reserve banks. This passage is accomplished by "calls"—notices that on the specified date funds will be transferred. The calls on smaller banks are less frequent and have considerable advance notice. Larger banks face more frequent calls with less notice; major money-market banks face frequent calls with little or even no notice. So far as is equitably possible, the Treasury Department attempts to avoid nasty surprises to the major commercial banks. However, since tax receipts often cannot be precisely forecast, some flexibility is needed.

The Treasury Department makes use of short-term borrowing to even out the patterns of cash receipts and payments. The Treasury bill, which we will examine later in more detail, is a major money-market instrument. New bills are sold every week and maturing bills are redeemed every week.

The Treasury Department, however, uses short-term securities for a much larger fraction of its "permanent" debt than is generally done by private corporations. A part, although not a very large part, of the Treasury debt is financed in the long-term capital markets.

The Treasury has one last-resort safety device, a source of funds on which it can always depend: the Federal Reserve System. Although the framers of the System were at pains to limit direct Treasury access to the credit of the System, there are provisions for short-term accommodation which are used rather infrequently.

FOREIGN HOLDERS OF DOLLARS

The United States has had a deficit in its balance of payments every year except one for more than twenty years. The dollar has been de facto inconvertible since 1968 and de jure since August 15, 1971. As a result of the deficit, foreigners have more dollars than they really like to hold, but they have little choice but to keep on accumulating them. They can, however, put these dollars to work in our money markets. The biggest fraction of these dollars is held by foreign governments directly or through their central banks. But some dollars are held by foreign commercial banks or even by businesses. What is more, a number of foreign commercial banks and branches of our commercial banks located in foreign money markets carry or "buy" dollar denominated deposits, which form the basis of the Eurodollar market.

Foreigners who have dollars may employ them by investment in U.S. Treasury securities. To encourage (and to some extent to placate) foreign governments and central banks to hold dollars, our Treasury Department even offers them special higher-return nonmarketable dollar securities. But the more ambitious holders may venture out into other forms of dollar investment: bankers' acceptances, commercial paper, and negotiable certificates of deposit (CDs). (Many foreigners venture even further into our stock market and other segments of our capital markets.) As Table 7-1 shows, the amounts have been important factors in our money markets.

Our money-market commercial banks act as money-market correspondents for foreign central banks, foreign commercial banks, and other foreign interests. However, the major balances of most foreign central banks and governments tend to be held by the Federal Reserve. Foreign holders of dollars have not had liquidity management problems, as we have elsewhere described them, since the dollar became a redundant currency.

COMMERCIAL BANKS THEMSELVES AS LIQUIDITY MANAGERS

The foregoing account must have made it clear that commercial banks, particularly the large money-market commercial banks, feel the impact of liquidity management by their own customers and other sectors of the monetary system. Those they consider customers—corporations, financial intermediaries, well-to-do individuals, and others—tend to depend on them for a kind of residual protection. And they attempt to serve the needs of these customers even if at the expense of their own liquidity position.

Commercial banks themselves have one of the most demanding liquidity requirements of all: rigid reserve requirements put on them by law and regulation. Every commercial bank, no matter how small, faces such requirements. Commercial banks that are members of the Federal Reserve System face these requirements in particularly explicit forms: collected balances at the Federal Reserve bank. "Country" or regional commercial banks use city correspondents as a buffer in reserve managements, much as do nonfinancial corporations. However, these banks often do not push aggressively in using liquidity and therefore tend to have surplus reserve funds ("Fed" funds) which they can "sell" (lend) to their city correspondent. When they need reserves, they can generally count on being able to "buy" Fed funds from their city correspondent. However, they cannot enter the central market for such funds, since their transactions tend to be too small and infrequent to be acceptable in these markets.

Major commercial banks, however, directly enter the central money markets. Most of the big banks of New York City and the leading banks of all the other major cities are linked together in a communications network that permits all the transactions involved in the money markets: Fed funds transfers and transactions.

In the liquidity management of a commercial bank, some factors are not subject to day-to-day management but must be accepted as a part of the financial balance to which the "money position manager" must adjust over the reserve computation period (one week):

While a commercial bank may influence the level of its demand deposits over the long run by promotion and management of its customer relationships, day by day it must honor deposit withdrawals whether expected or not.

Bank loans can be promoted or discouraged over longer periods of time, but during the reserve computation period only money-market loans can be adjusted. A bank cannot foresee exactly how fast a loan commitment will be exercised. Loans show up, of course, in the movement of deposit balances, given borrowing customers.

The manager of the tax-exempt portfolio can be given both objectives and limits on his investment operations; but within the reserve computation period, this portfolio cannot be readily adjusted to the needs of money management. It must be taken as a given by the money position manager.

In funds management, a bank can control the amount of funds it gets from negotiable certificates of deposit (generally in units of $100,000 or more) by adjustment of the offering rates against the computing rates in the market. But since the maturities of these CDs run beyond the reserve computation period, this is more a part of general funds management than reserve position management. Other time deposits tend to be reasonably stable, and the bank in the short term is largely passive about them.

Eurodollar deposits on an "overnight" or one-day basis may be used as a short-term source of reserves. But since most Eurodollar deposits available are for periods longer than the reserve computation period, they are more a part of the general funds management sphere than that of reserve position management in the short run. But they can and have played such short-term roles.

The market for short-term U.S. government securities, but particularly the bill market, is large and active. Since purchase or sale of Treasury bills for Fed funds (that is, immediate that-day settlement) is possible during the first part of the trading day, these securities can be used for fine-tuning adjustments of reserve position. However, bid-and-ask spreads are such that excessive in-and-out-of-the-market activity is not economical except for a dealer bank. (We shall explain this more fully in Chapter 8.)

The best day-to-day adjustment device for reserve funds is the market for Fed funds. Large money-market banks have tended to be large net debtors in the Fed funds market, and other banks have tended to be net creditors. However, considerable and rapid adjustments can be made in this market. This is the biggest and most dependable instrument used by the money manager of the big money-market commercial bank.

Usually, as a last resort, if other channels are not available or are too costly, the money manager can borrow money at the Federal Reserve. The policies of banks vary widely with respect to the use of this facility. The money-market position manager for a bank must be (and always is) well informed about the top-management policy of his bank with respect to Fed borrowing. Some banks want to use this facility freely when the Federal Reserve rediscount rate offers the opportunity for profit. The Fed itself generally discourages such use and puts direct pressure on a bank that, according to its standards, overuses the facility. At the other extreme, some banks avoid Fed borrowing and make it an impermissible alternative to the reserve position manager—except in dire emergencies.

THE FEDERAL RESERVE: THE OTHER SIDE OF MONEY MANAGEMENT

By its consitutional nature, the Fed itself can have no liquidity "problem," since it creates money. It is a public agency, however, and, in a sense, manages the liquidity of the economy. The general objective is national economic well-being. The Fed uses its three credit market instruments—reserve requirements, the discount rate, and open-market operations—as the tools for influencing money-market liquidity. Reserve requirements can be considered a structural tool. They set the rules of the game, and these rules are changed only with advance notice and rather infrequently. In a larger sense, the issue behind this instrument is who should get the earnings from the money creation process. The discount rate has an influence to the extent that some banks try to use the facility for profit-making purposes. But the number of such banks is not large, and the main influence of the rate is as a public display of the Federal Reserve's feelings about the proper level of market interest rates. The day-to-day credit instrument for Federal Reserve liquidity management is open-market operations.

Federal Reserve open-market operations are guided by an exceedingly cumbersome administrative system: the Federal Reserve Open Market Committee (FOMC). This body meets every month or oftener and gives general guidance to the day-to-day managers of the System Open Market Account (SOMA). Their operations are remarkably similar to the process followed by the "reserve position managers" of the big money-market commercial banks—but with vastly different objectives. (Indeed, the alumni of the Fed open-market function find ready employment in money-market banks. They change objectives radically but work in the same market with the same credit instruments and much the same techniques.)

DEALERS, BROKERS, AND UNDERWRITERS

One money market category was left out of the earlier description because we were not yet ready to explain its function: the dealers in U.S. government securities, dealers in commercial paper and bankers' acceptances, commission brokerage firms which arrange credit for their customers who buy securities "on margin," and the underwriting departments of the investment banking firms. United States government security dealers will be described much more fully in Chapter 14. But we must borrow from that chapter to explain the unique money-market role of dealers in general.

A dealer, to be an effective dealer, must have an inventory. These dealers must be highly leveraged to operate profitably and therefore need large credit resources. Bank borrowing is one such source: from both the banks in New York City and big banks elsewhere. These dealers also finance positions by repurchase agreements (RPs) with various customers, including banks and nonfinancial corporations. And to furnish a very short-term investment outlet for corporate customers, they have developed rather open-ended RP deals. Sometimes the Federal Reserve, wishing to put money in the market for specified periods, has offered RP money to both banks and nonbank dealers. Each dealer must balance his position each day, and that involves a continuous scramble for money.

The underwriting departments of investment bankers attempt to sell the issues they underwrite before the contractual delivery date, and this is usually possible. However, if a new offering does not sell promptly, then to pay for the securities for which they are obligated to accept delivery requires access to credit for a short but uncertain period of time. If a syndicate is involved, the managers usually arrange the credit for the entire syndicate (although individual members can request delivery of their unsold portion of securities if they have funds for the financing of them).

Commission brokerage firms generally offer their customers margin accounts, which means that (subject to the regulated limit of credit allowed by the Federal Reserve) the customer can buy securities in which he has an equity fraction less than unity. Since some customers have unemployed cash in their brokerage accounts, a commission brokerage house generally has to borrow only a part of the funds needed for its debit balance customers. These funds are usually arranged in the open money market as "brokers' loans."

These forms of credit are basically one-day, but sometimes they may be extended to as much as fifteen days (or even longer). This is the very heart of the money market. The amounts involved are not large (as Table 7-1 shows), but it has a strategic significance beyond its dollar value. Since banks do not feel the usual customer responsibility to arrange credit for these customers, they are fully exposed to the swings of ease and tension in the money markets. The ability to make money in a financial dealership is almost as much the ability to search for money as it is to buy and sell on good terms.

WHAT DOES "OPEN MARKET" MEAN?

An open-market transaction is usually considered to be one which is impersonal and competitive; in which the lender of funds seeks competitive quotations without regard to an established "customer relationship." The open-market borrower of funds seeks out the lowest cost, again by competitive bids. For example, the open-market operations of the Federal Reserve involve asking for bids from several dealers, selling at the highest prices bid (lowest yield), and buying at the lowest prices offered (highest yield). As a result, true open-market transactions have to be in virtually riskless credit instruments which are uniform in character and well understood by both buyer and seller. The price is "open," although the identity of buyer and seller need not be.

In fact, the degree to which markets are "open" is a bit less than is usually assumed. A nonfinancial corporation usually buys the negotiable CDs of its lead bank only after a look at competitive rates. If it needs the cash at maturity, it will ask for and get it. But it may renew even at noncompetitive rates rather than ask for cash if it knows that its bank is under pressure for funds. Another example: Money market banks often "accommodate" dealers who are good customers even when the banks are in a tight pinch themselves. The circle of participants in central money markets is small, and they know each others' telephone voices if not their faces. There is a bit of "give" in these markets, not so much in price as in "accommodation."

However, one requirement is never relaxed: To be an admitted member of this inner circle a person or a firm must be of unquestioned financial strength and integrity. The money market could not function if credit risks were more than trivial and exceptional. A man's word has to be good and his net worth substantial.

Most commercial bank loans are not considered open-market transactions. The borrower does not seek competitive bids. The nature of the loan agreement may contain requirements or understandings that violate the idea of homogeneity which is needed for an open market credit instrument. Nevertheless, commercial banks have to be competitive with the open market for those customers of such strong credit standing that they could enter the open market with commercial paper. The prime loan rate was at one time set largely by price leadership, although it always had to be reasonably in touch with open-market interest rates. In recent periods the prime loan rate has come to be set more often by a formula that explicitly links it with open-market rates.

Bank short-term loans are more nearly open market than might be thought at first glance, just as other money-market instruments are not quite as perfectly "open" as is often assumed. The differences are relative and not absolute.

MONEY MARKETS IN A MORE GENERAL SENSE

The central money markets, which have occupied our attention up to this point, provide an element of leadership for the financial system. The rates of interest determined in these markets are widely published and are often followed in other credit transactions. Central money markets also serve the important function of leveling out the national supplies and demands for funds. Money is fluid and moves about with agility, seeking employment on the best terms. Central money markets, however, do not embrace all segments of the financial system that might be thought of as money markets. The principal section yet to be covered is the regional commercial banking system. Before embarking on a survey of short-term credit in the commercial banking system, at least two other features will be noted—but rejected for inclusion in our survey of money markets.

Some descriptions of money markets include in them the markets for intermediate-maturity Treasury securities. This is thought to be appropriate since these securities are dominantly bought by commercial banks and through them have a link to money-market credit. This broadening of the money-market sphere by lengthening the maturity could be done, and the decision to do so would not be without some logic. The principal reason for not doing so here is that, in practice, the interest rates on intermediate-maturity securities seem to be more closely allied to long-term interest rates than to short-term interest rates. It seems more useful to treat the central money markets as being those in which fluidity of funds is very great and in which the credit instruments involved are true alternatives to the holding of money in the management of liquidity. If managers of liquid funds started using longer maturities, perhaps the intermediate maturities would then be true money-market instruments. However, very few corporate managers of cash go beyond one-year maturities in their portfolios, and much of the time they observe limits considerably shorter than that.

A second type of credit that might be thought of as relevant to money markets in a general sense is trade credit. This is short-term credit, and it is a significant source of funds. It is also a significant employment of funds for those businesses that use liberal extension of trade credit as a merchandising device. Furthermore, trade credit can be considered competitive with bank credit. Used as a merchandising device, it has made the large suppliers bankers of a sort to their customers. However, it cannot be said that a true market exists for trade credit. There is an implicit price for it, certainly, but this price is bound up with the price of the goods sold, and so credit is not bargained for apart from the goods purchased. No market transactions take place in trade credit. Without such market procedures, it would be hard to give trade credit any meaningful analysis as a money-market factor.

BANK LOANS AS MONEY-MARKET CREDIT TRANSACTIONS

The central money markets are largely open or impersonal markets. They are made homogeneous by the high quality of credit and competitive by the openness with which transactions take place. A few of the large money-market banks are true wholesalers of money; they do business mainly with other financial institutions and very large corporations. Most of the money-market banks, however, are both wholesalers and retailers of money. Since these banks have nationwide contacts, they tend to create a national market in bank credit. This national market is closely related to the central money markets; indeed, the banks are often the money-market agents of their customers. But these relationships are not impersonal open-market ones; they are customer relationships.

Aside from these giant banks, many fairly large ones operate on an essentially local or regional basis. Most banks, however, are wholly local in character. Those businesses (and individuals and others) that do not have the size to attract the attention of the big banks must depend on such local banking connections. In this sense, regional money markets exist. The terms and arrangements that govern these markets, however, are not detached from central money-market influences. Although interest rates charged by these banks fluctuate less than the prime rate and much less than central money market rates, they are not static. The availability of funds probably also varies.

This system allows for a great deal of flexibility. Central money markets emphasize standardized credit transactions and are practical only when they handle a large volume of virtually identical transactions. Local credit arrangements are tailored to the needs of individual customers. Much of this tailoring is an unconscious application of common sense but reflects sensible variations from national standards and practices.

INTERREGIONAL FLOW OF FUNDS

The credit needs of some areas tend to exceed the saving done in those areas. Other areas have much more modest demands and far more liberal supplies of credit. The central money markets serve to bring about some national leveling in the availability and cost of funds; it might be asked whether there are further devices within the commercial banking system for the accomplishment of this process of redistribution. The question is particularly relevant in the United States, since this country is characterized by a unit banking system. In a few states, statewide branch banking is permitted, but that is the farthest any new banking extension can go (not nationally as in Canada or England). In most states of the United States the limits are even narrower. In some states, branch banking is prohibited altogether.

The correspondent banking system provides for some connection between areas. However, the chief funds transfer incident to correspondent banking is the movement of deposit balances from country banks to city banks. This movement is not always in the direction that would be taken if a leveling of funds were desired. Probably the more important part of the banking system that has led to some interregional movement of funds has been loan participations or the handling of "overline" parts of loans.

When a large loan is originated by a bank, it may offer "participations" in it to other banks. This system works in many directions. A small bank may offer a participation to its city correspondent; money flows from the city to the country. On the other hand, small banks with inadequate loan demand have sometimes been offered participations in loans by their city correspondents. Then again, a small bank with a loan application that exceeds it legal loan limit may sell the "overline" portion to a city correspondent. Participations are also shared by banks of equal size, generally in cases of very large loans. Participations are offered and accepted in both short- and longer-term credits, but they probably have been more common in the latter.

CONNECTIONS BETWEEN THE MONEY AND CAPITAL MARKETS

Any observer of the money and capital markets can testify that strong interconnections exist. Federal Reserve policy is expressed wholly in the money markets, but its influence spreads quickly to the capital markets. Strong demands for funds in the capital markets spill over into the money markets and can cause money-market interest rates to increase. The nature of these interconnections is worthy of special observation.

Many suppliers of funds (savers or holders of savings) are clearly limited as to the market in which they place funds. For example, the foreign central banks and monetary authorities are limited to the money markets; they would be very foolish to commit monetary reserves to the capital markets. On the other side, savings institutions almost always employ their funds only in capital markets; they sometimes resort to money-market investment to bridge the gap between the flow of funds and investment opportunities, but this is rare. Some supplier institutions, however, do participate in both markets. Commercial banks are the leading example.

Commercial banks are traditionally more money-market than capital-market institutions, but events have changed their operations. In the first place, the commercial banks in the United States are large and important savings institutions in that they hold large amounts of time deposits. The use of such funds tends to put them into the capital markets. In prolonged low-interest-rate periods, commercial banks are also driven into capital market investment for the sake of survival. Low short-term interest rates during the 1930s would have starved banks if they had been their sole source of income. On the other side, some of the best customers of commercial banks—corporations—have long- as well as short-term credit needs. Commercial banks have found that good customer relationships often require a willingness to extend intermediate-term credit (often just called "term" loans) to leading customers.

The shifts of commercial banks between money and capital markets are partly determined by relative interest rates. Shifts in the use or availability of funds themselves tend to tie together the two markets. However, many of the shifts back and forth are not for rate reasons but are caused by other circumstances. For example, many commercial banks would prefer to do less term lending and certainly not to do it for the small differential in interest rates. But the overriding requirements of customer-relationship solidarity force them into extending such credit.

On the demand side, some borrowers are fairly well limited as to markets. Home buyers can get suitable credit only in the long-term capital markets. State and local governments finance a small part of their needs in the money markets, but most canons of prudent public financial management suggest mainly capital-market borrowing. On the other hand, U.S. government security dealers would be foolish (and would not be permitted by lenders) to borrow in the capital markets (except for firm capital); with imperfect foresight they could not afford to commit themselves to use money for long periods of time.

Some borrowers, however, can prudently shift back and forth between markets. The federal government has already been mentioned as one example of an institution that can act in this way. While the federal government probably should not have too large a part of its debt in floating form, the power to create money and the prime credit of the federal government mean that it can go much further than most other borrowers in financing essentially long-term needs for funds in short-term markets.

Large corporations can also shift between markets with relative safety. Public utility concerns need mainly long-term capital. Their record of income stability, however, is such that they can safely finance new construction with short-term bank credit and even carry complete properties for a while until conditions in the capital markets are fully to their liking. Other corporations can also choose to a considerable extent. Sales finance concerns have great flexibility. Interest rates are usually at the heart of their choice, but the matter is more one of timing than of ultimate differences in financial structures. In the end, a large part of business capital needs are long-term and go to the capital markets. Well-managed corporations, however, have some latitude about just when they do their long-term borrowing.

The material on the term structure of interest rates reviewed in Chapter 6 is relevant to this matter of interconnections. When yield curves are relatively flat, there may be little choice between money and capital market rates *at that time*. But if a flat yield curve presages a general decline in interest rates, as has often been the case, then shrewd borrowers can afford to pay higher short-term rates to wait for lower long-term rates. On the other hand, yield curves with a lot of early slope may put strong pressure on investing institutions, but particularly on commercial banks, to extend maturities. If interest rates later rise, as has often happened after such a yield-curve shape, then they will regret this action. Relative interest rates are at the heart of the arbitrage between these two sectors of the markets.

Chapter 8

Money-Market Instruments, Intermediaries, and Rates

The previous chapter introduced the major money-market participants: the Federal Reserve, commercial banks, dealers and brokers, U.S. Treasury Department, and corporations. In the course of this introduction it was necessary to mention some of the money-market credit instruments they used as they adjusted their liquidity. However, in order to keep that chapter focused on the functional nature of the liquidity adjustment process, these money-market credit instruments were not described in adequate detail. The role of intermediaries was also noted in the prior chapter, but little was said to indicate either their methods of operation or their economic significance. Such points will be elaborated in this chapter. The prior chapter also had quite a bit to say about the moving force of relative interest rates. Chapter 6 also dealt with interest-rate relationships in general. However, several details of money-market rate structures need further notice. The function of this chapter will be to examine closely the money-market credit instruments and intermediaries and the interest-rate structure on such instruments. Some puzzling and unanswered questions about rate structures will be raised.

INSTRUMENTS

Money-market credit instruments share the common characteristic of being (1) short in maturity, (2) issued by strong creditors and therefore of high credit quality, and (3) generally in large unit amounts as befits a wholesale market. The first two characteristics make the money-market credit instruments good liquidity vehicles or money substitutes. The short maturity reduces the money-rate risk to small proportions and the high credit quality avoids credit risk; these instruments are therefore nearly riskless on both scores.

Although homogeneous with respect to credit risk, money-market credit instruments are not homogeneous with respect to maturity. As was argued in Chapter 7, the difference between a one-day and a one-year credit instrument may be much greater than the difference between a one-year and a twenty-year credit instrument. It can also be said that the difference between a one-day and a one-month credit instrument is greater than the difference between a one-month and a one-year instrument. (Before going further in this chapter, the reader may wish to refresh his recollection of Figure 7-1 on page 128. This figure shows both the range of maturities and the approximate average maturity.) Money-market instruments are quite diverse in maturity for reasons that will become evident as this chapter unfolds. But more important, strong market forces tend to link the rate structures for these various instruments. They are competitive with one another, in varying degrees, for the attention of investors—or as sources of funds.

Treasury Securities

Since Chapter 14 will be devoted to the financial operations of the Treasury Department, this section will necessarily be brief. The Treasury borrows in the open market with:

1 Treasury bills of an original maturity of ninety days to one year.[1] The one-year and nine-month bills are dated to mature at the end of each month and are offered at separate auctions near the end of the month, often on Tuesdays. The total amount of one-year bills offered recently has been $1.2 billion and the amount of nine-month bills has been $500 million. The majority of bills are offered with original maturi-

---

[1] The Treasury Department formerly issued open-market one-year certificates of indebtedness (CIs). The success of the one-year bill suggests that this form of obligation may be obsolete, though the power to issue it still exists. Some dealer sheets still include the words in their titles, even though no CIs are outstanding, nor have any been for several years. However, the Treasury Department has recently sold short-term (twenty- to ninety-day) obligations to foreign branches of U.S. banks to absorb Eurodollars. These are labeled "certificates."

ties of thirteen weeks and twenty-six weeks, both arranged so as to mature on Thursdays (unless that should be a legal holiday). Each thirteen-week maturity simply adds to the issue sold thirteen weeks before and is indistinguishable from it. As a result, the Treasury bill market consists of thirty-eight issues. In the past, tax anticipation bills were also offered, but they have not been used recently. Since the Treasury bill is a discount obligation, only the face or par value is paid at maturity. As a result, bill yields are not exactly comparable with bond or note yields. The auction of thirteen- and twenty-six-week bills takes place on Monday (unless it be a holiday), and the results of this event often set the tone of the money-market week. The Federal Reserve itself engages in the auction and has no more explicit knowledge of bids than other participants until the bid boxes are opened. In the last hour before 1:30 P.M., when the Monday auction closes, a lot of frantic telephone calls are exchanged between dealers and others, which may account for the relatively close groupings of final bids.

2   Treasury notes. These obligations are issued with a maturity of from one to seven years. (Until a few years ago, maturity limit on notes was five years.) Although not money-market instruments according to traditional definition, the shorter ones belong in this category. They now constitute the largest segment of the Treasury direct debt, about $135 billion. The Federal Reserve has large note holdings, and this category dominates commercial bank portfolios. Treasury note issue maturities are trimodal: 15 months to 18 months; 3 1/2 to 4 years; and 7 years.

3   Marketable Treasury bonds. Not very important in money markets and less than $40 billion of the total Treasury debt. Most of these were issued several years ago; new issues are infrequent.

Agency Securities

The following agencies of the federal government issue nonguaranteed securities: Bank for Cooperatives, Export-Import Bank, Farmers Home Administration, Federal Home Loan Bank, Federal Intermediate Credit Bank, Federal Land Banks, Federal National Mortgage Association, Federal Home Loan Mortgage Corporation, and Government National Mortgage Association. Several of these agencies are related to the mortgage market in such a variety of ways that they will be described in more detail in Chapter 16. Total outstanding obligations of these agencies amount to $50 billion (December 1970). About one-fourth of the total has a maturity of one year or less.

These obligations compete in the money markets. For example, they can be used as collateral by commercial banks for securing public deposits. The yield differential of agency over direct Treasury obligations is sometimes less than 1/4 of 1 percent and almost never as much as 1/2 of 1 percent.

The federal government does not have a legal obligation to support the credit of these issuing agencies. This ambiguity accounts for most of the yield differential. However, it is almost beyond belief that Congress would ever allow any of these agencies to default on its obligations. If the Congress felt that we should come to the rescue, at least in part, of the Penn-Central and the Lockheed corporations, what would its attitude be toward financial difficulties of an agency which it had created?

Agency debt does not come under the Treasury Department's debt ceiling. This debt ceiling has become a halter that Congress keeps on the Treasury to force other concessions from it. The very existence of an agency debt outside this limit thus can be viewed as an economic irrationality produced in the naked use of political power.

Negotiable Certificates of Deposit (NCD)

These obligations are a part of commercial bank time deposits. The reporting definition of these obligations is certificates of deposit of $100,000 denomination or greater having common law negotiability. They have been used since 1961 and now account for more than $35 billion of the funds collected by banks. Maturities range from one month to one year. They are theoretically open-market instruments, but in practice a large fraction is sold by banks to customers. This gives rise to a market anomaly with respect to rates. Each bank posts rates for various maturities which signifies a rate that it is willing to pay all comers with money in their hands. However, this posted rate is almost always a bit less than the rate prevailing in the secondary market. As a result, an investor would generally be foolish to accept posted rates; he could do better from a dealer. (However, a dealer is often unable to supply large amounts of each maturity.) The implication of this fact is that commercial banks presumably write NCDs for their customers at rates which are a bit above posted rates. However, if a bank is anxious to attract money, it may move its posted rate above that of other banks and, in fact, a bit above the secondary market so as to attract money from the street.

The greatest barrier to the growth of the NCD has been the Federal Reserve Regulation Q which limits interest paid on time deposits. During some periods the Federal Reserve has held the Regulation Q ceiling below market-rate levels. Under these circumstances it would be expected that banks would lose all these funds as fast as the NCDs matured. In fact, this did not happen. This anomaly implies that consideration of good bank relationships persuaded some corporate customers to renew the NCDs for the sake of cementing their banking relationships, even if they could have done better elsewhere in the short run. The money markets may be open, but they are not impersonal!

The Federal Reserve made Regulation Q inoperative with respect to NCDs in mid-1970. It also appears from public statements that the Federal Reserve has less enthusiasm for use of this regulation to limit time deposit acquisition. However, Regulation Q still applies to certificates of deposit in smaller denominations. These CDs cannot be considered money-market instruments. This instrument has been used more actively by banks in the search of money, and this source of bank funds has recently been growing very rapidly. It is possible that there may be some further evolution in the form of both NCDs and CDs which might change the face of banking. Such an evolution, of course, would require a retreat from Regulation Q, which is not impossible.

Commercial Paper

This form of open-market borrowing is widely used by corporations with first-class credit. Corporations which use this market with special intensity include sales and personal finance companies. These types of companies generally place their paper by direct sales to customers. Such issuers offer tailored maturities of from 3 days (weekend) to 270 days. One-bank holding companies have also been issuing commercial paper (usually directly) and using the proceeds to acquire loans or other assets from their subsidiary banks. Most other corporations issue commercial paper through dealers. Commercial paper totals tend to reach their peaks during periods of tight money when corporations go into the commercial paper market with the blessing and encouragement of their banks. Commercial paper is "unsecured."

While commercial paper is relatively free of credit risk, losses do occur. The collapse of the Penn-Central Railroad was marked, if not precipitated, by the default of its commercial paper. A number of other corporations with marginal credit standings were forced to retreat from the commercial paper market at that time.

Commercial paper is normally (but not always) issued and traded on a discount basis. For this reason the paper is like Treasury bills in that some adjustment must be made in the quoted yield to make it comparable with yields on interest-bearing obligations.[2]

Bankers' Acceptances

These instruments are almost wholly related to the financing of international business, mainly of exporting or importing. In effect, a bank

---

[2] In a discount obligation, interest is figured on the face amount of the obligation but is then deducted, which is equivalent to collecting interest in advance. The effective yield is therefore greater than the nominal yield. This differential becomes particularly significant on longer-term discount obligations such as one-year Treasury bills or 270-day commercial paper. The differential is also more significant when money rates are high.

guarantees the credit of or arranges for the guarantee of the credit for a customer who engages in foreign trade. Acceptance credit can also be used to finance trade transactions between other countries, as when a U.S. bank facilitates the purchase of raw materials, purchased in still another foreign country, by a foreign subsidiary of an American corporation. For tax reasons (they are exempt from income taxes when owned by a nonresident) bankers' acceptances have been bought mainly by foreign investors in our money markets. The Federal Reserve also purchases a small but steady amount of acceptances. All Federal Reserve purchases are of acceptances based on real commodity transactions.

While most bankers' acceptances are still trade-secured documents, some money market banks with multinational corporate customers have used acceptance credit to supply working capital for the foreign subsidiaries of their customers. Since the market for acceptances has been somewhat more sheltered from tight money markets than other instruments, this device has been used mainly in such circumstances. However, this use has continued to grow. In the 1920s a similar expansion of "clean" or "finance" bills occurred. (This means a bill without the accompanying documents indicating an underlying trade transaction.) Finance bills were criticized then as now and were abandoned in the 1930s. If pushed too far, this practice could lead to withdrawal of the special tax status.

Short-Term Tax-Exempt Obligations

Although the bulk of state and local government financing is, as it has been, on a long-term basis, an increasing amount has been done with short-term obligations. Some short-term borrowing by local governmental units is more nearly a customer-negotiated transaction than a true money-market operation. However, a fairly large volume of short-term tax-exempt financing takes place in the open money markets. The most visible financing is that of the various U.S. government housing agencies. A number of large cities also borrow on a tax anticipation basis. These types of short-term tax-exempt notes include project notes, bond anticipation notes, budget notes (really tax anticipation notes), public housing authority notes, and urban renewal authority notes.

This segment of the money market appears to differ from other segments in two important ways. First, some of the cities selling short-term notes have such tangled financial problems that their longer-term bonds have been downgraded in terms of credit. While it would be wrong to attribute a great deal of credit risk to the short-term obligations of such cities, credit risk is not as absent as in most money-market instruments. A related technical difference is that some tax warrants do not have a specific maturity and thus are nonmarketable. The other difference is that the secondary market in these obligations is small. An investor doubtless could sell a short-term tax-exempt note before maturity but with more discount than would be true of most money-market instruments. Lack of a secondary market is indicated by the fact that yield quotations for such obligations almost never appear in the financial press.

Fed Funds

Although they do not have the largest outstandings of the money-market instruments, Fed funds transactions are most carefully watched, partly because they are thought to reveal Federal Reserve open-market policy. Fed funds are, as their name implies (if spelled out fully), Federal Reserve funds; in other words, an immediate claim to a Federal Reserve deposit. When held by a member bank, this deposit can be used to satisfy its reserve requirements. For this reason, Fed funds transactions are mainly among member banks. However, exceptions exist. Nonmember banks cannot use Fed funds themselves but can "sell" them off to a member bank if they are to be used. An increasing number of rather large commercial banks have withdrawn from Federal Reserve membership, so this is a growing source of sales. In addition, U.S. government and other security dealers often come into possession of Fed funds (payment for security sales in Fed funds has become increasingly common), and as a result such holders "sell" Fed funds, but mainly through a bank.

The basis for the market is simple: A bank with excess reserves wants to sell the excess for income; a bank with a reserve deficiency usually prefers to cover this deficiency by "buying" Fed funds rather than borrowing directly from the Fed (as will be explained more fully in Chapter 10). Because the market is so completely centered around the satisfaction of reserve requirements, it follows the rhythm of these requirements. For most money-market banks the weekly averaging period starts with deposit liabilities *beginning* Thursday morning and ends with the deposit liabilities the following Wednesday morning. The balance needed to meet the requirements starts with the *close of business* Thursday and ends with the close of business the following Wednesday. Saturdays, Sundays, and holidays count. Most Fed funds transactions are for one day, but weekend deals are for three days; over a holiday, two days. (The right combination of a weekend and a holiday can give rise to four-day transactions.)

The Fed funds market has two major sections. The wholesale section consists of transactions of unit size of $1 million or more (almost never less than $500,000). In addition, there is a kind of "flow-through" market from little banks to city correspondent banks. With the advent of the computer, many city banks now keep books for country correspondents. In doing so, they manage their reserve positions. Any excess funds of the country correspondent are purchased by the managing bank. The unit amounts are often somewhat less than common for open-market Fed funds transactions. The city correspondent, in effect, assembles these funds from its various country correspondents in its own reserve position and then resells any excess it has in the wholesale Fed funds market. Thus there is a steady trend: Small and country banks tend to be net sellers of Fed funds, and correspondent banks tend to be net buyers. A big proportion of banks tend to persist on one side of the market: to be net sellers or net buyers. While many Fed funds transactions are carried out by direct deals among banks, some banks perform a dealer function in Fed funds, both buying and selling to make a market. However, if such banks have problems settling their own reserve position, they may have to retreat from one side of the market. In addition, two nonbank firms "broker" such transactions.

Because Fed funds are so perishable, the market has certain rhythms of its own. Early in the morning, while banks are trying to figure out what check clearings have done to their reserve positions, business may be slow. Around ten o'clock business picks up. But since banks do not dare wait too long, business slacks off in the afternoon. Friday is always an exceptionally important day since that involves three-day commitments. Wednesday, which ends the reserve computation period, is the payoff. If unexpected developments have pinched reserves more than the Fed expected, the Fed may be busy putting money into the market by repurchase agreements (RPs) or other means. Any banks which miscalculated fight hard to find money. Conversely, any bank which overestimated its needs may find itself with excess funds and no buyers. Even in times of generally tight money markets, Wednesday afternoon Fed funds rates can sink backward. However, improved computer forecasting is making the market steadier over the weekly cycle than formerly was the case.

The departure of Wednesday Fed funds rates from the average of other days is graphically brought out in Figure 8-1. The Wednesday rates were materially below other days on April 12 and 19 and moderately below on May 3, 10, and 24. Wednesday rates were above the surrounding days materially on March 29 and April 26, and somewhat above on May 31. If the Wednesday rates are not counted, the rates of other days stayed fairly close to the 4 1/2 percent Federal Reserve discount rate that prevailed during all this three-month period. It would appear, in fact, that the target rate for that period was from 4 to 4 1/2 percent.

Money Market Rates

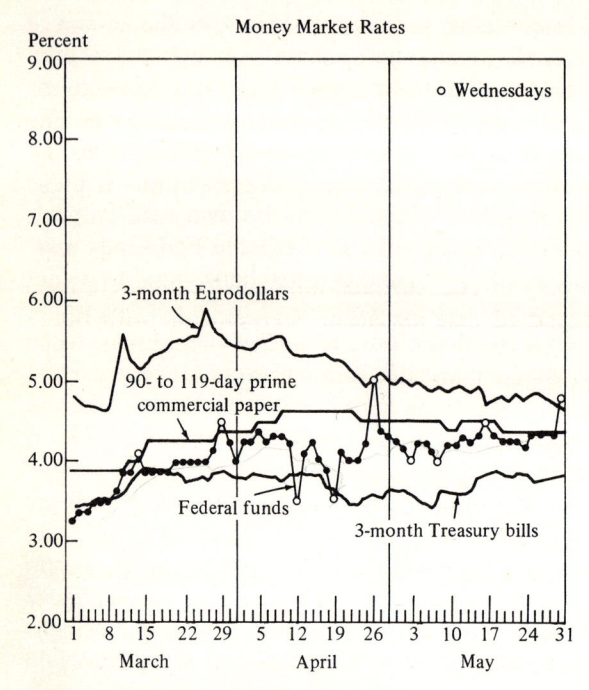

[Figure: Money Market Rates chart, Percent axis 2.00–9.00, March–May, showing 3-month Eurodollars, 90- to 119-day prime commercial paper, Federal funds, and 3-month Treasury bills. Wednesdays marked with open circles.]

Note: Dates are shown for business days only.

Figure 8-1 Selected interest rates, March–May 1972. Money-market rates quoted: Bid rates for *three-month Eurodollars* in London; offering rates (quoted in terms of rate of discount) on *90- to 119- day prime commercial paper* quoted by three of the four dealers that report their rates, or the midpoint of the range quoted if no consensus is available; the effective rate on *federal funds* (the rate most representative of the transactions executed); closing bid rates (quoted in terms of rate of discount) on newest outstanding *three-month bills*. (Source: Federal Reserve Bank of New York, Monthly Review, *June 1972, chart 1, p. 146. Wednesday indications added.)*

Repurchase Agreements (RPs): Direct and Reverse

Fed funds transactions are not secured. Since they are mainly among commercial banks, it is assumed that these short-term credit extensions do not need to be protected. However, the dealers in U.S. government securities (see pp. 156–159) and certain other participants in the money markets operate with such thin capital structures that creditors require that all credit extended to them be secured. A repurchase agreement secures credit: The "seller" sells securities to the creditor but simultaneously contracts to repurchase these same securities, either on call

MONEY-MARKET INSTRUMENTS, INTERMEDIARIES, AND RATES 155

or at some stated date in the future, at a price which will produce the agreed effective yield. Conversely, a holder of idle funds can buy securities with a simultaneous contract to resell. Dealers use this instrument both with the Federal Reserve and with other customers. Maturities with the Fed are usually quite short and never in excess of fifteen days. With other customers, however, somewhat longer terms are possible and, in fact, used.

The manager of the SOMA (see pp. 199–205) has used this device to extend credit to the money market through nonbank dealers. He has also used the reverse "matched sale-purchase" agreements with both bank and nonbank dealers in order to sop up excess money from the money markets for a foreseeable short period.

Eurocurrencies: Mainly the Eurodollar

In the strict sense of the word, Eurocurrencies are not traded in United States money markets. However, transatlantic communications have been perfected to the point that they are now, in reality, a steady competitor in our money markets. They furnish a vehicle by which banks can secure reserves; they also furnish an outlet for investment of idle funds by our multinational corporations and others who might otherwise use domestic money-market outlets. Chapter 12 will give a fuller account of how these currencies developed.

A Eurocurrency (which can also be an Asiancurrency) is simply a deposit account in a bank denominated in a currency other than that of the host bank. A deposit account denominated in dollars in a London bank is a Eurodollar. London is, in fact, the leading center for off-country denomination of deposits, and the dollar is the leading currency for such denomination. However, Frankfurt, Zurich, Singapore, and Tokyo banks now bid for deposits in nonnational currencies. Likewise German marks, French francs, British sterling, Dutch guilders, Swiss francs, and Canadian dollars are deposited in banks in countries other than their origin.

Why is this done? One reason is that banks in London and other foreign centers are free of Regulation Q. They can pay interest on deposits without legal limitation. In addition, other types of governmental controls such as exchange controls (and including income taxes) are more easily evaded when dealing in a currency away from home. Freedom has created the markets. Those who have dollars and wish to remain in dollars can find a better deal in the Eurodollar market.

Why do borrowers borrow in Eurocurrencies? Again because they can escape regulation such as on security margins or security taxes and taxes on foreign investment. Speculators betting on the devaluation of the dollar may prefer to borrow in dollars, exchange the funds for a stronger currency such as German marks—and wait for the devaluation. The Eurocurrency markets are for the sophisticated. But as the impact of regulation becomes more onerous in domestic markets, so much will these "refugee" markets prosper.

The Eurocurrency market offers a very wide range of maturities: from overnight or call transactions through seven-day, one-month, and various months up to one or two years and apparently longer in a few circumstances. However, a tabulation of the maturities of Eurodollar liabilities of the foreign branches of U.S. banks showed that one-month maturities dominated the market.[3]

It is significant that the foreign (mainly London) branches of U.S. banks account for a very large proportion of the total market. This relationship explains the way in which money-market banks could use the Eurodollar market to supplement their reserve funds. A bank's London branch would bid for Eurodollar deposits and transfer the funds to the head office where it would clear on the bank on which drawn and then be used as reserves. Such transactions did not, of course, increase the total of reserves available to U.S. banks, but once one bank started to use the channel, other banks were forced to do likewise to hold their share of total reserves.

United States banks with foreign branches are now required to carry reserves against Eurodollar deposits. The Bank for International Settlements has suggested that the market needs regulation. However, the market persists and often supplies an important part of the profit base of our great money-market banks.

MONEY-MARKET INTERMEDIARIES

Most of the institutions dealing in the money markets are large enough and expert enough to deal directly as principals with other money-market participants. However, in some cases intermediaries service specialized purposes with great skill. The most important of these are the dealers in U.S. government securities. A number of other dealers and agents also serve between the principals of the market.

United States Government Security Dealers

The market for both direct obligations of the Treasury Department and for Federal Government Agency securities is centered in a group of

---

[3] Federal Reserve Bank of Chicago, *International Letter,* June 11, 1971.

twenty-four dealers.[4] Ten of these dealers are specialized departments in commercial banks, and the others are nonbank dealers. Several of these nonbank dealers are departments of general financial houses, but the majority are independent firms. In addition, quite a few large commercial banks informally conduct fairly large dealer operations. The distinguishing mark of a dealer is that he "makes a market," which means that he buys or sells on either end of the bid-and-ask spread. He makes a "good" market if this bid-and-ask spread is moderate in size and if the amount he is willing to both buy and sell is reasonably large. What is "reasonable" for a spread and for amounts? This is hard to pin down because this depends on the security. Examples will help: A dealer would be considered to make a good market if his spread on ninety-day bills were 4 percent bid and 3.90 percent ask. He would be expected to go $1 million either way; and if he were a really substantial dealer, he probably would make a market of $5 million to $10 million or even more for a good customer. Since customers make counter offers, the effective spread might be smaller than the ten basic points (4 – 3.90 percent). On a five-year note the security would be quoted in terms of price rather than yield and the spread first quoted probably would be 4/32. A dealer would expect as a minimum to stand on both ends of the quote for $100,000, but a substantial dealer would go up to $1 million. Amounts above that would be less certain and might require "taking the order" so as to search.

The institutional significance of the U.S. government security dealers is that they are always the link between the Federal Reserve and the money market. The Fed executes orders for various customers (foreign correspondents mainly), but it always deals with dealers. At one time the Fed had a group of formally "recognized" dealers, but it now operates rather informally and will deal with any dealer who demonstrates financial responsibility and the willingness to make what the Fed considers a good market. It is thus the dealers who get the first wind of Fed market operations.

Since three excellent descriptions of this market are available to the student, the analysis at this point will be relatively brief.[5] This is a classic over-the-counter market. It is without a central meeting place and is governed much more by tradition than by such laws and rules that are

---

[4] Dealers reporting to the market statistics division of the Federal Reserve Bank of New York, as listed by *The New York Times,* September 10, 1972, sec. 5, p. 3.

[5] The best and most detailed account is *A Study of the Dealer Market for Federal Government Securities* published by the Joint Economic Committee in 1960. The second is found in various portions of Robert J. Roosa, *Federal Reserve Operations in the Money and Government Securities Markets,* Federal Reserve Bank of New York, 1956, particularly Chaps. III to V. The Treasury–Federal Reserve study of this market is a more diffuse and less relevant document for the serious student. The third source is Ira Scott, *Government Securities Market,* McGraw Hill Book Company, New York, 1965.

found in stock exchanges. It is, of course, an "over-the-telephone" market. The willingness of dealers to "make markets" varies greatly with conditions—and their relationship with the customer at the other end of the telephone. The primary income of dealers is presumed to be in the spread between their bid and ask prices. While this income provides their core support, the potential for income and the risk of loss on changes in price of their inventories of securities is also important and sometimes of dominant importance. To act as both a buyer and seller, a dealer must have inventories or "positions" in individual Treasury issues. Due to short selling, these positions can sometimes become negative, but this is not at all common. However, the dealer's fundamental ability is that of being able to find willing buyers of available securities and willing sellers of needed securities—at prices which leave the dealer a modest profit. Whether the dealer first sells the securities wanted and then replaces them in his own inventory or acts as a broker in the transaction, he must service his customers to stay in business.

The amount of business capital employed by the nonbank dealer community is relatively small. It furnishes a rather narrow margin when it is remembered that dealer holdings of securities have sometimes reached $6 billion. Dealers thus are able to carry positive positions in securities primarily to the extent they can find financing; capital is mainly just a guarantee fund. This search for financing is one of the principal reasons government security dealers are such important elements in the money markets. The bank dealer departments, of course, do not require external financing but are parts of the financial positions of the banks operating them. The cost of money is thus an important part of the nonbank business. Money-market banks have been the traditional source of such credit. This tradition goes back to the London money market in which the discount houses (very much like our dealers) depend on bank financing, and banks in turn use the dealers as an outlet for surplus funds. While commercial banks also lend surplus funds to dealers, the development of the Fed funds market has given banks an outlet for surplus funds. Dealer loans are not as favorably viewed as in London. A few money-market banks feel a responsibility to support dealer financing, but this is not a universal feeling. As a result, the dealers themselves have not felt content to depend solely on money-market banks for financing. With a unit banking system there are many banks outside the central money markets. The dealers very early learned to canvass the banks outside the money markets in efforts to locate low-cost one-day funds. But the most novel development in dealer financing has been the use of temporary funds from nonfinancial corporations.

Many of the giant corporations operate their financial affairs to cover their liquidity needs without bank borrowing even at the peak of such needs. This means that in slack periods they have surplus cash. Employment of this cash in the money markets was a natural consequence, particularly in the postwar period when interest rates went up to a level that made this worthwhile. This was not a new development, of course; during the 1920s many nonfinancial corporations loaned money on the call loan market.

The initial money market investment of corporations was directly in short-term Treasury securities, mainly bills. Dealers, however, found that they could offer corporations outlets for funds that were exactly tailored to the time money would be available. If a corporation has a scheduled dividend or tax payment, it may keep idle funds on hand for such purposes. If no Treasury bill matures on the payment date, this leaves a slightly untidy margin. Dealers found that they could offer to borrow the funds (secured by Treasury obligations, of course) for the exact period for which they were available. Rather than being a formal borrowing-lending transaction, these deals often took the form of a sale from the dealer to the customer accompanied by an agreement to repurchase at a fixed and predetermined price. These repurchase agreements or "repos," were generally negotiated at a rate which was below bank lending rates to dealers but often just slightly above the Treasury bill rate or at least the Treasury bill rate to the maturity date involved. The dealers save money in comparison with bank borrowings, but they can afford to pay a bit more than the bill rate, often because the average earnings on the portfolio they carry exceed the bill yield.

Commercial banks are the best customers of U.S. government security dealers, but the next best group of customers are the big and liquid corporations. There is, however, considerable specialization in this market. Some dealers are strong with banks, some with corporations, and a few consider themselves money-market specialists; they trade for other dealers.

The primary qualification for success in this market is the ability to read Federal Reserve signals and to interpret the evidence of pressures in the commercial banking system and the nature of expected business developments. The market is a tender one, and it can be swayed by rumors and random bits of news. Changes in business conditions are always very important; bearish business news is bullish news in this market—and the other way around. Steel strikes and foreign political developments have been known to move prices quite a bit. The reason for sensitivity to Federal Reserve policy is obvious, and it is notable that a fair proportion of the managers in this market are alumni of the Federal Reserve System open-market account operations.

Dealers in Commercial Paper and Bankers' Acceptances

There are about a dozen dealers in commercial paper and seven in bankers' acceptances. Most of these dealers are departments in investment banking firms. The sensitivity of investment banks to the financial condition of issuing companies makes them particularly fitted for commercial paper dealings. Dealers in bankers' acceptances are mainly those with good connections in the community of foreign banking offices and representatives in New York City. As is true of U.S. government security dealers, these firms carry a moderate inventory of these instruments and finance this inventory mainly by day loans from the money-market banks.

MONEY-MARKET INTEREST-RATE STRUCTURE

Chapter 6 in Part One dealt with two major problems of interest rate relationships: risk and maturity. Since the money markets tolerate little risk, risk discussion is more applicable to capital markets. The discussion of maturity-rate relationships—usually referred to as the "term structure of interest rates"—extended considerably beyond the short maturity limit usually associated with money markets. However, even within the traditional one-year maturity limit of the money markets, differences can be observed. Unless a flat yield curve prevails, there is usually more difference between ninety-day and one-year yields than there is between one-year and two-year yields. Further along the yield curve, the differential for a given unit of time is even less.

Observations at the short end of the yield curve, however, are subject to a number of qualifications. One of the most important is that very short-term rates may be quite volatile without much affecting other interest rates. For example, fluctuations in the Fed funds rate do not have much visible effect on other interest rates. Money-market participants know that the rate is sharply influenced by the short-term influences of reserve position management. In fact, the participants are more likely to ascribe such wide swings to inept defensive management by the Fed than to any general economic factor. Strictly speaking, there is no term structure to the Fed funds rates since it has no long-term counterpart.

In the market for Eurodollars, there is a counterpart characteristic. At times of international monetary crises, the overnight or call rate for Eurodollar deposits may jump very high for a day or two (it hit 20 percent in the early summer of 1972) with little change in the Eurodollar deposit rate for longer maturities.

Quotations of interest rates or yields often are more nominal than real. A Eurobank may feel required to post a rate, but there may be no takers. In other words, posted rates are opinions but do not necessarily represent real transactions.

The nominal character of quotations has another dimension. The rates known to those who are not insiders in the market are often those reported to the financial press after the close of the business day. A bored trader in a dealer firm is called by a bored newspaper writer putting together his standard money-market story. The bored trader "reads" his list and it is published. The list may, in fact, as it usually does, represent a fairly honest reflection of market conditions at the close of business. But who knows? Was most of the business done near the bid end of the range or the ask end? Or was a lot of business done outside the quotes? Real transactions are private matters and an outsider is justifiably dubious of nominal quotes.

An example already mentioned was the persistent excess of the secondary market yields quoted on NCDs over the rates posted by banks. The hypothesis advanced there was that the rates for real transactions are probably usually above the posted rates. A close reading of money-market yield quotations raises other questions:

1 Published yields on agency issues often cover an irrationally wide range. Can investors, in fact, get the high ask yields that are quoted? Conversely, are the bids at lower yields real? An outside observer cannot help but feel that the real market must be considerably more rational than the published quotes.

2 Published yields quoted for commercial paper almost always have far less maturity differential than the maturity differential of Treasury bills at the same time. However, the 90- and 180-day yields on commercial paper generally show a much more reasonable relationship to the T-bill rate than either the 30-day or the 270-day rate. Does this mean that since most of the business is done at the middle range, that the outside limits are more nearly nominal?

3 Why should the yields on NCDs lie above the commercial paper rate, and particularly the longer commercial paper rate, so persistently? It is hard to believe that the quality of bank paper is not as good as that of corporate paper. Is it possible that holders of the NCDs feel more hesitant about asking for cash at maturity than do the holders of CPs?

4 Why is the rate quoted on bankers' acceptances so stable? Is this really a sheltered market not closely arbitrated with the rest of the money market?

Chapter 9

Commercial Banks in the Money Markets

Chapter 7, which opened the money-market section, has already described the important and central role of commercial banks in these money markets. As the other sectors of the economy adjust their liquidity, the resulting impact is felt by the commercial banks as deposit shifts or loan demands. Commercial banks are in the business of supplying liquidity to their customers. But in the process of accommodating customers, commercial banks themselves face liquidity problems. In Chapters 7 and 8 some attention was given to the ways in which commercial banks do this job of "money position" management.

    What was left out of these chapters was adequate recognition of the diversity in the banking structure and how it is unified by correspondent banking. This is our first task. We should also show how the profit objective dominates commercial bank operations and how it affects their money-market operations. Commercial banks are profit-making institutions. Whatever else they may attempt to achieve, profits are the heart

162

COMMERCIAL BANKS IN THE MONEY MARKETS

of their operations. In this regard they differ greatly from the Federal Reserve, which is not a profit-motivated institution (although it does in fact make large profits from its money creation powers). The Federal Reserve has objectives of economic and money-market stability.

The central concern of commercial banks with moneymaking means that they must focus on two sets of interest rates: those that they receive as lenders or investors and those they pay (in money or implicitly) in securing money. Commercial banks are complex institutions with many sources of income—but the income from lending and investing money still dominates their revenue calculus. And while commercial banks have many costs, the most variable cost has been that of securing money. To understand how commercial banks operate in the money markets, therefore, we shall examine the relationship of interest revenues and interest costs.

INTEREST REVENUES AND COSTS: INTERRELATIONSHIPS

The opportunities that banks have to employ money determines how much they are willing to pay, directly or indirectly, for money. The growing importance of this line of causation is one of the great developments of contemporary commercial banking. At one time banks were rather passive with respect to securing funds. They solicited the business of depositors and adjusted the rates paid on time deposits—but they did not "buy" money in a very aggressive sense. For more than a decade, however, banks have been active searchers and bidders for money. The degree of search activity and bid rates have depended on the rates available in money employment opportunities. Thus revenue rates and cost rates are interrelated.

The problem, however, is that the process of money employment involves various terms of commitment into the future. If banks are to be able to grasp money employment opportunities, they must have much of the money on hand; it is not technically feasible to go out and "buy" large amounts of money on short notice. Thus banks are forced into the activity of forecasting both demand and supply in the money markets and then planning their balance of funds so as to be able to take maximum advantage of the opportunities that they believe to be before them. Banks were among the first to employ economists for financial forecasting, and they continue to be large employers of economists relative to other types of business. The reserve adjustment activities described in the previous chapter is essentially a short-run operation correcting for the variations in realized experience from forecasts. But a bank must also engage in a longer-range planning operation in which it marshals the funds it will need to meet its expected opportunities.

The plan of this chapter will be to look first at correspondent banking, the glue in our banking system. We will then examine the nature of employment opportunities for bank funds. The next part will be an examination of funds-marshaling operations. The final section will then deal with money-market volatility in the availability and cost of funds encountered in the reconciliation of funds marshaling and funds employment.

CORRESPONDENT BANKING: THE LINKAGE OF MONEY MARKETS

By now it must be evident that the commercial banking system is the principal private institution in the money market (and the Federal Reserve System is the principal public institution in the market). Now we shall address ourselves to the arrangement that gives cohesion to the commercial banking system: correspondent banking.

No bank can establish a branch outside the state in which it is located. In many states, branching is severely limited and in a few it is prohibited altogether. Although this restrictive legal structure is being loosened a bit, it remains a dominant feature of banking in the United States. No other economically developed nation has such a fractured banking system.

This restriction would make banking enormously inefficient, perhaps almost impossible if it were not for the correspondent banking system. Each bank, no matter how small, has at least one city correspondent. Intermediate-sized banks have several. City correspondents perform the required money-market services for their country correspondents that the latter cannot perform for themselves. Improved communications have put country banks into much closer touch with central wholesale money markets. Although some regional differences in interest rates persist (see Chapter 6), they have tended to lessen. But perhaps more important, the quality of services a country bank can make available to its customers has been greatly improved. It is something of a symbol that the prime loan rate, which was formerly noticed only by the city financial press, has in recent years often reached the television news programs.

COMMERCIAL BANK INCOME FROM LOANS

Loan and investment income accounts for five-sixths of commercial bank revenues. Loan income is about two-thirds and investment income about one-fifth. Each of the two broad groups of assets which dominate the income generating process must be broken down into further subgroups in order to make commercial bank profit management reasonably clear.

Business Loans and the Prime Loan Rate

Commercial banks make the largest part of their loans to businesses. A very large fraction of the dollar volume of business loans (although not so large a fraction in terms of numbers) is made at the prime loan rate. The prime loan rate was, until a few years ago, set by leadership within the banking community. The identity of this leadership was clear: About half a dozen very large banks took the initiative in raising or lowering the prime loan rate. Other big (but not quite as big) banks usually went along. The prime loan rate would be raised when money was short. This might be signaled by increases in various open-market interest rates, but it would also be justified by strong customer loan demand. A decrease in the prime loan rate would come at an opposite time: when open-money-market rates were going down and customer loan demand was weak. The actual announced decrease might come after a period in which there had been some covert and not fully concealed cutting of rates to especially good customers. A change was viewed as the expressed judgment of a money-market leader that such change was both needed and justified by money-market conditions.

Recently the prime loan rate has lost this simple nature. More banks have gotten into the act of announcing rate changes, sometimes, apparently, only for reasons of getting some cheap and quick publicity. But a few banks (five in mid-1972), rather than basing their prime loan rates on judgment, now use a formula related to the rate on commercial paper for doing so. Of course, the very act of selection of the elements in a formula involves judgment. The action, however, is no longer so clear a case of price leadership. Multiple prime loan rates have prevailed during some recent periods.

Banks away from central money markets do not adhere as closely to the prime loan rate, but most banks are influenced by it. For all banks, big and small, the rate should be viewed as one determined largely by market forces over which the individual bank has little or no control. What the individual bank can do, and what most banks do do, is to attempt to use their prime loan rate to solidify and extend their customer relationships. When money is easy, customer loans probably are the more profitable ways in which to employ money. It pays to promote loan business with customers. In times when money is tight and loan demand high, margin for negotiation remains in the level of compensatory balance requirements put on customers. Even compensatory balance arrangements are subject to considerable competitive pressure, and a bank cannot get far out of line with the market as a whole. But within margins, a bank can so arrange the nature of the requirement as to get the maximum balance from customers but to fit it most conveniently into customers' cash flows. Banks are increasingly offering cash management services to their customers, a part of which is that this is a way of getting the most for both sides of the bargain.

In the end, the prime loan rate should be considered closely allied to the more volatile open-market money rates, particularly the rate on commercial paper which, for many customers, represents a practical alternative as a source of funds. As mentioned already, the formulas now used by those banks that set their prime rates in this way generally put most weight on the commercial paper rates. The transmission route for influence is about this: general open-market money rates to the commercial paper rate, and from that to the prime loan rate. Two kinds of "add ons" to the prime loan rate are important: a higher rate for lower-quality customers and a higher rate for longer-term loans.

As the name indicates, this rate is for "prime" customers. Although there is no clear and unambiguous definition of what a prime customer is, many customers, and some of the most profitable, are not prime. The interest rates on business loans compiled quarterly by the Federal Reserve are always materially above the prime loan rate for the period covered by the report. For very big loans the margin is from 1/4 to 1/2 percent, but for smaller loans the differential is much greater. There is also a regional differential (see Chapter 6) which may or may not be due to differences in quality. However, even for those customers that do not rate as prime, the prime loan rate may still determine borrowing costs: Banks often classify a customer as "prime + x percent."

There are also differences for maturity. Short loans have the prime rate and longer-term loans will be made with some differential. The size of this differential cannot be quantified with available data. However, it appears that this differential is usually less than the slope of the yield curve. In other words, banks do not demand as clear a maturity differential as is demanded by the open money and capital markets.

Loans to Financial Corporations

Sales finance companies, both independent and affiliated with nonfinancial corporations, and several other types of financial corporations are often important participants in the money markets. These corporations are usually able to finance their short-term needs directly in the money markets by issuing their commercial paper. Since differentials between their lending rates and their borrowing rates are also important to their profit calculations, they tend to be careful money shoppers. However, since they usually cannot enter the commercial paper market without a backup line of commercial bank credit, they must maintain a good set of banking relationships. Since its borrowing needs are large, a big financial corporation will have needs beyond the borrowing limits of even the biggest banks and therefore must have principal relationships with several banks.

Loans to these customers must be competitive with the open money markets, and so the prime loan rate and the compensatory balance requirement are both carefully reviewed by both borrower and lender.

Business Loans Beyond the Prime Rate

Almost all banks make some business loans that lie outside the orbit of the prime loan rate. Loans to small business and to farmers usually fall in this category. The importance of such credit to money-market banks is not large, but it is often important to smaller banks that are remotely located.

Real Estate Loans

This is a special category of business loans with a wide variety of characteristics. Almost all banks make some mortgage loans to customers individually. This is often more an accommodation than a matter of direct profit. But construction loans to builders and real estate developers (including real estate syndicates) is a big and dangerous business. In many cases this form of credit is tied in with arrangements for follow-up financing of the real estate under construction. A Federal Reserve survey taken as of mid-1971 found almost $10 billion of construction loans at commercial banks.[1] Some banks act as mortgage bankers and so originate a great deal of mortgage credit; they sell the loans to investors located in areas of less loan demand, but service it while it is outstanding.

Consumer Credit

The rate charged on loans of this sort is so high that they are usually given a high priority. Availability of money in this area is not much affected by money-market conditions.

COMMERCIAL BANK INCOME FROM INVESTMENTS

The two big classes of investments at commercial banks are both government securities: about $60 billion of the federal government and about $80 billion of state and local government. Commercial banks also hold

---

[1] *Federal Reserve Bulletin,* June 1972, pp. 533-542.

almost $20 billion of "other" securities. All these classes of securities, but particularly the first two, are rather closely related to money-market developments.

Treasury Securities

At one time, the main significance of these securities to commercial banks was as a joint source of both liquidity and income. The liquidity function of Treasury security holdings has dwindled in importance. Commercial banks now hold Treasury securities mainly for the purpose of giving them collateral, which is required for public deposits. A few banks located where loan demand is weak hold Treasury securities in excess of their collateral needs; but this use has its limits, since the income potentials of tax-exempt state and local government securities have been far better for quite some time.

**Tax-exempt State
and Local Government Securities**

Commercial banks are now fully exposed to the impact of the corporate federal income tax. They can no longer give capital gains treatment to income from investment securities, and so about the only shelter left is that of investment in tax-exempt state and local government securities.

In recent years, when the rate on long-term tax-exempts has usually been between 5 and 7 percent, the attraction of these securities has been fully understandable. Back in late 1969 and early 1970, when short Eurodollar rates went above 10 percent, banks could still afford this rate and preferred it to foregoing the 7 percent yield on a tax-exempt (equal to a 13 1/2 percent taxable rate with a 48 percent marginal income tax rate on corporations).

The problem with tax-exempts, however, is that these high yields are available primarily on quite long-term bonds, and the marketability of these long bonds is not always the best. Although banks buy many short-term tax-exempts, they have tended to push out into longer maturities. If a bank commits itself to longer-term tax-exempt securities or even those of intermediate maturity, it may find some problems in trying to change its investment posture quickly.

Furthermore, the yields on tax-exempt securities are quite volatile. Since they depend very much on the bank market, yields are likely to be the highest when banks are pinched for funds and under the pressure of good customer loan demand. When this is not true and money markets are easier, other banks will also be easy and will be active buying tax-exempts—and driving down the yields. Therefore, it is very difficult for commercial banks to buy tax-exempts with good timing. This difficulty is further compounded by the fact that banks do not like to report sharply fluctuating income to stockholders, and the reservation of liquidity to wait for good buys in this market would tend to unstabilize income.

Because of the special role commercial banks play in this market, it tends to be tied more closely to money-market developments than almost any other sector of the capital markets. Commercial banks are important underwriters in the issuance of these securities as well as being the leading customers. The new-issue tax-exempt market, therefore, is more vulnerable to bad money-market news and more responsive to good money-market news than almost any other type of security.

MARSHALING BANK FUNDS

Deposits are the principal source of bank funds. Time deposits are now more important than demand deposits—and also often more volatile. In the past five years, time deposits have accounted for about three-fifths of the new funds available to commercial banks; demand deposits less than one-third.[2] Banks also have fairly large retained earnings, which accounted for about one-tenth of available funds during the past five years. Capital-market financing in the form of common stock or notes and debentures accounted for about 1 percent of bank funds in the past five years.

Most of these sources of funds are not very responsive to short-run managerial approaches. The large negotiable certificates of deposit (NCDs; see Chapter 8) are the most responsive and are related to the rates offered by banks. Over a period of months a bank may press on this source of funds or retreat from it. However, NCDs are good sources of funds only for the large money-market banks. Even for them, NCDs are not the largest source of funds.

Although the modern emphasis in banking is on "liability management," there are limits to this process. The way in which liabilities are managed is nevertheless central to the cost of funds secured by banks and therefore to their profitability. If a bank locks itself into a rather high average cost of funds expecting a strong high-rate demand for funds but the demand fails to materialize, its profits will be considerably cut. Thus the art of liability management (which means money-market participation) is that of securing an adequate volume of funds—but without cost commitments at a level which jeopardizes future profits.

[2] *Investment Outlook, 1972*, Bankers Trust Co., Table 24.

Time Deposits as a Source of Bank Funds

In the early history of commercial banking in the United States, time deposits were found mainly in middle-sized and smaller banks and those which aimed at "retail" banking business. Money-market banks secured most of their funds from demand deposit accounts. In 1961, however, money-market banks started to use the NCD, which was described in Chapter 8 and mentioned earlier in this chapter. The NCD was a pathbreaking innovation in liability management. It was first aimed at getting the surplus funds of nonfinancial corporations, but it has come to be used as an investment outlet by state and local governments, foreign investors, and other investors of short-term money.

Although popular attention has been focused mainly on the NCD, banks have also innovated in the use of other forms of time and savings accounts. Passbook savings accounts are now offered in a variety of forms. Nonnegotiable CDs are available to depositor-investors in moderate unit size. Federal Reserve Regulation Q controls the rates that banks can pay on smaller time deposits (NCDs have been exempted from such regulation since mid-1970). Within these regulatory limits, banks use many devices for the attraction of time deposits: monthly, daily, even continuous compounding of interest; various contract terms; and a variety of depository relationships that function as passbook accounts but are legally and technically much nearer to CDs.

The important feature of Regulation Q, however, is that it has made time deposits a rather undependable source of funds when funds are most demanded. The limitation on the rate of interest paid on time deposits was originally adopted in order to avoid what was feared would be ruinous competition for such deposits. However, the Federal Reserve has used Regulation Q in a somewhat different way. In 1966 and 1969 Regulation Q ceilings were held down even when market rates of interest rose. The purpose of this action was to avoid an attraction of time deposits from savings and loan associations to banks. In addition, the Federal Reserve appeared to view Regulation Q as a monetary instrument and welcomed the limitation that it indirectly imposed on the expansion of bank loans. However, it now appears that the Federal Reserve itself (or at least an operational majority of policy making officials within the Federal Reserve) no longer feels the need for Regulation Q.[3]

This monetary use of Regulation Q made time deposits a less useful source of funds. Since the ceiling rates tended to be most restrictive when interest rates were rising, it denied banks access to time deposit

---

[3] *Federal Reserve Bulletin,* March 1972, p. 223, "Ways to Moderate Fluctuation in the Construction of Housing."

funds just at the very time when the most profitable opportunities were available for the employment of added funds. However, if Regulation Q should be abandoned or at least made less restrictive, which now seems possible, then time deposits would offer even more appeal to banks in their search for funds.

Even with the restrictive influence of Regulation Q, the greater emphasis on time deposits as a source of funds has vastly changed the competitive position of commercial banks.

Demand Deposits as a Source of Funds

Although demand deposits have dwindled relative to time deposits as a source of funds, they are still important; the fraction of new funds coming from these accounts has varied between one-third and one-fourth in recent years. What is more, demand depository services furnish one of the important elements in the customer relationships of banks.

Several background economic facts account for this new position of demand deposits. Higher interest rates have made depositors more conscious of the advantages of careful cash management. When interest rates were low, as in the early postwar years of the late 1940s, a depositor might leave idle funds in a demand account beyond the need to compensate its bank for services because alternative employment did not yield very much income. But when short-term interest rates go up as they have in recent years, then such slack management of cash is no longer defensible. The other side of the story is that the volume of payment by check has grown more rapidly than GNP. In the past decade GNP in current dollars has just about doubled. During the same time, the dollar volume of check payments has grown by a multiple of five! Demand deposit turnover, even outside New York City, has doubled! The check collection system operated by banks is important to all depositors, but particularly to big businesses. As described in the previous chapter, they receive and disburse funds at many different places both here and abroad. The cost of this vast check collection system would have been enormous if it had not been for the advent of the computer and other related electronic devices for the automation of the check handling and collection process.

The higher interest rates, the larger volume of check payments, and the automation of check collections have combined to change the relationship of banks to several of their most important customers. The same law on which Regulation Q is based also prohibited the payment of explicit interest on demand deposits. However, banks have developed various service charge or other cost-of-service approximations which are used in figuring how much it costs banks to use various types of demand deposit accounts. Then, by use of some implicit rate of return on demand balances, it is possible to calculate how much of a demand deposit account must be maintained to make such an account profitable to the bank. This sort of cost-benefit calculus is monitored by the larger demand deposit customers by comparisons among banks, and thus there is a kind of implicit competitive rate on demand deposits even when no explicit payment is made. Customers have a fairly clear idea of just how much of a balance must be maintained and so know what are excess funds that can be employed in the money markets.

Although commercial banks are reluctant participants in this game of converting "idle" demand deposits into earning assets for their corporate customers, they know that this is the price for maintaining viable customer-depositor relations. Thus banks are more and more offering their customers cash management services. For the big nonfinancial corporations this service takes the form of planning the system of cash collection and disbursement which is most efficient. Many banks now have computer simulation programs for the estimation of such efficiency. With this planned system, they offer a full line of service for the investment of any excess funds—or a line of credit for the supplying of needed funds during periods of deficiency. Surplus-funds customers will be offered a wide variety of money-market investment outlets by trading departments of money-market banks, including commercial paper, bankers' acceptances, repurchase agreements against Treasury or Agency securities, its own or other negotiable CDs, and short-term tax-exempt securities.

The country correspondent banks of money-market banks are offered even more comprehensive services. In the first place, where physical location makes it possible and feasible, city correspondents often do all the accounting for country correspondents and handle check collections for them. The big computer installations of city banks are often able to handle this volume of work very efficiently. By this process, the city correspondent can, as mentioned above, manage the reserve position of its country correspondents. Explicit charges are made for some of these services but, in addition, balances held by the country correspondents with their city correspondent furnish a buffer for reserve position management. Funds that are in excess of reserve needs and in excess of the agreed balance held by the country correspondent with its city correspondent will be bought by the city bank as Fed funds. These Fed funds purchases are really residuals and not a part of the true open market for Fed funds. However, the rate set for such purchases will be the open-market Fed funds rate or close to it.

The computer has even made it profitable to offer checking account services for customers that, in the past, would not have been able to keep adequate balances to cover service charges. "Free" checking accounts have been advertised and combined with all sorts of consumer credit provisions. Retail banking has been made more profitable in this process.

Banks Earnings Retained as a Source of Funds

Although commercial banks are highly leveraged operations, retained earnings, as indicated earlier, have accounted for about one-tenth of new bank funds over the past five years. This fact is explained by the more rapid growth of bank earnings than of dividends. Since it is by no means clear that this trend can continue into the future, this source of funds may be a dwindling one.

New Funds from the Capital Markets for Banks

The new profitablity of banks has led to the organization of new banks. In addition, supervisory authorities have pushed some banks into seeking added capital, mainly in the form of capital notes or debentures. Some of these debentures have been issued in convertible form. Recently some banks have sold intermediate-term rather than (or in addition to) long-term capital notes or debentures. However, capital-market funds are still a small source of bank funds—about 1 percent.

BIG BANKS AND LITTLE BANKS

The increased aggressiveness of commercial banks is most evident in the central money markets. It is here that the pencils are sharpest (or the computers most efficiently programmed) and the action the fastest. It is here that the most dazzling use is made of fast communications and systems analysis. But country banking is also changing. The branching and chartering policies of the bank supervisory agencies, so far as existing law permits, have been made more liberal. Competition has been more encouraged. Higher interest rates helped by making banking more profitable, but with the attraction of this profit and the potential opened up by more liberal supervisory policies, smaller banks have been pushed into more aggressive postures both in seeking sources of funds and in employing them. At the same time, smaller banks have become more aware of the events in central money markets and sensitive to them in their own pricing and credit policies. Merely the act of selling excess reserves as Fed funds to their city correspondents, described above, has increased this awareness. The money markets of the United States can be said to have been more nearly unified by these forces than at any time in the past. And the degree of unification probably will become greater.

GREAT CHANGES IN THE LIQUIDITY MANAGEMENT OF BANKS

At one time, almost all the liquidity needs of banks were met from assets called "secondary reserves." The prime secondary reserve asset was short-term U.S. government securities. This type of liquidity management has not altogether disappeared, but most banks now look to other means of management. Several of the newer methods are uses of instruments that have already been mentioned and will come up again in Chapters 10 and 11. However, they will be brought forth here in connection with their liquidity management role.

For central money-market commercial banks, the three biggest changes are (1) the increased dependence on NCDs, (2) the maintenance of a persistent net debtor position with respect to Fed funds, and (3) Eurodollar borrowings from their foreign branches. The Fed funds "purchased" position can be "fine tuned" to meet shorter-term liquidity needs. The repurchase (direct or reverse) is also used for fine tuning. Such money-market banks often view their U.S. government security accounts as mainly a source of collateral for public fund deposits, and they sell off any excess above collateral needs. Smaller banks use their net creditor or seller position with respect to funds as a buffer for fine tuning reserve needs. Since smaller banks do not have the facilities to buy money, they have less freedom of action than large banks.

FLUCTUATIONS IN THE SOURCES AND USES OF BANK FUNDS

One useful view of money markets is that they are residual to the broader sweep of the capital markets. The basic long-term real and financial capital needs of business and government are met in the capital markets. Investors put the major share of their funds into the capital markets. Money markets are used to make shorter-term adjustments both in the need for funds and the employment of temporarily idle funds.

Any residual system tends to be more volatile than the basic system to which it is related. If, as is now widely thought, consumption spending is related to expectations of lifetime income, then saving will be more volatile in the short run than income. In the money markets, both the availability and the prices of funds are more volatile than in the capital markets, and for much the same reason.

Within commercial banks there are degrees of priority both in the use of funds and in the securing of funds. This system of priorities explains some of the extreme examples of volatility that are found in commercial bank participation in the money markets.

High-priority Sources and Uses of Bank Funds

The "good" and long-standing customers of banks account for the principal priorities as to both sources and uses. Since the services banks perform for their demand deposit customers and the expected compensatory balances to "pay" for these services are clearly spelled out, demand deposits can be considered both high-priority and remarkably stable as a source of funds. Customers have seasonal flows of funds which are easily measured and well understood; therefore, while balances are not static, they meet the test of stable expectations. Passbook savings accounts also tend to be reasonably stable, as do some other types of time deposits.

Banks also have high-priority uses of funds. No matter how tight money markets may be, consumer credit loans are so profitable that a commercial bank is not likely to ration this use of funds. Rates may be adjusted upward, but funds will be available at these rates. Business loans to good customers also command a high priority. Since customer needs will vary depending on business conditions, the volume of business loans may vary; but banks generally try to have money for these customers.

Intermediate Priorities among Sources and Uses

Public deposits are notoriously unstable in a seasonal sense; those of the Treasury Department fluctuate widely, but the swings can be anticipated to some extent by observation of Treasury cash management and financing operations. By nimble management of collateral for such deposits—U.S. Treasury securities mainly—these deposits can be used profitably. Banks also secure funds from the money markets by careful management of the rates offered on their NCDs. Although these rates are "open-market" rates in theory, we have pointed out above that some direct negotiation does take place.

Investment in tax-exempt securities can also be considered an intermediate priority in the use of funds, although some banks would dispute this assessment. Since investment in this form can be one of the most profitable of all uses of funds, it might be thought to deserve a higher priority rating. Nevertheless, the statistical record is clear; banks have been volatile investors in tax-exempt securities, and so—in action if not in theory—they have treated such investment as subsidiary or residual to customer lending. Lending to new customers must also be given a lower priority. While banks are constantly promoting business, a new customer cannot expect to stand as near the head of the line of credit applicants as a long-standing customer. Since investment in Treasury securities no longer has as much liquidity significance as before, and since it has much more significance as a collateral for public deposits or repurchase agreements, or both, this type of investment must also be treated as an intermediate priority.

Residual Sources and Uses of Funds

When money-market banks with foreign branches are hard pressed for funds, they can instruct these branches to "buy" dollars in the Eurodollar market and then borrow these funds from the branches. Banks without foreign branches can do about the same thing through the international bank correspondent system. These funds, however, tend to be very expensive, and so this source is used mainly as a last resort. In addition, they now must be backed by reserve balances. Such debt is reduced at the first possible opportunity. Some Fed funds might be considered an intermediate source of funds, but more often this is a residual source. Borrowings at the Federal Reserve are also clearly residual.

INTEREST-RATE VOLATILITY AND THE PRIORITY SYSTEM FOR BANK FUNDS

A short maturity tends to make for a more volatile interest rate. A one-day rate moves more than a one-week rate, etc. But the bank priorities also contribute to variations in volatility even for comparable maturities. Yields on intermediate-term tax-exempt securities fluctuate more than bank loans of comparable or even shorter maturities. Rates actually paid by banks for NCDs fluctuate more than good customer loan costs or the prime loan rate. Among the most stable of all rates are those that apply implicitly to the deposit balances held by customers to compensate banks for the services they perform for these customers.

ROOT CAUSE OF VOLATILITY

Money-market banks expect and are prepared to cope with considerable volatility both in the availability of funds and the interest rates that prevail on money-market instruments. Even more than that, they try to make money out of the process by shrewd anticipation of the direction that the root causes of such volatility may take.

Such volatility is mainly random. Interest rates and availability may swing for reasons that are not clearly evident to anyone, including such powerful and omniscient participants as the Federal Reserve. But the most important root cause of volatility lies in changes in business conditions—or, more accurately, the expected direction of such changes.

In the capital markets, the basic forces of real supply and demand dominate the markets. While expectations of both borrowers and investors can either delay or hasten the real ultimate economic factors, their power to do so is limited. But in the money markets, the short run is more important and both expectations—whether right or wrong—can make a great deal of difference.

By the same token the influence of the Federal Reserve may be of limited significance in the long-term capital markets, but it clearly has great power in the money markets.

COMMERCIAL BANKS: INTERNATIONAL FINANCIAL INTERMEDIARIES

Commercial banks are at the center of international monetary operations. They are the channels through which most of the short-term money transactions flow. They provide the basic services and operate in foreign money markets both for their own accounts and for those of their customers.

The central international function of commercial banks is that of acting as dealers or agents in buying and selling foreign money—that is, foreign exchange. Aside from a few very specialized foreign exchange brokers, the international departments of commercial banks do the major part of this business. To act as dealers they must have some inventories of foreign moneys, but in general this function is performed with a minimum of such holdings. The big banks with strong international departments are the true wholesale dealers; most other banks sell or buy foreign exchange as agents for their correspondents.

The market for foreign exchange is a rather close one. At the wholesale level, the spread between bid and ask prices is usually quite small, seldom much more than one part in five thousand. Even at the retail level, the range is not large. For this reason, profits in the process of buying and selling foreign exchange require large volume—and negligible losses. It is at this point that the matter of currency inventories becomes important. Even modest shifts in rates, well within the normal limits, can produce losses which are large relative to the dealer's small spread.

But this is not the whole risk. As will be related in Chapter 12, the present international monetary system of fixed exchange rates is subject to rupture from time to time. Devaluation of a currency, if it caught a bank with much of an inventory, could wipe out profits for a long period of exchange dealing. Accordingly, banks are very sensitive to the economic conditions of the countries in whose currencies they deal. Since the history of most devaluations has shown that they are likely to occur over weekends, banks are very disposed to balance out their positions in "weak" currencies as the weekend approaches. They may even allow themselves to have a "short" position in weak currencies—which, of course, makes them one of the much-abused speculators in foreign exchange.

Buying and selling foreign exchange, however, falls far short of an adequate description of the functions performed by commercial banks in the international sphere. The range of service performed for large business customers is wide and very important. For customers who are trying to export to foreign markets, banks provide a great deal of highly technical and important service. For example, the legal problems of selling in other countries are often complex; banks frequently provide a great deal of advice on such matters as quotas, duties, health regulations, and other related matters. Because of their long experience, they are frequently able to advise on such matters as political stability of foreign countries and other hazards of a noneconomic nature. They can also provide market information, as on incomes, tastes, and the character of existing competition. When a business locates customers for the product it is exporting, its bank can provide credit information about these potential customers; they may also help in the financing of exports. The banker's acceptance, described in Chapter 8, is such an instrument. If the buyer in a foreign country can get a local bank acceptable to our banks to guarantee the credit by means of this instrument, it is possible that such an instrument, endorsed by a United States bank, can be sold on our market more readily than in the money market of the country to which the exported good was sent. The choice of whether the transaction will be carried out in dollars or in the currency of the country in which the sale is made will often be important in deciding in what market the transaction will be financed.

Services of commercial banks to customers which are importing tend to be of the converse nature. Our own legal regulations, quotas, and other matters relating to importing are well known to banks, and they can offer useful advice. They can act in the guarantee of payment where required and supply the currency if payment is made in foreign moneys. One very special form of service "importing" is the foreign travel of our nationals. Banks are eager retailers of travelers checks and of letters of credit used by those going abroad. In recent periods banks have moved in the direction of almost acting as travel agents.

COMMERCIAL BANKS IN THE MONEY MARKETS

Business concerns contemplating larger-scale international activity such as locating plants abroad or even purchasing foreign companies make extensive use of their banking connections. Still another service some commercial banks provide for their multinational corporate customers is to execute the "working capital" acceptances described in Chapter 8. This does not use any funds of the accepting bank (and so tends to be used primarily when money markets are tight); but it does given the corporate customer a considerable cost-of-credit advantage, since acceptances tend to discount at relatively low rates. Under the existing balance-of-payments regulations which limit business capital export, banks can be helpful in arranging foreign long-term financing. The access to the great Eurobond market will be described in greater detail in Chapter 17.

Because of growth in the amount of multinational business done by our giant corporations, banks have had to extend their services. One of the most common forms of multinational operations for corporations is the establishment of foreign subsidiaries which engage in varying degrees in manufacturing, assembling, servicing, and marketing of various products and services. When foreign subsidiaries are established, they require the whole range of banking services required by a domestic corporation except possibly transfer, registration, and dividend distribution services. With the capital transfer regulations of the Treasury Department in effect, even the most liquid corporations need access to foreign capital markets.

Our great money-market banks provide these foreign services by direct establishment of foreign branches or through correspondent relationships with foreign banks. In addition, our money-market banks have sometimes purchased complete or partial interests in foreign banks but left them to operate with their original name, charter, and personnel. Whatever channel is used to provide foreign services, these operations have become one of the more profitable of outlets for commercial bank capital. At one time only a few dozen central money-market banks had foreign branches and only a slightly larger number had direct correspondent relations with major foreign banks. In recent years, however, a much larger number of banks have sought direct foreign outlets. London continues to be the largest concentration of operations by U.S. banks, but Zurich and Paris have long histories of interbank relationships. South America has long been a site of U.S. banking. In recent years, Tokyo, Frankfurt, and Amsterdam have become more important centers for branches or correspondents of our banks. Canadian banks relate to us mainly through their branches which are in our money markets, although U.S. banks have some ownership interest in Canadian banks.

This extensive system of foreign branches and foreign correspondents provides the major link between national money markets. The first reflection of this link is in the balance of supply and demand in the foreign exchange markets. But since credit is involved as soon as forward transactions enter, then relative money-market interest rates become relevant to the profit calculus. When an international operation involves a demand for funds, it tends to move into the market that offers the lowest net cost. Those with surplus funds tend to move them into the market with the highest protected return. This constant profit-oriented search is what links the money markets of the principal nations. When risk—such as fear of devaluation—attends the transfers of funds, the linkage may be weak. But when risk is small, as between two solid economies, the relationship tends to be closer—very close if true currency convertibility exists.

Chapter 10

The Federal Reserve: Evolution of Economic Goals, Monetary Instruments, and Operating Criteria

The pervasive role of the Federal Reserve System in the money and capital markets can be illustrated by the fact that the earlier chapters of this book have been unable to avoid mentioning the Federal Reserve System frequently, even though this chapter was in prospect. The Federal Reserve System, as the central banking agency of the United States, is mainly a public agency, but its operational characteristics bring it very close to the markets. While the Federal Reserve Board in Washington often seems indistinguishable from other federal government agencies, the Federal Reserve banks and particularly the Federal Reserve Bank of New York are closely integrated with the financial communities in which they are located. In terms of physical aspects they are often almost indistinguishable.

The public aspect of the system is that it expresses one of the major economic policy instruments of government. The control of this instrument has been subject to a long and frequently interrupted evolution. Central banks in some countries evolved from private money-market institutions—first into quasipublic institutions and finally into full-scale governmental central banks. However, the Federal Reserve was, from the very beginning, a public institution. As we shall see later in this chapter, the early Federal Reserve bankers sometimes could not curb their profit-making habits. At the present time, however, the Federal Reserve is clearly a public institution that is not motivated by profit. It does, as a matter of fact, make large profits out of exercise of its monetary function, but these profits are promptly turned over to the Treasury.

Because this evolutionary process is so important, we shall deal with it at a number of levels in this chapter. The first section will give a very brief history of the system so as to put the evolutionary process into a valid time framework. The second section will then deal with the evolution of economic goals. The concept of goals as used in this section will be of the broadest sort. The third section will describe the evolution of monetary instruments employed by the Federal Reserve. In order to make the impact of these instruments clear, a short exposition of the operation of our monetary system will be essayed. The fourth section will present the evolution of operational guides to money-market operations. The selection of the appropriate operational guides, the "monetary operators," depends on the role assigned to money in the process of economic causation. Because economists are still debating this question, it will turn out that, of all the evolutionary strands, this one is the most controversial and subject to change. Because this evolution is still very much in motion, the account will be more of the nature of a progress report than a definitive description. Since the various evolutionary strands overlap in time, the chapter will be concluded with an unusually extended summary. This summary will show in abbreviated form the sequence of ultimate economic objectives, the monetary operators which are presumed to help achieve these objectives, the way in which the monetary operators are controlled by the reserve management process, and finally the various methods by which the management process is monitored. Since these various steps in the monetary process are very much parallel to the decision-making process in the Federal Reserve System, this discussion will serve as a transition to the next chapter. There the nature of day-to-day Federal Reserve operations will be described so as to give a full and realistic account of the way in which United States money markets are influenced by Federal Reserve operations.

A BRIEF HISTORY OF THE FEDERAL RESERVE SYSTEM

The six decades of Federal Reserve history do not break down into neat and logical intervals. However, for the sake of brevity, a rather arbitrary segmentation will be used in the following paragraphs.

THE FEDERAL RESERVE

1   When the Federal Reserve Act was passed in 1913, the prime accomplishment expected of the new system was to avoid the money-market panics, and accompanying hard times, which had hit the country a half dozen times after the Civil War. The panic of 1907 was the specific precipitating event that first led to a study of the financial system and then to creation of the Federal Reserve System.

2   Before the system could get going in an independent way, World War I required it to be subservient to the financing needs of the Treasury Department.

3   The monetary expansion required for war finance may or may not have led to the sharp price rises of World War I, but such price advances were sharp and then there was an equally sharp postwar price reversal and depression. The Federal Reserve was blamed for this.

4   In 1923 the Federal Reserve discovered that the open-market powers it already had gave it considerable influence in the money markets. Until the crash in 1929, the system congratulated itself that it now could manage the economy. Others joined in the congratulations. This was, of course, premature.

5   From 1929 until World War II, the Federal Reserve did not play much of an economic role. However, during this period two important events influenced the future course of the Federal Reserve greatly. First, the publication of Keynes's *General Theory* persuaded a large fraction of the economics profession that the level of economic activity was influenced mainly by the balance of the government budget rather than by money. Keynes's role for the central bank (as many interpreted it) was to influence interest rates. The second event was the settling of a power struggle within the Federal Reserve System. During the 1920s and with the development of open-market operations, the real power within the system was in the Federal Reserve Bank of New York. Much of this was due to the great ability of Ben Strong,[1] who headed the New York bank during this period.

Strong's success was doubtless aided by the weakness of a number of political appointments to the Federal Reserve. However, under the pressure of Marriner Eccles, a man of great intuitive economic ability, the Banking Act of 1935 shifted the balance of system power from New York to Washington. This act created the Federal Open Market Committee (FOMC), which will be mentioned many times later.

6   World War II again required that the Federal Reserve be subservient to the Treasury Department, but this time its role was not simply supplying money but also controlling the interest rate at which it was supplied. This control of interest rates was continued in the postwar period until 1951.

7   In 1951 the Federal Reserve won its independence from the Treasury Department. It is a fascinating political story. The financial significance of it was that interest rates, while allowed to fluctuate, were

---

[1] Lester Chandler, *Benjamin Strong, Central Banker*, The Brookings Institution, Washington, D.C., 1958.

still a central concern of the Federal Reserve. Their significance has dwindled, but it has not vanished by any means.

8 The first professional economist appointed to the Federal Reserve was Adolph Miller in 1914. The second professional economist was appointed forty-seven years later in 1961. The next three consecutive appointments were also of professional economists, making them a majority of board members by 1966. By 1970 five of the seven board members had a background in professional economics. About half of the Reserve bank presidents are professional economists.

9 As will be described more fully in the last section of this chapter, the operational objectives have been gradually swinging attention toward the so-called monetary and credit aggregates but without full retreat from the older operational guides. Interest rates are in this limbo—less important but not discarded.

EVOLUTION OF GOALS

Although the United States did not get around to a formal legislative expression of the goals it set for public economic policy until 1946, a concern with such goals goes back to Alexander Hamilton. However, the emphasis changed depending on the nature of the problems faced. When the nation faced a shortage of capital in its developmental days, the emphasis was on inviting the import of capital. When hard times hit agriculture, the emphasis was on monetary measures to expand currency and therefore raise prices. When hard times hit growing urban populations, the emphasis was on creating jobs. When panics hit the money markets, it was on strengthening the financial system. The Federal Reserve has gone through a similar evolution of goals. At the same time, it has always been primarily concerned with general economic conditions. Although a financial agency, the Federal Reserve was a pioneer in developing retail trade statistics and statistics of industrial production.

1 The first decade of the system's existence did not develop clear-cut goals; war finance dominated the early years. A sharp economic downturn after the war did not bring out a clear-cut policy response from the system. However, the discovery of open-market operations in 1923 (described in the next section) led to increasing emphasis on general business conditions. In addition to interest in trade and production, the system concerned itself with restoration of postwar European monetary systems—and also with the booming stock market. The quest for economic stability was clearly a goal of the Federal Reserve System in the late 1920s. However, when the system was faced with the demand that it stabilize commodity prices, its spokesmen denied the system's ability to accomplish this specific stabilization goal, even though they admitted to its desirability.

2 The severity of the Great Depression that began in 1930 caught the Federal Reserve System off guard. The system made some feeble efforts to stem bank failures but otherwise took no steps of a vigorous counter-cyclical nature. Their faith in open-market operations shattered, the system did almost nothing to resist the drastic liquidation of bank credit and therefore of money. In the continued though less severe recession of the mid-1930s, excess reserves appeared in the banking system, so that the Federal Reserve was largely out of touch with the money market. Since the one aggressive leader in the Federal Reserve of this period—Marriner Eccles—had more confidence in fiscal policy than in monetary policy as a cure of economic slack, the system did very little. Its goal was economic recovery, but it disclaimed much ability to foster it. It is significant that the major development of new economic statistics during the 1930s took place not in the Federal Reserve System but in the Department of Commerce and in a private agency, the National Bureau of Economic Research.

3   From 1941 to 1951 the Federal Reserve was the somewhat reluctant administrator of the Treasury Department's policy of interest-rate stabilization. It also administered a wartime selective consumer credit control. Economic goals were not evident. However, the system tried to avoid supplying too many bank reserves; the goal was to achieve "enough" but to avoid "too much." A fear of postwar inflation started to develop.

4   This fear of inflation was given some justifying substance by the post-price-control run-up in prices in 1946 and the sharp jump in prices at the time of the Korean episode. A feeling that the system should play some anti-inflationary role grew stronger within the system. By a combination of superior staff work and political courage on the part of several board members, the Federal Reserve won its independence of the Treasury Department in 1951. The goal involved was simply avoidance of a monetary expansion that would lead to inflation. Very soon, however, the system developed a clear counter-cyclical credit policy. Its timing and strength of action were often criticized, but in 1954, 1957 to 1958, and 1961 there was a clear and sensitive responsiveness to general economic developments. Furthermore, public statements of William McChesney Martin—the new Federal Reserve chairman who took office in 1951, at the time of the "Accord" described above—clearly adhered to the policies of the Employment Act of 1946. The goal of the system, once more, was economic stabilization. In a later section, changes in the operating criteria of the system will be described. However, these changes in criteria do not reflect a change of goals. For more than two decades the system has viewed itself as a central agency of economic stabilization operating to offset excesses of either inflation or depression.

THE MONETARY SYSTEM AND MONETARY INSTRUMENTS

In order to understand the evolution of the monetary instruments, it will be helpful to preface that section with an exposition of the workings of the monetary system. We shall do this by graphic means. The relationship of the Federal Reserve to the availability of reserves to member banks is shown in Figure 10-1. As this figure shows, the "sources" of Federal Reserve funds are either in gold certificates they hold or the credit they extend. Treasury currency is also a modest but generally rather constant "source." The "uses" are primarily monetary in form: currency in circulation or deposits left with the Reserve banks. The nonmonetary uses are mainly the capital account of the Federal Reserve banks. The deposits of foreigners or of the Treasury Department can be considered special uses, but most of the deposits which are owed by the Federal Reserve are asset reserves of member banks.

The chart in Figure 10-1 shows that currency as supplied to the public by the Federal Reserve and Treasury is direct and on a one-for-

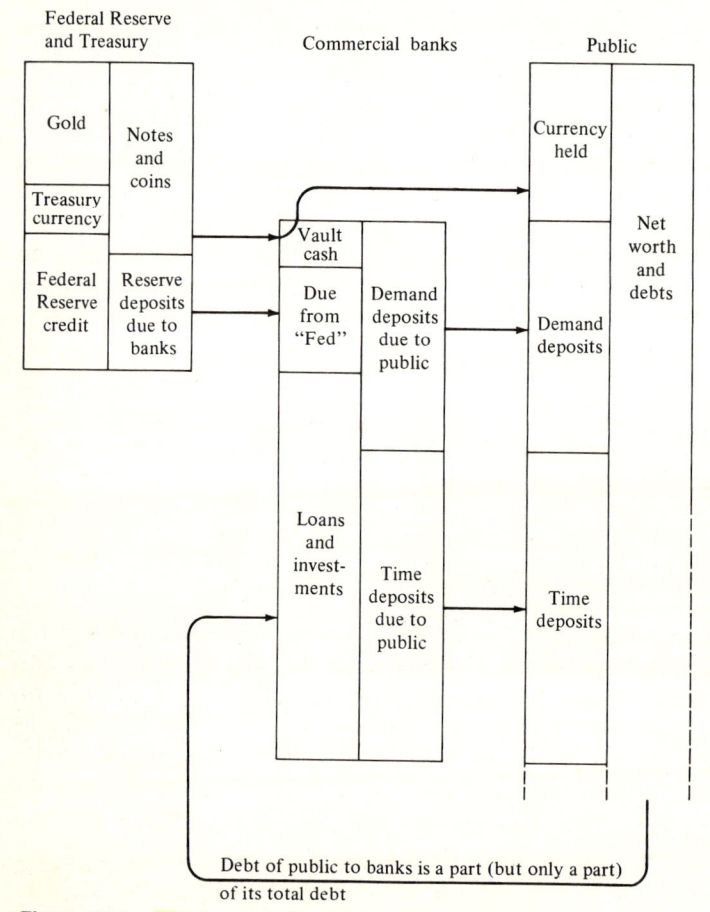

Figure 10-1 Monetary relationships (approximate).

one basis. Though it goes through the vault cash of the commercial banks, each dollar of currency held by the public is one dollar of Federal Reserve or Treasury liability. On the other hand, when reserve balances are supplied, multiple expansion of demand deposits up to the reciprocal of the reserve requirement ratio tends to take place. If the volume of currency held by the public were a constant proportion of deposits, then the average expansion multiple of the whole monetary system could be computed as the weighted average of one for the currency segment and the reciprocal of the reserve ratio for demand deposits (with allowance for the reserve balances needed to cover time deposits). Currency, however, is not a constant, particularly in the short run. This is the reason there was some ambiguity about the average multiple when it was mentioned in an earlier discussion.

While the management of the Federal Reserve cannot control the amount of currency demanded by the public, statisticians can forecast the demand reasonably accurately even though it varies. The Federal Reserve thus can control the reserves available to member banks by making forecasts of the public's currency demands and by supplying the volume of reserve deposits that will support the remaining deposit money thought to be needed by the economic system.

One other ambiguity or variable relationship exists between Federal Reserve credit and the deposit liabilities of commercial banks. The reserve requirements on demand deposits are higher than those on time deposits. Reserves can be used to support either. One dollar of reserves will support many more dollars of time deposits than of demand deposits. However, this ambiguity is not a major deterrent to precise reserve management. The demand-time deposit relationship is subject to reasonably good statistical forecasting.

THE EVOLUTION OF
THE FEDERAL RESERVE INSTRUMENTS

Discounting was the original credit instrument. When the Federal Reserve Act was passed, it was expected to be the only formal channel for extending Federal Reserve credit to the market. In the beginning it was expected that discount rates would vary from district to district depending on local credit conditions. In fact, it was soon discovered that we have a national money and credit market, and for most of the life of the system the discount rate has been reasonably uniform among districts. The present significance of the rate is mainly that of a signal to the market. However, since the Federal Reserve has tended to keep the rate a bit under market rates, it has had to curb bank rediscounting by a series of informal moral sanctions. The Fed funds rate often goes above the discount rate, indicating that a great majority of banks have responded to the moral sanctions by hesitating to borrow even when it would be profitable to do so. Recent experience suggests that the Fed may in the future keep the discount rate nearer to market rates.

Open-market operations were discovered by accident. From the very beginning the Federal Reserve banks had authority to buy U.S. government securities. After World War I, when the volume of discounts shrank, some Reserve bank presidents, accustomed to the profit calculus of commercial banking, started to put the funds released to work by buying U.S. government securities at a discount. They quickly discovered that this supplied credit to the market and only hastened the decline of discounts. They then retreated from this attempt at profit maximizing. However, Ben Strong grasped the significance of the new tool and started to use open-market operations as a positive market instrument. At this stage the system passed from being a passive credit agent, as it had been before, to being an aggressive manager of the money markets.

Reserve requirements were fixed rigidly by law for the first two decades of Federal Reserve history. The power to make such changes administratively was given the Federal Reserve System in 1933 so that it could absorb any excess reserves that would have been created by the issuance of fiat currency, which was the pet hobby of Congress at that time. The power never was used for its original purpose but was soon converted into a general credit control—and used with rather disastrous effects in 1937. Since then the system has mastered the technical problems of using this instrument without extreme upset to the money markets. This power has been used four times in the past ten years.

We are now in a position to use a segment of Figure 10-1 to illustrate more precisely the way in which the Reserve management instruments of the Federal Reserve are fitted into the entire monetary process. Figure 10-1 showed the bare bones of the monetary relationships but it did not include any of the currently used monetary instruments. That is done in Figure 10-2. In effect, this figure adds a graphic account of the two ways in which Federal Reserve credit is extended and also how the amount of required reserves is set. The Federal Reserve offers discounts and advances to member banks, which service is at the initiative of banks. The Federal Reserve sets the rate charged on such credit extensions and influences the availability of such funds by the indirect process of moral suasion on banks. But the principal way in which the Federal Reserve influences bank reserves is in the open-market operations it undertakes on its own initiative. Each of these three instruments of monetary policy is accompanied by a brief working description in Figure 10-2.

The role of the Federal Reserve in the monetary process is thus a multistage sequence. First the Federal Reserve sets the operating con-

THE FEDERAL RESERVE

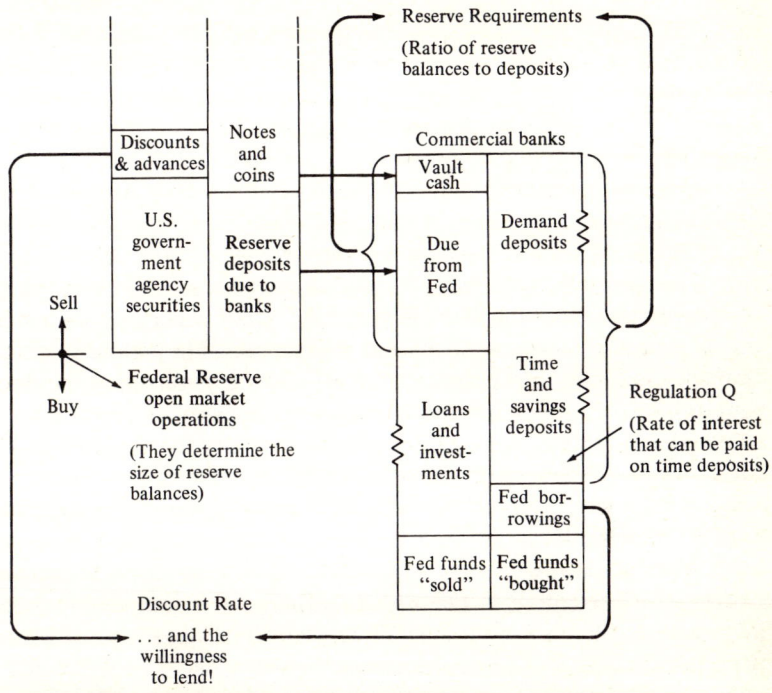

Figure 10-2 Major instruments of Federal Reserve monetary policy. (This is a smaller segment of Figure 10-1 with more detail.)

ditions faced by the banking system: the percentage reserve requirements and the price on discounts of funds by banks. Second, the Federal Reserve actively influences the ease or tightness of the reserve positions of banks by its open-market operations. The reserve positions of banks, in turn, determine the amount of credit they can extend and, at the same time, the amount of bank deposits. If the public holds constant its proportions of currency, demand deposits, and time deposits, the immediate monetary impacts of the Federal Reserve are fairly predictable.

Although there have been small legislative changes in the basis of these three instruments, they are, in broad terms, the same as they were forty years ago. What has changed is the sophistication with which the Federal Reserve uses these instruments. In the use of these instruments, the operational criteria have changed, and it is now to that subject that we turn.

EVOLUTION OF OPERATING CRITERIA

In order to develop operating criteria, there must be some underlying economic philosophy. Since the Federal Reserve System has many people in it, both official and staff, there are bound to be many economic philosophies within the system. And since the decision-making process involves groups, the decisions will often be compromises which do not have their origins in any one single strand of economic thinking. While it would be almost impossible to define the composite of thinking in the Federal Reserve System, it is certainly possible to do that for some of the leading individuals who played a large role in the system's history.

The first clear-cut economic philosophy to be found was that of Ben Strong, president of the Federal Reserve Bank of New York from 1914 to 1928. Having had experience as a commercial banker, he had a strongly traditional view of the money markets. He believed that the use of bank credit for trade and production was a good thing. As a central banker he believed in creating a reserve base on which commercial banks could service this sort of legitimate demand. At the same time, he took a dim view of "speculative" uses of bank credit such as holding commodities for price increases, or stock market or land speculation. Therefore, he thought that the Federal Reserve should withhold credit from such uses. This was a qualitative theory of bank credit. Unfortunately, these various efforts to be selective in the way in which Federal Reserve credit was used necessarily failed. Reserves are homogeneous and once created, the system could not control how they were used. As a result, there was a tendency to extend Reserve bank credit when it was felt that business conditions were healthy but to hold back when it was felt that business conditions were becoming too speculative. It was also under Strong that the open-market operations were first used to protect the money market from seasonal influences, Treasury balance variations, international movements of short-term money, and other random factors.

Negatively, the system denied its responsibility for price movements. And while the system clearly felt a responsibility to protect the money markets from panic events, it did not believe that it had the power or responsibility to counter severe depressions.

Marriner Eccles believed that it was fiscal policy, not monetary policy, that had the major impact on the economy. As a result, he tended to view the system's function as that of helping the Treasury Department meet its financing and interest-rate goals. However, it was in his regime that the number of professional economists on the staff was greatly increased and their voice was given greater weight. Staff thinking shifted from a sole preoccupation with bank credit to a recognition of the broader role of the central bank as a monetary agency.

William McChesney Martin was in some ways like Ben Strong; he had had Wall Street experience and thought in such terms. However, he had done night school work in economics. He recognized that Federal Reserve credit impact was quantitative, not qualitative, and he accepted

THE FEDERAL RESERVE

fully the idea of public responsibility for stabilizing general economic conditions. During his regime, a clear pattern of counter-cyclical action developed. During this period the managers of the System Open Market Account (SOMA) came to be drawn from among professional economists. While the majority of the economists in the Federal Reserve System were (and are) best described as eclectics, it was inevitable that a certain number would be strong monetarists drawn from the Chicago school of economics which has a long tradition of monetary emphasis. The Federal Reserve Bank of St. Louis led in this movement.

The development of operating criteria parallels this story of changing leadership. For many years the criterion for supplying bank reserves was mainly a "feel for the market." Ben Strong and those who followed him trusted instinct more than statistics. It was felt that those with long practical experience in the market could, virtually intuitively, determine when a market was sound and when it was becoming too speculative or unsound. Money-market statistics could be quoted, but no one of them assumed the role of a criterion that guided system actions. The nearest there was to a single criterion was that of member-bank borrowings. And when borrowing vanished in the 1930s, then the volume of excess reserves was the mirror image of this magnitude. However, the Federal Reserve was almost inert during the period of high excess reserves. When World War II finance was uppermost, considerable attention was paid to the structure of interest rates.

The revival of positive and at times aggressive Federal Reserve credit management after the Accord in 1951 led to a combination of the two former criteria: Member bank borrowings minus excess reserves, or net borrowed reserves (which could be negative as well as positive), came to be one of the first active criteria. Although its origins are not clear, it was clear that the FOMC spelled out its operating instructions to the SOMA manager in these terms at about this time. This magnitude evolved further. First, the SOMA manager turned to "unborrowed" reserves: simply total reserves less borrowings. This gives practical recognition to the fact that with more efficient reserve management, excess reserves have dwindled to a not very significant magnitude, on the average. The final form evolved, reserves to support private deposits (RPDs), will be described in the next section. In addition, the emergence of the Fed funds market gave an added criterion: the Fed funds rate.

The rise of professional economists to greater and finally dominating importance inevitably led to the development of far more sophisticated criteria for Federal Reserve operations. The system did not compile money supply statistics until the late 1950s and they were not used much for some period after that time. But in the past decade the number of criteria has grown.

FEDERAL RESERVE MONETARY MANAGEMENT: A SUMMARY

Up to this point Chapter 10 has had a strongly historical cast. This is useful, since history shows how much we change and may prepare us to cope with and accept further change. But this approach can also be confusing. The purpose of this section is to summarize where Federal Reserve monetary management stands now, as this is written, in the summer of 1972.

In terms of objectives, there has not been a great change in the past quarter of a century. The instruments used now are about the same as those that were available for use four decades ago. The mechanics are also quite similar. However, there has been a real change in system thinking with respect to which monetary aggregates are most efficient in achieving ultimate economic objectives. For this reason, there has been some change in the process of both setting targets and monitoring reserve action effects. Techniques of monetary management have been improved. In this section we shall attempt to reflect the current position. In doing so, we shall follow the general sequence of Figure 10-3. This figure attempts to show in brief diagrammatic form the sequence of steps by which the process takes place.

Ultimate Economic Objectives

Since the Employment Act of 1946, there has been little dispute about the general objective of maximizing real economic income—often represented by GNP in constant dollars—and minimizing unemployment. That act did not mention price stability, but it has been argued that its more general language comprehended a price objective. There is no doubt, however, that avoidance of excess price instability has become an accepted national economic goal. Our nation's goal with respect to its balance of payments is hard to state. The goal is not balance itself, because there are times when a deficit is desirable; just as there are times when a surplus is desirable. Current account balance and capital account balance must be considered separately. The phrase used in Figure 10-3—"Maintenance of a sustainable balance between payments to and from other countries on current and capital account combined"—is an effort to recognize the allowable variations from precise zero balance. The matter is not widely understood, but this seems to express a reasonable consensus of informed opinion.

These various objectives may conflict one with another. Stable prices and a sustainable balance of payments posture might require more unemployment than most of the nation would accept. Economic growth

THE FEDERAL RESERVE

Ultimate economic objectives: Maximum real economic income
                                  Stable prices
(Query: if these objectives   Minimum unemployment
conflict, which is to   Maintenance of a sustainable
be given priority?)   balance between payments to and
                                  from other countries, on
                                  current and capital account combined

Monetary operators (intermediate targets):
 (Which operator achieves   Bank credit (? Total or are some
 economic objectives   kinds of bank credit more
 most efficiently?)   significant than others:
                              i.e., "speculative" credit?)
                              Interest rates (? Short, long, and
                              does this include equity yields?)
                              Money: M_1 and M_2 (or even M_3?)

Control of monetary operators by bank reserve management:
 Instruments: Price and availability of Federal Reserve discounts
                Reserve requirements
                Open-market operations: outright purchase and sale,
                repurchase agreements, and matched sale-
                purchase agreements

 Preliminary requirement: filter out and offset random movements in
                          reserves caused by check collection float,
                          currency in circulation, Treasury and foreign
                          balance variations. Requires ex ante short-term
                          forecasts of reserve factors. ("DEFENSIVE")

 ?Focus on: Total reserves
              Net free or borrowed reserves
              Unborrowed reserves
              Reserves available to support private nonbank deposits

Monitoring the reserve management process (on target?)
 Feedback from the market: "Feel of the market"
                             Short-term interest rates,
                             particularly Fed funds rate
 ex post Reserve factors

 Estimate/forecast constantly updated of:
        Adjusted bank credit proxy. This is statistically
        more prompt than a direct measurement of bank credit
        M_1: Adjusted demand deposits and currency outside banks
        M_2: M_1 + commercial bank time deposits excluding NCDs

Figure 10-3 Federal Reserve monetary management in brief diagrammatic form.

is still the accepted goal of the majority although it is now much under attack by environmentalists, and may also conflict with price and balance-of-payments stability. In general, Federal Reserve officials may have tended to put a little more weight on prices and balance of payments while politicians holding elective office may have put a little more on employment and growth. But differences exist within the system as well as within the nation.

Monetary Operators for Efficiently Achieving Economic Objectives

This is an area in which opinion has recently changed and the process of change is still in motion. The monetary aggregates themselves get more attention, but bank credit and interest rates have not been discarded either. Bank credit (which is measured for current operational purposes by the Federal Reserve as the "adjusted bank credit proxy") still rates attention. However, in practice this tends to be quite parallel with M_2, the monetary aggregate favored by Milton Friedman.[2] M_1 may become less significant simply because demand deposits are growing less rapidly than commercial bank time deposits.[3]

An even broader view of the monetary process would include not only commerceial bank time deposits but also the time deposits of non-bank thrift institutions. This combination, labeled M_3, has not yet been given formal recognition by the Federal Reserve System, but it is computed by them and published in their *Bulletin*. It appears that while reserve management has some influence on M_1, its best fit is with M_2. It would be expected, however, that its fit with M_3 would be the poorest of all.

Interest rates have had a long history both as objectives and as monetary operators. More than small traces of this influence still exist. It is possible that our placement of interest rates as only a monetary operator in Figure 10-3 can be criticized; it also sometimes seems to be an objective. However, it is dwindling in importance even if it has not vanished. As we shall see below, it is still very clearly a monitor signal.

Reserve Management

Chapter 11 will have quite a lot to say about the mechanics by which the monetary operators are controlled by reserve management. The instruments have already been described; their use will be outlined in detail in Chapter 11. However, it is important at this point to recall the evolution of magnitudes on which this process has focused. Total reserves were the first point of focus, but this was soon replaced by the net

---

[2] See Figure 10-3 for definitions.
[3] Ibid.

THE FEDERAL RESERVE

balance of free and borrowed reserves. When excess reserves dwindled with more efficient reserve management by commercial banks, the focus shifted to unborrowed reserves. The recent further shift to "reserves available to support private nonbank deposits" (RPDs) grows out of a technical superiority rather than a fundamental change in economic philosophy: RPD is thought to be more closely related to the monetary aggregates than the other reserve measures.

Monitoring the Reserve Management Process

Chapter 11 will have quite a bit to say about the mechanics of this monitoring process. However, explanation of its significance should not be deferred to that point.

Reserve management often takes place when the managers have no adequate idea of the economic and financial facts of the time at which decisions are being made. Always, of course, these managers have no knowledge of the future. The Federal Reserve System has worked very hard to hasten the collection of statistics, and it has reduced the lag between events and the reporting of them to remarkably short times in many cases. But because the process is not certain, it is important to use such evidence as there is. Some feedback signals hit the monitor very quickly. If the manager of the SOMA takes positive open-market action in the morning, he will look for its influences on the Fed funds rate by noon or early afternoon. Other feedback loops are longer and less precise. This is why the process of monitoring is so important. Some monitor factors are also nothing but early estimates of the monetary operators. Others are proxies for them. But some are quite indirect and vague, as for example the "feel of the market." Although this old-fashioned element may be given less recognition these days, it is probably still true that the managers cannot help but use intuition when the figures seem to be wrong. (And they can be wrong; errors have been publicly admitted.)

Chapter 11

Federal Reserve Operations

TRANSLATION OF GENERAL ECONOMIC AND FINANCIAL OBJECTIVES INTO MONEY-MARKET ACTIONS

The way in which general economic and financial objectives are translated into more specific money-market actions depends, of course, on the beliefs of the Federal Reserve with respect to the role of money in determining economic activity and also with respect to the lags with which such results are achieved. As described in the previous chapter, the Federal Reserve has gradually been attaching more importance to the direct effect of money and has therefore given greater weight to the monetary and credit aggregates. At the same time, the older ideas have not disappeared, so that Federal Reserve operations can often be described as torn between conflicting ideas and objectives.

This multiplication of goals creates added complications in understanding Federal Reserve translation of its general policy posture into explicit money-market actions. This chapter will describe in general terms how this translation process takes place and also some of the problems that are encountered by those outside the Federal Reserve in trying to understand these actions for purposes of practical money-market analysis.

Since ideas are changing, this chapter should be viewed as a progress report. Further changes are likely, and the prudent analyst must be sensitive to such changes in ideas, mechanics, and the signals that are used to guide action.

The Federal Open Market Committee (FOMC)

The first step of translation of general economic, monetary, and financial policy takes place in the most exalted organizational element in the Federal Reserve structure: the Federal Open Market Committee (FOMC). The FOMC formally consists of all seven members of the Board of Governors plus five Federal Reserve bank presidents. The president of the Federal Reserve Bank of New York serves continuously, but the other four are selected from among the other eleven Federal Reserve bank presidents and serve on a formal rotation.

In fact, all twelve Reserve bank presidents almost always attend the meetings and enter discussions freely. In addition, a formal staff of sixteen, including the manager (or managers) of the SOMA, serve the FOMC. This staff is usually supplemented by close to a dozen other staff members who are privileged to attend FOMC meetings. Thus the meetings, at four-week intervals or oftener, consist of close to fifty persons.

The sequence of materials presented to and discussed by the FOMC are indicative of the problem this body faces. The starting point is generally a review of business and financial conditions, with emphasis on the past month. The areas covered include national income, industrial production, employment, prices, and trade—both domestic and international. Financial developments are covered in even more specific detail: banking, the capital markets, and balance of payments position. Reports of current position are usually supplemented by cautious forecasts for the next month or quarter.

The FOMC, after extended informal discussion by the members, then adopts its formal "directive" to the manager of the SOMA. In recent years this directive has been in a fairly rigid stylized form. It consists of two paragraphs, the first of which has two parts. It almost inevitably starts with the words, "The information reviewed at this meeting suggests that . . . ," and then reviews both the general business and financial developments of the past month. Still in the first paragraph there then follows a sentence which again almost invariably starts: "In light of the foregoing developments, it is the policy of the FOMC to foster ...," followed by a general description of the credit and money-market conditions to be "fostered." The second paragraph almost invariably starts with the phrase "To implement this policy ...," which is followed by rather more specific guides to credit and interest-rate directions expected. This second paragraph may also contain a "proviso" clause which allows the manager of the SOMA some latitude in the event of a possible but not certain development (such as a major strike). Although the second paragraph is more explicit than the general words of the concluding sentence of the first paragraph, it is not in specific quantitative terms. However, such terms are clearly used in the informal discussion that precedes adoption of the directive.

A sample of a directive with the indicated sections marked appears in Figure 11-1.

Although the growth rates for the monetary and credit aggregates and the range and levels of Fed funds rates are not specified in the directive, they are freely discussed in quantitative terms, and some of these discussions are reflected in the analysis that accompanies the publication of the directive. This discussion usually faces bluntly the possibility that there may be conflicts between objectives in "money-market conditions" as reflected in the Fed funds rate and the desired rate of growth in any monetary aggregate. It often gives the manager of the SOMA some guidance as to which element is to be given priority if such conflict appears.

It is usually such points of emphasis—rather than any element that appears in the directive—that lead to dissents of individual FOMC members. Mr. Francis's dissent in the illustrative FOMC directive specifically mentions a 5 percent annual growth rate for M_1, which clearly indicates that other percentages were discussed at the meeting—as indeed was the case. It is inevitable, however, that differences of opinion within the FOMC arise out of different values given to basic economic objectives. The Federal Reserve System has probably been more concerned about inflation than other parts of the federal government.

The directive is published by the Federal Reserve—with a three-month lag—together with an accompanying analysis of about 2,000 words. This analysis is a summarization of the longer analysis presented at the FOMC meeting, and it also includes a summary of the discussion by members and other participants in the meeting. While this analysis carefully refrains from direct forecasting, it is clear the "expectations" expressed at prior meetings are often disappointed. In fact, the discussion at the FOMC meetings in recent years appears to put more and more emphasis on such expectations.

The more important point, however, is that the monetary and credit aggregates have clearly been given a larger weight, not only in the informal discussions but also in the formal directive to the manager of the SOMA. The 1971 report of the manager of the SOMA, published in edited and abridged form, shows this clearly.[1]

The manager's reports make clear the dilemma he faces in giving full expression to the direction in the market actions he takes. The increasing emphasis on monetary and credit aggregates that has been included in the policy and directives of the FOMC has not been paralleled by a withdrawal from older interests in interest rates and general money-market conditions. As a result, the manager may be faced with a conflct of objectives; he can take actions that support the rate of expansion of monetary aggregates indicated, but this may be possible only if he neglects the interest-rate objectives specified by the FOMC.

The FOMC performs the role of coordinating all of the elements of monetary policy within the system. The Board of Governors, not the FOMC, has the power to change member bank reserve requirement percentages (within limits set by law). However, all such proposed changes are thoroughly discussed at FOMC meetings so that the actions will be fully coordinated. Discount rates are proposed by individual Federal Reserve banks subject to the approval of the Board of Governors, but proposals for discount-rate changes are discussed at FOMC meetings. The Board is thus almost never faced with unexpected proposals. Indeed, it is the other way around; directors of local Reserve banks may find that discount-rate changes have already been decided upon and that they are being asked to supply the rubber stamp.

The coordinating role of the FOMC is of great importance. The policy-making organization might be described by a person who prized neat organization charts as "chaotic," but the results are what count and the FOMC tends to produce a real sense of unity within the system. On the other hand, it has not tended to discourage originality. Dissents from FOMC directives are frequent, often emphatic and eloquent—and sometimes more revealing than the bland prose of the formal analysis. Monetary ideas within the Federal Reserve System have been pushed by the Federal Reserve Bank of St. Louis, and the frequent dissents of this bank have had increasing impact over time.

The Manager of the SOMA

The FOMC has two managers, both chosen from the staff of the Federal Reserve Bank of New York. The "special manager" deals with foreign exchange operations, and his function will be described in a separate

[1] *Monthly Review of the Federal Reserve Bank of New York*, April 1972, vol. 54, no. 4, pp. 79-94.

Review of business developments

The information reviewed at this meeting suggests that real output of goods and services, which declined in the fourth quarter of 1970, is rising in the current quarter primarily because of the resumption of higher automobile production. The unemployment rate remained high in January. Wage rates in most sectors are continuing to rise at a rapid pace, and recent increases in some major price measures have been relatively large.

Review of financial developments

Interest rates have fallen considerably further in recent weeks despite continued heavy demands for funds in capital markets, and differentials between interest rates in the United States and those in major foreign countries have widened further. Federal Reserve discount rates were reduced by an additional one-quarter of a percentage point to 5 percent. Bank credit increased considerably further in January, as business loan demands strengthened somewhat and banks made substantial further additions to their holdings of securities. The money stock narrowly defined grew modestly in January following a stronger December rise, but money more broadly defined expanded sharply further as a result of continued rapid growth in consumer-type time and savings deposits. The over-all balance of payments deficit in the fourth quarter was about as large as in the third quarter on the liquidity basis; on the official settlements basis the deficit increased further from the very high third-quarter level as banks continued to repay Euro-dollar liabilities. More recently, the issuance of a special Export-Import Bank security to foreign branches of U.S. banks helped to moderate the flow of dollars to foreign central banks.

Figure 11-1 FOMC directive for February 1971.

FEDERAL RESERVE OPERATIONS

In light of the foregoing developments, it is the policy of the Federal Open Market Committee to foster financial conditions conducive to the resumption of sustainable economic growth, while encouraging an orderly reduction in the rate of inflation and the attainment of reasonable equilibrium in the country's balance of payments.

General policy statement

To implement this policy, System open market operations until the next meeting of the Committee shall be conducted with a view to maintaining prevailing money market conditions while accommodating additional downward movements in long-term rates:

Directive to SOMA manager—greatly amplified by discussion at the meeting

provided that money market conditions shall promptly be eased somewhat further if it appears that the monetary aggregates are falling short of the growth path desired.

Proviso clause

Votes for this action: Messrs. Burns, Hayes, Brimmer, Daane, Heflin, Maisel, Mitchell, Sherrill, Swan, and Mayo. Vote against this action: Mr. Francis.
Absent and not voting: Mr. Robertson. (Mr. Mayo voted as alternate for the late Mr. Hickman.)

Vote

Mr. Francis dissented from this action for reasons similar to those underlying his dissents from the directives adopted at the two preceding meetings. Briefly, he favored placing less emphasis on money market conditions in implementing policy, and he thought that expansion in M_1 at an annual rate of about 5 percent would be best suited to the needs of the economy.

Mr. Francis, who dissented, is president of the Federal Reserve Bank of St. Louis, which has led the system in increasing stress on the monetary aggregates.

section. In this section we shall examine the role of the manager of SOMA.

The function of the manager of the SOMA is to accomplish the money-market results directed by the parent body. The problems he encounters in doing this job are illustrative of both the nature of the monetary process and also the operations of the money markets in practice. The manager faces several problems. The central one is that, while his actions are powerful, they do not have an immediate impact. He cannot change the direction of money supply formation quickly; he is often uncertain by how much the results will lag behind his efforts.[2] Another problem is that he may face conflicting evidence as well as deal with conflicting objectives. The Fed funds range given him by the FOMC may seem to be inconsistent with the growth rates for money supply he is expected to "foster." The account of operations given below, therefore, represents an effort to illustrate the many problems he faces in discharging his obligations to the FOMC.

The manager of the SOMA operates at two levels. Before he can effect any credit actions that are intended to have a positive effect on credit conditions and the monetary aggregates, he must offset the random factors that influence bank reserves. This offset process was called "defensive" open-market operations by Roosa.[3]

The biggest of the random factors is the amount of float in the banking system—the difference between the volume of checks in Federal Reserve collection channels and the amount for which the Fed has delayed credit. At present the Fed is working to reduce the amount of float. However, as long as check credit and payments depend on physical transport, float is likely to be a large and variable item. Currency in circulation is highly variable, but it is a reasonably predictable variable. In addition, other factors such as variations in the Treasury Department and international deposit balances at the Fed cause random variations in reserves. Furthermore, defensive reserve adjustment must take account of carryover in excess and deficient reserves as well as shifts in reserve requirements due to shifts among classes of banks and deposits. A final problem is that reserve requirements for major banks are averaged over the week ending Wednesday. Since the SOMA must be in the market almost every day, it must work with weekly patterns of the ways in which banks manage their reserves.

Defensive operations cannot be precise; the manager reports an error range of from $100 million to $250 million in such operations.[4]

The sequence of steps in the influence of the manager's actions is

---

[2] Ibid.
[3] Cited in Chap. 8, p. 157.
[4] *Monthly Review*, loc. cit., p. 81.

FEDERAL RESERVE OPERATIONS

not precise, but an approximation serves to illustrate the problems he faces. Such a sequence is roughly as follows:

1   The immediate impact of the actions taken by the SOMA is to increase or decrease the unborrowed reserves of member banks. If the SOMA buys securities or enters into repurchase agreements (purchase with agreement to resell one to fifteen days later), unborrowed reserves are increased. If the SOMA sells securities or enters into matched sale-purchase agreements (reverse RPs), then unborrowed reserves are decreased. The emphasis is on unborrowed reserves because member bank actions may and often do offset SOMA actions. If SOMA withdraws reserves from the market, member banks may be forced to restore these reserves by borrowing. Added reserves supplied may not increase reserves but be used to repay prior borrowings. RPs are used when the SOMA manager wishes to offset some temporary factor in the market; regular purchases and sales are made when the purpose is to have a more enduring reserve influence—and possibly also to influence security prices. RPs presumably have negligible direct security price impact.

2   Unborrowed reserves have an immediate impact on the Fed funds rate. Indeed, the range of Fed funds rates specified by the FOMC gives an immediate target to which the manager can respond in a meaningful way.

3   The Fed funds rate has an important impact on the profit calculus of member banks. Fed funds sales or purchases are more nearly marginal or incremental to bank operations than any other use or source of funds. As a result, the Fed funds rate tends to have a causal relationship to other short-term market interest rates. But, more important, banks adjust their operations, both in seeking funds and in the employment of them, to their marginal cost of money—which is best reflected by the Fed funds rates.

4   Bank adjustments to the Fed funds rate are ultimately reflected in the amount of credit they extend—and that in turn determines the volume of bank deposits, which are the monetary aggregates. However, at this stage it is necessary to bring demand elements into the stream of influences. The amount of deposits the public is willing to hold appears to vary with interest rates and—possibly even more important—their expectations with respect to economic developments. The amount the public borrows is likewise influenced by a complex of these same considerations. Because both circumstances are important to the profit calculations of banks, the amount of bank credit and therefore the monetary aggregates do not follow meekly in the path of unborrowed reserves and the Fed funds rate. Tightness may be successfully resisted and ease may not induce expansionary action. In other words, this phase in the transmission of SOMA influences is neither exact, prompt, nor even wholly dependable.

Because of this variable link in the transmission process, the manager of the SOMA must operate with a complex of reports, projections, and a nonquantitative "feel" for the market that defy systematic explanation. This problem is one that has certainly retarded the move toward more emphasis on the monetary aggregates. The older concentration on money-market conditions gave the SOMA manager reasonably explicit guides with which he could work and by which his stewardship could be judged. But when goals are introduced that are of magnitudes that do not respond closely and predictably to the manager's influence, his stewardship is harder to judge and the process is subject to second guessing.

Variations in accomplished results from the intended results in the monetary process get progressively greater as we move from the center of the reserve supply process to the monetary aggregates. The errors in forecasts for defensive actions have already been reported; they appear to be less than 1 percent of the base figures to which they apply. But at the next step, the manager of the SOMA aims at some level of unborrowed reserves. Since no figures of error have been published, the departures from expectations are not known; but they are almost certainly greater than 1 percent. But it is total reserves, not unborrowed reserves (or some variant such as the new RPD described below) which are related to the monetary aggregates and, by the admission of the manager of the SOMA, variations of this magnitude from unborrowed reserves are material.

The FOMC has recently started giving more attention to the reserves available to support private nonbank deposits (RPD). Since the figure is relatively new and a background of its variations is not yet available, an error range cannot be reported. It seems clear, however, that since this is one more step removed from total reserves, its variations from planned levels will almost certainly be a bit larger than those of total reserves. However, RPDs appear to have a more direct relationship to M_2 and the adjusted credit proxy, so it is preferable.

And at the final step, the loose link between RPD and the level of both bank credit and the monetary aggregates must accept an even wider error range. The nonquantitative discussion of the analysis accompanying the publication of the "directive" shows that FOMC members are often quite surprised at the difference between intentions and results. Since the public lacks the sophisticated data base on which they operate, it is not surprising that public and press analysis is often wide of the mark.

One of the problems is that there are not only lags in the process of transmitting the manager's monetary actions into final changes in the monetary and credit aggregates, but these lags are quite variable in time and degree. Although lags have been extensively studied, the results are far from dependable. However, it is clear that the manager of the SOMA operates with much doubt in his mind about the results of his actions.[5]

One small clue to the degree of variation of plan from actuality is contained in a chart published in the manager's report which was cited on page 199 above. The chart[6] is published without accompanying figures, so the estimate below is an approximate chart reading. The tracking path if money supply objectives were to be realized varied from actual money supply by only about $1.33 billion—a variation from the base figure of less than ½ of 1 percent. However, if this variation is compared with amounts required to meet rates-of-change objectives, the results are more startling. If a 5 percent annual growth rate had been the objective, the growth objective for the year of about $11 billion would have been $2.75 billion for a quarter. Thus, the variation of $1.33 billion meant that error variation could be almost a half of the objective goal. In other words, 5 percent ± 2½ percent.

The "Special Manager" of Foreign Exchange Operations

For many years the Federal Reserve Bank of New York has been the agent for both the Treasury Department and the Federal Reserve System in the conduct of foreign exchange operations. Since 1967 the manager of this function is also a "special manager" for the FOMC. The principal role of this manager is to give market expression to the international monetary policy of this country in the markets for foreign exchanges. His main obligation, therefore, is to the Treasury Department, since it formally dominates our international monetary policy. However, his operations relate to domestic monetary policy in at least one very important respect.

As described in Chapter 12 in greater detail, when currencies are reasonably convertible, the short-term interest rates of the major nations of the world tend to be subject to reciprocal influences. One cannot say that the levels of rates are the same, because the barriers to money movements are still too great to achieve this uniformity. But they are related, even if in an indirect way. Specifically, if interest rates in the United States are lower than those abroad, international investors are likely to move from the United States to other markets—which has an adverse effect on our balance of payments. Thus domestic monetary policy goals with respect to interest rates are of considerable importance to our balance of payments. By the same token, developments in other countries

[5] *Monthly Review*, loc. cit., pp. 90 and 94.
[6] Ibid., p. 84.

influence our money markets and therefore the arena in which our monetary policy is developed. The special manager, therefore, serves both functions in the FOMC: to represent the Treasury view on interest rates in our money markets and to inform the FOMC about current and expected developments in other money markets. Foreign exchange operations also affect the volume of reserves in the money markets and must be absorbed in the defensive operations of the domestic manager of the SOMA.

Federal Reserve open-market operations sometimes face a very specific problem with respect to interest rates: a conflict between domestic and international goals. The Federal Reserve may be placing more emphasis on the monetary and credit aggregates, but it has not lost its interest in interest rates. Many times the FOMC wishes to put downward pressure on interest rates for economic (and political?) reasons. If the student will refer back to the directive in Figure 11-1, he will note the phrase " . . . while accommodating additional downward movements of long-term rates."

But lower interest rates can make our money markets less attractive hosts to foreign holders of dollars and thus can lead to an outward movement of short-term capital. For this reason, the manager of the SOMA has sometimes made his open-market purchases in the long-term end of the U.S. government securities market while making sales in the short-term end of the market. This effort to shift the yield-curve (see Chapter 6) slope has been called "operation twist." It was first practiced in 1963. Later efforts were labeled "minitwists." It is of considerable economic interest that the efforts have not been rewarded with clear success.

Feedback from the Demand Side of the Money Market

As should be evident, the FOMC and its manager of the SOMA do not *control* the money markets, they *influence* them. Thus there is a constant process in which the results of their actions are monitored in an effort to evaluate the results. In effect, this is observation of what is the more vague and unmeasurable element of demand in the money markets. For example, the manager of the SOMA keeps an hour-by-hour watch of the Fed funds rate to see if it is moving as he would expect it to in light of the supply of reserves as he sees it. Since reserve requirements are computed on a weekly basis, he must note the day of the week and the usual pattern of bank response to such facts (see note 1, page 199). If the Fed funds rate departs from the expected track, this departure may be caused by either of two elements: errors in the reserve projections or elements of demand in the market that are not fully expected. So the manager must make a quick judgment as to which cause is the more probable one. If an error in estimate has been made, then some further market adjustment may be called for. But if demand elements in the market are changing, this is viewed as a more fundamental economic factor. The manager often has to ask himself: "What is the market trying to tell me?"

When the FOMC makes some change in the availability of bank reserves, an aggressively managed bank does not supinely and meekly accept the fact; if it faces demands for funds from its customers, it will intensify its own efforts to get funds from the money markets. To repeat what has been emphasized before, money-market commercial banks are profit-oriented institutions. They make money out of supplying customer demands. The cost of funds may be increased by tightness in the money markets, but the rate of return they can get from customers or from the market may go up even more. It pays them to resist the reserve withdrawal by the FOMC by every means at their command.

Of course, in the aggregate, the FOMC can win in this struggle. It can limit the total volume of reserve funds. It can put a halter on the banking system and on the monetary and credit aggregates. But in the process of enforcing its will, it may produce a degree of strain in the money markets—higher interest rates and shifts in the channels through which funds flow.

In a larger sense, the FOMC cannot wholly win this struggle in the long run. While it can limit the flow of funds through banking channels, it cannot stop the flow of funds in channels outside banks. If rates go high enough, depositors can take funds away from banks and go into the commercial paper market. Some borrowers can get funds from the commercial paper market if their normal banking sources will not meet their needs.

It is this feedback process which the manager of the SOMA, the whole FOMC, and finally the entire financial community watches with the greatest of interest. The Federal Reserve can have probably the largest influence on the volume of unborrowed reserves and almost as much on the Fed funds rate. It has, after a considerable and variable lag, an important influence on the monetary and credit aggregates. But demand elements intervene, and in the end it cannot balk the pressure of this demand without facing the risk that it will change the structure of the money market by pushing more and more of the money-market transactions outside the banking system and into an arena in which it has less influence.

THE OUTSIDER'S VIEW OF FED OPERATIONS

Although the Federal Reserve lags the publication of its official FOMC directive for three months, it scrupulously publishes comprehensive money-market statistics with very little delay. For many years the Fed released to the press on Thursday of each week the full statement of the Federal Reserve balance sheet and also the daily average figures of the Fed and Treasury monetary factors of the week ended the day before the release. This was done long before the advent of computers. Even more recently, the Fed has been releasing the principal figures which are used in guiding the Fed's operations:

Money supply, both conventional (M_1) and with time deposits (M_2)
Total reserves
Net free or borrowed reserves
Reserves available for private nonbank deposits
Member bank borrowings
Adjusted credit proxy
Other data

With a one-week delay, the Fed also publishes the weekly balance sheets of "large" commercial banks.

An outsider thus has almost instantaneous access to the same market data on interest rates available to the Fed: the Fed funds rate and interest rates on all other money-market instruments. The outsider probably has less ability to judge the amount of business done at these rates than money-market insiders, including the manager of the SOMA. For example, the posted Fed funds rate may be almost nominal with little business done—or it may be a rate which prevails for a large volume of transactions. To some extent the same is true of the rates posted by commercial banks on negotiable certificates of deposit. Rates at which business is largely done may vary a bit from the posted rates.

Very few outsiders, however, have either the access to knowledge or the competence to develop the elaborate "projections" which are so basic to the process of money-market management. For example, on a day-to-day basis the transactions of foreign central banks may be very important in the market. The Fed, as agent for these banks, knows exactly what they are doing in our markets. Others may be able to surmise after a bit of lag, but they never have the same degree of knowledge. Likewise, Treasury transactions are ultimately disclosed by published Treasury figures on a net basis, but outsiders cannot have the degree of knowledge of these transactions that is had by the Fed itself.

Even with these limitations, however, the outsiders who work hard with the available figures and guess shrewdly on the points about which they do not have exact knowledge can come surprisingly close to the right track in figuring current Federal Reserve policy. This is, of course, a desirable thing. While it would not be practical for the Fed to disclose much more about itself, its operations, or its current formal directive than is now done, viable money markets would be affected negatively if the principal participants had to operate in the dark. As it is, knowledgeable private managers in the money markets, knowing the general direction of Federal Reserve intent, take actions which reinforce these actions rather than thwart them. A money market of poorly informed participants would be an irrational one.

Chapter 12

The International Monetary System in Turmoil and Transition

During the early chapters of this section on money markets, it was necessary at a number of points to refer to international aspects of our national money markets. This was done in an introductory way in Chapter 7. When reviewing money-market instruments in Chapter 8, the Euro-currency deposits were described and discussed at length. In Chapter 9 the international operations of commercial banks in the service of our multinational corporations were outlined. The discussion of the Federal Reserve policies and operations both in Chapters 10 and 11 faced the subject in connection with the interest-rate problems. However, none of these chapters could convey the degree to which the international monetary system has changed and is under pressure to change still more. Furthermore, it would not have been appropriate in any of those chapters to have looked with sufficient detail at the exact nature of the balance of payments problems of the United States (and other countries) and the relationship of these problems to the construction of a viable world money system. This chapter, which concludes the section on money markets.

will try to bring together these various strands—to describe the postwar growth of both trade and international money markets and the problems that have often threatened their fabric.

As this is written (summer of 1972), a formal program of conferences is under way trying to construct a set of new international monetary arrangements that have some chance of survival. At the same time, it must be confessed that revived forces of nationalism are at work. Extreme nationalism would threaten the workability of any such arrangements. The most that this chapter can do is to launch the student into a more penetrating understanding of these forces as they unfold.

INTERNATIONAL ASPECTS OF OUR MONEY MARKETS

International influences on our money markets are of growing importance. Improved communications and transport extend our boundaries. War has also taught us the importance of political harmony (where possible) and the need to have some regard for the well-being of other nations. But in spite of the fact that all these factors push us nearer to "one world," there are still barriers. And at no place are these barriers more evident than in the money markets.

Technology and economics are bringing about closer world relationships. The forces of national pride, cultural provincialism, and differing political systems, however, interpose some barriers to this process. Just as the self-sufficient hermit becomes an anachronism in this world of specialization and exchange, the isolated nation cuts itself off from the advantages of trade and cultural exchange. For these reasons, an understanding of the many ways in which international influences appear in our money markets requires resort to much more than economic analysis; it needs the perspectives of world politics and even of cultural relativism.

The Money Barrier: Multiple Monetary Systems and Foreign Exchange

The principal barriers to the completely free international passage of financial influences is the multiplicity of monetary and legal systems. As we emphasized in the very first chapter of this study, money is the vehicle through which both short-term credit and longer-term investment operations proceed. Money is the universal solvent to the financial system. Within the borders of a nation with a unified money system, financial transactions can take place over wide areas without encountering any barrier. A dollar in New York is virtually the same as a dollar in San Francisco.

National borders, however, give rise to monetary barriers. Each nation has adopted its own monetary system. Most financial transactions in each nation take place with that nation's own money. There are some exceptions to the rule that anyone who travels with dollars can usually buy goods and pay his bills with dollars. This only means, however, that the exchange of moneys will be done by the vendor of goods and services (and probably at a little extra profit). We have already been introduced to a money market in our dollars that developed outside our borders. However, this is an exception. Passing over a national boundary usually requires some kind of exchange of money.

Just how much of a barrier this proves to be varies with time and circumstances. In the nineteenth century a large proportion of the leading nations made their currencies convertible into gold. As long as this was true and gold could be freely imported and exported, the rates of exchange between currencies were set by the ratios of the physical definition of monetary units. Variations from this parity were limited to the cost of physically transporting gold. Thus reasonable stability prevailed, so that business planning could take place on the assumption of such rates.

The system, however, broke down from time to time. The usual reason was that monetary expansion in some countries would proceed to the point where convertibility into gold could not be maintained in the face of loss of confidence. Only when confidence was restored would convertibility become possible. It was a system that worked well as long as money holders had confidence that they could exercise the right and thus did not feel compelled to do so.

Some countries maintained the effect of such convertibility, by holding stocks not of gold but rather of leading currencies that were convertible into gold. This gold *exchange* standard is important, since it furnished the example on which most of our present world monetary arrangements have been based.

The nineteenth century was an era of internationalism. Its critics also call it an era of colonialism (although this system had started much earlier), but the net effect was the development of many areas rather more rapidly than would have been possible without colonialism. The network of reasonably stable monetary relationships permitted not only a growth in world trade but also the movement of capital from country to country. Much of the rapid development of the United States was due to the inflow of foreign capital which built our railroads and cities and aided the rapid push from an agrarian economy to an industrialized one.

But the system of gold convertibility always carried with it the risk of collapse. When money expanded faster than gold reserves, this exposure was increased. The First World War was accompanied by a general suspension of gold convertibility of currencies, but at the time it was widely assumed that the system would be restored after the war. Efforts at restoration were made, but most of them collapsed in the Great Depression or even before. The Great Depression was followed by a period of nationalism, and the currency systems of the great nations were generally separated by systems of exchange control. And then came World War II.

For many, the principal political and economic lesson of World War II and of the events that had preceded it was that internationalism had to be restored. The political aspects of this restoration were to be found in the United Nations and the financial aspects in the Bretton Woods agreements which led to the establishment of the International Monetary Fund (IMF) and the International Bank for Reconstruction and Development (the "World Bank"). Our interest is mainly in the system of monetary relationships created by the IMF.

The great stability of the United States during an era in which many foreign nations had suffered great instability had led to the accumulation of a great gold stock. At the peak, the United States had two-thirds of the world's visible gold supply (an uncounted but large amount was in private hoards or unreported Russian reserves). In the negotiation of the Bretton Woods agreements for the IMF, gold was kept as a basic part of the international monetary system. But its part was a new and somewhat reduced one. In the panics of the 1930s, the private ownership of gold had been outlawed in the United States and in some other countries. Gold was made an asset of official monetary agencies. Its significance became more international than national. The United States, to its later embarrassment, insisted on the retention of gold in this international role. Each IMF nation was required by the agreements to denominate its currency in terms either of gold or of a currency convertible into gold. The United States was the only one to denominate its currency in gold; the others denominated their currencies in dollars! This restored the system of fixed exchange rates which many felt was so essential to world trade and capital movements, But it left the United States and its dollar with a special role; the dollar came to be a kind of international as well as national money. As long as the United States preserved a monetary and fiscal balance which commanded the confidence of the world by being strong so that the dollar would be in demand, the system could work.

The system has been brought into great jeopardy: The United States has not controlled its balance of payments effectively and so has brought the whole world system of money relationships into jeopardy. This failure was not merely a matter of economic significance: The prestige of the United States as a world power was high when its currency was strong, but when its currency weakened, this had a damaging effect on its political stance—it undermined the influence that the United States could exert in other areas of world interest. Near the end of this chapter we shall return to the current and unsolved problems of both the United States and the world in making the international monetary system work. It is worth adding at this point, however, that (at least in the opinion of the authors) this problem has been badly aggravated by the persistence of the United States in fighting an absurd and immoral war.

The system of fixed exchange rates has not worked with complete smoothness for other reasons. The original IMF agreements recognized that from time to time some nations might be forced to change the parity of their currencies with the dollar ("devalue" their currency) and made provision for such changes. But in practice the need for change has been rather larger and more often contemplated than in the original IMF agreements. This must therefore be taken as the general background to our study of international influences in the money markets: The participants watch one another carefully and a "weak" currency (one for which a change in parity or devaluation is quite possible) gives rise to pressures which destabilize and sometimes almost paralyze these markets.

**Balance of Payments:
Weak and Strong Currencies**

If the citizens of a nation are free to import and export and to move their capital to the most favorable location, the net balance of a nation's payments—in and out of the country—may depart materially from equality. A country with stable prices and many investment opportunities tends to export goods and to attract capital to the country; it is likely to have a surplus in its balance of payments. This will give it a "strong" currency. If a nation has high costs of production and rising prices, if it does not present many investment opportunities, and if its domestic capitalists are anxious to send their funds elsewhere, it is more likely to have an outflow than an inflow of funds. Its currency will be "weak."

A nation with a "strong" currency will tend to receive an excess of payments of other currencies over its own payments and therefore can convert this excess into gold or dollars—which is its international monetary reserve. A weak currency has to draw on its reserves to make payments to other countries, and sooner or later these reserves may be depleted to the point where some adjustment must be made—and devaluation is the most frequent adjustment.

This is the background against which the foreign exchange market works. Ordinary transactions are carried out by foreign exchange dealers, which are mainly departments of commercial banks. As long as these private dealers are dealing with currencies in which they have confidence, the small price adjustments in foreign exchange rates are mainly a reflection of the ebb and flow of demand. However, a currency that is persistently strong will bump the upper limits within which price fluctuations are presumably to be contained by the IMF or other agreements. When a currency is bumping against the top, the country of issue, through its monetary authority (usually its central bank), will supply its currency. In this way it collects other currencies which it may elect to hold or to convert into either dollars or gold. When a currency is weak and its price threatens to breach the lower boundaries, then the country of issue must buy up its own currency, paying for it with dollars or other acceptable currencies—which tends to deplete its monetary reserves. In other words, foreign exchange markets are normally conducted by private dealers (mainly commercial banks, as we said above), but monetary authorities intervene when necessary to avoid breach of either the upper or the lower boundaries. In practice, the various monetary authorities have formed themselves into an informal union so that each authority is the agent for foreign monetary authorities in its domestic market. Our Federal Reserve Bank of New York is the agent for most other monetary authorities and will intervene in the New York foreign exchange market for these other authorities as their agent. (Some countries make use of the agencies of their own banks; Canadian commercial banks, for example, have agencies in New York City and may act for the Bank of Canada in the foreign exchange market.)

Another force in the international money markets must be noted. Many of the large corporations in the United States have greatly expanded their multinational operations. The direct export of long-term capital mentioned elsewhere is reflective of this development. In the process of multinational operations, these corporations have both receipts and expenses in a number of different currencies. They must maintain some minimum cash balances in the countries in which they operate continuously, but they are very sensitive to the difference between weak and strong currencies. They are also influenced by relative interest rates. As a result, these corporations move their cash about, attempting to make it both as safe and as profitable as possible. The "gnomes of Zurich" have been blamed for foreign exchange speculation but the great corporations are probably just as much involved in such operations. The corporations, of course, use their banks as agents for such dealings. They also depend on such banks for advice about cash movements in search of safety and profitability—but many great corporations employ extremely well-informed managers for this purpose and have themselves excellent intelligence networks with respect to international currency developments. These corporations are major forces in the money markets of the world.

Channels through Which International Factors Influence the Domestic Money Markets

The balance of payments, of course, embraces all the various ways through which economic forces exert their influence over national borders. Exchange rates are the usual signals of imbalance in the passage of forces. The analytical task is that of abstracting from these general forces the ones that are sufficiently visible to give money-market analysts a tool they can use. At the very simplest level, relative prices and relative interest rates are the forces at work. Except for the barriers of transport cost and tariffs, goods should cost about the same throughout the world; price-level changes should be parallel. However, the barriers are such that price-level influences are only imperfectly felt across national borders.

The same is true of capital and interest rates. If exchange rates were fixed and all market participants were confident that they would remain fixed at the same rates, money-market interest rates for riskless credit forms ought to be the same in the various money markets. But the assumption of exchange-rate fixity is unrealistic. Exchange rates do vary through moderate ranges even in the absence of devaluation. But devaluation is the great fear of foreign currency holders, and it happens fairly often. Even more relevant, the fear of devaluation and the potential losses are so great that short-term investors are unwilling to move into foreign markets except as they are assured of a return trip without loss. There is one channel through which two-way transit for money can be arranged: the forward exchange market. A simultaneous cash purchase of a foreign currency together with a forward sale of the same currency is, in effect, such a guaranteed round-trip ticket. With such a "covered" arrangement, funds can move temporarily and safely into other markets. With allowance for this factor, there is some relationship between these four factors: The interest rates in two markets and the spot and forward exchange rates between these two markets. This four-way relationship is shown in the chart in Figure 12-1, which was originated by the Federal Reserve Bank of New York.[1]

This chart is essentially a comparison of the premium or discount of

---

[1] Allen R. Holmes and Francis H. Schott, *The New York Foreign Exchange Market*, Federal Reserve Bank of New York, New York, 1965. This account is strongly recommended as a clear and authoritative description of foreign exchange markets. This chapter owes it a large debt.

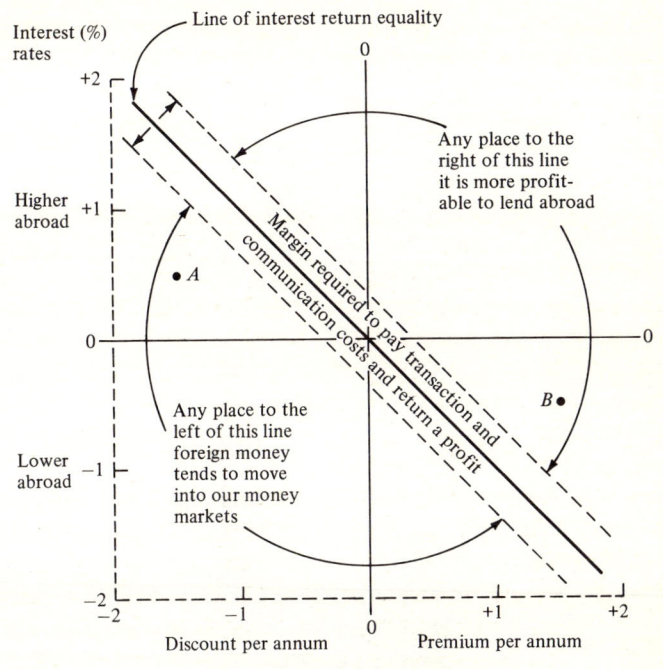

THE INTERNATIONAL MONETARY SYSTEM IN TRANSITION

Point A: The foreigner could get 1/2% more at home but the forward exchange rate discount (premium to him) of 1 1/2% gives him a full percent point advantage in our money markets!

Point B: Money rates are 1/2% lower abroad but the forward exchange premium makes it profitable for U.S. money market investors to go abroad for a net 1 percent advantage.

Figure 12-1 How forward exchange-rate premiums and discounts can push money into lower interest-rate markets. *(Adapted from Holmes and Schott,* The New York Foreign Market, *Federal Reserve Bank of New York, New York, 1965, p. 54.)*

the forward exchange rate (converted to an annual basis) with the interest-rate differential. Along the declining diagonal, any gain or loss on forward exchange is exactly offset by a loss or gain on the interest-rate differential. When actual market rates give a relationship which is not on the diagonal, then an arbitrage opportunity exists. For example, if London exchange had a forward discount of 2 percent (annualized) but London Treasury bill rates were 8 percent when ours were 5 percent, then the gain on London investment would more than offset the forward exchange loss. In a frictionless market, money would move to London. If forward rates have a premium, it is possible that funds can flow to a lower rate market. For example, suppose the premium on forward Swiss francs was 1/2 percent for 90 days, which is the same as 2 percent per annum. Even if Swiss bill rates were 1 percent below New York rates, money could flow to Switzerland. And if the differential is the other way around, money will flow into our market. For example, if there were a market premium on forward Canadian exchange of 1 percent but our Treasury bill rate were 2 percent above the comparable Canadian rate, we would expect an inflow of Canadian funds.

Arbitrage does not bring all exchange-interest relationships as close to the diagonal as theory suggests it should. The principal reason is that the market for forward exchange is not large enough to absorb the full burden of arbitrage transactions, so that enough funds to erase the rate differential cannot flow. While the forward market is used by the monetary authorities for support purposes, there is a tendency to attempt some discrimination in purchase so that "foreign exchange speculators" are not accommodated. In other words, the market forces of arbitrage are not allowed to work freely.

Another force, though one not always fully recognized, is that the assumption of freedom from credit risk is never quite absent from these transactions. While the solvency of the great financial institutions that deal in the international money market is widely assumed, in times of crisis it is not thought prudent to lean on this assumption with too much weight. An instantaneous or "spot" transaction in foreign exchange involves virtually no credit risk. A forward transaction, however, is tinged with just a small shade of such risk. While the risk is small, older traders' memories of the hectic days of the 1930s still remain.

International developments have an influence on domestic money markets in still one more way. The very fact that monetary reserves move from one country to another has an effect on the availability of bank reserves. In the days of the classic gold standard it was assumed that gold movements would have an influence on bank reserves and would thus automatically help correct an imbalance. A country losing gold had tighter credit, and this held down inflationary developments and might even cause some deflation—which was expected to correct the factors that led to the gold outflow.

In the United States the influence of international monetary movements on bank reserves is presumably offset by Federal Reserve action. Such action offsets reserve changes for the banking system as a whole, but individual banks can feel such pressure, and at times the whole community of banks in an area such as New York City can be pinched by international reserve losses for which offsetting Federal Reserve action is nationwide and not focused just on New York City. Furthermore, at times the Federal Reserve, by design, allows international factors to tighten domestic markets if it is felt that such action is in keeping with overall economic objectives.

The Linkage of Monetary Systems

The lines of influence described above show both theoretically and practically the way in which monetary influences are conveyed from one country to another. The theoretical link is in a highly developed system of currency exchange. It is strongly assisted in practice by the banking systems of this country and other countries. Banks furnish the institutional links or channels through which these influences pass. Countries that enjoy freely convertible currencies tend to be tied together by trade, capital movements (both long-term and short-term), and travel. For a while the area of freely convertible currencies embraced all the nations of Western Europe. In the North American continent, Canada, Mexico, and the United States were included. Japan was also a member of this community. All other parts of the world were generally excluded: certainly all of the Communist bloc countries and most of Africa, and unfortunately most of the South American countries do not have really convertible currencies—though we do have strong trade relations with many of them. As we shall describe later, this situation is now somewhat less happy.

The significance of these links is as much political as economic. In general, close monetary relationships are not possible if political uncertaintly prevails. (And good monetary relations help to keep temporary bad feelings between nations from causing a complete rupture.)

POSTWAR WORLD MONETARY CHANGE

As already mentioned, the United States came out of World War II with about two-thirds of the world's visible gold stock. Even more important, its productive capacity had been expanded and modernized by war rather than destroyed, as was true of many nations. Now, a short generation later, Germany and Japan, the two defeated nations, have built powerful industrial economies and have accumulated the two strongest positions in terms of world monetary reserves. Even more striking, in 1971 the United States was finally forced to swallow its pride and devalue its currency. The story of this great switch is instructive.

The reconstruction of economic productivity in the war-torn nations took less than a decade. The United States helped in this process in two ways. The more visible one was the Marshall Plan aid in the very early postwar years. The less visible but perhaps more important way was that the United States opened its markets to foreign goods and at the same time exported a great deal of long-term capital in the form of direct investment by our multinational corporations. By 1958, the principal Western European countries were strong enough to make their currencies de facto convertible at fixed exchange rates. World trade grew (and continues to grow in spite of currency difficulties) at the rate of about 10 percent per annum. The United States continued to have a strong trade surplus (until about 1967), which, however, was more than offset by the large direct investment.

By the time the 1960s were entered, it became clear the U.S. balance of payments deficit was no longer a constructive world force. A very considerable redistribution of world monetary reserves had taken place. And the increased use of dollars as international monetary reserves was no longer so clearly advantageous either for us or for other nations. Still, the need for monetary reserves grew rapidly because of trade expansion.

Additions to the world's gold stock were far smaller than the growth of trade. Dollars took up the slack, and as long as the dollar was a strong currency, most nations preferred it to gold. Dollars could be invested in our money markets and earn a return; gold is a sterile asset. But the position of the dollar changed as our balance of payments deficit, no longer a constructive world monetary force, nevertheless persisted. In 1960 during the Kennedy-Nixon election campaign, a brief flurry of speculation against the dollar erupted. A similar period of pressure came in 1963, and we were forced to impose an "interest equalization tax." In 1965 it became necessary to institute "voluntary" programs of credit restraint for foreign lending by our commercial banks and also to limit foreign direct investment, also "voluntarily." In 1968, the quote marks on "voluntary" became even more meaningless as rather strong regulatory programs of capital export restriction were imposed. In real terms perhaps the sharpest blows to the international monetary position of the United States came from two sources: the Vietnam war, which required large offshore expenditures, and the gradual erosion of our export balance—so that by 1968 we no longer had a surplus on current account. In 1971 the United States was forced to take the humiliating step of devaluing the dollar and of stopping its convertibility into gold (which had already been de facto cut in 1968) or into other forms of international monetary reserves or both. The dollar, however, is still held as a reserve currency. The so-called gold shortage led the IMF to adopt the system of "Special Drawing Rights" (SDRs) in 1967. This "paper gold" expanded world monetary reserves—as long as the world had confidence in the future of the IMF. But dollars still earn money and SDRs do not; therefore, even in 1972, the major part of the world's monetary reserves is in the form of dollars. Eurodollar deposits grew by a sixth in 1971 and, at $54 billion, accounted for over three-quarters of the total Eurocurrency deposit market.

Fixed versus Floating Exchange Rates

Focusing on the sad story of the United States puts the whole picture out of perspective. Other countries have also had balance of payments problems and devaluation has been frequent elsewhere. In fact, the number of devaluations has been so large that many raise the question whether the system of fixed exchange rates should be preserved. Chicago school monetarists argue that exchange rates freely changed in the markets are an automatic cure of balance of payments problems. Traditionalists, particularly those who have had practical experience in the foreign exchange markets, argue to the contrary. But the traditionalists have been shaken by the repeated sudden ruptures caused by devaluation. Devaluation, of course, has usually followed a period of speculative shifts of short-term capital. One proposal (which we will not discuss since it has not been tried and probably will not be tried) is that of the crawling peg: a kind of stair-step devaluation. However, another proposal—wider trading margins—is now being tried and deserves brief notice.

The IMF specified that each member had the responsibility of maintaining its currency within a 1 percent band on either side of its adopted par with respect to gold and/or dollars. The Smithsonian agreement which followed the dollar devaluation in 1971 widened the margin to 2¼ percent on either side of the agreed pars, or a total range of 4½ percent. However, this was accompanied by a side agreement among Common Market countries in which the limits of 1¼ percent on either side or 2½ percent total applied within this group. This has been called the "snake within the tunnel." (Belgium, Luxembourg, and the Netherlands have an even more restrictive agreement: 1¼ percent! This has been called the "worm within the snake within the tunnel.")

The Common Market: A Unified Currency?

The subject of the common market runs far beyond this review of money markets, but it embraces one long-range goal which is of great significance. Although it is still in doubt, the Common Market countries adopted the long-range goal of a unified currency. Since it has been adopted only "in principle," no operational details have been developed.

The significance of this move, if it should ever take place, is that each of the countries would have to give up individual monetary sovereignty and to yield it to some supranational body. This was not done with the IMF. Whether the nations are ready for this step is more a political than an economic issue. But if it should transpire, the Common Market currency would then doubtless outshine the dollar. It might displace it as a reserve currency. How we could unwind a large short-term debt to foreign holders of dollars is not clear, but it would present a great challenge—unless we should join the system ourselves. But we are probably not politically ready for this internationalist step during the lifetime of anyone who might read these words.

The More Immediate Future

The 1971 Smithsonian agreement and the 1972 formal devaluation of the dollar were only transitional steps. Formal steps for negotiation of a new international monetary system or structure are in (slow) motion. Since agreement will most certainly be hard to reach, it is not at all impossible that a renewal of nationalism might take place. It is even possible that exchange controls might return. We already have forms of reverse exchange control in which countries with strong currencies such as the Swiss franc, the West German mark, and the Japanese yen have adopted measures which make it hard for a foreigner to come into speculative possession of such currencies. In addition, to protect their strong trade positions, the countries with strong currencies resist upward revaluations of them. The countries with strong currencies can resist de facto revaluation only by large purchases of the dollar. This is exactly what was done on a massive scale since our devaluation in 1971. It means that present exchange rates do not reflect true market forces, and so there are no guides to those attempting to plan reconstruction of a viable international monetary system. This is why the word "turmoil" was used in the heading to this chapter. Restrictions on capital movements, although nominally temporary, may linger on. And if they do, trade restrictions are more likely to grow than be erased. The outcome is in doubt.

The only safe forecast is that our money markets will continue to be shaken from time to time by currency crises of one sort or another. Money will move, but not so freely as to equalize interest rates among money markets. And, for the foreseeable future, the Eurocurrency market will continue to thrive.

Part Three
Capital Markets

Chapter 13

A Capital Market Overview

This chapter uses a device that careful scholars may think to be excessively crude: Dollar amounts are introduced, but they are very approximate. Estimates of real capital can differ among estimators by several hundred billions of dollars. The authors' estimates are made mainly to balance the financial amounts shown. Where financial magnitudes are involved, the error margin is much less but still material. The excuse for this cavalier treatment of numbers is pedagogical. The authors have always found it easier to understand new concepts if numbers, even very rough ones, were attached. In their experience as teachers they have found the same thing to be true: amounts help. The speed of light is an abstraction, but the fact that light takes eight minutes to travel from the sun to the earth is something one can grasp. (Whether it reveals the great speed of light or the remoteness of the sun is uncertain.) In any event, there has always been a large element of spurious precision implied in the publication of social (and business) accounting magnitudes to very many decimal places. The flow-of-funds statistics may tell us that the market value of corporate shares in the United States was $1,038.4 billion at the end of 1971—but we (and they) know equally well that this value was based on transactions involving only one-tenth of 1 percent of the total shares outstanding. Furthermore, by the time the figures are published some months later, a similar computation could be different by as much as $200 billion. Pedants may wish to skip this chapter; others should plunge into it only with a clear understanding of what it does and does not attempt to do.

In a number of important respects, our money and capital markets are quite similar. The lower tip of Manhattan, which is often identified as the center of the money market, is also the central location of many leading capital market institutions: the New York Stock Exchange and the offices of many investment bankers. Many financial institutions have roles in both markets. But there are great differences, and it will be the first function of this chapter to explore some of the differences.

Chapter 7 described the basic role of the money markets as that of liquidity adjustment. The central role of capital markests is that of putting capital to work; preferably long-term, secure, and productive employment. Chapter 2 described the basic economic processes of saving and investment. As the word was used there, "investment" means direction of economic resources into real capital: machinery, factories, housing, roads, and even the intangible capital goods of education and knowledge. A nation that directs its capital into tombs for kings is not as likely to prosper and advance as one that puts its capital into schools, laboratories, irrigation ditches, and sanitary sewers.

In the money markets, there is one major type of private institution—the commercial bank. Commercial banks could be considered money-market intermediaries in that they accumulate funds by deposits and then make them available in lending. The money creation process may seem to obscure this role, but it exists. The capital markets are served by a large variety of types of intermediary institutions (including commercial banks). Commercial banks are not just money-market intermediaries; they are important in the capital markets. The capital markets are facilitated, in addition to true intermediaries, by a variety of institutions that are not themselves intermediaries but service institutions: investment banking firms, commission brokerage houses, and investment advisers of all sorts, sizes, and shapes—including those dealing with the problems of law, accounting, engineering, and markets.

The money markets are closely and directly tied to the Federal Reserve. The capital markets feel central bank influence, but mainly indirectly and through the money markets.

In the money markets, commercial banks are closely regulated.

However, money markets themselves—for commercial paper, U.S. government securities, bankers' acceptances, negotiable certificates of deposit, and Eurocurrencies—are not generally regulated beyond the ordinary influence of the law of negotiable instruments. In the capital markets the institutions are not much regulated, but the markets are. Investment bankers are not regulated as are commercial banks. Commission brokerage houses are very little regulated except by some measure of industry self-regulation. But the new issues markets and the secondary markets for outstanding securities are regulated.

HOW MUCH CAPITAL?

The first point to emphasize is that capital markets serve the basic purpose of transferring savings from those with saving in excess of investment to those who must seek external financing. Real investment is the starting point, and its magnitudes are relevant to financial investment.

The social accountants have given us only fragmentary estimates of our national balance sheet. National income has been explored in detail, but not wealth. A very rough estimate of U.S. national wealth in the early 1970s would be an amount approaching $3 trillion. This is a market value estimate. With inflation, some increase in value is not planned voluntary saving but rather a form of ficticious growth. Net voluntary saving in the United States was roughly $100 billion a year. Depreciation on our stock of capital goods (including automobiles and other consumer durable goods) was close to $200 billion. These two sources financed the roughly $300 billion of capital goods produced. If one does not wish to include consumer durable goods as capital goods (which the Federal Reserve flow of funds does) but to exclude them (as does the Department of Commerce from the national income estimates of capital expenditures) then one must subtract about $100 million from both depreciation and capital goods produced. It can thus be said that our real national wealth was increasing at the rate of about $100 billion a year—but inflation was sometimes expanding the total by as much as another $100 billion.

These totals do not reveal the role of capital markets. To do that we must look at sectors. Although crude in a social accounting sense, we shall limit our review to three sectors—households, business, and government—and then take a brief look at the system of financial intermediaries. The "household" sector (which includes nonprofit institutions in flow of funds accounting) holds about two-fifths of the real assets. But the more important asset to the household sector is financial in form. A very rough balance sheet rounded to hundreds of billions of dollars and as of the end of 1971 would be as follows:

	"Households"		
Real assets	$1,000	Debt (mainly mortgages and consumer debt)	$ 500
Financial assets			
Money	$100		
Common stocks	800		
Equity in unincorporated business	200		
Equity in pensions and insurance policies	350		
Savings accounts	500		
Bonds and mortgages	250	2,200	Net worth	2,700
Total		$3,200		$3,200

And the income statement rounded to tens of billions of dollars would be:

Wages and salaries and professional income	$640
Interest, dividends and rents	120
income	$ 760
Saving	$ 90
Real investment in housing and durables	40
Net financial investment	$ 50
Increase in financial liabilities	40
Gross financial investment	$ 90

The last two lines of the income statement represent capital market magnitudes. The second line represents the property income from past capital market investments. The annual magnitudes vary greatly from year to year, of course, but they do tend to grow. It would be unwise to use them as the basis for forecasting or projection. Households appear to receive a property income return of about 6 percent and to save somewhat less than property income. Except for inflation, net worth grows at the rate of about 4 percent per annum. Much of this increase takes place automatically as equities in pension funds increase. And the increase in the value of common stocks is not due to the investment of new funds but rather through retained earnings and the growth in the value of the business sector.

The business sector consists of corporate business as well as unincorporated enterprises, including farming. In terms of income and employment, the unincorporated sector approaches a third of the amount

A CAPITAL MARKET OVERVIEW

of income and the number of persons employed. In terms of assets and equitable claims, however, it is near a fifth of the business total. The very approximate (market value) balance sheet of nonfinancial business at the end of 1971 (billions of dollars) was:

Nonfinancial Business

Financial assets (net of trade receivables)	$ 300	Financial liabilities (net of trade payables)	$ 600
Real assets	1,500	Net worth	1,200
Total	$1,800		$1,800

And income (not including professional income) was:

Before-tax income:	corporations	$ 90
	unincorporated business	30
Interest paid by business		30

Corporation taxes were slightly less than $40 billion (tax on unincorporated business income not included). As is evident, business produces about three-fourths of the property income enjoyed by households. The remainder comes from governmental debt and payments by some households to other households. What is even more remarkable is that the rates of earnings on the debt of business and on net worth (at market value) are both only about 5 percent—very moderate when compared with the market rates of interest recently prevailing.

Producing a balance sheet for government (federal, agencies, and state and local) is almost impossible. We know that the combined financial assets are about $250 billion and financial debts are about $600 billion. However, how much real property governments have is beyond even the freewheeling efforts of this chapter. The amount is probably less than this difference, and thus government as a whole probably has negative net worth as figured on this basis.

The financial intermediaries, however, can be measured. Including commercial banks and the monetary authorities as intermediaries, the balance sheet for the end of 1971 is about as follows:

Financial Intermediaries

Financial assets:	debt form	$1,200	Liabilities	$1,400
	equities	200		
Real assets		100	Net worth	100
Total		$1,500		$1,500

Financial intermediaries have a gross income of about $70 billion a year (mainly in the form of interest and dividends) and distribute about $50 billion. Some of the remainder represents services performed for customers, such as the collection of checks and the maintenance of credit lines in commercial banks. There is considerable duplication and overlap within the category of intermediaries; some of them hold the claims on other intermediaries or owe funds to other intermediaries. This is a combined, not a consolidated balance sheet.

This section of the chapter has looked broadly at the whole range of balance sheets and income statements for the principal sectors. The capital markets do not comprehend all magnitudes, however. The capital markets concentrate on those cases where net savings come from savings-surplus sectors and are borrowed by savings-deficit sectors. The capital markets also furnish vehicles by which outstanding claims are passed from owner to owner, the so-called "secondary" markets. In addition, the capital markets may also duplicate financial assets. When a closed-end bond fund or a real estate investment trust is formed, this increases capital market activity and the volume of financial claims without necessarily reflecting any new net saving at all. Bankers Trust *Investment Outlook* for 1972 showed the following estimate of capital market transactions in 1971:

Investment funds	$102.9 (in billions of dollars)
Short term funds	29.5
U.S. government and agency securities	19.4
	$151.8

Since these amounts exceed the volume of saving going into financial investment during the year, the excess is some measure of the duplication of financial claims as a result of intermediation. These amounts are also some indication of the relative size of money markets as against the capital markets.

RATE OF GROWTH AND MAGNITUDES OUTSTANDING

Capital market magnitudes have grown at unusually rapid rates during the postwar years. Figure 13-1 is marred by an inconsistency—corporate equity is at market value and others are on a liability or book value basis—but nevertheless gives a general notion of both magnitude and rate of growth. The private sector has grown at a rate close to 10 percent per

A CAPITAL MARKET OVERVIEW

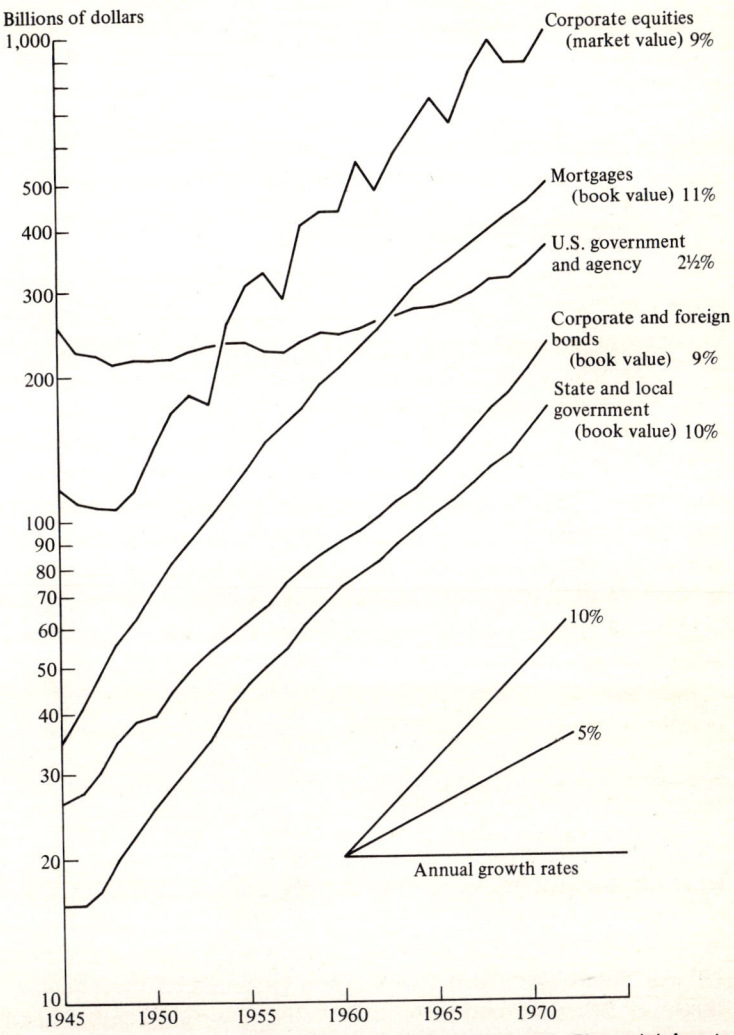

Figure 13-1 (*Source: Flow of Funds Accounts: Financial Assets and Liabilities 1945-1971*, Federal Reserve Board of Governors.)

annum. Federal government and agency debt (in spite of conservative worries to the contrary) has grown at a relatively slow rate.

TYPES OF FINANCIAL INTERMEDIARIES

Commercial banks, described at some length in Chapter 9, can be considered a type of financial intermediary. Other financial intermediaries have been classified by the Bankers Trust in their *Investment Outlook* as:

> Savings institutions—contractual type
>   Life insurance companies
>   Private noninsured pension funds
>   State and local government pension funds
>   Fire and casualty insurance companies
> Savings institutions—deposit type
>   Savings and loan associations
>   Mutual savings banks
>   Credit unions
> Mutual funds—open-end (closed-end are generally listed on the NYSE or traded over the counter)
> Financial corporations—factoring, sales finance, business loans

Efforts at classifying financial intermediaries are not altogether satisfactory. Intermediaries exist because they perform specialized services—most often for savers but sometimes for borrowers. The type labeled as "contractual" above really depends on actuarial principles. An individual cannot forcast fire or life expectancy (either before retirement when insurance is needed or after retirement when income is needed), but this can be done for groups. Each intermediary enters the capital market for investment outlets that presumably are in keeping with the needs of the group it serves.

DEGREE OF INTERMEDIATION

At various other places in this text, reference has been made to problems of stability and instability in the financial markets. Chapter 6 discussed the considerable instability of interest rates. Chapter 2 discussed the instability involved in the adjustment of saving to investment. Chapter 19 will discuss the general problem of financial market and economic stability. But this chapter will introduce one element of instability that inheres in the systemic structure of financial markets: changes in the degree of intermediation.

    Earlier in this chapter it was shown that about two-thirds of the debts created by basic sectors are held by intermediaries as over against claims by "households." In the case of equities, the degree of intermediation is smaller—about a fifth of the total. What these estimates did not disclose is the considerable instability in the degree of intermediation. The first demonstration of this, shown in Table 13-1, is drawn from the Bankers Trust *Investment Outlook* for 1972 (table 31).

    This process, which was particularly marked in 1966 and 1969, has been called, awkwardly and incorrectly, "disintermediation." In

A CAPITAL MARKET OVERVIEW 233

fact, it was a reduced use of the process of intermediation by households. A further fact is that this process does not have an even impact on all types of capital market obligations. Table 13-2 is not complete, but it shows changes in total holdings and holdings of households for U.S. government securities, state and local government obligations, corporate and foreign bonds, and residential mortgages. For these obligations, direct acquisition amounted to 48 percent in 1966 and 88 percent in 1969. In the other five years, direct acquisition accounted for 6 to 28 percent.

The impact was not even among these four types of obligations. The most erratic shifts were shown in the ownership of U.S. government and agency securities. Individuals liquidated holdings in some years and added to them greatly in other years. A very similar though somewhat less extreme pattern is shown in state and local government securities. Corporate and foreign bond purchases by individuals appear to have grown steadily with no special emphasis on 1966 and 1969. The influence of these two years on residential mortgages is equally hard to detect. This is particularly interesting because, as will be related in Chapter 16, disintermediation was particularly heavy on the savings institutions—savings and loan associations and mutual savings banks—which concentrate in mortgage lending. In this area, a shortage of institutional money and higher interest rates did not bring out increased participation by households as was true in both forms of government bonds. It is easier and more convenient for individuals to buy bonds when the rates are attractive than to make added mortgage loans.

Table 13-1 Degree of Intermediation

Year	Liquid funds*	Direct investment	Total	Direct/total
	Billions of dollars			Percent
1964	25.6	3.3	28.9	11
1965	28.8	−1.5	27.3	minus
1966	21.6	10.7	32.3	33
1967	35.8	−2.8	33.0	minus
1968	31.7	−1.0	30.7	minus
1969	16.1	18.2	34.3	53
1970	35.4	4.2	39.6	11
1971(est.)	69.5	−8.0	61.5	minus
1972(proj.)	52.9	12.0	64.9	18

*Deposits in mutual savings banks, savings capital in savings and loan associations, shares in mutual funds and credit unions passbook savings deposits and "other" time deposits at commercial banks.
Source: Investment Outlook, Bankers Trust Co., Table 31.

Table 13-2 Degree of Intermediation, Private Sector

Year	U.S. government securities	State and local government obligations	Corporate and foreign bonds	Residential mortgages	Total	Percent of total
1965: Total	2.3	7.3	6.0	17.9	31.2	
Direct	2.3	2.6	1.4	−.8	5.5	
Intermed.	−2.3	4.7	4.6	18.7	25.7	82
1966: Total	5.4	5.7	10.3	10.7	32.1	
Direct	8.8	2.7	2.5	1.3	15.3	
Intermed.	−3.4	3.0	7.8	9.4	16.8	52
1967: Total	5.7	8.3	16.0	15.6	45.6	
Direct	−1.3	−2.0	5.3	.9	2.9	
Intermed.	7.0	10.3	10.7	14.7	42.7	94
1968: Total	13.3	10.1	13.8	15.8	53.0	
Direct	7.7	.3	5.1	1.8	14.9	
Intermed.	5.6	9.8	8.7	14.0	38.1	72
1969: Total	5.4	7.9	12.6	11.8	37.7	
Direct	16.0	7.5	7.6	2.0	33.1	
Intermed.	−10.6	.4	5.0	9.8	4.6	12
1970: Total	6.2	13.8	20.5	12.9	53.4	
Direct	−7.6	1.7	10.4	2.2	6.7	
Intermed.	13.8	12.1	10.1	10.7	46.7	52
1971: Total	−4.0	20.2	20.0	31.9	68.1	
Direct	−13.1	5.7	8.6	2.4	3.6	
Intermed.	9.1	14.5	11.4	29.5	64.5	94

Source: Flow of Funds, Federal Reserve Bulletin, June 1972, A73.2. ("Intermediation" is here defined as any form of acquisition except by households.)

SERVICE FUNCTIONS AND INSTITUTIONS IN THE CAPITAL MARKETS

The capital markets employ a wide range of institutions that perform the functions necessary for effective market performance. Figure 13-2 shows this in schematic form. The most distinctive of the institutions are investment banking firms. Unlike commercial banks, which tend to a considerable degree of similarity in scope of function, investment bankers are diverse. Some are "full service" institutions; some develop certain areas of special competence. Some are international in interest and scope; others are strictly domestic. Some investment banking firms serve many types of industries; others specialize. Some are active in competitive bidding; some interest themselves only in negotiated financing. Some make venture capital financing a central feature of their operations; some do not enter this area. Some are more active as (secondary) market makers than others.

Commission brokerage firms also vary greatly in character. Some aim at widespread public participation and invite individual participation. Some concentrate on the area of servicing institutional investors. A very few commission brokerage firms also have underwriting or "investment banking" departments; almost all are members of the selling groups used by the underwriters.

Around these central institutions are clustered many small specialty firms such as those advising on corporate or tax-exempt financing or acting as investment advisers.

MEASUREMENT OF IMPORTANCE: TRADING VOLUME OR INTEREST COST?

Comparisons of money markets and capital markets get muddied by efforts to illustrate importance or economic significance with figures that reflect only one dimension. For example, the Fed funds market is the biggest financial market of all if volume of trading is used as a measure; turnover often exceeds $5 billion a day. This is far more turnover than in any other financial market. A typical trade in the Fed funds market is for $1 million. At the rate prevailing on the day this was written (fall of 1972), which was 5 1/8 percent, the interest involved in such a deal was $142.36. On the same day the prevailing interest on mortgages was about 7 percent. On an active day in the mortgage market, about $200 million of new loans will be made. A modest mortgage of $20,000 on a home at 7 percent for twenty-five years will involve the debtor in paying almost $23,000 of interest if the mortgage runs to its contractual termination.

Is the Fed funds transaction 50 times as important (if measured by

Agency	Function

Investment bankers	Marketing new issues
	    Corporate bonds
	    Corporate stocks
	    State and local government bonds
	Venture capital negotiation

Commission brokerage firms	Brokerage service for:
	    Individuals
	    Institutions
	Information and research
	    Market technical analysis
	    Security analysis
	    Portfolio evaluation

Dealers	Marketing outstanding issues
	    Market support operations
	    Over-the-counter transactions

Organized stock exchanges	Secondary market services
	    Continuous face-to-face trading
	    Competitive auction pricing
	    Information and protection

Consultants and advisors	Advising
	    Corporate finance
	    Security analysis
	    Portfolio advice

Commercial banks	Trust services for:
	    Individuals (living or dead)
	    Corporations
	Contacts with other agencies

Note: There really is not a one-to-one relationship between agency and function because some agencies serve more than one function, and some functions are served by more than one agency. Moreover, some firms are multi-agency firms.

Figure 13-2 Capital market functions and agencies.

trading volume) or is the mortgage 160 times as important (if measured by interest cost involved in the contract)?

Is the total Fed funds *market* 25 times as important (as measured by trading volume) or is the total mortgage *market* roughly 30 times as important (as measured by the volume of interest it generates in the national income accounts)?

STABILITY OF SIZE RANKINGS IN CAPITAL MARKETS

The money markets may be volatile in terms of interest rates, but the major private money-market institutions—commercial banks—are amazingly stable with respect to market ranking. The list of the 100 largest

Table 13-3 Size Ranking of Investment Houses—1968 and 1971

1968 rank	Net worth (000 omitted)	Date of report	1971 rank	Total capital position (000 omitted)	Date of report
1 Merrill Lynch	$254,368	12-27-68	1 Merrill Lynch	$393,000	12-31-71
2 Bache & Co.	96,423	12-31-68	2 Bache & Co.	128,042	1-31-72
3 Allen & Co.	91,031	7-31-68	3 Salomon Brothers	101,700	9-30-71
4 Loeb, Rhoades & Co.	76,541	3-31-68	4 Paine, Webber	79,600	3-31-72
5 Lehman Brothers	69,752	11-30-68	5 duPont Glore Forgan	78,219	4-30-72
6 Francis I. duPont & Co.	66,330	12-31-68	6 Dean Witter & Co.	77,346	11-30-71
7 Salomon Brothers	58,700	9-30-68	7 Loeb, Rhoades & Co.	75,400	12-31-71
8 Walston & Co.	58,391	11-30-68	8 Allen & Co.	75,381	12-31-71
9 Dreyfus & Co.	55,037	12-31-68	9 Walston & Co.	56,603	12-30-71
10 Eastman Dillon	53,000	12-31-68	10 Hornblower & Weeks	53,023	12-31-71
11 Dean Witter & Co.	51,023	12-31-68	11 Goldman, Sachs	53,000	12-31-71
12 Goodbody & Co.	49,600	8-30-68	12 First Boston	51,828	12-31-71
13 Hayden, Stone	49,478	12-31-68	13 Eastman Dillon	51,300	12-31-71
14 E. F. Hutton	48,095	1- 2-69	14 Reynolds Securities	51,238	12-31-71
15 Burnham & Co.	44,300	12-31-68	15 E. F. Hutton	50,789	12-31-71
16 Gruss & Co.	41,158	11-29-68	16 White, Weld	49,112	12-31-71
17 Goldman, Sachs	41,038	8-31-68	17 Donaldson, Lufkin	48,439	3-31-72
18 White, Weld	40,749	12-31-68	18 Blyth & Co.	42,810	12-31-71
19 Stephens, Inc.	36,982	11- 2-68	19 Shearson, Hammill	42,669	3-31-72
20 Reynolds & Co.	36,224	12-31-68	20 Oppenheimer & Co.	41,000	8-29-71

Source: *Finance Magazine*, reprinted by *The New York Times*, September 24, 1972, sec. 5.

Table 13-4 Financial Market Matrix: Claims and Sectors*

Claims \ Sectors	Monetary: Federal Reserve System A	L	Commercial banking A	L	Financial: Dealers, brokers, underwriters A	L	Intermediaries A	L	Corporations A	L	Individuals A	L	Government: Federal A	L	State and local A	L	Rest of the world A	L
Money markets: M_1, "money"†	55			180		3		16	38		150		5		17		6	
Open-market credit instruments	44		76	71	10	17	7		48	31	44	2	3	155	32	19	59	4
Short-term loans			150		8		2			100		50						10
Intermediary claims: Time and savings deposits				239				273			482				30			
Insurance, pension, investment companies, and REITS								430			480							
Capital markets: Equities	31		132	33	3	2	185	56		946	827						21	
Bonds: Government							59				105		214		13	147	17	
Corporate and foreign			4	3			172		214		47				6		2	14
Mortgages			83				337		89		45	410	32		2			
Directly negotiated intermediate and long-term loans			50				40	10	60	140	30	30	30					

*Amounts (in billions of dollars) are more suggestive than definitive. Date: approximate end of 1971.
†$M_2 = M_1$ + commercial bank time and savings deposits (NCDs are in money-market credit instruments): 235 + 239 = 474. $M_3 = M_2$ + other intermediary time and savings deposits: 474 + 273 = 747.

238

commercial banks changes relatively little from year to year, and shifts in ranking are exceptional. On the other hand, in the capital markets, the ranking of investment houses changes materially and sometimes drastically. Recent changes may have been unusually severe because of the solvency crisis in stock exchange firms which will be described in Chapter 18. But the shifts are material even in more quiet times. The ranking of investment houses, shown in Table 13-3, drawn from *Finance Magazine* and reprinted by *The New York Times,* illustrates this extremity of change. Seven of the twenty houses at the top in 1968 had dropped out of the top twenty by 1971 or had vanished completely. In other cases, rankings were greatly changed.

CAPITAL MARKETS IN THE FINANCIAL MARKET MATRIX

Chapters 4 and 7 made use of the flow-of-funds system to illustrate relationships in the financial markets. The matrix of amounts outstanding shown in Chapter 7 was introduced, among other purposes, to show relative magnitudes. The same can be done for capital markets. Table 13-4 shows capital markets as a part of the whole structure of financial markets. This matrix also shows the intermediary financial institutions as a sector and their claims as a functional part of the system.

As Table 13-4 clearly shows, individuals are the dominant sector. They use intermediaries more in the debt markets than with respect to equity ownership. This figure also shows the much greater size of capital markets. The mortgage market alone exceeds in size the total of money-market credit instruments. The total of capital market claims (if corporate equities are treated as a "claim") is roughly 4 1/2 times as great as money-market claims. If allowance is made for the fact that long-term interest rates have generally exceeded money-market interest rates, the capital market property returns must be at least six or seven times as important as money-market property returns.

Chapter 14

The Market for U.S. Government Securities

The market for securities of our federal government developed out of the two circumstances that brought most of the great federal debt into existence. These two prime causes have been war (both hot and cold) and depressions. Management of this federal debt by the Treasury Department has proved to be one of the major problems of public affairs.

The private market mechanism that handles this debt has been shaped by the nature of the debt itself. With a large federal debt, it has been necessary for the Treasury to offer many types of securities and to appeal to several sectors of the capital market. Part of the public debt has been lodged in nonmarketable form, but the section of most interest is the share—a major one—that is in marketable form.

The one overriding characteristic of Treasury securities is that they involve no credit risk; the only risk their holders incur is associated with fluctuations of interest rates. Treasury securities thus appeal to investors interested in liquidity. In meeting this demand, the Treasury may have ended up with a debt that is mainly short-term. As a result the private market mechanism is geared mainly to the provision of liquidity. The dealers in Treasury securities and the commercial banks are both suppliers and demanders of liquidity. In other words, the Treasury debt, even the longer-term portions of it, tends to belong as much in the money as in the capital segments of financial markets.

Treasury securities have no credit risk because the federal government has sovereign monetary powers. The federal government never needs to default a debt; it can create whatever money is needed to pay its debts. Treasury securities are valued according to the prevailing yields in the market. The price of these securities fluctuates in a direction opposite to movements in yields and rates.

The discussion in this chapter, and in later chapters that deal with market structure, is organized in a twofold pattern. The first part deals with the nature of demand in the market. Why has the federal government been a borrower? Several related questions also emerge. What sort of timing has characterized this demand; when has the federal government been required to borrow for its basic needs? What kinds of securities has it used to meet its needs? Maturity is usually the leading dimension of securities, and this plays an unusually important role in the federal debt.

The second part deals with the buyers of Treasury securities. What portfolio use do these buyers make of Treasury obligations? What has been the history of their market participation? If the first section could have been labeled "the demand for funds by the federal government," this section could be thought of as "the supply of funds"; the investor's side of the market. This section is mostly a detailed examination of the principal investing sectors.

FEDERAL GOVERNMENT DEMANDS ON THE MARKETS

The federal government operates under a statutory budget that makes no distinctions between capital expenditures and current expenditures. The budget document offers the analyst only a few shreds of evidence for the reconstruction of such a distinction. More important for the work here, federal finances are not dominated by the tradition that governs many other areas, that long-term capital expenditures are more justifiably financed by borrowing than by current expenditures.

Capital budgets for the federal government have sometimes been proposed. Since federal finance differs greatly from private and other forms of finance, however, it is not clear that such a distinction has a great deal of merit. One of the principal expenditures of the federal government has been for national defense. During peacetime some of these expenditures are for military installations or ships or other objects that could be thought of as "capital." Yet once hostilities break out, all these objects become expendable. Can one put wars fought and won on a national balance sheet as an asset? An affirmative answer would be cynical and Machiavellian; a negative answer implies that our federal government is bankrupt. Neither answer is really true.

The timing of federal government ventures into money and capital markets is not to be judged by rules that apply elsewhere. The timing that dominates such activity is the balance of the federal budget. Although much economic controversy has raged over the economic principles that should govern the balance of this budget, expediency has largely governed actual events. This is particularly true of war. Economic logic indicates that large national expenditures for war or defense should be paid for with taxes when incurred. This has never proved to be practical; a great lag in raising taxes always occurs during a war. The major share of federal government borrowing is accounted for by war.

When economic conditions turn slack and labor and other economic resources are not fully employed, many have come to feel that the budget should not be balanced but that a deficit should be encouraged. This principle, however, does not have universal endorsement, though it is certainly true that most professional economists would support it. A downturn in business activity is, in fact, usually accompanied by a drop in federal government tax receipts, which are sensitive to corporate profits, personal income, and related factors. Federal government expenditures, however, tend to be rather fixed or at least to resist cutting, so that a downturn in business activity is automatically accompanied by a tendency toward a budgetary deficit. Thus it is said somewhat cryptically that the federal debt is a legacy of our wars, our national quarrels, and our depressions.

This might be expected to produce balance in the markets. The federal government would tend to be a larger demand factor in the money and capital markets when private economic units tend to reduce their demands. Low demand during war is due to restrictions on private capital expenditures: during depressions it is due to slack demand. To a very great extent this expectation is realized.

The federal debt, however, has become so large that even when it is not growing, the Treasury Department, as fiscal agent of the government, must constantly refund or "roll over" the existing debt. Every capital and money market analyst must be prepared for and understand the role of the Treasury in the markets. It is so large that at times it tends to swamp other financing. Treasury financing sometimes triggers sharp changes in the levels of interest rates; inept Treasury financing can be, and unfortunately sometimes has been, the cause of market disturbances.

Size of the Federal Market Debt

At the end of 1971 the total debt of the federal government was about $424 billion. Quite a bit of it, however, was not "in the market." In the first place, some of this debt is nonmarketable; other portions are held by the trust funds of the federal government, which are inactive market operators. The portion of the marketable Treasury debt privately held was just about $173 billion, almost exactly the same amount as in 1962. For the sake of fairness, however, it would be necessary to include the Treasury securities held by the Federal Reserve, because this institution is very much "in the market." These holdings were $70 billion on that date. The market could thus be thought of as having amounted to something more than $243 billion at that time. This is a large amount. The short-term portion of maturities under one year amounts to $119 billion and was a major factor in money markets. The roughly $124 billion of over-one-year maturities is a somewhat smaller segment of the capital markets but is material by any reasonable quantitative test.

Treasury Cash Balance Management

The Treasury is very much like all other financial managers; it must keep a minimum cash balance. As indicated in Chapter 7, the Treasury makes all expenditures out of its Fed deposits. The Treasury keeps this balance from $1 to $3 billion. The major cash reserve of the Treasury is kept in balances at commercial banks in so-called Treasury tax and loan accounts. The size of the balance is related to the expected cash payments to be made by the Treasury, but these balances also serve another purpose. Although it is probably inconceivable that a Treasury financing operation will ever fail, the Treasury cannot assume so; in fact, it would be bad strategy to present such a desperate face to the market since it would be more exposed to strategic pressures. The cash balance is expected to cover the contingency of a financing failure, remote as it may be. In practice, the Treasury tax and loan accounts have been between $4 billion and $10 billion, with occasional variations slightly outside these margins. These balances have usually been maintained at around $6 billion. Based on gross cash expenditures of the federal government, which average over $200 billion annually, this means that the average cash balance would cover from one to two weeks of spending. Treasury outlays are irregular in timing, however, and this period varies considerably. The Treasury often carries a larger balance than needed right after a new cash financing, but it may run this down to a rather bare margin before expected tax receipts or the next borrowing. (Professors and students should have no trouble understanding managing on a narrow cash balance even though at a much lower absolute level of dollars.) The condition of the cash balance together with the expected schedules of receipts and expenditures is the device used by money-market analysts in trying to anticipate Treasury financing operations.

These cash balances have still another point of market significance. Tax and loan accounts are kept in commercial banks, as noted above. These deposits, when withdrawn, tend to draw reserves from the banks holding them. The Federal Reserve usually tries to smooth the money market to minimize the total effect of the Treasury "calls" on tax and loan accounts. Calls are notices that depository banks must pay out some fraction of these deposits to the federal government, where it will be spent by the Treasury. In spite of the federal government's smoothing efforts, individual banks often vary enough from the averages to feel the effects of calls with unusual severity. Treasury calls are therefore a factor of considerable significance in money-market analysis.

Debt Management

Treasury debt management may be broken into two aspects: new cash borrowing and refunding. The first tends to be important when the debt is increasing but slackens when the debt is stabilized (except for short-term or seasonal borrowing). Refunding, however, is a never-ending process. The maturity structure of the federal debt, for reasons discussed below, has tended to be somewhat shorter than that of most other major debtors, so that Treasury obligations come up for refunding more frequently.

Net cash borrowing has a much greater impact on the money and capital markets than refunding: It takes a net amount of money out of the markets. The capital markets can be viewed as the focal point of a process in which the inflow from saving is taken up by borrowers. The flow of saving probably tends to be fairly steady, but borrowers queue up impatiently and irregularly. A borrower as massive as the Treasury Department can almost exhaust the current flow and leave relatively little for private borrowers and others.

This risk is one of the major conundrums of Treasury operations. Once Congress has fixed tax rates and made appropriations for expenditures, the Treasury must honor these mandates. To do so, it must offset the excess of expenditures over receipts with a schedule of demands on the markets. This schedule is never exactly fixed; even though Congress sets the tax and expenditure rules, the amounts of tax collections and the timing (mainly of expenditures) are often in doubt. This is one of the reasons why the Treasury needs to keep a healthy cash balance. The Treasury faces a hard choice; if it groups its expected borrowing operations into a small number of trips to the market, the average size of each one will be so large as to strain and possibly drain the sources of the market. On the other hand, if the Treasury reduces the average size of cash borrowings, then it "disturbs" the market more frequently.

The second element in Treasury financing is the refunding of debt that is already outstanding. As already mentioned, about $119 billion of the debt outstanding at the end of 1971 and maturing in less than one year required refunding at the rate of $2.5 billion a week. The $124 billion that has a maturity over one year also presents a problem. Since a very large proportion of it is in maturities of less than five years, the rate of turnover is rather fast. Experiments in "advance" refunding have been aimed at this latter segment of the market. This will be discussed later.

Since refunding does not take "new" money from the market, several issues can be bunched into a single operation. This reduces the number of times the Treasury must come to the market. When huge amounts are refunded, however, the market mechanism may be strained.

Even though there may be no net withdrawal of funds from the market as a whole, considerable redistribution of ownership usually takes place. If one of the new securities offered in exchange for the maturing ones has a rather long maturity, the capital section of the market can suffer very real pressure. Treasury obligations approaching maturity probably had drifted into the hands of money-market holders. If the new security offered in a refunding has a fairly long maturity, a switch of ownership is needed. The holder of a maturing security has the "right" to apply for exchanges into the new security or to take cash. A holder of a maturing security who himself does not want the newly offered security may sell his maturing security (which is then called a "right" since the right of exchanges attaches to the security itself) to someone else who wants the new security, which at that moment is not for sale for cash. The churning about in the market caused by those who sell out because the exchange does not fit them and those who buy to get rights may adversely affect security prices.

One of the most important market choices that the Treasury must make both in a cash and in an exchange financing is the maturity of the new security or securities to be offered. The market for longer-term obligations is thinner than that for short-term obligations, so fewer of them can be sold at any one time.

The average maturity of the public debt was a subject of considerable concern at one time. As shown in Figure 14-1, it declined rather sharply from 1949 until 1952. Much of this decline resulted from the dispute between the Treasury Department and the Federal Reserve

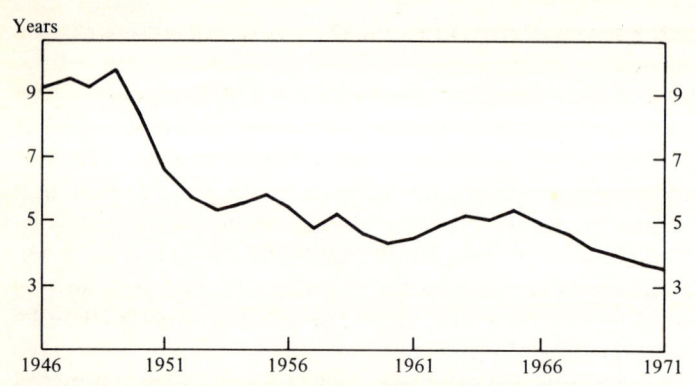

Figure 14-1 Average length of marketable treasury debt. *(Source: Economic Report of the President, 1972, Table B-69, p. 276.)*

described in Chapter 10. The Treasury wanted low interest rates and the Federal Reserve was increasingly reluctant to cooperate. In fact, market interest rates were tending to go up in spite of Federal Reserve efforts, so the Treasury Department was unable to sell long-term obligations at rates it was willing to pay. With the yield curve upward-sloping, the Treasury did all its financing in short-term form; thus, the rapid decline in average maturity. The "Accord" of 1951 terminated the Treasury/Fed dispute, and thereafter interest rates were allowed to move up as the market dictated. However, until it left office, the Truman Adminstration refused to pay the slightly higher rates that would have been necessary for longer-term refunding. This was an issue of some importance in President Eisenhower's first presidential election campaign. True to his concern, the Treasury Department started a vigorous effort to lengthen the debt in 1953. The chief method used was advance refunding. Rather than waiting to the last moment of maturity, the Treasury Department picked a favorable time in the market and then offered reasonably generous terms so as to attract exchanges from the holders of the not-yet-matured securities that were being refunded in advance. The "reasonably generous" terms were possible since the Treasury Department was no longer hung up on the low-interest-rate obsession that had hamstrung it until 1952. The effort was carried over into the Kennedy Administration and even the first two years of the Johnson Administration. This policy however, was a casualty (an unimportant one) of the Vietnam war.

The nature of public concern with the average length of the public debt is illustrated by the position taken by the Commission on Money and Credit in 1961. This quite liberal and forward-looking group recommended that the Treasury Department " . . . arrest the shortening of the outstanding publicly held marketable debt . . . [and] pursue a program which, over a period of time, would lead to a more balanced maturity structure for the debt."[1]

At the present time there is far less concern with respect to the length of the public debt. The capacity of our money markets to absorb short-term credit instruments in large volume was shown in Table 7-1, p. 132. The Treasury Department could lengthen the public debt if it wished, but there is no sense of urgency with respect to the problem. The large short-term debt is rolled over easily. There are even times when the market complains of a shortage of bills. The issue is dead. Advance refunding is still used, but it has become wholly an instrument of convenience and not of principle.

One of the persisting problems of Treasury debt management is the considerable seasonal variation between receipts and expenditures. Deficits are particularly great in the second half of the calendar year. July, August, October, and November are almost always deficit months. (September and December are tax collection months.) Another problem is the lag in tax collections. If times are good and income is increasing, this does not show up in better tax receipts for a period of six months to a year. In spite of long experience and sophisticated techniques, the budget estimators often are wide of the mark in forecasting budget receipts. Even more surprising, expenditures are not always well anticipated. The budget message of the President in January 1972 overestimated budget expenditures for the first six months of 1972 by almost $8 billion. During recent years, the Treasury Department has carried slightly higher cash balances than formerly, apparently because of such uncertainties.

Informal Underwriting of Treasury Offerings

Treasury offerings are not formally underwritten except for two small issues of long-term bonds which were sold by competitive bidding in 1962 and 1963. Jay Cooke helped finance the Civil War by selling bonds—at a price. Since then the Treasury Department has been its own salesman and market manager. The Federal Reserve has sometimes assisted in Treasury financing by actual market support buying, but this has not been done for almost two decades, with a few minor exceptions.[2] In order to secure informal underwriting of Treasury offerings, pricing must be attractive to the market. When pricing is attractive, most of the underwriting support is given by commercial banks and dealers in

---

[1] "Money and Credit," *Report of the Commission on Money and Credit*, Prentice-Hall, Englewood Cliffs, N.J., 1961, pp. 102–103.

[2] The Federal Reserve handles the mechanical details of all Treasury financing operations, but this is done as fiscal agent, not as a principal.

Treasury securities. Commercial banks are both investors and underwriters. They are often induced to support cash offerings by the privilege of paying for the securities bought with a credit to their tax and loan accounts. When the funds are called from these tax and loan accounts, they ultimately must pay for them, but having use of the funds for a few days yields them a moderate but tidy profit. Above, it was noted that the average time money is held in the tax and loan account is about a week and a half, assuming an average cash balance. A ten-day delay in paying for a $1,000 bond with a 6 percent coupon is worth about $1.67. This is equivalent to $167 on each $100,000 bought, an amount which would be within the capacity of even the very smallest bank. At this rate the profit is $1,667 per million bought and paid for in the tax and loan account. When tax and loan account cash offerings are sold at auction, as is true of tax anticipation bills, active bidding often wipes out much of this profit. Banks prefer to give tax and loan credit for short-term securities, since there is less risk of price fluctuations, but the profits on underwriting longer-term securities and their later reoffering on the market is sometimes attractive.

The other principal informal underwriters of a Treasury offering—both cash and refunding—are U.S. government security dealers. Since these dealers get no advantage from tax and loan credits, a cash offering has no advantage to them over a refunding offering. Since refundings are sometimes slightly more generously priced, they may even slightly prefer them, though the statistics do not clearly indicate such a preference.

Pricing, of course, is at the heart of Treasury debt management. A price that is too high will not sell securities. A price that is too low is wasteful, results in early premiums, encourages public speculation in new offerings, and invites criticism. But between the two, the second is clearly the lesser evil. Because of its enormous weight and size, the Treasury cannot escape the role of market leadership. It is generally useful to have had recent financings give investors and underwriters a modest profit. Too large a speculative following, however, can have bad sequels, but the results are not as bad as if recent offerings had left investors with securities selling at a discount and underwriters with losses. Such customers are not likely to be enthusiastic repeat buyers. In the capital markets as elsewhere, nothing succeeds like success.

Large seasonal variations should be mentioned as a cause of Treasury financing. Cash needs may arise owing to a concentration of Treasury tax receipts. Federal expenditures are not evenly spread throughout the year, but they are far more so than tax receipts. Taxes are paid on conventional dates, most of them quarterly. At such periods the Treasury may have an abundance of cash; later this position will be reversed.

So that the Treasury will not hold large amounts of idle cash after tax dates, short-term Treasury securities are timed to mature around or soon after tax dates. Special tax-anticipation bills (TABs), which have a modest yield advantage when used to pay taxes, have also been sold. Even with allowance for these efforts at smoothing and equalizing receipts and payments, the process still results in considerable unevenness. Short-term borrowing covers this gap, and the Treasury bill issues are usually used for this purpose.

Since 1970, the Treasury Department has been experimenting with the auction sale of Treasury notes. So far the auctions appear to have reduced debt costs slightly. More important in some ways, they appear to leave the market in better shape. The auction price may be lower than expected, but an auction cannot be a failure in the same way a sale at an announced price and coupon can be and has been a failure. When announced sales have gone badly and required massive intervention by Treasury trust accounts, the whole Treasury security market has generally been "poor" for some time afterward. A poor market is one that does not have depth, breadth, and resiliency.

THE BUYERS OF TREASURY SECURITIES

The Federal debt is so massive that it must be lodged in many groups of holders. Since a great part of the debt was originally issued during World War II, the original buyers were induced to buy these securities partly by patriotism. But they were also moved by more practical considerations. During the war private capital expenditures, such as those for nondefense housing and capital equipment, were curbed. Private demands for funds were thus at a low level. Old debts were also being repaid. In many ways federal borrowing supplied survival rations for the financial intermediaries. Many who would have preferred some other investment outlet bought Treasury securities as a matter of necessity and not through patriotism.

The result was a large redistribution of the federal debt during the postwar period. Because original holders were shifting out of such amounts that they felt surplus to their normal needs, the Treasury had to hunt for new buyers. Marketing of the federal debt has been a large and unsolved problem. Not the least of the reasons has been the large increase in interest rates in the postwar period. Interest on the federal government debt now exceeds $20 billion. This, however is an average cost of less than 5 percent.

The principal utility of Treasury securities for investors is liquidity. Short-term securities are liquid not only because maturity is near at hand but also because the secondary market in these obligations is a large one, with great absorptive capacity. An investor selling no more than $5 million worth of long-term bonds may have a bit of a marketing problem unless he is willing to concede an appreciable margin. The amount conceded may not be more than a fair marketing cost, but such costs are often of a magnitude to give investors pause. Investors are notoriously close figurers. For this reason they are impressed with the fact that $100 million of Treasury bills can be sold almost casually without much of a ripple in the market. The spread in bid and asked prices levies only a very small marketing cost.

The market for intermediate-maturity Treasury obligations is large enough to allow for rather sizable shifts at least for expert managers. The great commercial banks operate in this maturity area, and they often engage in rather large switching operations. The range of price movements of intermediate-term securities has proved to be somewhat larger than usually expected, but the size of the market is considerable. In light of this, the market also serves a liquidity purpose for many investors.

Long-term bonds of the Treasury admittedly have a more limited market. The amount that can be sold quickly is often small. Sometimes a skillful dealer will be able to move fairly large amounts without disturbance to the market, but this takes time. Even with this qualification, however, the market for Treasury obligations as a whole is a large one that offers considerable liquidity.

In reviewing the various buyers of Treasury obligations, no notice will be given to the government itself. The Federal Reserve is obviously in the market in a major way, but its motives are those of public policy realization and so cannot be easily considered along with a review of private investors. Their operations were covered in Chapters 10 and 11.

Commercial Banks

The commercial banking system in the United States has stabilized its holdings of Treasury securities at about $60 billion during the past several years. This level is a decline from over $90 billion at the end of World War II. Present holdings account for about one-fourth of the privately held marketable securities of the Treasury.

At one time, Treasury securities were regarded as liquid or "secondary" reserves by commercial banks. That function has become far less important, as recounted in Chapter 9. The use for Treasury obligations that is of growing importance to banks is as collateral for public deposits—for federal, state, and local government. When so used, Treasury obligations tend to be a rather frozen asset. With banks getting

THE MARKET FOR U.S. GOVERNMENT SECURITIES   251

liquidity more by liability management, this has subtly shifted the function of the Treasury portfolio. Since agency securities serve as collateral, more of them are owned. Collateral use, of course, tends to freeze the holding of a security so used. If holdings are to be frozen, then the average maturity held might as well be longer—at least when the yield curve is favorable for this posture. As a result, average maturity of bank holdings has tended to increase while the average maturity of the total Treasury debt has been going down. There have been times when nonfinancial corporations in the New York money market have owned far more Treasury bills than the money market commercial banks.

At one time commercial banks were able to play a game of tax switching, charging capital losses against current income in one year and then taking capital gains and paying taxes at a capital gains rate in a later year. The device is no longer available to them. The effect of this is that banks no longer view Treasury securities so much as cyclical outlets for funds. (Cycles in business and interest rates were the foundation of the tax switching game.) At present, tax-exempt securities are more used as a cyclical vehicle, as we shall explain in Chapter 15.

Foreign Monetary Authorities

Since the dollar has become the most important reserve currency, many foreign monetary authorities hold large dollar funds. Some are deposited in banks in time deposit form, but some are invested directly in our money markets; the amount has recently been between $30 billion and $40 billion. Maturities are short, but not as short as they used to be. In addition, some private foreign interests hold dollar balances in this form.

During the past decade, but particularly since 1968 and emphatically so in 1971, the greatest increase in holdings of Treasury securities has been by foreign monetary authorities. As explained in Chapter 12, they are somewhat unwilling holders. The dollars they have acquired originated in their support of the dollar in the foreign exchange markets. This was not altruism. When de facto convertibility of the dollar was terminated in 1968 and our balance of payments deficit continued, there were two choices open to them: to acquire the dollars or let their currency appreciate against the dollar. If their currency had appreciated against the dollar, this would have hurt their trading position vis-à-vis the United States. German and Japanese goods would have cost Americans more. So they took the dollars—reluctantly, grudgingly, but in large amounts. And since they saw little chance of getting rid of the dollars soon, they put them to work—sometimes in the Eurodollar market but often directly in our money markets. They started out purchasing short-term Treasury securities; but as they came to envisage a longer and longer holding of the dollars, they appear to have pushed out quite a way into longer maturities.

Individual Investors

Moderate-income individuals seldom invest in marketable Treasury obligations; the unsophisticated moderate-income buyer can meet his needs with nonmarketable savings bonds. Individuals, presumably those with higher incomes, have nevertheless been the beneficial owners of more than $20 billion worth of marketable Treasury securities in recent years, an amount of considerable importance.

Presumably most of these individual holdings are for investment purposes. Conservative trust accounts of which individuals are the beneficial owners often include Treasury securities. Some of these holdings are accounted for by a special tax circumstance. All but the recently issued over-ten-year-maturity Treasury bonds, which have recently been selling considerably below par, can be used to pay estate taxes at par if in estate prior to death. A wealthy individual, seeing the possibility of early demise, can give his heirs a "tax break" by acquiring a certain number of such bonds. Speculation is another factor accounting for some individual investment. From time to time individuals have bought Treasury issues (at time of offering) hoping to make a capital gain. A few may have been frozen into such holdings. The most common explanation for holding of Treasury marketable bonds by individuals, however, is simplicity. Many quite wealthy people are without a great deal of financial sophistication. Some remember the past and mistrust the stock market. If they have funds beyond their savings bond limits, they may buy marketable Treasury obligations simply because of the lack of knowledge of alternatives.

State and Local Governments

State and local government accounts are surprisingly large investors in Treasury obligations. The explanation is partly the need for liquidity to bridge the gap between borrowing for a capital expenditure and the making of the expenditure. Many state and local govenmental units are required to borrow before a capital expenditure project is started, sometimes before the contracts are let.

Another factor enters into the willing acceptance of this rule. Since the interest on state and local govenment obligations is exempt from federal income taxes, the coupons and yields on these obligations tend to be lower than those prevailing on Treasury obligations, which are subject to income taxation. As a result state and local governments have sometimes been able to make a modest profit on bridging transactions: The interest they earned on short-term liquidity funds was more than they were paying on their indebtedness. Borrowing in advance actually became profitable, and it has never been very costly. Maturities of the Treasury securities they buy and hold are, of course, quite short. Such "arbitrage" investment is now restricted though not prohibited by federal tax law.

Savings Institutions

The two leading savings institutions—savings and loan associations and mutual savings banks—together hold $6 billion worth of Treasury obligations. The mutual savings banks once held over $10 billion, but their holdings have dwindled to less than $3 billion. This decline, however, has not been as drastic as that of the life insurance companies.

Savings and loan associations are required to keep liquidity reserves. Treasury securities now account for about one-fifth of this liquidity reserve.

The Treasury securities bought by savings and loan associations are now limited to intermediate-term obligations.

Nonfinancial Corporations

During World War II a great many nonfinancial corporations were limited in the amount of capital expenditures they could make. As a result they had very large net cash flows from depreciation charges as well as retained earnings. They were encouraged to invest these funds in Treasury securities, and many did so. In addition, the tax liabilities were large because tax payments were somewhat less current than under present law and regulations. It was considered the part of wisdom to fund these tax liabilities, and the Treasury Department encouraged this practice by offering TABs.

In the postwar period, corporations have gradually drawn down their excess liquidity. At the peak, nonfinancial corporations held more than $25 billion of the Treasury marketable debt—about 15 percent of the amount then outstanding. At present the amount has dwindled to about $5 billion or about 2 percent of the total. Funding with TABs is still practiced by a few corporations when such bills are available, but the practice is dwindling. As mentioned in Chapters 7 and 8, some corporations supply funds to U.S. government security dealers by means of repurchase agreements which are tailored to their funds availability. Such arrangements are competitive with the tailored maturities of commercial paper directly placed, as mentioned in Chapter 8.

Insurance Companies and Pension Funds

At one time life insurance companies were quite important investors in Treasury obligations; right after World War II they held about $20 billion worth of them. The amount has been steadily dwindling, and at present they hold only about $4 billion worth. Since life insurance assets have grown a great deal over the same period, the shrinkage in percentage terms is even more drastic: from about 45 to 2 percent of total assets. Life insurance companies do not need liquidity, and since that is the prime virtue of Treasury obligations, they have little appeal to that group of institutions.

Other insurance companies, mainly casualty insurance companies, do have some use for liquidity and they own about $4 billion worth of Treasury obligations. This amount is between 6 to 8 percent of their assets. While the life insurance companies mainly hold long-term maturities, the casualty companies usually buy intermediate-term obligations.

Private pension funds are not important buyers of Treasury obligations. These funds have no need for liquidity since their outflows of cash are quite predictable and they have large cash inflows. The amounts held by these funds dwindled from $8 billion in 1960 to $3 billion in 1970. Maturities, of course, are always rather long.

State and local government pension fund holdings of Treasury obligations have slowly dwindled to about $7 billion. The Civil Service Retirement System, which is one of the Treasury Trust accounts, holds almost $25 billion of special nonmarketable Treasury issues. Social security and U.S. government insurance accounts hold over $40 billion of similar securities.

Dealers in Treasury Obligations

On some occasions dealers have been important investors in Treasury obligations; the total has occasionally been as high as $6 billion. Size of holdings, however, does not adequately express the function of dealers. The market for Treasury securities is the largest secondary market for debt securities in the United States (or the world). Turnover of all maturities of Treasury securities is greater than that of comparable maturities of any other securities. This is true even in the money markets. Commercial paper, bankers' acceptances, and NCDs tend to be held by the original purchaser until maturity. There is a secondary market in each of them, but it is small compared with the secondary market in Treasury bills. No other intermediate or long-term securities turn over as much as Treasuries. The reason is the "depth, breadth, and resiliency"[3] given to this market by the dealer function. Dealer portfolios turn over about every two or three days.

The Treasury Department was, and potentially still is, inhibited by a statutory limit on the coupon interest rate it could pay on bonds: 4 1/4 percent. Rates on bills, certificates, and notes were not so limited. This was one of the problems in trying to lengthen the public debt. In 1971 Congress relaxed the interest rate ceiling in part: it permitted the Treasury Department to issue up to $10 billion of bonds without regard to the ceiling. So far about one quarter of this amount has been issued. In terms of financing opportunities, this may be about as much as is feasible; but any extensive effort to lengthen the average maturity of the debt would require further relaxation.

Treasury bills have always been sold by auction, as described above in Chapter 8. Recently the Treasury Department has been using the auction method for sale of longer-term securities, but mainly in small and experimental amounts. To encourage wider use and participation in the auctions by less sophisticated investors, the Treasury has tried the use of an auction in which bidders who offer a price high enough to buy securities in a normal auction are required to pay only the marginal or "stop-out" price. In other words, an unsophisticated bidder need not fear paying too high a price (which, however, would be true only so long as the marginal or "stop-out" price were still determined by sophisticated bidders).

AGENCY SECURITIES

The market for securities for a number of agencies created by the federal government is included here for several reasons. One of the most important is that these securities are traded in very much the same channels as direct Treasury obligations. They also appear to be purchased by about the same group of investors. And since most of the agency securities can be used for the same collateral purposes of banks as direct Treasury securities, they can be considered functionally equivalent. And finally, although not guaranteed, they are widely thought to be almost a moral obligation of the federal government. The yield differentials of these

---

[3] This phrase was first used in a study commissioned by the Federal Reserve at the time of the "Accord."

securities with respect to direct Treasury obligations has been so small and so constant that the market, in fact, treats them as very good substitutes.

The largest volume of securities is issued by corporations sponsored but not owned by the federal government. They include (with acronym and date of organization):

Banks for Cooperatives (COOP), 1933
Federal Intermediate Credit Bank system (FICB), 1923
Federal Land Banks (FLB), 1917
Federal Home Loan Banks (FHLB), 1932
Federal National Mortgage Association (FNMA), 1938, 1954, 1968

The government-sponsored agencies are subject to neither the 4 1/4 percent interest rate limitation nor to the debt ceiling. They have enjoyed the umbrella of government sponsorship without having to suffer the penalties of governmental limitations.

By this narrower definition, these agencies had total outstanding securities in the markets of about $45 billion and in 1971 made offerings of new securities with a maturity of over one year of more than $10 billion.

Each of the agencies has a fiscal agent who furnishes the leadership in the marketing of its securities. These fiscal agents operate through selling groups of several hundred dealers and banks who receive small dealer commissions. These fiscal agents keep in touch informally not only with each other but also with the Treasury Department so that, so far as possible, traffic jams in the markets for these very similar securities are avoided. All these fiscal agents were formerly located in the Wall Street area so as to be in touch with the markets. The current tendency, however, is to return them to Washington.

The governmentally owned agencies include the following:

Tennessee Valley Authority (TVA)
Export-Import Bank ("Ex-im")
Government National Mortgage Association (GNMA)
Federal Home Loan Mortgage Corporation (FHLMC)
Farmers Home Administration (not to be confused with FHA)

Each of these corporations uses a marketing system somewhat different from the basic one described above, and their securities are not quoted by most dealers. The operations of GNMA and FHLMC will be described in Chapter 16, which deals with the home mortgage market. The Farmers Home Administration offers an "insured" package of its own credits to the market. Total debt of agencies owned by the federal government is approaching $15 billion. The average maturity tends to be somewhat longer than that of the sponsored agencies. Not included here are the public housing or urban renewal authorities, since their securities are not only guaranteed by the federal government but are also tax-exempt. They will be treated in Chapter 15, which is devoted to the tax-exempt market.

At the fringe of the agency market are a number of other federal-government-guaranteed types of obligations, such as Merchant Marine bonds, bonds of the Rural Electrification Authority and of the Rural Telephone Bank, and the very recently created New-Community Development bonds.

Each of the "sponsored" corporations was created by the federal government, and in the beginning some stock in these corporations was owned by the Treasury Department. However, this Treasury stock has now been retired and each corporation is now owned by its members. The FNMA, a secondary market maker and price supporter for mortgages, was put in the private sphere by congressional mandate in 1970. At present it is listed on the NYSE and for a while its stock was a speculative favorite.

AUTOMATION OF THE U.S. TREASURY DEBT INSTRUMENT

The U.S. Treasury debt instrument may soon become mainly a fully automated book entry. It will exist only in a computer memory bank and not on paper. The very large volume of paper work in this active market had led many years ago to centralization of much of the physical aspects of security transfer and hypothecation in one large New York City money-market bank. But even that system was not adequate. There was an early pressure for as much automation as possible, one form of which was wire transfer of Treasury obligations between Reserve banks.[4] A second reason was a series of thefts of securities, including some Treasury securities, that took place in and around the Wall Street area. The large losses led the leading company insuring security safety to threaten to cancel all delivery insurance. As a result of these costs and risks, a special drive was put on to automate this market. The system now appears to be fully tested and operational and is available for such banks as

---

[4] "The Program for the Automation of the Government Securities Market," *Monthly Review*, Federal Reserve Bank of New York, v. 54, no. 7, p. 178, July 1972.

elect to open book-entry accounts. These banks can do so not only for their own Treasury securities but also those of customers. This is particularly important for the dealers who have the largest volume of transactions. How fast the system will spread is not certain, but the cost and risk factors are strong incentives. The physical Treasury debt instrument, with its rococo engraving, is already obsolete and may soon disappear.

The significance for the rest of the securities market is great. If the system can work for Treasury debt, why can it not work for all other stocks and bonds? However, anyone who has struggled with repeated uncorrected errors in his computer-prepared brokerage account statement must hope that control of the input for the book-entry system can be improved. After all, at some stage a human action must initiate the first entry to the machine. If that entry is wrong, the whole magnificence of computer technology is wasted.

Chapter 15

The Market for State and Local Government Securities

The principal characteristic of this market is that it is of securities with coupon interest income exempt from the income taxes of the federal government. This income may be taxed by states (other than the one in which the securities are issued and sometimes even by or in the issuing state). Capital gains on these securities can be taxed by the federal government. However, the basic exemption of coupon income from taxation sharply sets these securities aside from the securities issued by the federal government itself, those issued by corporations, and the interest income on mortgages.

These securities are sometimes colloquially called "municipal" bonds; but, in fact, tax-exempt securities are issued by all levels of state and local government as well as by some special authorities created just for this purpose. Since more than 80,000 units of state and local government exist, the multiplicity of this market is evident. Table 15-1 shows the principal types of issuers in the year 1971. This distribution is typical of other recent years.

THE BORROWING DEMAND OF STATE AND LOCAL GOVERNMENT BODIES

Capital expenditures account for most state and local government borrowing. State and local government capital expenditures are also more likely to be financed by borrowing than corporate capital expenditures are, though not as likely to be so financed as new housing construction. Exceptions to this rule exist. A few state governments borrowed during the postwar period to pay bonuses to veterans residing in their states. Other examples of borrowing for noncapital purposes can be found, such as borrowing to refund debts; but this is rare. Some short-term borrowing, in anticipation of tax receipts or of long-term borrowing, is also done, but this market is a limited and specialized one, confined mainly to commercial banks. Such short-term loans may be sold through the open market, but bond or tax anticipation notes are often sold directly to banks.

Our comments should not imply that most state and local government capital expenditures are financed by borrowing. Capital expenditures, such as state road building, made on a regular and scheduled basis are often financed out of current receipts. This is particularly true where special earmarked taxes are used for such expenditures. However, many capital expenditures, even at state levels, are too "lumpy" (large in size relative to regular stream of expenditures) to be financed out of current receipts. Smaller government bodies, such as school districts, find almost all capital expenditures lumpy and tend to finance them by borrowing.

For most of the postwar years, educational capital expenditures

Table 15-1 Type of Governmental Agency Selling Tax-exempt Securities—1971

Issuer	Billions of dollars
States	6.0
Counties	1.8
Municipalities	6.0
School districts	2.4
Special districts*	1.3
Statutory authorities*	7.4
Total	24.9
Type	
General obligations	15.2
Revenue bonds	8.7
New housing authorities	1.0
Total	24.9

*Mainly revenue
Source: Securities Industry Assoc., *Municipal Statistical Bulletin*, February 1972, Tables 1 and 2.

have led the list of purposes for state and local government borrowing. This purpose still is in first place, as Table 15-2 shows, but its relative importance is declining and it probably will fall from first place soon. The postwar educational plant has been built and the birthrate is declining. However, other uses, particularly for local utilities (water, sewer, municipally owned light and power plants, etc.) and for roads have grown.

For many of the postwar years, borrowing accounted for about half of the total construction expenditures of state and local government, but this proportion has been increasing as state and local government struggles with increasing problems of local finance. At the same time, tax-exempt borrowing has sometimes been used for purposes of capital construction that have been greatly changed from the original idea of public capital expenditures. The Port Authority of New York and New Jersey has built and operated the tunnels and bridges in the New York Metropolitan area, which is quite different from operating a seaport. The operation of airports at LaGuardia, Kennedy, and Newark airports, however, is reasonably well in keeping with the original idea of the authority. But what about the two World Trade Center towers that now dominate the skyline of lower Manhattan? They were tax-exempt financed, but they compete with the office buildings that had no such exemption for their financing. And how different is this from the industrial bonds used by cities and some states to attract industry with low-cost industrial plants based on tax-exempt financing? This practice has been curbed for larger projects, but the validity of the principle remains open to question.

A similar comparison is not available by levels of government, but it would almost certainly show that the proportion is smaller for states; for local governmental units it would be much larger. The year-to-year correspondence of borrowing and capital expenditures is not exactly constant, however. The explanation seems to be that borrowing almost always precedes construction, often by long periods. State and local government finance officers attempt to borrow when markets appear favorable, so the lead time of borrowing over expenditures varies. Bond anticipation notes can be used by some governmental bodies, but such borrowing is prohibited for others.

The basic demand for borrowing by state and local governments has a strong demographic basis; it is caused by increases in population and by movements of population. These movements may be nationwide, but they can be important even if only for short distances, as movements to the suburbs. In that respect, state and local government needs are very much like the demand for mortgage credit to finance housing purchases. The movement of population from the center of cities out into the suburbs has tended to create new governmental service needs: for new roads, new schools, new sewers and other sanitary facilities, and for

Table 15-2 Purpose of Tax-exempt Borrowing—1971

Purpose	Billions of dollars
Education	5.3
Transportation*	4.3
Water, sewer, and other utilities	5.2
Public housing	1.9
Other "social welfare"	1.9
Industrial	0.2
Public services	0.6
Unclassified and miscellaneous	5.1
Refunding	0.5
Total	24.9

*Roads, bridges, tunnels, ports, airports, and miscellaneous transportation.
Source: Securities Industry Assoc., *Municipal Statistical Bulletin*, February 1972, Table 2.

new fire and police protection facilities. States receiving large population inflows have tended to be heavy borrowers, and those with dwindling populations or little change have made fewer capital expenditures and borrowed less. The general prosperity of the postwar period, however, has led to some upgrading of governmental facilities; even in those areas where population is not increasing, newer school buildings are being built and some roads improved.

Since state and local governments are less affected by business conditions than is true of corporations, their capital expenditures do not tend to be related to business cycle movements. On the other hand, as we shall show later, the actual borrowing process has been very much affected by changes in interest rates. In turn, interest rates are, of course, closely related to business conditions.

CREDIT RATINGS AND THEIR CONTROVERSIAL IMPACT

Sophisticated investors generally make their own evaluation of the credit quality of the securities they buy. However, the vast majority of individuals and many smaller institutional investors undoubtedly rely very heavily on agency credit ratings. Two agencies that also rate corporate obligations—Standard and Poor's and Moody's—rate a large fraction of the tax-exempt bonds sold. However, as Table 15-3 shows, an appreciable margin of issues go unrated.

These credit rating are controversial in two ways: First, many of the evaluations by the rating agencies are challenged; second, the issues

THE MARKET FOR STATE AND LOCAL GOVERNMENT SECURITIES 263

too small to be rated may be discriminated against by the absence of ratings. A small business may be presumed to have a questionable credit rating just because smallness is a problem in a highly competitive business environment. But smallness in a local government unit is not necessarily a sign of poor credit. The sewer bonds of a small sanitary district in a high-income suburb may have very great credit strength.

In 1965 both rating agencies lowered the bonds of New York City from an A rating to Baa, and this set off a controversy that is still not settled. (In early 1973 the A rating was restored.) Investigation of the rating process by Congress was proposed. Suggestions were made that such credit rating might better be done by some federal agency. Nothing came of these suggestions, but the problem remains. Many factors have tended to increase the operating costs of state and local government. For one thing, welfare rolls have increased even in times of good business conditions. Upgrading of the level of welfare payments has been spurred by minority militance and by the impact of inflation. Another factor causing increased costs of local government has been the increased organization for wage bargaining of state and local government employees: public school teachers, firemen, police, garbagemen, and others—and now even college teachers!

These factors have pushed state and local government finances to a point at which a larger share of capital expenditures requires borrowing. When interest rates were somewhat lower, the burden of this debt was not as great. But as we shall outline in the closing section of this chapter, such rates have increased considerably. Tax exemption no longer guar-

Table 15-3 Credit Ratings of Tax-exempt Bonds—Total of Years 1970 and 1971

	Billions of dollars	Percent of total
Aaa	4.9	11.4
Aa	10.4	24.2
A	15.1	35.2
Baa	7.7	18.0
Ba and lower	0.1	0.2
Unrated	4.7	11.0
Total	43.0	100.0

Source: Securities Industry Assoc. *Municipal Statistical Bulletin,* February 1972, Table 5.

antees low borrowing costs. And thus the budget burden continues to increase. The effect of this will be to aggravate the problem of credit ratings. As debt and debt costs mount, any credit analyst, whether public or private, would have to conclude that the quality of the debt was no longer as good as it had been.

Nevertheless, it would be a mistake to belittle state and local government credit. As Table 15-3 shows, more than three-quarters of the rated debt has an A rating or higher and almost two-fifths of the total is in the two top ratings.

INVESTORS IN TAX-EXEMPT SECURITIES

The generally strong credit of tax-exempt securities makes them a preferred outlet for conservative investors who face high marginal tax rates and who nevertheless want current income rather than capital gains. Tax-exempt securities also have an advantage over other kinds of tax shelters since the investor is almost certainly assured of this shelter over the full life of any security he purchases. This is not true of such tax shelters as investments induced by oil-depletion allowances or cash-flow real estate investments where a change of legislation could strip the shelter from those now holding it. Most of the proposals for tax reform of these latter areas have, in fact, been along these lines. This has not been true of tax exemption on state and local government securities. The only serious legislative effort within the past generation (since 1940) of any significance with respect to these securities came in 1969. This effort was only to give an interest differential subsidy to those state and local government issuers who would voluntarily forego the privilege of tax exemption on the new securities they issued. This would have left the outstanding issues untouched. (It probably would have also given them a premium or scarcity value and upped their price.) Thus it can be said that the state and local government bond tax shelter has superior durability.

Tax exemption has a long legal and constitutional history. In Civil War times, such interest income was taxed, but in the later part of the nineteenth century taxation of any income by the federal government was declared unconstitutional. The Sixteenth (income tax) Amendment permitted the federal government to tax income "from whatever source derived." Since there was some feeling that this exposed interest income from state obligations to federal taxation, Congress passed a law exempting such income from federal taxation, a law which has remained untouched since that time. With this statute on the books, the constitutional issue has never been tested. Opinions on this point differ and the differences generate much heat. The issue, however, is not important to the capital market analyst. Except for the relatively mild proposal described above, no serious legislative challenge has been made in the past generation. The political balance of power is such that Congress would almost certainly not repeal the existing statutory exemption (though many economists, including the authors, feel it to be inequitable). For practical purposes, the present situation can be taken as a firm basis for examination of the effects of tax exemption on the investment process.

Where tax exemption exists, it is used mainly by investors exposed to income taxation. The more they are exposed, the more likely they are to invest in tax-exempt securities. A large portion of institutional investors are tax-exempt per se: pension funds and nonprofit institutions such as university endowment funds and charitable foundations. Some intermediary institutions are technically subject to federal income taxation, but the exemption rules have been liberal until recently; the mutual savings banks and the savings and loan associations are examples of such cases. Some institutional investors, though generally taxed, are taxed at lower effective rates than apply to the unsheltered investors: life insurance companies are the principal example.

The "unsheltered" or fully exposed investors having a large stake in tax exemption of interest income are principally commercial banks, nonfinancial corporations, high-income individuals (or the trustees who manage their investment affairs), and casualty insurance companies. As might be expected, this group constitutes a somewhat narrow market. All the buyers of tax-exempt securities are important investors in other markets; they, in fact, view these other markets as more basic to their investment needs than tax exemption. This leads to an unusually complex set of crosscurrents between the tax-exempt market and other segments of the capital markets. One result of these complexities is that tax-exempt yields, while lower than other interest rates (as would be expected), are also quite variable. Market understanding of these variations requires some detailed attention to the behavior of these other investors.

Commercial banks are basically lenders to business and to other customers. They invest in Treasury obligations for reasons of collateral coverage and liquidity. However, the interest income from both sources is exposed to federal income taxation: Tax exemption has a powerful appeal to them. In addition, as we shall develop more fully later, some bigger commercial banks also act as underwriters and dealers in these obligations. As a result of these factors, commercial banks are large but erratic investors in tax-exempt securities. If loan demand is high, they buy very few and may even be net sellers of them. When loan demand is low they become large investors.

This erratic participation in the tax-exempt market is dramatically

Table 15-4 Net Acquisition of Tax-exempt Obligations (Gross Acquisitions Less Sales and Retirements—Billions of Dollars)

	1964	1965	1966	1967	1968	1969	1970	1971
Commercial banks	3.6	5.1	1.9	9.0	8.6	.4	10.5	13.7
Nonfinancial corporations	.2	.5	1.0	−.2	−1.1	5.1	1.4	4.0
Individuals	2.2	1.9	2.5	−1.4	1.3	1.6	−1.2	.7
Fire and casualty insurance	.3	.5	1.0	1.5	.8	1.1	1.3	2.0
Other*	−.5	−.7	−.6	−.3	−.1	—	−.2	.3
Total†	5.8	7.3	5.8	8.6	9.5	8.1	11.8	20.7

*"Other" investors include state and local government general and pension funds (which have been liquidating holdings almost every year) and life insurance and mutual savings banks (which were also liquidating holdings until 1971).

†The total does not include U.S. government loans to states and cities.

Source: Bankers Trust Co., *Investment Outlook 1972*, Table 12. (These figures vary slightly from those published by the SIA used in Tables 15-1 to 15-3 and also the flow-of-funds figures of the Federal Reserve used in Table 15-5.)

illustrated in Table 15-4. In 1966 and 1969, when money markets were relatively tight, commercial banks almost dropped out of the market. The withdrawal of commercial banks led state and local government issuers to delay market offerings so that the total was also lower in each year than the year before or after.

Nonfinancial corporations were formerly rather small participants in this market. However, the increase in short-term offerings in the last several years offered them a vehicle in keeping with their money management needs. Thus the nonfinancial corporations tend to be important factors in the market for short-term tax-exempt obligations. The gross holdings of this group, however, are not large, as is shown in Table 15-5.

High-income individuals have even more compelling tax reasons for investment interest in these securities. Individuals who are subject to marginal rates of income taxation above 50 percent, or even less, find that fixed income from taxable obligations has little appeal. High-income individuals concentrate their attention on corporate equities. With capital gains taxed at lower rates, this investment outlet has much appeal. However, the attractiveness of the stock market is notoriously variable. Higher-income individuals thus appear to move back and forth from equities to tax-exempt securities, depending on changes in this attractiveness. The market for tax-exempt securities is thus considerably influenced by stock market developments; more so than any other fixed-income security market. Changes in the degree of individual participation in the tax-exempt market are shown in Table 15-4.

The participation of individuals in the tax-exempt market has been greatly reduced in recent years because of inflation and the fear of it. Tax

THE MARKET FOR STATE AND LOCAL GOVERNMENT SECURITIES 267

exemption does not exempt the investor from the devastating losses of inflation. Corporations and banks whose liabilities are in dollar form can invest in fixed-dollar assets feeling that inflationary erosion will hit both sides of their balance sheets equally. Not so for individuals. The yields have been attractive but not large enough to offset loss of purchasing power. As the closing section of this chapter will show, tax-exempt interest yields have gone up considerably relative to other interest rates. If it were not for inflation, even very moderate-income individuals could benefit from tax-exempt investment. Indeed, the investment bankers marketing these securities have sought to expand this market. Mutual funds of tax-exempt securities have been formed and sold. Some investment bankers now advertise in a way that is aimed at middle-income investors. But the problem of inflation remains. Individuals continue to be the second-largest holders of tax exempt obligations, as shown in Table 15-5, even if they have reduced purchases recently.

Casualty insurance companies participate in this market because of a rather special set of circumstances. These companies write a form

Table 15-5 Holdings of State and Local Government Obligations—End of 1971*

	Billions of dollars
Total state and local government debt	171.7
Owed to U.S. government	5.2
Marketable tax-exempt securities owned by:	166.5
Commercial banks	82.9
"Households" (individuals)	52.3
Fire and casualty insurances companies	19.3
Life insurance companies	3.5
Corporations (mainly nonfinancial)	3.2
State and local government general funds	2.1
State and local government pension funds	1.8
Dealers and brokers	1.0
Mutual savings banks	0.4
Total	166.5
Maturity	
Long-term	147.3
Short-term	19.2
Total	166.5

*These figures vary slightly from those of the SIA and the Bankers Trust used in earlier tables in this chapter.
Source: Federal Reserve Flow of Funds Accounts, Financial Assets and Liabilities, June 1972, p. 41.

of insurance that is less subject to precise actuarial expectation than life insurance; a hurricane, for example, can give them a nasty bunching of losses. Thus, they need far more liquidity than life insurance companies. Casualty insurance net income is also variable; these companies have little taxable income in years of unusually heavy casualty losses and a great deal of income in other years. They are also more exposed to federal income taxation than life insurance companies. For these reasons individual companies are important investors in tax-exempt securities—but also erratic investors.

Table 15-4 showed that, in the aggregate, these companies are less variable than the other investors in this market. Individual casualty insurance company experience, however, often differs from industry experience. One company may have little use for tax exemption in a year and so be selling off its portfolio of tax exempts when other companies are buying heavily—also for tax reasons. Thus the aggregate figures often conceal a lot of churning about among individual companies.

THE MARKETING PROCESS

The marketing of state and local government obligations is a good example of the way in which competition encourages efficiency in our private economic system. Bidding for these securities is usually competitive, and the process is fully exposed to public surveillance. As a result, the investment banking community has developed economizing practices that result in low-cost borrowing to state and local government bodies, even rather small ones. This result occurs even though the investment bankers face a rather volatile market. A further obstacle overcome is the fact that the number of borrowers is large and diverse and the obligations are usually serial bonds, both of which facts would seem to lead to complexity.

Competitive bidding is required as a safeguard against connivance. Fraud and graft, which have not been unknown in governmental management and financing, offer an opportunity for skullduggery if not fully exposed to public view. Most states govern the borrowing of lower levels of government by statute, and most of these statutes require public competitive bidding. State governments generally follow the same practice.

The mechanics of competitive bidding require advance notice of the intention to sell bonds and the terms attaching to these bonds. An "invitation to bid" is the signal for the formation of buying groups or syndicates among investment bankers. Large issues usually require the formation of large groups; small issues, much smaller groups. Very small issues are occasionally bought by a single buyer. Syndicate structures tend to be fairly continuous. Leading commercial banks and investment bankers assume the responsibility for the formation of the groups and their management. In this process, traditional relationships and leadership patterns develop. A large bank may traditionally lead or manage the group formed to bid on the bonds in the city in which it is located. The managing head or heads of a syndicate invite other firms and banks that were members of similar earlier groups to participate in bidding for the new bonds, and the sale of the bonds if the bidding is successful. Managers of one syndicate may turn up as nonmanaging participants in other groups, but very likely with some of the same partners in the group they managed. Traditional relationships tend to be maintained for long periods of time and reciprocity is expected. While invitations to participate are reciprocal, one of the best ways for a firm to attract invitations is to have a good record as an aggressive selling house. "Free riders" (weak sellers) get fewer repeat invitations.

New groups are seldom exactly the same as old ones. Smaller members may drop out of a group if they do not agree with the bidding proposals; they may not be asked a second time if their selling performance is poor. What is more, the relative importance of investment banking houses changes more rapidly than expected. A house that has enjoyed many years of leadership may dwindle in importance if it loses dynamic leadership; a single man has often made a great deal of difference to a firm.

A few investment banking firms specialize in state and local government obligations, but most state and local government security marketing is done by departments of firms that engage in somewhat broader financial activities. The presence of commercial banks in this underwriting process also differentiates this market from the one for corporate bonds; banking relationships tend to be long-standing and enduring and groups formed for underwriting ventures may parallel other long-term relationships.

The widespread use of serial obligations in state and local government finance is the result of adverse experience with term bonds. In earlier days state and local government often used term bonds in financing. Following corporate practice, they also purported to establish sinking funds for the retirement of such debt. Such sinking funds, however, were too often subject to fraud. In addition, some governments failed to meet sinking fund payments. Serial bonds were found to be a far better assurance of debt retirement; they require no sinking funds which can be plundered by sticky-fingered public servants.

The serial bond, however, imposes a somewhat more complex task on the selling groups. Commercial banks and nonfinancial corporations tend to be buyers of the short maturities. Intermediate maturities are bought by casualty insurance companies and trustees. Individuals and mutual life insurance companies tend to buy the longest bonds. These generalizations, however, have many exceptions. Since the principal buyers are all somewhat volatile in their attraction to this market, the underwriters of state and local government financing attempt to adjust the yields on the various maturities to expected market preferences as far as the underwriters can foresee these preferences: yield curves that measure this term structure of interest rates were discussed in Chapter 6. However, with all the skill and foresight applied to this market, the selling of serial obligations involves more complexities than are encountered in the corporate bond market, which is (except for rail equipment obligations) almost wholly on a "term" or one-maturity basis. The variety of yield differentials is also sometimes further complicated by odd coupon structures which are used for technical reasons.[1]

The selling process in this market is not as rapid as that in the corporate bond market. A popular state and local government issue may be sold out in one day (fifteen minutes would be a comparable record for the sale of a desirable corporate issue), but more often than not a state and local government issue of any size will require several days or even weeks for its marketing. As a result, dealers and underwriters tend to carry larger inventories of new but unsold issues. Much of this inventory is advertised in a special marketing vehicle: the *Blue List*. This daily publication lists issues alphabetically, first by state and then by city or issuing authority. The total of issues advertised in the *Blue List* is often cited as a kind of inventory figure in this market. It is generally believed, however, that dealers do not regularly advertise all the issues they own, so that this figure understates market inventories by varying amounts. Normally a dealer may prefer to show almost everything he has for sale; the *Blue List* is widely used by investors as a source of information as to where particular issues may be located. But a dealer may decide to conceal some of his holdings for strategic reasons. He may be able to bargain better on inquiries if he shows only half of his holding of a given issue.

Although no systematically collected facts prove it, this market is almost certainly of smaller unit size than that of other segments of the capital market; it is more parallel to the mortgage market in this respect. Five-bond transactions are common and the odd-lot designation is applied only below this level. Big transactions take place, but many small ones are the heart of the market. With smaller unit size, it is almost inevitable that the sale of a given dollar volume of bonds requires more time.

[1] See Appendix B of Roland I. Robinson, *Postwar Market for State and Local Government Securities*, Princeton, Princeton, N.J., for the National Bureau of Economic Research 1960; see also pp. 112 and 170.

The efficiency mentioned in the opening paragraph of this section is all the more remarkable in the light of the facts subsequently surveyed. The market is one of many issuers, many issues, and some degree of technical complexity. Withal, the margins taken in the underwriting process are remarkably small. These margins vary, but a high-quality borrower frequently markets its obligations with a cost of less than 1 percent of the capital sum involved. What is even more amazing is that this modest margin is often accorded quite small borrowers *if they are of very high credit standing.* Many bond issues of under $1 million have been sold for less than 1 percent of their par value. Low-quality issues and very small ones (under a quarter of a million) encounter costs materially higher, of course.

This efficiency raises an important question which will be considered elsewhere: Is it size or credit quality that accounts for the high cost of raising capital for small corporations?

REVENUE BOND MARKETING

The majority (but a dwindling majority) of state and local government obligations are "full faith and credit," or general credit obligations of the issuing bodies. The taxing power of their issuers protects these obligations. Some governmental authorities, however, have no taxing authority and can support their obligations only out of specific kinds of revenues. For example, sewer bonds are often of this nature; they are serviced and repaid from service charges or specified assessments on users in the areas in which they are installed. In addition, governmental authorities have sometimes been created to construct special facilities such as bridges, tunnels, or airports and have been given borrowing power to finance such construction. Payment of their obligations, however, is based only on the revenues that they can earn. The credit and value of these bonds depends on the ability of the projects they finance to earn revenues. The record is not without some failures.

The bonds issued by such authorities are "revenue" bonds; that is, they depend on the revenue they can raise, and the issuers have no power to tax. In the credit analysis of such bonds, the general wealth of the area, tax rates, the assessed value of property, and similar matters have no relevance; the one relevant factor is the ability of the authority to raise revenues from the users of the facility it provides. In the case of many sewer systems, this assurance is pretty high; unless an area is abandoned, sewers are likely to be used and paid for. However, the demand for the services of some revenue projects is elastic, even if they are a monopoly supplier of their service as in the case of a bridge. The amount of revenue is not under the exact control of the managing authority. Raising charges can discourage use, as some toll road operators have found. The price elasticity of demand may be relatively elastic; that is, raising prices can actually reduce total revenues. Of course, the elasticity is more often relatively inelastic.

At one time commercial banks were denied participation in the underwriting of revenue obligations, although they could invest in them if they were of sufficiently high grade. For a decade, however, they have been allowed to underwrite securities if they were of a quality in which they could invest. This has been an important right for the big commercial banks. As was shown in Table 15-1, the proportion of revenue obligations has grown until it averages about one-third of new offerings. What is more, the underwriting margin on these obligations is wider than on "full faith and credit" obligations and so offers more profit opportunities.

Other differences in the marketing system may be found. Financial advice is more important in the initial arrangement of revenue projects. Some special agencies for handling this part of the problem have developed: Engineers and other experts are frequently consulted in planning these projects. Furthermore, the investment banking connection is more often arranged by negotiation and not quite as universally by competitive bidding; the need for an advisory relationship may account in part for this difference.

The buyers of the bonds tend to be a rather different group of investors, individuals more often than not. Since many of these projects must be financed before their revenue-producing potential can be estimated with any precision, there is a degree of speculation in the initial investment in these obligations. Once such projects have been in operation for a period, their standing as investments becomes clearer. However, an agency such as the Port of New York Authority, which has built many revenue projects (several Manhattan bridges, tunnels, and airports as well as dock facilities), comes to have a recognized financial standing. For reasons noted below, the secondary market for some revenue obligations is rather large and active.

POLLUTION CONTROL REVENUE BONDS

In an effort to respond to the environmental hazards of industrial pollution, the Congress authorized the use of tax-exempt revenue bonds for the financing of capital expenditures, the prime purpose of which is to reduce industrial pollution. In the first instance a private industrial corporation, faced with the need to make such expenditures, plans such a project. If the project is given approval by the federal environmental authorities, the bonds then qualify for tax exemption and are marketed as such. Most of these bonds have been sold on a negotiated basis rather than by competitive bidding. The credit basis of these bonds is the sale of the project to the sponsoring company by the local governmental unit, usually the county, in which the "project" is located. This local governmental unit is the nominal owner of the project in the first instance. Since the payments by the sponsoring company to the county or other local governmental body involved are tax deductible, this form of financing turns out to be a relatively expensive form of subsidy. For this and other reasons, the Securities Industry Association (the trade association of investment bankers) opposed the use of pollution control revenue bonds.

PUBLIC AUTHORITY HOUSING OBLIGATIONS

One other sector of the market has quite special characteristics: the market for obligations of the public housing authorities. The deficits of such authorities are guaranteed by the Department of Housing and Urban Development (HUD) under certain circumstances, and through it by the federal government. These local public housing authorities, however, are considered state and local governmental instrumentalities for purposes of taxation. As a result, their obligations combine the tax exemption of state and local government obligations with the credit standing of a federal governmental agency. Since a fairly large volume of these obligations has been issued in the postwar years—4 percent of the total in the postwar period and 5 percent since 1968—a fairly distinctive market in these obligations exists.

Public housing notes are both short-term and as near liquid obligations as can be found in this market. The use of these notes has represented a most interesting strategic device of the public housing authorities. When interest rates are considered high and likely to fall, they may finance on a short-term basis and then fund these short-term obligations later when the market is expected to be more receptive to tax-exempt offerings. Thus, this is one of the few tax-exempt market areas in which long-term financing is not always in advance of construction expenditures.

As irrational as it may seem, local housing authorities' bonds do not always sell on as good a basis as other Aaa state and local government obligations. This can only be explained by the large volume of local housing authorities' offerings in this postwar market. Some investors like to have a variety of good "names" in their portfolios. Aaa obligations of cities that rarely issue securities have several times sold on a better basis than local housing authorities' bonds of the same city.

SECONDARY MARKETS FOR TAX-EXEMPT SECURITIES

The secondary market for tax-exempt obligations is moderately active, particularly in periods of credit stress. Its size relationship to the secondary market for corporate bonds is not clear, but a rough guess is that the two are about equal. It is, of course, far smaller than that for securities of the federal government. The reason for the relative viability of this secondary market is that few of the principal investors tend to be "hold-until-maturity" investors. The life expectancy of individuals buying tax-exempt securities is often less than the maturity of the securities. This point is particularly relevant when one recollects that tax-exempt securities appear to be concentrated in the portfolios of fairly old and high-income investors: those beyond the age of aggressive investment. Commercial banks, as already noted, are sometimes sellers as well as buyers.

The "credit crunch" of 1966 had the unintended result of broadening temporarily the secondary market in tax-exempt securities. Many banks, under the pressure of credit demands made on them by corporate customers, sold off rather large parts of their tax-exempt portfolios to get liquidity. At that time the tax laws also allowed these losses to be charged against current income. The yields in secondary markets were so high that new investors were attracted—nonfinancial corporations among others—as Table 15-4 showed. In 1969 these nonfinancial corporations were even larger buyers as many banks again sold off holdings.

Some dealers specialize in this market. Most are legitimate. A few, some of which operate from former auction barns near a middle-south city, use high-pressure sales tactics to encourage less sophisticated customers to switch holdings. For example, small banks have been "twisted" in the effort to conceal portfolio losses and increase reported earnings. The margins taken by these houses is reputed to be much wider than in more legitimate sectors of the market.

Margins in the secondary market are wide at best. No public data exist, with one small exception. This study suggested that the bid-and-ask margin was about 2 1/2 percent, which is almost double the selling margin on new issues.[2] Trade association standards suggest a maximum margin of 5 percent.

On the buying side, small investors often can find exactly the bonds they wish in the secondary market without waiting for a new issue that is to their taste. The secondary market is conducted by dealers most of whom are also underwriters, but some pure brokers also operate in this field.

The secondary market is one of negotiation (as is true of almost all secondary markets), but the relationship of new-issue prices to secondary market prices is probably more favorable than is true in corporate bonds

[2] *Business Review,* Federal Reserve Bank of Philadelphia, June 1968, p. 9.

and U.S. government obligations. Although the brokers are primarily secondary market institutions, they are sometimes used to sell new issues; in one famous case a small house bought a very large issue and used brokers successfully to market the issue. This was an impressive demonstration of the flexibility of financial institutions in responding to new conditions in the market.

The secondary market probably tends to dwindle in activity when the new issue market is active and to increase in activity when new issues are in smaller volume. This is almost clearly true over longer periods of time; whether or not it is true for short periods of time is not as clear.

RATES AND YIELDS

Because of tax exemption, the yields on state and local government obligations are below those of comparable maturity and risk in all other sectors of the capital markets. In addition, a number of special points appear to have at least transitory significance.

1 This differential varies a great deal. When state and local government offerings are heavy, it is likely to narrow, so that most of the advantage of tax exemption is passed on to investors and much less is retained by borrowing state and local governments. At other times, when demand for state and local government obligations is high, most of the advantage can be retained by state and local governments, and investors get only a modest remainder.

2 The differential between lower grade (Baa) state and local government obligations and those of the highest grade is often more than the differential between comparable grades of corporate obligations. This circumstance has been less true in recent years than earlier, but it has not vanished. Why? So far only conjectural explanations have been advanced.

3 Prices and yields in the tax-exempt market are subject to greater short-term fluctuations than almost any other long-term interest rate series. The hypothesis has been advanced that this market is subject to a short inventory cycle very much like the one that prevails in some merchandising fields. It is true that large holdings by underwriters have a temporarily depressing effect on this market and that a shortage of prospective offerings has a strongly bullish effect.

4 The term structure of interest rates in this market is almost always an ascending one, even when the yield curve for U.S. government obligations has become flat or humpbacked. The sole exception appears to be the last five months of 1966, when the tax-exempt yield curve was flat. The tight money of 1969 and early 1970 did not produce a return to a flat yield curve in spite of market pressure. No descending yield curve has appeared since modern yield records have been maintained.

    5   The yields on bonds of untested revenue projects are often fairly high. After a project has demonstrated capacity to cover its debt service adequately, then yields tend to fall toward, but never quite fully to, those of general obligations. This results in the capital gains possibilities anticipated by some speculative buyers of new revenue bonds in this market.

Chapter 16

The Mortgage Market

The mortgage market is based on real estate. A mortgage is a legal instrument by which a lender can keep a contingent lien on title to land and the structures attached to the land. Residential use of real estate, including both single- and multiple-family properties, accounts for about three-fourths of the volume of mortgage credit. Because of the social interest in housing and the deep conviction that a good quality of it should be made available widely, government has become very much involved in the mortgage market. However, an appreciable part of the mortgage market is devoted to leveraging the financing of real estate properties producing "cash-flow" income that is partly shielded from income taxation.

Because of this diversity, the chapter will start with a review of a few basic facts about this market. It will then turn to our analysis of the demand for mortgage credit. The demand for housing is, indirectly, a demand for mortgage credit. The demand for mortgage credit to leverage income properties is only about one-fourth of the total market, but because it is both interesting and complex, its explanation will take somewhat more than a proportionate space. The chapter will then turn to the supply of mortgage credit. Here the role of the federal government will have to be reviewed. The chapter will end with a review of the mortgage interest rate structure, which is the product of the impact of the forces of supply and demand that will have been reviewed.

MORTGAGED PROPERTIES AND MORTGAGE BORROWERS

Figure 16-1 shows the basic facts about the properties which were mortgaged and the economic sectors that had used the mortgage as a source of funds. This figure is based on the amount of mortgage credit that was outstanding at the end of 1971. The amount of new mortgage credit being extended is rather more heavily weighted with mortgages on income-producing types of properties and less on the single-family home. High costs of construction and demographic factors have reduced the proportion who can afford the single-family home. Apartments and mobile homes have grown relatively much faster. (Mobile homes, not being firmly attached to the soil, are financed more like automobiles and other consumer goods.)

This figure shows the near identity between the borrowings of households and the mortgages on one- to four-family residences. While a few households live in one unit of a two- to four-family residence (and thus get some income), the amount is small. At the same time the number of one-family residences that are basically (not just occasionally) held for rental is very small. This diagram also shows the overlap between residential and income properties. Income properties account for almost one-third of mortgaged properties, even though three-quarters of properties are for residential purposes. Nonprofit borrowers are presumably churches and private educational institutions that do not have access to the tax-exempt market. The types of properties mortgaged by nonprofit borrowers is not disclosed by available statistics.

Mortgages differ from other capital market instruments in one important respect: mortgage lenders put more reliance on the value of the property on which the mortgage lien is placed for security than on the debtors. Some corporate bonds involve mortgage security, but most realistic security analysts count on the income-producing ability of the borrower more than on the liquidating value of the underlying property. A great many real estate mortgage investors, however, still depend more on the value of the property than on the creditworthiness of the borrower. Uniform mortgage terms are offered in most speculative housing develop-

THE MORTGAGE MARKET

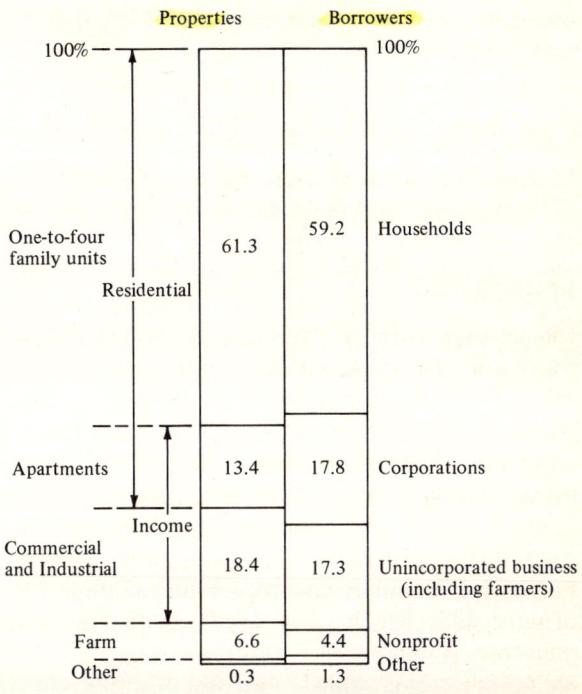

	Properties	Borrowers	
One-to-four family units (Residential)	61.3	59.2	Households
Apartments (Income)	13.4	17.8	Corporations
Commercial and Industrial (Income)	18.4	17.3	Unincorporated business (including farmers)
Farm	6.6	4.4	Nonprofit
Other	0.3	1.3	Other

Figure 16-1 Mortgages: properties and borrowers, end of 1971, percent of total. (Condominiums are treated as single-family residences and not as apartments because they are individually financed.)

ments whether the borrower be marginal or an excellent credit risk. In this respect, mortgage credit has much in common with loans on automobile and other consumer durables. Lenders on automobile loans or home mortgages try to assure themselves that the car or home buyer is not a flagrant deadbeat, but they do not go very far beyond this point in credit checking.

Mortgages also have one other characteristic in common with consumer credit arising out of the purchase of consumer durable goods: the downpayment and maturity terms are often critical factors in the merchandising process. Mass markets have required accommodation of marginal buyers who can put up only small downpayments either on homes or automobiles; owner's equity thus tends to be modest. The maturities of such loans also determine the size of their monthly payments. Before the Great Depression, most mortgages were written with lump-sum maturities. In fact, they were seldom paid at maturity but were renewed often. The monthly payment amortized loan has made the final maturity a more critical matter in finding qualifying buyers. These monthly payments are often viewed as the equivalent of rent and are budgeted in much the same way.

VOLUME OF MORTGAGE CREDIT EXTENDED

The net gain in mortgage credit outstanding fluctuated within the range of $20 billion to $30 billion during the 1960s. In 1971 it abruptly jumped to over $48 billion. The volume of mortgage credit extended, however, was materially higher than these net gains. Unfortunately, statistics with respect to the gross volume of mortgage lending are incomplete except for selected lenders. However, it is possible to make rough estimates from other known facts about mortgage practices.

It can be estimated that regular contractual payments on outstanding mortgages in the year 1971 were about $20 billion. To produce a net increase in the mortgage debt of the amount noted above, mortgage loans which are "new" in every sense of the word must have been written at the rate of $45 billion to $70 billion a year. However, many mortgages are retired in advance of maturity, frequently as a part of the refinancing of a real estate property at the time of a sale. The actual amount of mortgages which were "new" in the sense of a new legal contract, therefore, is much larger. Mortgage financing thus appears to be responsible for at least one-third of the net flow of saving in the United States. No other factor commands such a large fraction of our national resources, at least in peacetime, and no other institutional sector is as important in our peacetime capital markets.

THE DEMAND FOR MORTGAGE FUNDS

For purposes of analysis, the demand for mortgage funds should be divided between those that arise out of home buying and those for funds to finance the acquisition of rental properties. Most owner-occupied dwellings are single-family homes, although a small number of condominium apartments are included in this category. On the other hand, most residential rental properties operated as such continuously are multifamily dwellings.

Another classification of demand can also be used: the distinction between the demand for funds involved in the acquisition of newly constructed homes or rental properties as against the credit involved when an exiting property is sold. The financing of new homes or rental projects usually must be arranged before construction can even be started. Indeed, the terms on which mortgage funds are available may have a decisive influence on the rate of housing starts. The rates on, and availability of, funds for mortgages on existing real estate properties cannot influence their basic supply; they can only influence the price at which they trade.

Mortgages on Owner-occupied Homes

The basic source of demand for housing, of course, goes back to demographic factors such as the number of marriages, the number of children born to such marriages, and the social role of home ownership. In most families in the United States, the home is the largest single asset, the greatest cause of expenditures, and the basis of the largest personal debt. Home ownership is encouraged by our social mores and by the tax collector. During the postwar years the portion of owner-occupied homes has risen substantially to an all-time high level, slightly above 60 percent. Although an increasing proportion of persons and families are moving into apartments, this proportion appears to have stabilized at just about the 60 percent level.

A closely related development occurred during the postwar period. The construction of new homes prior to sale by "speculative" builders has been a common phenomenon for many years. The average size of speculative building firms, however, was generally small. Construction was one of the bulwarks of small business. In the postwar years, a much larger share of home building has been done by rather large operators—builders who scheduled more than a hundred homes a year rather than a dozen or a score as was true in prior periods. Merchandising devices include the prearrangement of financing for buyers. Builders found that mass selling of new homes is greatly aided by the existence of prearranged financing. To some extent commercial banks have extended short-term construction loans only where prearranged financing was available. The mortgage commitment, which will be discussed in later sections, has come to play a central role in the operations of these larger-scale builders.

Prearrangement of financing by builders usually involves the submission of building plans and estimates of construction costs. A speculative builder also needs to own or have options on enough vacant land in acceptable locations to make the merchandising of his houses feasible. After this hurdle has been passed, an institution providing the final financing may be prepared to give a firm commitment to acquire the mortgages generated or "originated" in the final sale of these homes.

The parties to this prearranged financing may include more than the builders on one side and the institutional lenders on the other; an intermediary frequently makes the arrangements. A large part of the negotiation of such prearranged financing during the postwar period has been done by so-called mortgage bankers. The role of this institution will thus have to come up for extended comment at a later point.

Several characteristics are associated with large-scale speculative building covered by committed or prearranged financing. In the first place, the formality of prearrangement increases the chance that the mortgage loan value will coincide with sales price. Since a small required downpayment is frequently one of the principal attractions advertised by builders, they must be prepared to deliver at time of sale. This is, in effect, covered in the early inspection and approval of plans, sites, and the other elements by lenders to such operations. Another characteristic is that mortgage financing under these circumstances is likely to have the longest possible maturity so as to require the smallest possible monthly payments. One of the principal sales inducements is the argument that purchase of a home really costs no more than rental.[1]

One result of prearranged mass financing has been greater national mobility of mortgage funds. A one-mortgage real-estate deal is likely to be financed with local money or by the loan correspondent of a life insurance company. Mass mortgage banking operations, however, particularly when the originating and servicing functions of the mortgage banker are available, can be between remotely located lenders and local homeowners.

The market for existing houses is also dependent upon the availability of credit that will finance such purchases and sales. When existing houses are marketed, the credit arrangements are usually made by the sales agent, although buyers sometimes make their own arrangements. Since this is a smaller market, credit is usually supplied by a local financial institution. Such credit is usually in the form of a conventional mortgage.

One difference is quite likely to distinguish the mortgage credit given in the sale of an existing house as against the credit involved in the sale of a new house. Existing housing has served a part of its useful life; the maturities allowed by lenders on such housing are likely to be somewhat shorter than on new homes. Furthermore, the appraised value for loan purposes is more likely to depart from sales price than is true in the case of speculatively built new housing. For both these reasons the buyers of existing housing are more likely to find the credit terms a bit more exacting in such purchases than would be true of new housing. A larger downpayment will have to be found, and the monthly payments will tend to be a bit larger relative to the capital sum involved. When downpayments are onerous, there is a greater chance that some form of second or junior mortgage financing will be involved in such transactions. Junior financing has, in fact, rather more often than not, been identified with the sale of quite old, often badly depreciated and run-down property. Housing often passes through various stages of depreciation and downgrading, and terminal owners are more likely to be drawn from minority

[1] This matter can be debated endlessly and without conclusive results. Rental and owner-occupied residences are almost never comparable in terms of facilities, so no precise resolution can be made of this issue.

races or lower-income groups that can buy housing only with the aid of junior financing.

Income Real Estate in the Financial Markets

The federal government pervades the market for mortgages on single-family homes, as we shall explain in a later section. The participation of income-producing real estate in the financial markets is almost exactly the opposite. This sector of the market is private and unregulated. It is also often secretive.[2] However, recent public offerings of some of the larger partnerships or syndicates have required the filing of registration statements, which action has reduced the degree of secrecy and has opened these operations to public scrutiny and evaluation. Public ownership of the real estate investment trusts (REITs), discussed later in this chapter, has also exposed more of this market.

The principal types of income-producing real estate include apartment houses or complexes; motels and hotels; office buildings, including those with specialized clients such as doctors, dentists, and lawyers; shopping centers; industrial parks; amusements parks; post offices; and even brand new cities.

The principal difference in the financing of income-producing real estate is that it requires equity capital as well as debt capital. In order to give a picture of the way in which income real estate comes into being, a hypothetical illustration might help: A real estate firm becomes aware of the demand for apartments of a given type and in a given location, possibly from the inquiries it receives with respect to rentals. The firm may locate and take an option on a vacant site that would be appropriate for the type of apartment structure needed. It will then get a firm of architects and engineers to prepare preliminary plans for such a structure. The plans will then be bid by a construction firm. (Some real estate firms have affiliated construction departments.) With the plans and a price on them, it will then seek a commitment from a mortgage lender. With the option, the plans, the bid, and the mortgage commitment, the firm will then seek equity investors. It may do this by organizing a syndicate,

---

[2] The secretive nature of this market is seen in the following two examples. The author of this chapter was asked by a doctor of medicine to evaluate a proposal to join a partnership which would have financed an apartment building aimed at student occupancy. Since the information in the proposal was quite inadequate, I went to the real estate firm which was sponsoring the project. At first they refused to acknowledge that such a proposal existed. When faced with the document itself, they refused comment—and with a show of hostility. Second illustration: An ad in *The Wall Street Journal* invited participants with funds in units of $100,000 or more to join in a real estate venture that promised a cash flow rate of 9 percent. I wrote to the postal box address given and, while denying the possession of $100,000 for such a purpose, explained that, as a textbook author, I wished to educate both myself and my audience. I received a reply saying: "Ask me no questions and I'll tell you no lies!"

usually in the legal form of a limited partnership, which seeks investors from upper-income groups, such as doctors of medicine, who can take advantage of the special tax-shield character of rental real estate.

The special character of income from rental real estate is directly related to two factors: (1) the provisions of tax law that allow the deduction of depreciation charges that are considerably in excess of real economic depreciation from gross income and (2) the widespread belief that inflation will continue to boost the value of real estate. An illustration of how this works is as follows:

Cost of land	$ 200,000
Cost of structure	1,000,000
Total cost	$1,200,000
Loan of 2/3 (8 percent interest rate)	800,000
Equity needed	$ 400,000
Rental income after real estate taxes and all other cash expenses except interest and income taxes	$ 120,000
Interest on loan	−64,000
Accelerated depreciation (first year)	−60,000
Net *loss* for tax purpose	($ 4,000)

But after-tax cash flow ($120,000 − $64,000) of $56,000 is 14 percent on $400,000. The equity holder also has a loss charged against his other income.

Of course, the accelerated depreciation declines as time goes on and more and more of the income becomes taxable. But this opens up the next step. If real estate does continue to go up in price as a result of inflation and if the accelerated depreciation is greatly in excess of real economic depreciation, the owners of this project may sell the apartment to a new set of owners, perhaps at the same price of $1,200,000. The new group can start depreciating on the new higher basis. The selling group, according to present tax rules, will have to pay taxes at regular rates if it sells before 8 1/3 years (100 months); but after 16 2/3 years (200 months), all excess of sales price over book value is treated as capital gains. Between 100 and 200 months, the excess is prorated between regular income and capital gains at the rate of 1 percent a month.

Variations on the system are many. For example, the land, which is not depreciable, may be sold to an investor who does not pay income taxes, such as a pension fund or a university endowment fund. This land is then leased back to the project with a long-term contract or "ground rent" which is net of all real estate taxes or other expenses. The income from this lease would be fully subject to income taxes if held by a taxed investor. The remaining or depreciable part of the property will then be syndicated to investors who can use a tax shield. The holder of the ground rent inherits the full structure at the end of the lease, together with any renewals available and taken. Columbia University owns the ground under Rockefeller Center and, if the structures last long enough, will someday own it all.

The illustration given above can be varied to show how this would work. Suppose the land is sold to a tax-exempt pension fund for its cost of $200,000 with a leaseback at the net rate of 10 percent. The leaseback may run for thirty years, with two fifteen-year renewals available to the renters. The calculation of equity return is now as follows:

Rental income	$120,000
Less interest	−64,000
Accelerated depreciation	−60,000
Land rent	−20,000
First-year tax loss	($ 24,000)

Cash flow ($120,000 − $64,000 − $20,000 = $36,000) is 18 percent on the $200,000 equity; and the tax loss is an even bigger charge against other income! For investors in a 50 percent tax bracket, this amounts to a first-year tax-free income of 24 percent!

Junior Mortgage Demand

The inventors of the insured mortgage hoped that the higher permissible loan ratios would make junior financing unnecessary: No buyer would be forced to pile a second layer of debt on top of the first one for home purchase. In the insured and guaranteed mortgage field, this hope has been realized to a fair extent. Indeed, such additions are contrary to the rules at time of original granting of these loans. On conventional mortgage loans, however, the loan-to-assessed-value ratios often leave margins to be covered. The second mortgage is still with us.

A second mortgage is not supposed to accompany an FHA[3] loan when it is first made. VA loan values have been so high that the need for them at a time of original extension is not clear. The interest rates on many of these loans made in earlier years, however, were so low by current standards that when houses subject to such mortgages have been

[3] FHA and VA mortgages will be explained later in this chapter. In addition, the glossary lists and explains the various acronyms used in the mortgage market. These terms may vanish as HUD (again see glossary) reorganizes its housing operations and subsidies.

sold, it has often been advantageous for buyers to assume the existing mortgage. Its amount, however, may be less than the new purchaser needs to finance the transaction, so a junior mortgage may be added on the second transfer. Various kinds of junior mortgages have been developed in the financing of income properties. The rates involved are often quite high.

Such financing is usually for the purpose of facilitating the sale of property. Since the sellers often resell or "discount" second mortgages, the process involves a concealed higher interest rate and lower cash value of properties involved. Second mortgages are also used for other purposes, as to finance improvements.

The nominal contractual interest rate on junior mortgages is often limited by the usury statutes. If the mortgage is salable only at a discount, its true yield may be materially higher. Since junior mortgages are usually for shorter terms than first mortgages and are now usually amortized by monthly payments, any discount increases yield materially. For example, if a 7 percent five-year junior mortgage with equal monthly payments were sold for "90" (which means 90 percent of the par or face value), its annuity yield, if paid according to contractual terms, would be nearly 14 percent. This computation is never precise in practice. Although most junior mortgage loans are ultimately collected, default of the contractual terms is not at all uncommon.

The borrowers on second mortgages tend, as already hinted, to be lower-income buyers, often members of minority races and without much financial sophistication. There are exceptions, however; second mortgages are sometimes put on income or rental properties by quite sophisticated investors in order to attain a higher "leveraged" rate of return.

Second mortgages are marketed through brokers who may perform this function on a part-time basis. The full-time job of such brokers is often that of real estate salesmanship, management of a savings and loan association, or even management of a bank. The investors in junior mortgages are almost all individuals, usually a rather specialized kind of investor. They are frequently older men with some knowledge of real estate who are willing to keep an eye on such investments and to apply personal collection pressure if necessary. This market is completely local, but within such markets junior mortgages may be quite salable and even enjoy some liquidity. After a period of seasoning which demonstrates the payment record of the buyer, they may be resold at a lower yield or higher price. Some brokers are also investors and hold junior mortgages through a seasoning period before reselling them. In some cases they are even held with bank credit, which can produce a surprising degree of leverage.

THE SUPPLY OF MORTGAGE FUNDS

The supply of mortgage funds is more than a matter of economic analysis; the subject has become an issue of political importance. The supply of funds has been described as "erratic," although a survey of the record suggests that this description is extreme. However, in 1966 and again in 1969 and the greater part of 1970, funds from private sources were indeed short. As a result, federal government programs were geared up to fill this gap. Institutional participation has also changed both in character and amount. In this section of this chapter we shall first examine the changed nature of the market participation. We shall then review the changing and increasingly complex role of the federal government in this market. Finally, we shall note some specific factors in the participation of various institutional lenders in this market.

Figure 16-2 shows the distribution of mortgage holdings both in terms of dollars and as a percentage distribution for three dates: 1945, 1958, and 1971. Because the growth has been so large, the upper part of this figure shows little discernible detail in the bar for 1945. The lower section, however, reflects the changes in relative importance of holders. Households were the largest holders in 1945, with a third of the total. They actually increased their holdings almost four times in the next twenty-six years, but in spite of this their relative holdings declined to less than a tenth of the total! The most important feature of this figure, however, is a demonstration of the emergence of the savings and loan associations as the dominant mortgage lenders.

The type of mortgage preferred and the methods of acquiring mortgages vary greatly among these institutions. Since the relative tightness or ease of these various institutions do not always follow the same patterns, the market is subject to shifts in flows. Nevertheless, it is generally true that a high degree of competition prevails in this market. The great success of the savings and loan associations in the postwar period has attracted the envy of other financial institutions and forced them to modify their operating methods. Interest rates on mortgage funds have risen, but not because the competitive drive to acquire mortgages was absent. It can also be said that savers have gained because of this keen competition; the rates paid to secure the funds with which to make mortgage loans have increased more during the postwar years than the mortgage rates themselves.

Savings and Loan Associations

These associations are primarily mortgage lenders. The original form of their title—building and loan associations—emphasized this purpose.

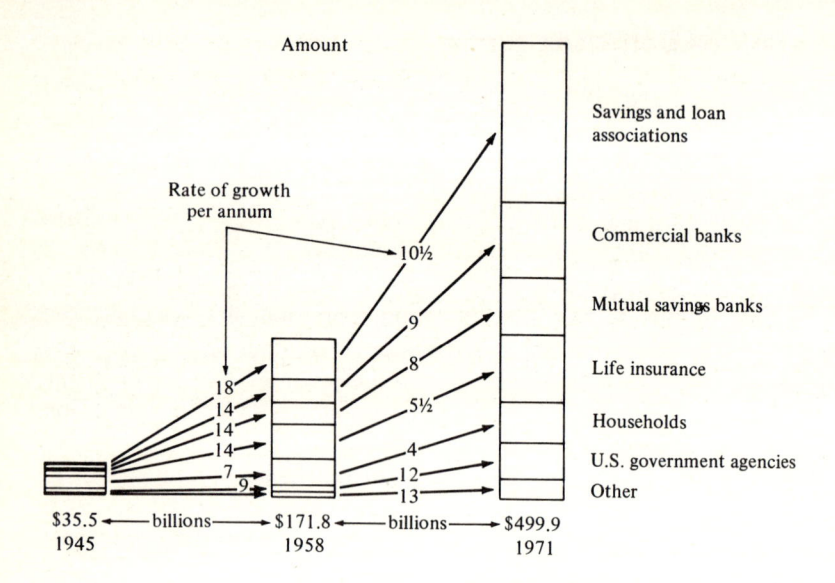

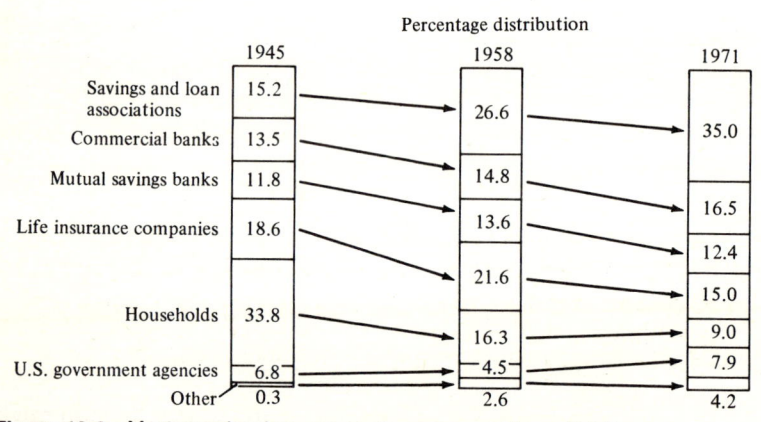

Figure 16-2 Mortgage lenders: amounts and percentage distribution for 1945, 1958, and 1971. (Growth rate for "other" 1945 to 1958 not significant since starting base was negligible.)

Early associations were expected to facilitate the pooling of members' savings so as to permit each member to build a home. The order in which that privilege was exercised was sometimes settled by lot. Some associations expected to disband once the objective of home building by the original members had been accomplished. Since then they have evolved into rather different institutions. More emphasis is put on the promotion of saving. Those who borrow from them are not the only ones who use them as vessels for their savings.

THE MORTGAGE MARKET

Until the early 1960s savings and loan associations grew more rapidly than any other major type of mortgage lender. They competed vigorously for savings and used them all for mortgage lending. However, in the mid-1960s banks became more vigorous competitors for funds and also more active mortgage lenders. In the "credit crunch" of 1966, the flow of funds into savings and loan associations dwindled and mortgage lending was brought almost to a standstill as they attempted to fulfill previous mortgage loan commitments. It was only by massive recourse to funds that the Federal Home Loan Bank System was able to raise in the capital markets that they were able to maintain a reasonable degree of current lending activity. At that time Federal Reserve Regulation Q (see Chapters 9, 10, and 11) was used to curb bank competition. A similar but somewhat less drastic pattern followed in 1969 and 1970. This led to the extension of the so-called secondary market for conventional mortgages. This rather complex arrangement will be described in a later section of this chapter.

Since savings and loan associations originate most of the mortgages they hold, they seldom buy mortgages from the mortgage bankers. Many associations are located in parts of the country with strong mortgage demand; additional sources of mortgage supply have not been necessary. On the other hand, some savings and loan associations have originated more mortgages than they could finance themselves. Some of the oversupply of mortgages originated by such savings and loan associations has been sold to other savings and loan associations in areas with weaker loan demand. Thus, this system has provided some of its own mortgage banking facilities. Savings and loan associations also tend to service their own mortgages; that is, they collect payments, keep records, and enforce liens when necessary. Savings and loan associations make some construction loans, but they do not look for such business. Sometimes they give commitments to make loans both on large-scale housing projects and on individual homes.

The savings and loan association started as a mutual or nominally nonprofit institution, and four-fifths of the assets of these institutions are still of this type. However, a number are organized as profit-oriented institutions with stockholders and even holding companies. Several of these are listed on the NYSE. Two-thirds of the assets of California institutions are of this type. They also are important in Texas and in Ohio. It is a tribute to the profit motive that the most rapid and aggressive development of this industry has taken place in states with profit motivation.

Savings and loan associations originate a large fraction of the mortgage loans they hold. Most loans are on individual homes, but recently these institutions have become more aggressive lenders on apartments and now hold more such mortgages than any other type of lender. Most of their mortgages are made in "conventional" form, but they have small holdings of both FHA and VA mortgages. The savings and loan system originally opposed FHA insurance of mortgages, but that issue is no longer of much importance.

Mutual Savings Banks

The basic character of mutual savings banks is quite like that of savings and loan associations. Both are "mutual" in theory but nonprofit self-perpetuating bodies in practice. Both are primarily mortgage lenders. Both like to emphasize their savings promotion. They differ greatly in one respect, however: Savings and loan associations are located throughout the United States, many of them in the growing areas of the country where mortgage demands, at least recently, have outrun local supplies of funds. The mutual savings banks are mostly concentrated in New England and North Atlantic seaboard states.

Mutual savings banks also seem to have a slight preference for conventional mortgages, but when forced to acquire their mortgages in national markets through mortgage brokers, they have turned more and more to the FHA-insured and the VA-guaranteed mortgage. Indeed, the appearance of discounts on these mortgages stimulated interest in these obligations. Some buyers of mortgages, such as life insurance companies and some large mutual savings banks, have been rather important sources of loans for rental real estate; in this market they are national factors.

Mutual savings banks do not have inflows of funds as regular as those of life insurance companies and thus have not been able to use the same mortgage acquisition techniques. Some mutual savings banks prefer to buy mortgages from mortgage bankers after the mortgages are originated rather than to give early commitments. However, commitments have been given by some of the bigger mutual savings banks. The mutual savings banks in both New York State and in Massachusetts use central agencies in the acquisition of out-of-state mortgages.

Most mutual savings banks make construction loans when this facilitates the acquisition of desirable mortgages, but some mutual savings banks have close ties with one or two commercial banks and prefer to channel construction loans to such banking associates.

One of the problems faced in the management of mutual savings bank mortgage operations has been some irregularity in the inflows of savings funds. These inflows have varied more than those of savings and loan associations and much more than the inflows of life insurance companies. Since mutual savings banks have had fairly large liquidity reserves, they have been able to make some forward morgage commitments and to honor them. They make local mortgage loans and invest in out-of-state mortgages, but local mortgages get preferred treatment when a pinch of funds develops. In the national mortgage market, mutual savings banks are not counted as continuous investors.

Life Insurance Companies

Life insurance companies have relatively fewer mortgages and a much more diversified asset structure than either of the two types of savings institutions so far considered. Furthermore, since the number of life insurance companies is much smaller and since only one of the major companies operates its own agency system for acquiring mortgages, these companies are more or less forced into using intermediate agencies for acquiring mortgages. The mortgage bankers, already mentioned, furnished the principal means for doing this. Owing to the fact that they operate through intermediaries, life insurance company mortgage operations tend to be national. This circumstance has doubtlessly helped to reduce regional differentials in interest rates, since insurance companies hesitate to vary rates greatly between areas for fear of adverse publicity.

Life insurance cash inflow can be predicted with far more success than that at savings institutions. Life insurance companies receive a steady stream of premium payments. Even new sales can be forecast with fair success. With such foreknowledge and with a more diversified asset structure, the life insurance companies can commit themselves with more confidence than other mortgage lenders can. When mortgages are scarce, as they were in the early postwar years, this assurance provides a competitive advantage in getting a supply of mortgages. On the other hand, when conditions are reversed, this factor has been used to improve yield. Some life insurance companies are reluctant to vary forward commitments to acquire higher-yielding mortgages. Some, however, have tried to extend their commitments when rates were high and to resist any softening of rates by allowing commitments to dwindle in periods of ease.

Knowledge of expected cash flow is obviously a help in complex investment operations; still, other institutional arrangements have been made to further this strategic position. At first, life insurance companies, operating through mortgage bankers, simply committed themselves to purchase mortgages when they had been processed and were ready for delivery. Since builders could not tell in advance just how long the building process would take and how fast their houses would sell after completion (and whether or not all purchasers would accept the prearranged mortgage terms), there was necessarily some ambiguity in forward commitments to buy mortgages with respect to time and amount. Some commitments are never exercised.

Rather than undertake an undated responsibility to accept delivery of blocks of mortgages when the mortgage bankers were ready to deliver them, some life insurance companies made commitments which permitted them to delay delivery of completed mortgages. This required that the mortgage bankers fall back on commercial banks for interim credit to carry the mortgages until the life insurance buyers were ready to accept delivery. This interim financing was sometimes supplied by the same commercial bank that had also provided construction loans for the builder. The mechanics of releasing the liens involved in construction loans could be coordinated with the registration of mortgages—a clear advantage if both credits are on the books of the same bank. Life insurance companies seldom advance construction loans, so this arrangement is considered a logical one. Some life insurance companies have themselves "warehoused" mortgages with commercial banks when an overcommitted position made them take delivery of mortgages beyond their current capacity to pay for them.

For many years life insurance companies have been more active in making mortgage loans for apartments, commercial properties, and farms than for single-family homes. Since they generally do not have regional offices, they were at a disadvantage in this area. In recent years this has reached the point where life insurance portfolios of mortgages on single-family homes are being gradually liquidated. Furthermore, many life insurance companies are interested in apartment and commercial mortgages only if they give them some degree of equity participation, a practice described in the next section.

Equity Participation—"Kickers"

While the tax shield of depreciation is a principal feature back of equity investment in income-producing real estate, a degree of leverage continues to be important. Also, to the extent that equity investment in real estate is built on the assumption of continued inflation, leverage has great appeal. As a result, the bargaining by borrowers with lenders on income-producing real estate is often almost as much with respect to the loan-to-value ratio as with respect to the interest rate. Indeed, the rate applied to many large income properties is higher than the rate on a small individual family home.

As a result of more risk with larger loan-to-value ratios, many lenders on income real estate have sought and secured some form of equity participation—"kickers," as this is known. One of the earliest forms was some share in gross revenues such as a fraction of sales above some minimum level in a shopping center. For example, a principal tenant in a shopping center might be given a fairly modest basic rent but would be expected to pay 1 percent of sales above some given level. Many more complex arrangements have been worked out. The lenders which have been most aggressive in seeking equity kickers have been pension funds, life insurance companies, and those for whom the residual and long-term values were important.

Life insurance companies apparently originated this practice and are still the most active in it. It was quickly adopted by those pension funds that participate in the mortgage market. It has even been used by profit-motivated savings and loan associations and by a few banks.

Commercial Bank Mortgage Lending

Although commercial banks are not appropriate mortgage lenders according to tradition, they are in fact rather important lenders in this market. Construction loans, of course, are frequently a necessary part of the building process, and being short-term credit, are quite appropriate for commercial banks. Commercial banks, however, hold appreciable amounts of time deposits and, as savings institutions, can appropriately hold mortgages. Indeed, national banks are permitted to hold mortgages according to a rule which is stated mainly in terms of the amount of time deposits held.

Commercial banks make mortgage loans of all kinds: conventional, FHA-insured and VA-guaranteed. Since national banks and some state banks are limited not only as to the total amount of mortgage credit that they can extend but also as to downpayment characteristics, the conventional mortgages made by commercial banks frequently have rather more restrictive terms than the conventional mortgages made by other lenders.

Commercial banks originate more mortgages than they keep, and they sell an appreciable volume. Some commercial bank mortgage departments originate mortgages for the trust departments of their own or other banks. While unit commercial banks are somewhat limited to the area of their location, these barriers are overcome to some extent by the workings of the correspondent banking system. Big banks sometimes sell participations in large mortgages to smaller banks in need of loan outlets. On the other side, a small bank facing a larger proposition than it can handle may call on its city correspondent for participation and sometimes for technical aid. Branch banking systems, particularly those on the West Coast, usually tend to be aggressive mortgage lenders. Commercial banks also participate in this market by making short-term mortgage "warehouse" loans to mortgage bankers and to life insurance companies and even, on some occasions, to savings and loan associations.

REAL ESTATE INVESTMENT TRUSTS (REITs)

These institutions are a relatively recently developed source of funds for commercial and income-producing real estate financing. The Real Estate Investment Act was passed in 1960, but few REITs were organized in the first eight years. The real surge of organization came in 1969 and 1970, when over a hundred were organized. To qualify as an REIT, a company must have 75 percent of its assets in and derive 75 percent of its income from real estate. In addition it must distribute at least 90 percent of its income to stockholders. If it qualifies by these rules, it then pays no income taxes itself, but all income to the stockholder recipient is taxed.

About half the REITs (a total of about 160) have been independently organized. The other half, which includes a great majority of the large ones, were sponsored by commercial banks, life insurance companies, mortgage bankers, or financial conglomerates. Assets of REITs have been estimated at more than $5 billion. Although this is an impressively large sum, it nevertheless amounts to only about one-twentieth of the total investment in income producing real estate.

REITs share the common characteristic of involvement in real estate, but the form of this involvement varies widely. Some REITs are primarily equity investors in real estate. To the extent they take this form, they are similar to the syndicate partnerships formed for the ownership of real estate. Cash flow rather than accrual income becomes significant. Some of the equity-type REITs have distributed this cash flow which makes them quite similar to the syndicate partnerships. Only a part of the distribution to shareholders is of taxable income. However, this tends to be a liquidating enterprise, and other equity-type REITs retain and reinvest cash above accrual income.

Another type of REIT is one which engages in real estate development and makes construction loans. During tight money, the effective interest rates on construction loans were very high, sometimes as high as 15 percent per annum. At all times, construction lending tends to be a high-risk and high-rate type of lending demanding unusual skill on the part of the lender. Some REITs of this type did very well during tight

THE MORTGAGE MARKET

money, but they started to earn far less when their loans were being paid off in an easier-money period.

Still other REITs appear to be mainly long-term mortgage lenders, although generally with some kind of equity participation. In fact, many REITs are combinations of these various characteristics. Some have changed in character as they operated. In other words, REITs do not lend themselves to clear-cut classification.

After 1970, relatively few new REITs were organized. However, a number of existing ones returned to the capital markets for additional funds. While equity furnishes much of the capital structure of REITs, many of them also have material amounts of debt outstanding. In most cases this is long-term debt. Such debt is often convertible into common stock. A few of the larger REITs, with prestige sponsorship, have used and use the commercial paper market for short-term financing.

REITs appeared to develop rapidly primarily during periods of tight money. They were sponsored mainly by institutions that may have had more real estate projects than they could finance. If so, are they a temporary phenomenon not likely to grow further if and when money eases? It is probably true that they can at least hold their present relative position because they open up a new investment outlet for a group of investors that did not heretofore have access to real estate investment.

MORTGAGE BANKING

Long before World War II mortgage brokers and mortgage bankers were functioning in the arrangement of mortgage credit. The large-scale development of this system, however, was largely a product of postwar developments. When life insurance companies and later the mutual savings banks started to go outside the area of head office location to acquire mortgages, mortgage bankers became the middlemen between the new larger-scale speculative builders seeking mortgage commitments and these lenders. Mortgage bankers also played a continuing role in the servicing of the mortgages that they originated. The usual fee for servicing—½ of 1 percent—is a fairly important part of most mortgage bankers' income.

The fairly simple commitment arrangements first used became complicated when the institutional investors did not always find it convenient to acquire the mortgages originated for them at the moment when they were completed. Before the 1951 Treasury–Federal Reserve "Accord," when Treasury security prices were pegged, insurance companies in need of funds could always sell long-term U.S. government securities. When price support was dropped, the timing of such sales became a much more critical matter. Commitment arrangements were consequently revised, so that mortgage bankers were expected to be able to carry completed mortgages for at least a short period before final delivery. This, of course, required access to bank credit. Still other devices were invented, including so-called "standby" commitments, which were often at prices below the market but at least enough to bail out projects so protected.

Why were commitments needed? Commercial banks, as short-term lenders, hesitated to give construction loans to a project without assurance that the sale of completed homes could be financed. They might be willing to assume the risk of sale when the builder had a good record and basic demand was strong. However, a housing project without financing could become a badly frozen asset if tight money markets should arise. Some savings institutions had been embarrassed by having let themselves become overcommitted, and new commitments have not always been easy to arrange. Thus the standby could serve to hold place pending a better deal.

Mortgage bankers hesitate to commit themselves to builders unless reasonably well assured of a final buyer of the mortgages to be generated; they also know that commercial bank credit for warehousing these mortgages is usually unavailable in the absence of a final commitment. Rather than turn down otherwise attractive offers from builders when institutional investors had no funds, mortgage bankers sought "standby" commitments. Commercial banks have been the most frequent source of such standbys, and this function has sometimes been linked with the supplying of warehousing credit.

FHA-insured and VA-guaranteed mortgages have been the preferred vehicle for mortgage banker operation, but the development of a secondary market for conventional mortgages has increased their participation in this form of mortgage. Mortgage bankers originally handled mainly loans on individual owner-occupied homes; however, mortgages on large rental properties are an increasing part of their business. Intermediate-sized apartment house financing has often been arranged by mortgage bankers, and they often service such mortgages after originating them.

Good mortgage bankers know the preferences of institutional investors and can often help builders to tailor their plans to the known taste of these final lenders.

FEDERAL GOVERNMENT AGENCIES IN THE MORTGAGE MARKET

For almost forty years the federal government has been using one means or another to support and stimulate home buying, home building, and the mortgage market. Not only have several new agencies been created but

THE MORTGAGE MARKET

the functions of agencies have been changed, enlarged, and sometimes shifted to other agencies. The present system can only be described as one of complexity, overlap, and ambiguity. Some programs have been very successful, but others have been marked by fraud and failure.

In the section below we shall start with a brief description of the federal government agencies involved in the field at the time this is written (summer of 1972). In order to make this description as clear as possible, it will be organized according to function and means. Figure 16-3 is a graphic display of the agencies and their functions and means. The principal functions are, as shown in the figure, to (1) insure and guarantee mortgages, (2) make secondary markets in mortgages, (3) support private mortgage lending institutions (principally savings and loan associations), and (4) subsidize home ownership or occupancy. The following sections will cover these four elements.

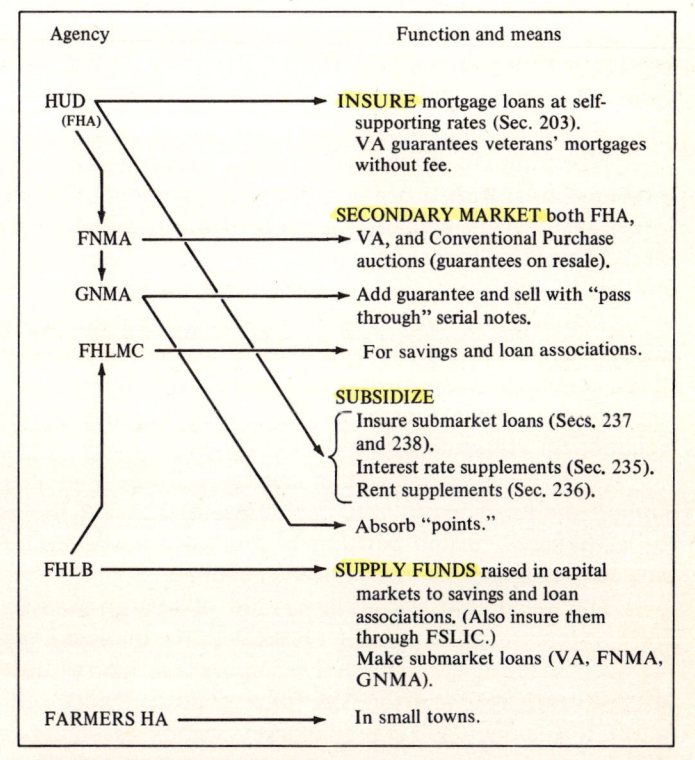

Agency	Function and means
HUD (FHA)	INSURE mortgage loans at self-supporting rates (Sec. 203). VA guarantees veterans' mortgages without fee.
FNMA	SECONDARY MARKET both FHA, VA, and Conventional Purchase auctions (guarantees on resale).
GNMA	Add guarantee and sell with "pass through" serial notes.
FHLMC	For savings and loan associations.
	SUBSIDIZE Insure submarket loans (Secs. 237 and 238). Interest rate supplements (Sec. 235). Rent supplements (Sec. 236).
	Absorb "points."
FHLB	SUPPLY FUNDS raised in capital markets to savings and loan associations. (Also insure them through FSLIC.) Make submarket loans (VA, FNMA, GNMA).
FARMERS HA	In small towns.

Figure 16-3 Federal government support to the mortgage market. (By the time this text is published, the FHA name may have vanished with the function performed by a division of HUD. The distinction between self-supporting and subsidizing insurance of loans is weakening.)

Mortgage Insurance and Guarantee

This is the oldest and most fully developed channel for federal government support of the mortgage market and of housing.

During the attempted recovery from the Great Depression in the 1930s, the federal government started a system of mortgage insurance under the FHA. This system of mortgage insurance has been revised and its terms changed many times. A brief expository account of the mortgage market should not undertake to describe the prevailing terms; they are almost sure to be obsolete before the account is available to readers. However, several points about this system should be noted. In the first place, insured mortgage loans are made for amounts much nearer to 100 percent of the appraised value of the underlying properties than is true of conventional mortgages. Furthermore, the lower the price range for the property, the larger the allowable debt-to-assessed-value ratio. An insurance fee ($\frac{1}{2}$ of 1 percent per annum) is charged and the rate on the mortgage is nominally controlled. The principal feature of the FHA mortgage, however, is that it is always "amortized," that is, retired by regular monthly payments. Before the 1930s most mortgages (except those of savings and loans associations) were lump-sum obligations. Now almost all are amortized.

When initiated in the early 1930s, the insured mortgage system was a method of restoring order in the mortgage market demoralized by the Great Depression and of aiding economic recovery. Later it became a kind of welfare measure. Greater benefits for low-income buyers are implicit in the larger debts permitted for lower-valued houses. Furthermore, the measure has become not just a general antidepression measure but is aimed at the relief of residential construction even when other parts of the economy are not particularly depressed. Whenever home construction activity slackens just a bit, the powerful home builders' lobby starts a clamor for still easier terms.

Governmental support of mortgage credit has also been used to support the financing of veterans' housing. The VA has been authorized to "guarantee" certain portions of mortgage loans made to veterans for purposes of home buying. No fee is charged.

The maximum permissible ratio of loan-to-assessed value under both systems was set at a high level with the implied hope of eliminating the second mortgage. The FHA imposes an interest-rate ceiling on its insured mortgages and the VA follows along. These ceilings have been adjusted to money and capital market conditions—but usually with some reluctance and delay, since interest rates are an issue of considerable political impact. The existence of the ceiling has given rise to the need for the so-called secondary market, described in the next section.

The "Secondary" Market in Mortgages

When interest-rate ceilings made insured and guaranteed mortgage loans unattractive to free market investors, there was political pressure for the federal government to support the market. At first this was a very simple system in which a government agency, the Federal National Mortgage Association (FNMA or "Fannie May") was expected to buy FHA and VA mortgages during tight money markets and then sell off its holdings during subsequent easier money markets. This is not, of course, a true secondary market any more than the government purchase of agricultural surpluses is a true secondary market. Recently the system has been greatly changed and enlarged to cover conventional mortgages. New devices have been invented to stimulate the flow of funds into mortgages. FNMA was spun off into a private corporation listed on the NYSE. Two new agencies of government have been created. The Government National Mortgage Association (GNMA or "Ginnie Mae") accepts bundles of mortgages from sellers—generally mortgage bankers in areas of excess demand—guarantees the package, and sells it to investors through two types of securities: "pass throughs" or serial bonds. In the first form the full cash proceeds, both interest and principal repayment, are "passed through" to investors after servicing charges are deducted by the originators. The serials do approximately the same, but at stated intervals. Investors may purchase whatever maturity they prefer. Both types have lives of about twelve years.

FNMA now conducts purchase auctions every two weeks for FHA and VA mortgages and about once a month for conventional mortgages. The sellers, mainly mortgage bankers, offer mortgages, and the FNMA accepts offers up to such rate as it decides. The FNMA both purchases and also makes commitments to purchase. Presumably the FNMA also sells mortgages, and in fact it does so occasionally. If a lower interest-rate period should come, or one in which mortgage demands should decline, it might sell off much or most of its portfolio.

In essence, both the FNMA and GNMA function to absorb the flow of mortgages when the regular channels do not have enough funds. They do this by borrowing from the agency market (described in Chapter 13) which has support if not direct guarantee of the federal government.

A new agency for making secondary markets in mortgages was created in 1970: The Federal Home Loan Mortgage Corporation (FHLMC) under the general guidance of the Federal Home Loan Bank System (FHLBS). It will make a secondary market primarily for savings and loan associations. Its distinctive service appears to be to offer commitments to buy mortgages at fixed rates of interest so that it, rather than the lender, bears the risk of interest rate changes.

At this writing (summer of 1972) it is still too early to assess the functioning of this multiple system. One interesting current development may have significance for the future. The savings and loan associations, flush with much new money in 1971, became one of the principal investors in the "pass through" securities offered by the FNMA. In other words, these agencies might turn out to be mainly involved in the redistribution of mortgages and funds *within* the system of mortgage lending institutions.

FHLBS: Support of Savings Institutions

The FHLBS was created in 1932, in the depth of the Depression, as an agency for using its market borrowing power to give liquidity to savings and loan associations. In the beginning it was not viewed as a way of supporting mortgage lending. However, in the rapid postwar expansion of the savings and loan system, it came to support savings and loan associations more often when faced with excess mortgage demands than with share cashing. At first, the FHLBS support came in years of unusual mortgage demand, but in the 1960s the savings and loan growth rate slackened a bit, and for several successive years FHLBS support was steadily increased. In 1966 and 1969, years of credit stringency, there was special demand for this support.

The degree of federal government support to the mortgage market through this agency and the "secondary" market purchases described in the previous section may be seen in Figure 16-4. In the year 1969, federal government support accounted for more than 40 percent of the mortgage credit extended, and in several other recent years the proportions were also high.

Subsidy: HUD and Others

The federal government has started massive programs of housing subsidy. Strictly speaking, this subject might not be appropriate for a review of capital markets except for one fact: One of the principal subsidy channels has been that of insurance of substandard mortgages and also direct payments which are passed through the mortgage market channels.

The entrance of Housing and Urban Development (HUD) into housing and mortgage subsidy is through a variety of programs too complex for description here. The programs are aimed at providing housing for those who could not afford it with their own means. As this is written, the FHA, which is under HUD, may disappear as an agency as such, and the distinction between self-supporting mortgage insurance and subsidized mortgage insurance may become blurred or even vanish.

THE MORTGAGE MARKET

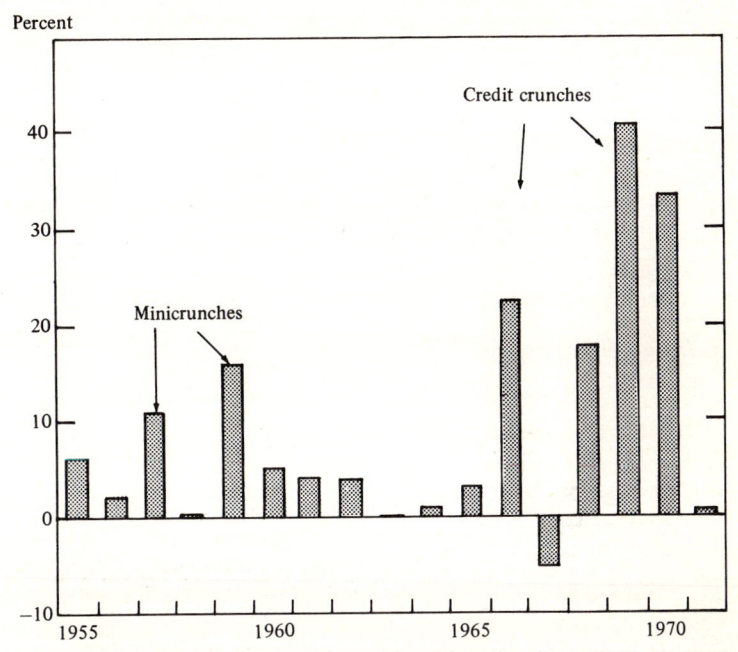

Figure 16-4 Support of the residential mortgage market by federal government agencies. (Net FHLB advances and FNMA and GNMA secondary market purchases as a percent of increase in total residential mortgage debt.) *(Source:* Savings and Loan Fact Book, 1972, *Table 33, p. 40.)*

In one sense, of course, it can be said that all the programs mentioned in the last few sections reflected government subsidies in one way or another. The new programs, however, involve more than the lending of the federal government's name to agencies and capital market instruments; they involve appropriated funds. Unfortunately, some of the subsidy programs appear to have become bogged down in fraud, graft, and incompetence.

PRIVATE INSURANCE OF MORTGAGES

The transformation of FHA from an agency of just mortgage insurance into one of social welfare has seemed to bog it down in enormous amounts of red tape, delay, and general inefficiency. Over the years the ½ percent mortgage insurance fee has proven to be more than adequate to insure mortgages of reasonably good quality; it is only when submarket mortgage credit is introduced that it becomes less than adequate.

Attracted by the potential profits in the insurance fee, eight private firms have started the insurance of mortgages. While they do not have the financial resources of the federal government, they have enough to make these insured mortgages quite acceptable in the secondary markets. The amount of business is still small, but the rate of growth is rapid. The scale of this development is yet to be shown. One of the private mortgage-insuring firms showed such large early profit growth that its stock became "hot" and attracted a great deal of institutional support. The traditional, though recently rather muted, opposition of the savings and loan industry to FHA will probably help the development of private insurance of mortgages.

INTEREST RATES ON MORTGAGES

At one time the interest rates on mortgages tended to be rather insensitive to shorter-term capital market influences. Conventional mortgages would be set at rates customary to a community and would stay that way for a considerable period. When the FHA insurance of mortgages was started, the ceiling rate went unchanged for long periods of time and it often became or determined the prevailing rate on conventional mortgages.

When the FHA tried to hold mortgage rates below market rates, investors retreated from the market. It was at that time that the FNMA secondary market operations became significant. In due course, FHA-insured and VA-guaranteed mortgages came to be traded at discounts. This, of course, is parallel to the case where a bond with a coupon below the market rate of interest sells at a discount. These discounts were called "points" and became a considerable feature of the market. Speculative builders nominally absorbed these points, but in practice it was quite clear that they were passed along to home buyers in the form of higher prices. The contract rate of interest understated the true interest cost.

The development of a more active secondary market has given the mortgage rate of interest rather more flexibility. Ceilings are changed more often and they appear to be more responsive to short-term capital market influences. For a period the effective rate of interest on conventional mortgages appeared to parallel the Baa rate on corporate bonds. Recently, however, mortgage rates appear to have drifted down relative to corporate bond yields. This is reflected in Figure 16-5.

Inflation and the Rate of Interest on Mortgages

As argued in Chapter 6, all interest rates have been influenced by the widespread expectation of continuing inflation. In the case of real estate, however, the impact has been particularly important. In the section dealing with the financing of income-producing real estate, it was pointed out

THE MORTGAGE MARKET

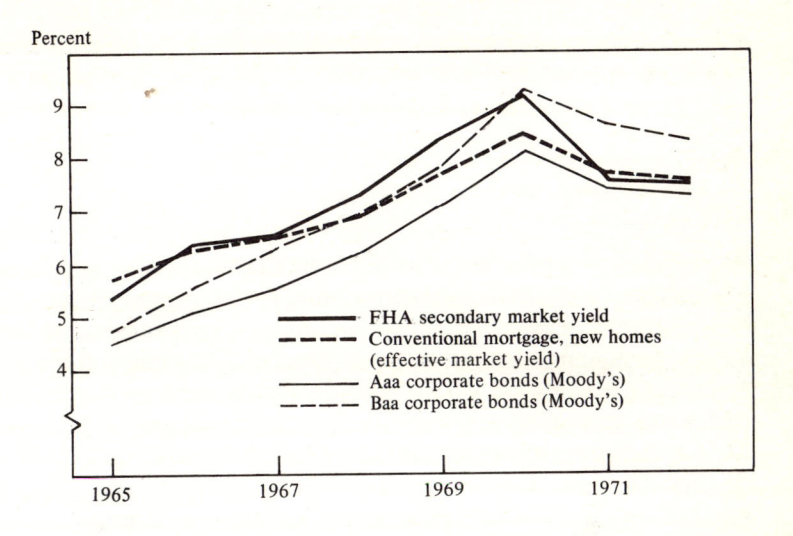

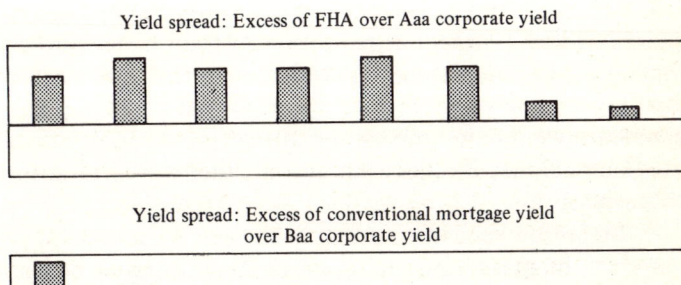

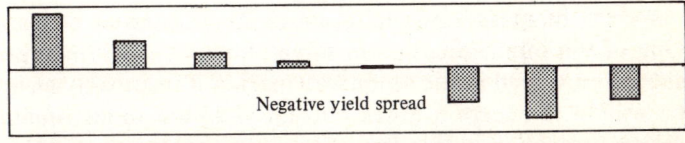

Figure 16-5 Mortgage and corporate bond yields, percent. *(Source:* Savings and Loan Fact Book, 1972, *Table 34, p. 41, and* Federal Reserve Bulletin, July 1972, A. 52.)

that accelerated depreciation permitted by the tax laws is widely believed to be much in excess of real economic depreciation. A large part of this excess is due to the expectation of secular inflation and the resulting increases in the price of real estate. Under such circumstances it is not surprising that the level of interest rates has such moderate impact on the demand for credit. The promoter of a tax-shielded-income real estate venture may find it more important to get a large loan and therefore more leverage than to get a lower rate of interest. Interest is, after all, a tax deduction. This is also one reason why lenders have increasingly demanded some form of equity participation: If they are to shoulder more risk, they wish a return that is not limited to the interest rate but is also geared to the income-producing potential of the property involved.

Variable Interest Rates on Mortgages as an Inflation Protection

One of the problems of savings intermediaries specializing in mortgages (savings and loan associations and mutual savings banks) is that, with fixed interest rates, they cannot afford to raise rates on their savings accounts when interest rates go up; there is too much lag in their income. Thus they not only cannot attract new money but face the risk of loss by withdrawals to other capital or money-market investment outlets.

If, however, their assets had interest rates adjusted to the market, then they could do so and protect their position. The variable-interest-rate mortgage has been proposed as a device to accomplish this result. It was recommended by the Hunt Commission and recently by the Federal Reserve. Both recommendations were accompanied by careful safeguards so that mortgage borrowers would not be led into contracts which they did not understand or which involved unexpected increases in monthly payments. (Most of the proposals contemplate that monthly payments would stay the same but that mortgage principal would be retired more slowly if rates went up—in other words, an automatic maturity extension.)

So far few such instruments have been created. However, it has been urged on the market by such sponsorship that it may be inaugurated soon. One of the interesting and unsolved questions is how these instruments should be valued in the secondary market. Presumably an investor should be willing to accept a lower current yield for an instrument that had inflation protection in this form. However, borrowers could also argue that they should assume this unspecified liability only if they get lower initial rates on any such mortgage. And if they bargain away most of the advantage, how much is it worth to investors?

An even more interesting question: If we should enter a low-interest-rate period in the future, would those instruments have downside variability too?

WALL STREET INTO REAL ESTATE

The widespread move of investors into tax-shielded outlets has pushed many Wall Street investment banking firms into various kinds of real estate activity. Some form limited partnership syndications (with the basic developers being the general partner or partners). These limited partnerships are registered like any other publicly offered security and then sold. Others have sponsored REITs. However, the large part of this business still appears to be in small, limited partnerships which do not have to be registered. A few firms have even attempted to establish secondary markets in the limited partnerships they have formed so that individual partners can "get out" if and when they so wish.

FARM MORTGAGE MARKET

The farm mortgage debt was over $33 billion in 1971; too large to dismiss completely without notice. Nevertheless, two factors justify brief coverage: A large part of farm mortgage debt has drifted into the hands of governmental agencies and thus is outside our primary interest in private capital markets; second, the ratio of farm mortgage debt to the value of farms is so low that no material credit problems arising from this source can be imagined.

Life insurance companies were formerly large farm mortgage lenders, and a few still participate in this market. After the Great Depression, many mortgages formerly held by life insurance companies were absorbed by the Federal Land Banks, the Federal Intermediate Credit Banks, and the Farmers Home Administration. The rates of interest fixed at that time, and since raised inadequately, are so far below market rates as to leave little incentive for private lending. Individual farmers who sold off their farms (sometimes to sons or sons-in-law) often held the mortgages on their farms. An Iowa farmer retired to Florida, Arizona, or southern California may be living on a mortgage held on the old farmstead. Commercial banks in rural areas still make a modest volume of farm mortgage loans.

Farm land values enjoyed a postwar boom far beyond that justified by farm income; city investors bought farms as inflation hedges, and farmers themselves enlarged their operations as machinery made it possible for one man to handle more land. As a result, farm mortgage credit is usually well protected by a thick layer of equity ownership.

Chapter 17

The Market for Corporate Debt

The corporation is the dominant form of business organization in the United States. It accounts for about two-thirds of all business income and a somewhat larger proportion of total business capital expenditures. If farming is excluded from noncorporate business, the dominance of the corporation in business affairs is even more pronounced. Unincorporated business gets some external financing from mortgages and bank loans, but it very seldom is able to enter the national capital markets. The next two chapters, therefore, will deal with the corporations in the capital markets; the next one with the market for corporate equities; and this one with the market for corporate debt.

Corporations are of many kinds. Manufacturing corporations still top the list in terms of volume of business done, even though manufacturing is a shrinking part of the economy in relative terms. An enormous diversity characterizes other branches of corporate business. We will be unable to deal separately with all these types, but several will be singled out for separate but brief mention in this chapter—financial corporations

THE MARKET FOR CORPORATE DEBT

particularly, since they make deliberate and extensive use of leverage in their capital structures and are therefore encountered more often in the capital markets than their proportion of business income would suggest.

The statistics presented in this chapter suffer from a number of limitations. For example, corporations organized solely for the owning of income-producing real estate properties, which were mentioned in Chapter 16, are unavoidably included. The flow-of-funds statistics will be used, but in spite of the great expertise in their preparation, surprisingly large and unexplained discrepancies remain.

CORPORATIONS IN THE FINANCIAL MARKETS

Corporations enter the financial markets for added funds when their internal sources of funds are not adequate to pay for the assets they feel they must add to their balance sheets. Conventional corporate finance often classifies the demand for capital into two forms: fixed capital expenditures and net increase in working capital. However, net working capital itself contains some important elements of financing, particularly short-term bank borrowing. For this reason, this chapter will use the somewhat more comprehensive form used by the flow-of-funds system. Table 17-1 illustrates this choice. The sequence within this table (rearranged somewhat from the way in which the Federal Reserve publishes the flow-of-funds accounts) is from the demand for funds ("uses") to the supply of funds ("sources"). This is based on the traditional logic of corporate financial management. The starting point is the need for funds. These needs are met from internal sources—retained earnings and noncash expenses (mainly depreciation)—and then external sources are used to meet any residual need for funds.

Several points emerge from this table. The rate of growth of fixed capital expenditure averaged about 8 percent for the eleven-year period. This is considerably faster than the growth of national income. While inflation accounts for a part of this growth (price indexes for capital goods have gone up more than the general price level), there has doubtless been an increase in capital intensity. The growth of wages at rates faster than productivity has increased and has pushed corporations into capital expenditures, not just to increase capacity but also to cut costs. In spite of an older traditional idea that capital expenditures were cyclically unstable, they have increased with surprising regularity. From 1961 to 1971 there was an increase every year.

The demands for financing inventory investment and the increased holdings of financial assets are considerably smaller than for fixed investment—and more erratic. The total of the two is somewhat more

Table 17-1 The Demand for and Supply of Funds by Nonfinancial Corporations (Billions of Dollars)*

	1960	1961	1962	1963	1964	1965	1966	1967	1968	1969	1970	1971
Demand ("Uses")												
Fixed investment	36.0	35.1	39.3	41.2	46.2	54.8	62.7	64.8	69.7	78.4	81.6	86.2
Inventory†	2.8	1.6	4.4	4.8	6.4	9.6	16.2	8.4	9.7	12.0	7.1	5.3
Financial assets‡	4.1	10.2	11.4	12.4	9.2	14.0	7.7	9.7	15.7	8.1	14.0	18.3
Total demand	42.9	46.9	55.1	58.4	61.8	78.4	86.6	82.9	95.1	98.5	102.7	109.8
Supply ("Sources")												
Internal:												
Retained earnings	10.0	10.2	12.4	13.6	18.3	23.1	24.7	21.1	19.9	15.8	12.3	17.2
Depreciation	24.2	25.4	29.2	30.8	32.8	35.2	38.2	41.5	45.1	49.2	53.8	59.0
Total internal	34.2	35.6	41.6	44.4	51.1	58.3	62.9	62.6	65.0	65.0	66.1	76.2
External:												
Stocks	1.6	2.5	.6	−.3	1.4	—	1.2	2.3	−.8	4.3	6.8	13.4
Bonds	3.5	4.6	4.6	3.9	4.0	5.4	10.2	14.7	12.9	12.1	20.3	19.4
Mortgages	2.5	3.9	4.5	4.9	3.6	3.9	4.2	4.5	5.8	4.8	5.3	11.2
Loans	3.8	1.3	3.0	3.9	4.7	11.2	9.3	7.8	12.4	18.0	6.4	4.5
Other	1.8	3.1	5.8	5.6	4.0	6.8	6.7	.9	5.9	−.2	−.2	.7
Total external	13.2	15.4	18.5	18.0	17.7	27.3	31.6	30.2	36.2	39.0	38.6	49.2
Total supply	47.4	51.0	60.1	62.4	68.8	85.6	94.5	92.8	101.2	104.0	104.7	125.4
Discrepancy (D-S)	−4.5	−4.1	−5.0	−4.0	−7.0	−7.2	−7.9	−9.9	−6.1	−5.5	−2.0	−15.6

*Nonfinancial corporations include those organized to own rental real estate. These corporations account for most of the mortgages in the external sources and for a roughly equivalent amount of fixed capital expenditures.
†Inventory is without valuation adjustment since corporations must finance to pay higher prices.
‡Financial assets are net of trade debt payable.
Source: *Economic Report of President, 1972*, Table B-76, p. 284, and FRS Flow of Funds.

THE MARKET FOR CORPORATE DEBT   309

stable than either part, however, suggesting that financial asset holdings may be a residual item. This interpretation, however, is not in keeping with the idea of conscious corporate planning of its liquidity position.

The sources of corporate financing follow a somewhat different pattern. Noncash expenses, depreciation mainly, continue to supply a substantial portion of the outlays for fixed capital investment. Depreciation grew at a rate of 9 percent per annum, faster than the growth rate for capital expenditures. This faster growth was very possibly the result of accelerated depreciation covering an increasing part of the total capital base. Retained earnings, however, have not kept pace. They increased rapidly from 1961 to 1966, but they have declined since then. The revival of profits in 1971 and early 1972 has not been enough to regain the 1966 level.

The result has been an increasing resort to external financing. External financing has grown at a rate of almost 12 percent per annum for the eleven-year period. Since neither loans nor mortgages have grown at such a rate, bond financing has grown at a rate of about 15 percent per annum. That will be the principal focus of this chapter. Common-stock financing, starting from a negligible base, has grown even faster, but that will be covered in Chapter 18.

The volume of corporate bonds shown as a source of funds in Table 17-1 is a net figure. Since the volume of corporate debt retired each year is now approaching $10 billion, the gross volume of new issues is currently running very close to $30 billion a year.

FORMS OF CORPORATE FINANCING

In this analysis of corporate debt we have elected to include both long- and short-term forms of debt. This gives us a somewhat broader scope than if we had limited our inquiry merely to the "market for corporate bonds." The reason for choosing the harder and more complicated alternative is that the two are so closely intertwined in corporate financial management.

From the side of money and capital markets it is quite easy to distinguish the instruments of finance. The corporate bond market stands apart from the market for short-term credit. But from the internal corporate point of view this is not the most important way of dividing the subject matter.

In the minds of corporate management, the important distinction in all financial judgments is between the stockholders' equity and the "outside" funds supplied by others, whether these funds be short- or long-term. Most corporate managements, even those of a professional sort and without a large ownership equity of their own, are conscious of their primary responsibilities to stockholders. Debt is an instrument to be used in such ways and to such extent as benefit stockholders. Whether the debt be long- or short-term is a matter of expediency but not principle. The traditional way of viewing short-term borrowing is that of covering seasonal needs. Such needs still exist and are serviced, but the prevailing management expectations of bank credit are somewhat broader. The preferred form of financing in almost all corporations is retained earnings. If profit opportunities or competitive pressures create demands for capital expenditures or require working capital expansion that cannot be met from retained earnings, then these expenditures and expansions must be financed in some manner. If there is no prospect that the debts can be repaid in the short run, then long-term financing is in order. Corporate managements of companies in volatile industries such as manufacturing often seem to hope that this debt can be retired before maturity from retained earnings. No long-term debt is truly long-term in the minds of corporate managements that hope to retire it quickly. In the fields of public utilities or communications (telephone), debt is used to create financial leverage, and then managements expect it to be with them for as long as human foresight runs. However, most financial managers recognize that leverage may be gained from either long- or short-term debt.

Short-term debt is used when the prospects are that the debt can be repaid fairly shortly or when the period for which it is needed is uncertain. Short-term debt is also used sometimes where the expectation of repayment is not very high but where current conditions in the long-term market make deferral of such financing desirable. Intermediate-maturity financing, such as the term loans granted by commercial banks, is frequently used by manufacturing and commercial corporations for very long-term capital expenditures, but where retirement out of retained earnings within a fairly certain intermediate period is thought to be possible. The term loan has not been much used in those industries that expect to have long-term debts for the indefinite future, such as the public utilities and telephone companies.

Short-Term Debt

Some forms of short-term debt arise more or less automatically in the conduct of a business: trade payables and tax liabilities, which have already been mentioned. These amounts have to be carefully controlled and provided for by a prudent financial management. As we have already said, however, these debts are not negotiated on the money or capital markets so will not be considered further here.

A few corporations issue commercial paper which is sold on the open money markets. Some even use bankers' acceptances when they do international business, which is the traditional way in which such financing is generated.[1] The principal form of managed short-term business debt is bank borrowing. Most bank borrowing in the United States is based on long-standing banker-customer relationships. Even though many individual bank borrowing transactions are short-term, they have back of them a quite different and often long-standing relationship. Banks stand ready to accommodate good customers of long standing for all legitimate purposes even at considerable cost to themselves. In tight-money periods banks reduce credit lines and discourage new borrowing customers. An old customer, however, can count on a great deal of support from his bank.

This residual use of bank credit leads to wide fluctuations in the amount outstanding. Bank credit tends to grow most during years of high business activity and may be liquidated during slow years. Short-term corporate borrowing is sometimes secured; many ingenious devices such as field warehousing have been invented to make bank lending to marginal businesses possible. Banks prefer customers, however, with a credit standing good enough to make unsecured lending possible.

Long-Term Corporate Debt

The principal form of long-term corporate debt is the corporate bond. The matter of form, however, may conceal far more important factors about the way in which such debt is generated. The corporate bond, as it is usually understood in the market, is a negotiable bearer instrument in units of $1,000. Some bonds are in registered form with higher denominations, but interchangeability of coupon and registered bonds is usually allowed. Bonds are often but not always generated by a public sale. The public sale may be one that is negotiated through an investment banker selected in advance and may be arranged by holding a competitive bidding in which a number of investment banking syndicates bid for the bonds, the award being made to the highest bidder. Most public utilities are required to use competitive bidding. Most other corporations, free of this requirement, do not use it, but they "negotiate" bond sales.

For a number of years, however, much long-term corporate borrowing has been directly negotiated with the ultimate lenders: "direct placements." Most direct placements have been negotiated with a single life

---

[1] This fact shows the influence of tradition in finance and business. In a technical sense there is no reason why domestic transactions should not be used to generate acceptances and to secure some quite low-cost financing from the money markets. Trade credit, however, has become so general that few buying customers would tolerate the practice, and so it is not used. This appears to be no-cost financing for buyers, but in the end it may prove to be costlier for both buyers and sellers than acceptance credit.

insurance company or a group of life insurance companies. These transactions, for reasons of convenience, are usually in the form of bonds, often registered bonds interchangeable with coupon bonds. In other words, the word "bond" is not necessarily indicative of the way in which a particular form of debt was originated.

Just to complicate the matter a little further, commercial banks have made longer maturity installment loans to corporations, which are commonly called term loans. The physical form of a term loan, however, is just that; it is not usually an instrument convertible into a bearer coupon obligation such as is loosely called a bond.

A bond is a debt contract. It is a mortgage bond if it involves a lien on some specific property, otherwise it is a debenture or "unsecured" bond. "Unsecured" is put in quotation marks because a debenture usually has fine security, but of an intangible kind: earning power! Almost all bonds, whether based on a mortgage or on the general earning power of the issuing corporation, have their terms spelled out in a detailed contract called an indenture. This agreement spells out the rights and obligations of both parties, mainly rights of lenders and obligations of the debtor. The terms of this indenture contract are usually left to the enforcement of a trustee who acts for bondholders collectively. The terms of the agreement and the duties of the trustee were spelled out in the Trust Indenture Act of 1939, the result of some irregularities which came to light during the dismal days of the Great Depression.

Maturities of corporate bonds have gone through a number of changes in fashion. At one time very long-term bonds, such as for a hundred years, were not unknown. Most of these very long-term bonds were in the era of railroad expansion when it was expected that bonded indebtedness would be a nearly perpetual part of the capital structures of such operations. Perhaps it was the bad experience with railroad finance that led to a shortening of maturities on corporate bonds.

At present, even public utilities, which expect to continue to use bonded indebtedness for the foreseeable future, almost never sell bonds with maturities exceeding forty years. Thirty years is far more common. Industrial bond maturities almost never exceed thirty years, and twenty- or twenty-five-year terminal maturities are quite frequent. Finance companies tend to sell rather shorter average maturities, probably to give them greater control over their future cost of capital.

Almost all bonds provide for retirement in advance of final maturity by call. Premiums are paid for early calls, but later calls involve lower premiums, and finally there is no penalty. A substantial proportion of bonds are called before final maturity.

Most corporate bond issues have only one terminal maturity. It is only in the financing of railroad rolling stock that serial issues (bonds with a sequence of maturities) have appreciable usage. Equipment financing, loans to finance the purchase of machine tools or other types of depreciable fixed assets, is also done with serial-payment or amortized types of loans.

Many term bonds have an indirect provision which may serve about the same purpose as amortization: the sinking fund for retirement of some or all bonds in advance of maturity. Sinking funds are of several complex types which may be reviewed in any good corporate finance textbook. They often provide for calls of partial lots of bonds at prices considerably less than call prices for retirement of an entire issue.

Industries needing large amounts of fixed capital usually depend on bonded indebtedness more than other industries do. Bonded indebtedness is also likely to be incurred at the time of major expansion. This can be illustrated from past railroad history and from past and present public utility history, and the gas and oil pipelines seem to be illustrating this generalization once more.

To some extent investors have changed their view of the value of mortgage security for a bond. Many railroad bankruptcies have shown that a mortgage on a property is of little value unless the property produces a good flow of income. Debentures, which are without mortgage security, have come to be quite acceptable when issued by companies with good earning power. Industrial concerns usually use debenture financing to avoid encumbering fixed property with liens.

In recent years, the largest part of new long-term corporate debt has been in the form of bonds. About half of these bonds have originated through open-market issues. Term loans have accounted for less than one-tenth of the net increase in corporate long-term debt. The ways of originating bonds have varied greatly by industry. Public utilities and telephone companies are usually required to make public sale of their obligations, and many of them are required to offer them for competitive bidding. On the other hand, one public-utility type of industry, the gas and oil pipelines, has financed large amounts by private placement. Manufacturing industry has used direct placement more than public sale, but some very large corporations appear to exceed the capacity of the direct placement system; these very big ones are so large that private placement with a single buyer is not possible. Once multiple buyers are needed, it seems to be felt that a public distribution is easier to negotiate. An investment banking group handles such transactions, and the indenture terms are tailored to the preferences of the issuing corporation (within the limits of investor prudence). In public offerings of the bonds of a large manufacturing corporation, the investment bankers managing the offerings are usually selected by negotiation and not determined by public bidding. The banker-customer relationship is not as much stressed as it once was, but many corporations clearly feel that there is a great advantage in maintaining a long-standing investment banker relationship. While fear of adverse publicity has led to minimizing the evidence of these relationships, they are undoubtedly close. As near as outside observers can tell, these close relationships are as beneficial for customers as for bankers.

Public regulation of the capital markets governs many of the sales practices, including the requirement for competitive bidding in the sale of light and power company bonds. In days gone by, investors were sometimes bilked by unscrupulous security salesmanship. Blue sky laws were enacted years ago in many states to counteract this possibility. They were not wholly successful, and, after the Great Depression, the marketing of large issues of debt to the general public came to be regulated by the Securities Act of 1933. The principal effect of this act is very simple: Issuers must tell the truth and the whole truth about themselves and their reasons for borrowing, first in the registration statement and then in the prospectus covering the sale.

Competitive bidding is discussed in greater detail in Chapter 15, where the market for state and local government obligations is surveyed. Competitive bidding dominates that market and has led to some quite interesting results. In the corporate market, the practice is concentrated mainly in the sale of public utility bonds. The purpose of the requirement has been to assure the public that the cost of capital was truly competitive and to avoid "banker domination" of these companies. The history of the requirement goes back to some of the abuses in public utility financing disclosed in the Crash of 1929 and dealt with in the Public Utility Holding Company Act of 1935. This is not our story, but it should be looked at by those with special interest in the capital market specializing in public utility obligations.

Competitive bidding requires investment banking firms with the capacity to form syndicates large enough to handle issues of whatever size may be offered. Since only one syndicate can win (and the sale may be called off if only one syndicate submits a bid), half the time or more a syndicate is unsuccessful. This requires flexible organization—the ability to form with minimum cost when a sale is announced, to stay together to sell the bonds if their bid is successful, to complete the sale whether the reoffering is sold easily or meets adversity, and to reform for new sales when announced. This cycle of activity puts special demands on the flexibility of the system.

Direct placement avoids the open capital market; the whole process is one of negotiation. However, investment bankers are often parties to these negotiations as financial advisers. Direct placement has some appeal because of lower cost, but in fact it may have emerged because it has some strategic advantages of other sorts. The greatest is that new or unusual financings, which require technical study and might receive poor reception in the open market, may be acceptable in the more limited sphere of highly sophisticated investors.

Life insurance companies' influence on the terms involved in direct placements has been considerable. Since these insurance companies have little need for liquidity, they have offered borrowers relatively long maturities in the form of direct placements, longer than commercial banks have offered in term loans. The repayment provisions have also been influenced by life insurance feelings on call provisions. When the capital markets were easy and investors avid for good bonds, call was permitted almost immediately after issue. While call premiums were a modest barrier to early call, when interest rates were declining a substantial drop in interest rates often made it advantageous for a borrower to call and refund a higher-coupon issue soon after it had been sold. Several large bond issues sold in 1953 were called and replaced with lower-coupon and lower-yielding issues in 1954. Life insurance companies felt the call option to be unfair and unsymmetrical in its working. They started refusing to buy bonds with early call provisions. Some borrowers had to concede no-call provisions for the first five years. However, some public utility commissions refused to allow the companies they regulated to accede to such terms, and for a considerable period life insurance companies have not been active buyers of public utility bonds.

Bearing this in mind, the life insurance companies have tended to put rather restrictive provisions on the prepayment of bonds directly placed. They permit retirement out of retained earnings (although often with fairly severe penalties), but retirement for purposes of refunding at lower rates is frequently virtually impossible.

On other scores, however, the indenture terms applying to direct placements have been reasonably consonant with borrowers' financial needs. Special situations were flexibly handled in this form of financing.

The bank term loan is really more nearly intermediate-term credit than long-term credit. Retirement for refunding purposes is generally prohibited or heavily penalized, as is true of direct placements, but prepayment out of retained earnings is usually allowed completely without penalty. As a result, the life expectancy of term loans as a whole is considerably shorter than their average contractual maturity. Furthermore, term loans are almost always in serial payment form, which makes their average maturity rather shorter than the terminal maturity. The practice with respect to direct placements is not known publicly in full detail, but the presumption is that the serial form of maturity is used less frequently.

For those kinds of business in which cash generation can be fairly rapid and where capital expenditures are limited to projects promising fairly high rates of return, the term loan has many business advantages.

The tailoring of terms is useful, but perhaps the most important feature is that the borrower is able to negotiate his entire credit needs with a single lender: his commercial bank. This intimacy of financial relationship is highly desirable when the borrower feels the needs for continuous contact with a financial adviser. Moderate-sized firms do not find continuous contact with an investment banker possible. They also find a financial relationship with a life insurance company to be rather barren with regard to help and advice. However, the commercial banking relationship has continuity and breadth in terms of financial services.

Term loans also have one material disadvantage: Bankers still have a basic preference for short-term lending. When money markets tighten, commercial banks may limit the amount of term credit they will make available. In the course of cyclical swings, commercial banks are not as dependable a source of longer-term credit as the open capital markets or the direct placement services of life insurance companies.

THE SUPPLIERS OF CREDIT TO CORPORATIONS

In the 1920s individuals were the most important buyers of corporate bonds: They held about two-thirds of those outstanding. During the low-interest-rate period of the 1930s, however, individuals lost interest in this market and it came to be dominated by life insurance companies and mutual savings banks. Commercial banks also bought some corporate bonds. Much of this interest, however, was expressed in the secondary market, since the amount of new issues sold by corporations during that period was small. Considerable refunding took place when lower interest rates made it profitable to call the older higher-coupon obligations and replace them with lower-coupon ones. While refunding does not take any net amount of money from the capital markets, it is likely to cause a fair amount of redistribution of ownership. This seems to have happened during the 1930s. The individuals who were holders of the high-coupon obligations might have been unwilling to accept the new rates; financial institutions, being under more pressure for current interest income, were forced to do so.

During this period, insurance companies developed the direct placement technique. At first, it was primarily a competitive tactic for assuring priority in access to the limited supply of investment outlets. Life insurance companies also saved the costs of marketing when they were large enough to handle such transactions. To some extent the same situation prevailed in the early days after World War II, when financial institutions were trying to lighten their holdings of U.S. government obligations and to convert portfolios into higher-yielding forms.

The basic shift, from that time when there was a shortage of investment outlets to the present time of high capital demand, has led to fundamental shifts in the marketing process. Faced with a much more active demand for loans, commercial banks virtually stopped buying corporate bonds (rail equipment obligations were a slight exception) and bought only tax-exempt securities or Treasury obligations. All long-term funds made available to corporations were in the form of term loans. Mutual savings banks continued to buy a few corporate obligations, but as mortgage demand revived, their interest in them dwindled. Life insurance companies were buyers for a while, but when they came to feel that the call provisions were unfairly weighted against them, the larger ones left the market and concentrated on direct placements. As near as can be read from public evidence, they changed the nature of direct placement in the process. Direct placements, at first, were competitive with open market rates. Under these new circumstances, however, life insurance companies started extending credit more at the margin of creditworthiness and charging much higher rates. They were making long-term corporate credit available to a group of borrowers that might have found the open corporate bond market a little hard to crack. The life insurance companies, however, charged them a good stiff price for this credit.

With so many buyers departing from the market, where was the slack taken up? During the postwar period it was taken up mainly by the pension funds, both public and private, but particularly the former. Later, individuals returned to the corporate bond market.

Pension funds had existed for a long period; their investment policies vary greatly. Some private pension funds consist mostly of the stock of the company sponsoring them, as in the case of Sears, Roebuck. Some favored the bonds of their sponsoring company, as did the pension fund of the American Telephone and Telegraph Company. Public pension funds (teachers' and other state and local government funds) were often limited wholly to governmental obligations.

The postwar emphasis on fringe benefits in the attraction of good personnel gave the pension fund a strong boost. Tax factors favored receiving a part of one's pay in such funds and security was still highly prized by persons considering changing jobs, particularly those who could remember the Great Depression.

Not only did the number of pension funds greatly increase, but for a variety of reasons the trustees of these funds came to be under greater pressure to increase the rate of return on them. Sometimes they switched from fixed-return types of investment such as bonds into common equities, a point that is noted at length elsewhere. Some funds shifted from lower-yielding bonds into better-paying bonds. One of the most dramatic changes was that of public retirement funds, some of which had been investing only in state and local government or federal government obligations. When the investment authority of many funds was broadened, they then became great buyers of corporate bonds. In this process the open bond market found quite a new set of customers. The salesmen of investment banking firms that had been calling on life insurance companies and mutual savings banks found themselves calling more and more on the trustees of pension funds.

Individuals in the Corporate Bond Market

When interest rates were low, individuals were negligible buyers of corporate bonds. The interest returns from savings accounts were often materially better than anything available in the bond market. When interest rates advanced moderately in the later 1950s, there was some revival of individual buying of corporate bonds, but not on a very large scale. Individuals seldom accounted for more than a fifth of the market. However, the rapid advance in long-term interest rates which started in 1966 brought individuals into the corporate bond market in a substantial way. This was an element in the "disintermediation" which was mentioned in Chapter 16. When savings institutions could not raise the rates paid on savings accounts to the level of return available elsewhere in the capital markets, many individuals withdrew funds from savings accounts and went into the bond market. From 1969 through 1971, individuals accounted for just about half of the net purchases of corporate bonds. Some corporations were even reported to be considering issuing bonds in small $100 denominations in order to reach for this market.

MARKETING INSTITUTIONS

When corporate borrowing is arranged directly, such as with commercial banks or with life insurance companies, no separate marketing institution intervenes between borrower and lender. In most other types of arrangements, however, the investment banker facilitates the financing process.

The investment banker is, traditionally, at the very center of capital market operations. In the nineteenth century investment bankers often were the midwives of great corporations, as when the elder J. P. Morgan created U.S. Steel out of an idea and a bold deal with Andrew Carnegie. Investment bankers sat on the boards of directors of the corporations that needed money from the markets; they also sat on the boards of directors of the financial institutions that were investors, such as banks and life insurance companies. Relationships were long-term and paternalistic. Investment bankers made, and then sometimes broke, the managements of the great corporations. Finance was frequently in the saddle of corporate control.

This picture has changed. The Great Depression put investment banking on the defensive. The ties between investment bankers and life insurance companies were weakened as long ago as before World War I by a great investigation (the Armstrong investigation in which Charles Evans Hughes played a large part). Legislation in 1933 prohibited individual institutions from engaging in both commercial banking and investment banking.

Probably the greatest change was that corporations broke their bondage to finance; slack demand for money and the availability of retained earnings made them bargainers on more nearly equal terms. Investment bankers are now wise and helpful members of corporate boards of directors, but they seldom control them nor make an effort to do so. They have been reduced more nearly to their core function: marketing corporate and other debt obligations.

In performing this function, investment bankers have developed great expertise. Some corporations prefer to maintain a continuing relationship with a single investment banking house. That firm forms and manages any syndicates needed to market public offerings that the corporation may make. The investment banker is expert in many ways, two of which should be mentioned. First, markets are changeable and the expert investment banker is a good judge of timing (When should a borrower come to the market?). Second, he is adept at picking the appropriate terms to be put in the bond indenture so they are acceptable to investors under prevailing preferences but leave the borrowing corporation the freedom and flexibility it needs to meet possible future contingencies. Though less noticed than the coupon rate on new bonds, variations in indenture terms are often of considerable significance.

Even though a single investment banking house may keep such a long-term and intimate relationship with a corporation, it usually cannot wisely assume all the marketing risk of underwriting (guaranteeing the sale of) a large issue. To spread this risk, syndicates (short-term joint ventures) are formed among a group of underwriters. The firm (or firms) heading a syndicate expect reciprocity. That is, they expect to be invited to join the syndicates their invitees may form. Reciprocity is a little like the exchange of dinner invitations by suburban housewives (who keep track of who owes whom a dinner as precisely as a racetrack bookie keeps accounts with his customers). Investment bankers many times are partners on one venture and competitors on another at the same time. Underwriters, as contractors of the sale of an obligation, are often joined by still other financial houses who share in the selling operations but are not involved in the core underwriting process. Part of the art of being an effective leading investment banking house and of managing syndicates is choosing good associates, keeping them happy, and having the expert judgment to avoid frequent losses or slow sales which tax the patience and financial resources of smaller members of investment banking syndicates and selling groups.

When bonds are sold by competitive bidding among investment

bankers, the connection of any one investment banker with an issuer is necessarily a more detached and impersonal relationship. Since an investment banker cannot know in advance whether or not he will "win" bonds in the bidding, he cannot spend a great deal of time or energy giving advice or helping the company prepare the issue. The issuing company's lawyers and financial advisers draw up the indentures. Most important of all for an issuing company, since it must announce its intention of selling bonds some time in advance of the sale so that bidding groups can be formed, timing cannot be as precisely judged. In any event, it must make its own decisions about timing. It can seek financial advice about the matter of timing, but in the end the decision is its own. Since the mechanics of competitive bidding are fairly costly and since issuers do not wish to lose the good will of possible bidders, an issuer is fairly well committed, practically if not legally, to selling bonds on the announced sale date once it has issued a firm "invitation to bid."

On the other side, competitive bidding does bring out rather close pricing. Underwriters experience difficulties in marketing competitively bought issues with enough frequency to suggest that they usually come rather close to the top price investors will pay in bidding to get bonds. No one can prove whether competitive bidding or negotiated sales bring lower borrowing costs, but in either case large American corporations have little to quarrel about; they get good bargains in bond money.

Once bonds are in the hands of investment bankers, whether by negotiation or by competitive bidding, the sale process is as rapid as possible. The offering of such bonds is announced by advertisement, but the detailed information required by security analysts and investors is in a prospectus prepared according to the regulations of the Securities and Exchange Commission and also in the even more detailed registration statement filed with that commission. Since the prospectus usually has been available in "red herring" form (without a final price but with some red printing on it indicating that it is a preliminary document), investors have already studied the issue and the current position of the company as revealed by this and other evidence. The only remaining fact to be disclosed is the price itself.

As soon as a syndicate has won a bid, telephone selling starts. With good luck and planning, an issue will be sold before its formal advertisement appears in the newspapers. Ability to buy an issue after the appearance of an ad for a corporate bond issue may indicate that it is not selling any too well. (This is not true of state and local government issues, as was shown in Chapter 15.) Negotiated financings are presold to a greater extent than bonds sold through competitive bidding. The current market among pension funds and smaller life insurance companies is concentrated, so that a relatively few teleophone calls often serve to move a whole issue. A successful issue is one that achieves a small premium soon after the sale. The premium satisfies investors that they have got a good buy: A premium more than "small" might lead borrowers to believe that they had paid too much for the money borrowed.

Although some investment banking houses are better known for their support of and skill in competitive bidding (Halsey Stuart) and some are better known for negotiated sales (Kuhn Loeb), most investment banking houses are prepared to operate in either fashion. Some houses pride themselves in taking leadership and some are mainly selling houses, but hard and fast classification of investment banking houses is not possible.

The efficiency of this system is high; it raises capital at low cost. On big bond issues, the margin is often less than 1 percent. Even on moderate-sized bond issues the cost seldom exceeds 2 percent. It is only on smaller bond issues (under $5 million) that the cost is likely to exceed these levels.

SECONDARY MARKET IN CORPORATE BONDS

Nobody knows exactly how large the secondary market in corporate bonds is or ever was. The volume of transactions in corporate bonds on the NYSE has grown more rapidly than the volume outstanding. (NYSE statistics of listed bonds appear to include some U.S. Treasury bonds, but in the postwar period the volume of them traded on the NYSE has been negligible.) Even with growth, the turnover of listed bonds is very low. However, it appears (no statistics exist to prove the point) that convertible and low-grade bonds dominate the NYSE bond trading. Within this group, the rate of activity may be fairly high.

The secondary market in corporate bonds, therefore, is largely an OTC market. A decade ago relatively few firms made OTC markets in corporate bonds. All underwriters nominally made such markets for a short time after a new issue was sold, but nonconvertible bonds appear to have found reasonably firm holders most of the time. However, the high interest rates of recent years may have increased the relative as well as the absolute size of the corporate bond secondary market. Some evidence grows out of the fact that more firms are in the business of making OTC markets in corporate bonds. It also appears that the portfolio managers for pension funds are more willing to shift position. Sometimes, secondary market movement appears to be related to the new issue market. A practice called "overtrading" is one in which an underwriting house, anxious to move its allotment of new bonds, will trade the new issue for an outstanding one and on such terms that investors get a better deal. The syndicate price is not violated in any formal sense, but the profit margin of the sellers certainly is thinned by this process.

INTEREST-RATE RELATIONSHIPS

The interest rates paid in the form of coupons on corporate bonds (modified to a yield basis by such small premiums as are received by the sellers or discounts granted by them) are rather closely geared to the whole interest-rate structure of the market. Interest rates are one of the more volatile of prices. While long-term rates move through smaller ranges than short-term rates, their movements produce fairly large price effects in bonds, putting interest rates in a class with agricultural commodities and world-traded raw materials.

The interest received on corporate bonds is taxable income to the holders to the extent that the owners are subject to federal income taxes. In this regard corporate bonds are quite different from the tax-exempt state and local government issues, but they are like those of the federal government, which made all its debt issues taxable in 1941. Nevertheless, all these interest rates tend to move together, depending on general conditions in the money and capital markets (Figure 6-3, page 114).

As this chart shows, yields on Aaa or highest-grade corporate bonds move in a fashion parallel with those of the government and just slightly above them. The rate movements are slightly less volatile than those of U.S. government obligations, but most major movements are mirrored one in the other. The average maturity of the so-called long-term U.S. government obligation, on which the statistical series shown in this chart is based, is actually somewhat shorter than the average maturity of Moody's Aaa corporate bonds; if maturities were comparable, the two curves would be even closer together.

This chart shows still another interesting fact: the surcharge of the capital markets for lending to corporations with credit other than the very best. This is measured by the differences between the Aaa and the Baa curves.

The rating of corporate bonds by Moody's and Standard & Poor's has not involved controversy similar to that with respect to tax-exempt bonds. A research study by Hickman, cited in Chapter 6, showed that the ratings were reasonably well supported by relative default experience. That test, however, was of bond performance during the Great Depression. Since there has been nothing even faintly approaching the number of large business failures or episodes of financial difficulties since that time, the applicability of the ratings to present conditions is not as clear. Some portfolios of bonds are often limited to only top-rated bonds—

state and local government pension funds, for example. However, more sophisticated bond investors have come to feel that the ratings exaggerate differences in credit quality and that the higher yield of the lower ratings may more than compensate for the credit risk assumed. Episodes such as the failure of the Penn-Central Railroad still shock the market into a retreat from the lower credit ratings, but some of the new bond funds aim frankly at increasing yield even at the cost of some risk.

The rates in Figure 6-3 are open secondary market rates. Secondary market interest rates seem to fluctuate less than those prevailing in primary new-issue markets. The levels of new-issue yields do not differ greatly from secondary market yields in lower-rate periods. The differences become material, however, in periods of tighter money and higher rates. One technical factor explains a part of the difference. The secondary market during the 1960s handled many lower-coupon issues which gave investors part of their return in capital gains form as the discount on such lower-coupon issues was accumulated. This gave a better after-tax yield than indicated by market rates. Some smaller tax-exposed bond investors sought out low-coupon bonds in the secondary market for this purpose. Overall, however, it seems likely that the new-issue yields are economically more significant. Larger investors can fulfill their investment needs only in this market. A parallel restraint exists on the other side of the market. If a bond is issued during a high-interest-rate period with an early call possible, the price of this bond will bump up against its call price in any subsequent decline in interest rates. Since investors shy away from a bond that does not protect their future income, the yield on this bond may stay above other bonds of comparable quality and maturity but with a coupon that does not bring their price near the call level. Because both low-coupon and high-coupon bonds are affected by special factors in the secondary market, the new-issue market yield appears to be more significant economically.[2]

The high-interest-rate period of the late 1960s and early 1970s showed clearly the influence of callability on yield. Although no extensive recent research on this has been published, it appears that a bond issuer, reserving to itself the right to an early call, had to pay possibly as much as half a percentage point more than on a comparable issue with call protection for five years. However, yield differences between five-year and ten-year call protection were not as evident.

Sporadic research on the subject of new versus secondary market yields has indicated that when yields were low and the corporate bond market was stagnant, new-issue yields tended to be *under* secondary market yields. However, when yields rose, the relationship would reverse.

---

[2] William H. White, "The Structure of the Bond Market and the Cyclical Variability of Interest Rates," *Staff Papers of the International Monetary Fund*, March 1962.

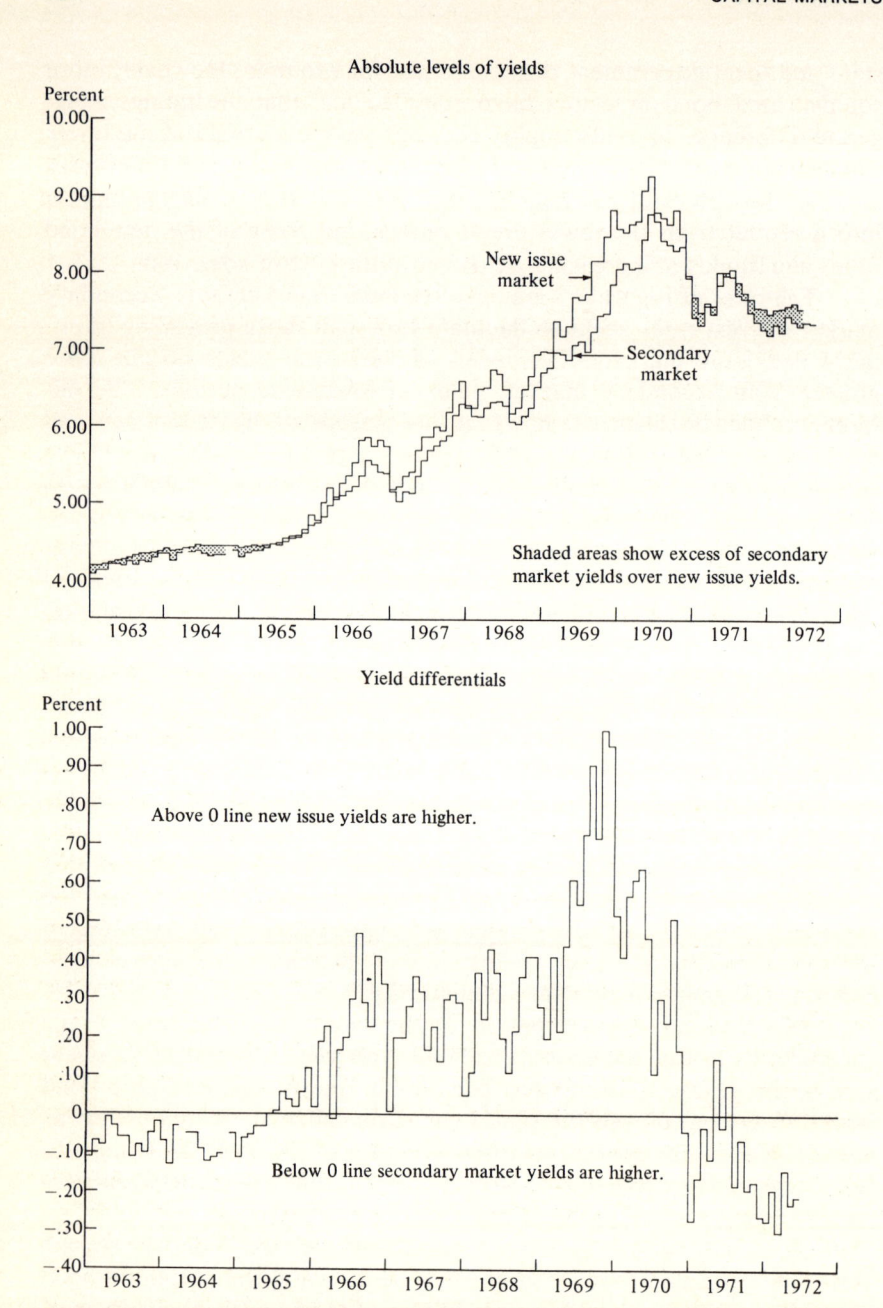

Figure 17-1 Corporate bonds: new-issue vs. secondary market yields. (New-issue yields: public utility AAA from Federal Reserve. Secondary market yields: Moody's public utility Aaa yields.)

This was consistent with the logic that when yield rose, outstanding bonds with lower coupons had two advantages: (1) part of the return was taxed at capital gains rates and (2) such bonds were more protected against early call. Until recently, however, no continuous statistical series on new-issue yields was available. The Federal Reserve is now publishing regularly (starting in the fall of 1972) a series of new issue yields for triple-A public utility bonds. This new series is shown in Figure 17-1. It shows the expected relationship through most of the period covered, but recently it has developed a most unusual and unexpected characteristic: Even at high interest-rate levels, the new-issue yield fell *under* the secondary market yields in spite of heavy market offerings. This circumstance prevailed during much of 1971 and throughout all of 1972. The differential, however, is not large. A possible explanation, so far not tested with research, is that the excess of secondary market yields over new-issue yields both now and in earlier times is accounted for by this fact: New-issue yields are essentially "ask" prices and secondary market quotations are essentially "bid" prices. The differential may be nothing more than the normal bid-and-ask spread.

A second difference is that these open-market yields, whether from secondary markets or new-issue markets, seem to vary somewhat from those reported to prevail in the case of direct placements. An extensive study of direct placements and the yields on them[3] found that the credit quality of direct placements was somewhat lower than that of the bonds offered in the public market. When allowance is made for this factor, yields on direct placements were shown to be higher than those in the public new-bond-issue market by approximately an amount equal to the greater cost of a public offering. In other words, the borrowers may not have paid materially more than they would have had to pay in the public market (assuming that they could have qualified for it at all), but the lenders increased their return by doing the work necessary for developing an effective and protective loan contract.

During the stock market boom of 1967 and 1968, the volume of convertible bonds offered the public market increased materially and has remained fairly high since then. However, the proportion has never been a large part of the total public bond market. Direct placements, on the other hand, were usually joined with some form of equity participation. In this respect direct placements were quite parallel to the mortgage loans on income-producing real estate ventures described in Chapter 16. It is also significant that the volume of direct placements did not grow materially during the upsurge of public offerings starting in the late 1960s.

[3] Avery B. Cohan, *Yields on Corporate Debt Directly Placed*, New York, Columbia University Press 1967. A part of the financial research program of the National Bureau of Economic Research.

FINANCE COMPANY DEBT

Finance companies extend consumer loans, buy installment paper from auto and other hard-goods dealers, factor accounts receivable for corporations, and lend on inventories. Some finance companies are "captive" subsidiaries of manufacturing concerns who use them not only for profit but also as a way of supporting their sales efforts. (General Motors Acceptance Corp., or GMAC, is a captive finance subsidiary.)

Finance companies use a high degree of leverage—not as much as banks, but much more than nonfinancial corporations. They are the main direct sellers of commercial paper mentioned in Chapter 8. They also borrow directly from banks. In addition they also sell debentures to the bond market. These debentures are unsecured and may be subordinated to other debts. The volume of finance-company debt is about one-sixth of the total corporate debt. The average maturity is slightly shorter than that of nonfinancial corporations: ten to twenty years rather than twenty to forty.

Banks supply about one-tenth of their capital structure with capital notes, a form of corporate bond. The volume of bank bonds outstanding is about 1 percent of total corporate debt.

EUROCURRENCY BONDS

When the United States imposed the interest equalization tax in 1963, it limited the access of foreign borrowers to our capital markets. At the same time, the Eurodollar deposit market was starting to develop with the excess dollars foreigners received as a result of the balance of payments deficit we were seeking to lower. Borrowers and lenders who were willing to make longer-term commitments were brought together in a Eurobond market. This first developed in London but later was taken up by a number of other centers. As was true of the Eurodollar deposit market, the lack of regulation was attractive to investors. It also offered many investors a way of evading income taxes on their investment income.

When the United States adopted its programs restricting the export of capital by our multinational corporations, first in 1965 and then more rigorously in 1968, these corporations soon became the leading borrowers in this Eurobond market. Many corporations that had done little borrowing in our capital markets because they had ample funds (General Motors, for example) were pushed into the Eurobond market.

The Eurobond market was mainly one denominated in dollars, but as time passed, it included other currencies, the West German mark particularly and also the Swiss franc. Even more recently there has been a small and experimental volume of bonds denominated in optional currencies: the European Currency Unit (ECU), which gives the investor the choice of the six common market country currencies, or the European Unit of Account (EUA), under which the investor receives interest and redemption payment in the same currency used to purchase the bond but with value guaranteed by a fixed gold currency relationship. Eurobond issues have a somewhat shorter maturity average than U.S. bond issues—about eleven to fifteen years—and the underwriting cost is two to three times as much—about 2½ percent.

The interest rate on Eurobonds has generally been above the rate prevailing in our bond markets, but by less than the interest equalization tax. Thus there has been no incentive for U.S. investors to buy them. About half of the bonds appear to have been marketed in Switzerland, much of them doubtless for the accounts of citizens of other countries who had transferred refugee money to Switzerland. When our stock market was booming, multinational corporations found a ready market for convertible Eurobonds. The interest cost could be reduced by about 1½ percent for Eurobonds that were given convertibility into the parent companies' stock at a premium of no more than 10 to 15 percent above the prevailing market. When our stock market turned down, this no longer attracted investors. Recently some Eurobonds have been marketed with floating rates; they have been set generally at ¾ of 1 percent above the six-month Eurodollar deposit rate.

At first the Eurobond market suffered from a poor secondary market. Underwriters did not assume a secondary market responsibility. The physical clearing of the bonds was irregular, with an abnormal number of "fails." One of our leading banks organized a clearing facility abroad, and recent efforts suggest that the secondary market has been improved, at least in a technical sense.

While our multinational borrowers still dominate the market, their role is becoming relatively less important. Capital expenditures of foreign subsidiaries of U.S. corporations now exceed $15 billion, but an increasing portion of this can be covered by internally generated funds (high profits and depreciation charges). European municipalities often find it a cheaper market than their domestic one. (They do not have tax exemption.) In 1971 the estimated volume of Eurobond issues exceeded $5 billion.

Chapter 18

Markets for Corporate Equities

The market for corporate equities is divided into two organizational sectors: (1) the markets provided by organized securities exchanges and (2) the so-called "over-the-counter" (OTC) market (which is, of course, an "over-the-telephone" market). The bond markets, reviewed in Chapters 14, 15, and 17, are dominantly over-the-counter markets. The equities market is concentrated more on the organized exchanges than the bond markets are. The New York Stock Exchange (NYSE) dominates the organized market. The American Stock Exchange (AMEX) is much smaller, though still larger than the regional exchanges that do moderate but recently growing amounts of business.

CORPORATE EQUITIES: DOMINANTLY A SECONDARY MARKET

Perhaps the leading characteristic setting this market apart from other segments of the capital markets is that it is so dominantly a secondary

MARKETS FOR CORPORATE EQUITIES

market; most trading is in securities that are already outstanding. New equity capital is raised by established concerns rather rarely, but ownership of their outstanding equities is transferred at a brisk clip.

This characteristic goes back to the way in which corporation finance is conducted. Corporate equity capital largely originates in retained earnings. This fact is even more true in an economist's sense than it is in an organizational sense. Most corporations start very small, with only the funds of the founders, their friends and families, and sometimes other backers. In terms of number, though not dollar size, most corporations continue throughout their lives to be so closely held. If they grow, they grow by virtue of retained earnings. After such growth, these companies may "go public" in the sense that some portion of the original owners' shares is sold on the impersonal public market. Such transactions dominate the statistics of so-called "new equity issues." In an economic sense, however, these are not new issues; new capital is not being raised—rather, the small group of original owners is selling out some portion of its ownership to the public. This is why it was said above that the equities market is even more a secondary market in an economic sense than in an organizational sense.

The volume of trading on the organized securities exchanges far exceeds that in any other segment of the capital market. In the year 1968 this volume reached $187 billion, and in 1971 it was also close to this level. If the volume of trading in the OTC were included, it is almost certain that the total would be considerably more than $200 billion. New issues of equity securities have also been increasing in recent years and in 1971 reached a level of $14 billion. Even so, this amount is small compared with the volume of sales in the secondary market.

Although the volume of trading in this secondary market is larger than in any other capital market, it is not particularly large relative to the value of securities outstanding. A comparison of the volume of trading with total market value suggests that the average holding period for equity investors appears to be about four to five years. However, this trading volume includes that of members of the NYSE who have much shorter holding periods. If the trading volume of members and other short-term speculators is removed from the figures, the average public investor probably tends to have a holding period that is much longer; possibly near ten years. As we shall see later, the gradual growth of institutions as holders of equities has led to some increase in trading activity; their average holding period is shorter than that of the individual investor.

An exception to the general rule that the organized stock exchanges are secondary markets should be noted. Preemptive rights of existing stockholders in some corporations give them a first chance at buying any new voting stock offered by such companies. In addition, existing shareholders may have the "right" to purchase any debentures that are convertible into equities. Even though not required to do so by law, some corporations employ rights financing as an economical means of raising new equity capital.

The volume of rights financing varies directly with the strength of the equity market. When stock prices are booming, rights financing becomes more frequent; when the market weakens, the volume drops off. Even so, the volume is never very great when compared with the larger magnitudes of financing for corporations.

When the stock market is looked at as a source of new capital and therefore a net drain on the flow of saving, it is far less important than several other capital markets. The $14 billion raised in the new-issue equity market in 1971 was far higher than in any other year of record by a considerable margin. In the other years of the preceding decade, the volume of new capital raised was between $3 billion and $9 billion and averaged only about $5 billion. Thus, mortgages, corporate bonds, state and local government securities, issues of the federal government, and even consumer credit drew more on saving than equity financing.[1]

It is entirely possible that future years will see a continued fairly high volume of equity financing. Corporations came out of World War II with high liquidity and little debt. For the first two decades, new financing was modest relative to capital expenditures. Such new financing as was needed could easily be done with debt. Furthermore, debt financing had clear tax advantages since interest, but not dividends, is a tax-deductible expense. While the tax advantage of debt financing remains, the capital structures of many corporations have now been expanded with about as much debt as is prudent, and thus further external financing requires some injection of new equity capital.

The positive economic contribution of secondary equity markets is frequently misunderstood. Many look upon these equity markets primarily as speculative outlets. The volume of trading tends to increase whenever prices are rising; it falls off greatly when prices stabilize, even at high levels, and increases again on declines. Excess emphasis on speculation, however, tends to conceal the economic function of equity trading. In effect, corporate equities are perpetuities. An individual owner, limited as he is to the natural life-span of a man, can realize on a market investment only by giving the equity to an heir or selling it in the market. Sale

---

[1] Professor Roger Murray, in the first Buttonwood lecture (published as an undated pamphlet by Columbia University and NYSE), suggested that retained earnings should be considered as capital "raised" by the stock market, since it is this market which gives investors the chance both to use new funds and to liquidate holdings increased by retained earnings. The idea is not without merit, but it strains the concept of markets beyond its normal boundaries.

MARKETS FOR CORPORATE EQUITIES 331

permits the individual to adjust his portfolio to changing needs, tastes, and expectations. The much-abused word "liquidity" reflects the purpose served by equity markets; they allow owners to liquidate their holdings quickly. Prices fluctuate (and some feel that equity prices fluctuate irrationally and excessively), but the existence of the equity market makes them more liquid—at a price.

The owners of shares in closely held corporations have a hard time liquidating such investments. Some of them are able to sell out to colleagues or friends, but they cannot all be certain of being able to do so. This shortcoming often explains why prosperous, closely held companies go public. Principal owners often have no need of cash but foresee the time in their personal affairs when they will need a market for their shares. In such sales, owners frequently sell only a portion of their holdings, but enough to create a fairly active trading market. This market serves to evaluate the remaining shares they own and to give them financial maneuverability.

THE OWNERSHIP OF CORPORATE EQUITIES

As we have seen, the majority of other capital market instruments are owned directly by intermediary financial institutions with individuals on the other side of the balance sheets of these intermediaries. In the case of equities, the dominant ownership is, and will be for many years, directly in individuals. The following estimates taken from the flow-of-funds statistics are:

	1961	1971	Percent change
	(billions of dollars)		
Households	502	823	+ 64
Institutions	60	185	+208
Foreign	12	21	+ 75
Total	574	1,029	+ 79

Thus, over the decade, the market value of equities increased by about 80 percent. At the same time institutional holdings increased by over 200 percent. Institutional holdings have increased more than the volume of new equity issues, so that individuals have been, on balance, net sellers of corporate equities. The amount of such selling has not been large—only about 1 percent of holdings in any one year; but such selling has taken place every year in the past decade. If new equity issues increase more than institutional net buying, the transfer rate may slow down.

The NYSE estimated that at the end of 1970 almost 31 million individuals owned corporate shares, directly or indirectly. The indirect ownership was mainly through investment companies, and it was estimated that more than 18 million persons owned shares listed on the NYSE. The savings accounts in banks and other savings intermediaries are doubtless the most common forms of financial investment. There are over 100 million such accounts in the United States. Share ownership, with 31 million, takes second place by a very wide margin. One of the interesting recent developments is the large increase in share ownership by those under twenty-one. The end-of-1970 estimate was for 2.2 million such holders. This was spurred by the "uniform gift to minors" acts, which now exist in all fifty states. Under these provisions, shares may be given to minors by doting parents or grandparents (with, it should be noted, some gift tax advantages).

Another surprising fact is the extent to which share ownership has penetrated down into lower income levels. The 1970 survey of share ownership indicated that 8.8 million persons with incomes of $10,000 or less were share owners. While some of these would be accounted for by the young holders, there must be many others, including probably some at the other end of the age spectrum: retirees who own shares but have incomes of less than $10,000.

Share ownership exists in all fifty states. It is clear, however, that the incidence of such ownership is relatively more common in the northeastern states than in the agricultural states; also that share ownership is more common in cities than in rural areas. Ownership of small blocks of shares doubtless imposes a considerable cost on corporations, but it is a burden they bear willingly for the sake of its public relations value.

The institutions in the stock market are of several different types. Some are virtually pure intermediaries; some are far more complex both in purpose and operation. The closest to a pure intermediary in the equity market is the mutual fund or investment company. This type of institution interposes professional investment analysis and portfolio selection between the ultimate investor and the equity market, and it charges a fee for the service. Most of these investment companies are "open-end," which means that investors can be added and can also withdraw. Some open-end investment companies have sales loading charges in addition to management fees; others are "no-load" in form. A small number of closed-end investment companies, most of whom were organized many years ago, are listed on the NYSE. Open-end companies cannot be listed; they are directly sold and redeemed.

MARKETS FOR CORPORATE EQUITIES 333

Life insurance companies and pension funds have come to be very large equity investors. The reason is fear of inflation. Both life insurance and pensions involve very long-term liabilities. Since the value of both life insurance and pensions is eroded by inflation, there has been an effort to offset this influence by investment in common stock. In fact, some pensions are now partly annuities that are related to the level of equity prices.

In the statistics of trading volume, the NYSE treats commercial banks as institutional investors. They are, in fact, the most important of such institutional investors in terms of trading volume. However, the basis for this is that commercial bank trust departments manage or operate many trusts. Total trust assets in 1969 were $280 billion, of which common stocks were $180 billion—$60 billion in pension trusts and the rest in personal trusts. Legally this is not an intermediary relationship; the commercial bank does not interpose its balance sheet between the investor and the market. Individuals are the direct beneficial owners of the trusteed shares. However, for all operational purposes, the investment activities of the trust departments of commercial banks are so similar to those of true intermediary investors that this is the more realistic view of the equity market. Treating equity securities in trust accounts as "institutional" raises such ownership to about a third of total equities. Since the volume statistics of the NYSE show that institutional trading exceeds that of individuals, this means that the turnover of institutional equity portfolios is materially higher than that of individual or "household" equity portfolios.

THE ORGANIZED EXCHANGES

The volume of trading in equity securities is reported in great detail for the organized exchanges, but only recently and still rather incompletely for the over-the-counter market. As a result, the importance of the two cannot be compared directly. Without specific statistical evidence, it is only possible to estimate. Organized exchanges dominate equity trading. The volume of trading on organized exchanges amounted to about nine-tenths of the total in 1949.[2] No recent estimate of this magnitude has been prepared from original research materials, but indirect evidence suggests that it is still a reasonably valid representation of the true facts.

The principal characteristic of an organized exchange is that it provides a physical place for trading and enforces rules of trading that govern all transactions on the trading floor as well as the relationship of

[2] Irwin Friend, C. Wright Hoffman, and Willis J. Winn, *Over-the-counter Securities Markets*, McGraw-Hill, New York, 1958.

traders to their public customers. The physical trading area involves a kind of face-to-face double auction. The spot at which a specific security is to be traded is designated. At this "post" records of past prices and trades are kept, and from it reports can be quickly dispatched both with respect to price (to the public) and execution (to the buyer and seller). All trades involve public "crying out" of bids and offers. A broker does well to have a voice that would be suitable for train dispatching without a public address system.

The trading rules not only require the public calling of bids and offers; they also require that the best price prevail, the highest available for sellers and lowest for buyers. No playing of favorites is allowed; a bidding trader must buy from the quoting trader who offers the lowest price. Furthermore, the rules forbid sham transactions used only to bull up prices or to bear them down. Any sort of rigging of the market or collusion between traders is forbidden. While these are hard rules to enforce and violations probably occur from time to time, trading almost certainly has become far more honest than was true in earlier and wilder days.

Among organized exchanges, the NYSE dominates. In terms of dollar volume, a far better measure than number of shares, the NYSE accounted for close to 80 percent of all trading on organized exchanges in 1971. American Stock Exchange volume fluctuates, but it has averaged around 10 percent of the total. The remainder is accounted for mainly by several regional exchanges of which the Midwest, the Pacific Coast, and the Philadelphia-Baltimore-Washington stock exchanges have been the three most important. The latter gained considerable volume by permitting institutional membership—a matter that will be discussed later.

On organized exchanges, trading takes place among members, who have the privilege of trading on the floor of the exchange. Some members act as specialists, a few trade solely for their own account, some trade for other members, but the great bulk of them trade for, and generally are partners in, commission brokerage firms. The major business of most commission brokerage firms is offering buying-and-selling service to the public. These members may trade for their own account, but they usually consider commission brokerage to be their principal activity. Commission brokerage houses may be linked with investment banking firms or departments of them, but some specialize in providing just this service. Commission brokerage business in securities may also be allied with commission brokerage in commodity markets or even other types of markets such as foreign exchange.

The members of an organized exchange are subject to its rules, including the rules of conduct governing their relationships with customers. Most of the exchanges now have extensive procedures for the policing of their members and the disciplining of those who violate their rules. This zeal is doubtlessly reinforced by the fact that the Securities and Exchange Commission stands ready to take over should their own zeal slacken. The principal purpose of trading rules and policing is to avoid the bilking of customers and the rigging of prices, practices that unfortunately were once rather more common than not. Violations may occur now, but they are the exception and not the rule in modern equity markets, particularly in the organized sector.

All the securities traded on the New York Stock Exchange are listed on that exchange. Listing is allowed only for the securities of companies that comply with the rules of the exchange, principally with respect to publication of pertinent financial data and the disclosure of all facts of relevance for investors, such as the trading in a corporation's securities done by its principal owners and officers. In order to qualify for listing, the volume of shares available for public trading must also meet certain minimum standards. For example, the shares of a big but closely held corporation would not be listed. A minimum number of public shareholders as well as shares is required to assure reasonably continuous and viable markets.

The American Stock Exchange (AMEX), with somewhat less stringent listing requirements, tends to be the market for smaller and often younger companies. Some companies have viewed an AMEX listing as an intermediate step between OTC trading and a NYSE listing. Many other companies have attempted to leapfrog AMEX listing and to go directly from OTC trading to NYSE listing. This differentiation did not extend just to companies; it also went to types of securities. For example, for many years the NYSE would not list warrants, so that a NYSE-listed company might have its warrants AMEX-listed. However, the NYSE has opened its doors to warrants of *some* companies (American Telephone and Telegraph led the way). During the speculative upsurge from 1965 to 1968, AMEX trading bulged briefly. Recently, however, it has returned to about its traditional one-tenth position.

Some companies have dual listings, on the NYSE as well as on one of the regional exchanges. Indeed, some of the regional exchanges get most of their trading volume from such dual listings. Transfer taxes, which are steep in New York, often account for the preference for a trade on a regional exchange. Where such dual listing exists, prices on the regional exchange are kept parallel with those on the NYSE by constant arbitrage. Arbitrage is the buying of a security or commodity in one market and selling the identical security or commodity in another market whenever a price differential appears. Arbitragers tend to equalize prices among markets. This arbitraging is mostly done by specialists.

The role of the specialist on an organized exchange is one of considerable responsibility but also opportunity. Brokers representing commission brokerage firms have to move around the trading floor of the exchange and cannot keep in constant touch with the individual stocks which are traded at fixed points or "posts." The specialist is more than a broker; he is a dealer in specific stocks. A "dealer" in a security deals for himself and therefore has an inventory in that security. The inventory, however, may be "short" or negative as well as "long" or positive. These specialist-dealers take orders from other brokers for both buying and selling, and when prices justify, they execute such orders. The rules of the exchange require specialists to give priority to customer orders, and they are charged with maintaining some continuity to the market for the security in which they specialize. Specialists are expected to buy when no other buyers appear or to sell when no other sellers can be found. Specialists often take losses in discharging this role. However, profits are not forbidden, and a specialist can serve as a buffer against irrational price movements and make a profit at the same time.

The information in the specialist's book of unfilled orders is of great strategic importance. If disposed to try to rig the market in his favor, he has a strategic advantage in launching such an operation. For this reason, specialists are constantly under the surveillance of the governors of an exchange; their order books and the records of their transactions are subject to scrutiny at all times. If they perform their duty conscientiously, they serve an important role in the market, but the margin between conscience and cupidity is not always a clear one.

The role of the specialist is very much like that of the dealer in the U.S. government security market already discussed in Chapter 14.

Institutional Membership on the Organized Exchanges

Until April 1971, institutional investors nominally paid the same brokerage commission rates as much smaller investors for all transactions involving 100 or more shares. There was no quantity discount. Because large economies of scale exist in brokerage, this made large transactions excessively profitable. To attract such institutional business, many brokerage firms offered various free services to institutional investors, of which security research and analysis or sale of mutual fund shares were the leaders. This was what made the payment of full brokerage commission "nominal."

Although such indirect rebates were permitted, they did not satisfy many institutional investors. Some of them sought to be permitted to become exchange members. This was and still is denied except in one regional exchange. The Martin report (see page 357 of this chapter) on the securities market also recommended against such membership. Negotiated commission rates on large transactions was the recommended alternative. This first took the form of negotiation of the brokerage charge on any portion of an order in excess of $500,000. This amount was later reduced to $300,000. While this solves the problems of some of the larger institutional investors, it leaves others without much help. Commercial banks, for example, have many trust department orders below these levels. Banks have been able to exact compensatory deposit balances from commission brokerage firms which are related to the amount of business done—but this is still an awkward type of arrangement. The money system was devised to overcome the clumsiness of barter, but these deals are essentially barter in nature.

The Paper-Work Problem

The volume of trading on the NYSE increased steadily during the 1960s as share prices rose and as public participation in the stock market increased and widened, but particularly as institutions speeded up portfolio turnover. In the year 1967 the rate of increase was unusually rapid. The operational facilities of some commission brokerage firms simply were not equal to the increased volume of work. Overtime was used, but it was often not enough to cure the problem. The most evident form of the paper-work problem in the street was the "fail" (a failure to deliver a security which has been sold). This may start a chain of other fails, since the buying firm then cannot deliver the security it has purchased in a subsequent transaction. The public also became aware of the paper-work problem in the form of frequent errors in brokerage accounts: the failure to credit accounts for proceeds of sales, failure to credit accounts for dividends, and frequent improper credits and debits. In August 1967 trading days were shortened by ninety minutes for nine consecutive days to help commission brokerage firms clean up the backlog of work.

The year 1968 was very probably the peak of the paper-work problem. Volume of trading went to record levels, particularly in unlisted OTC securities. Fails increased to an alarming extent. The trading day was shortened, and the settlement period was extended from four to five days. Overtime was used extensively, and the NYSE assumed a rather aggressive role of self-regulation in pushing some member firms into greater and more efficient operational efforts. One of the problems was the introduction of the computer. Some firms had done so earlier and had worked out the operational bugs, but many were in a state of transition and were unable to perform either by the old or yet by the new methods.

Markets were kept open only four days a week for the second half of the year.

By 1969 the situation started to improve, markets went back on a five-day schedule, and by early 1970 most of the street had returned to fairly normal operational conditions. One of the features that helped in the improvement was the introduction of a Central Certificate Service (CCS). The CCS acted as a depository for stock certificates, and participating members could effect delivery simply by a book entry at the CCS. At first the CCS covered only a limited number of NYSE-listed stocks, but it has since been expanded to cover most NYSE issues, most AMEX issues, and a large number of OTC issues; a total of 2,600 at the end of 1971. The participants include not only commission brokerage firms but also eleven New York City clearing banks. Collateral loans can be arranged through the CCS. At present further extension of the service to banks outside New York City and also to some institutional investors is being worked out.

A still more comprehensive system called the Comprehensive Securities Depository System (CSDS) has been planned, and implementation by mid-1973 has been promised. This "super CCS" is aimed at approaching the time when the physical stock certificate may be phased out entirely, as will soon be done in the U.S. Treasury security market, and when securities may be transferred simply by book entries as is now done with money in checking accounts.

Failure of Many Commission Brokerage Firms

The paper-work problem contributed to the financial distress of many commission brokerage firms, but it was only one factor in their final financial failure. Stock prices turned down in late 1968 and volume declined rather sharply until mid-1970. Many commission brokerage firms were themselves rather active market participants and had much of their capital tied up in market positions. The market decline impaired and in some cases wiped out firm capital. Since the commission brokerage business allows much leverage (the NYSE capital ratio required at that time was only 5 percent and has since been raised to 6 2/3 percent), even moderate losses are likely to impair capital rather quickly. In addition, the decline in stock market volume in 1969 and 1970 cut commission income. While operating losses aggravated the problem, it was position losses that cut most deeply into capital.

In 1968 one commission brokerage firm failed. The customers, however, were protected by a trust fund the NYSE had established for this purpose. In late 1969, two other commission brokerage firms failed.

But the major wave of failures came in 1970. The statistics are not precise, but the following facts appear reliable: During this period, 160 NYSE member firms disappeared. Nonmember firms also disappeared. Most of them did so rather quietly and without public notice. The NYSE beefed up its surveillance of member firms and doubtless quietly pushed some of them into sale of their businesses to member firms or into liquidating. However, public attention was focused on seventeen well-publicized cases of firms that went into bankruptcy or were acquired by member firms with indemnification agreements from the NYSE. In the process the NYSE increased its "Customer Assistance Program." Congress also passed the Securities Investor Protection Act in 1971. This is very similar to the insurance programs applying to banks and savings and loan associations. It appears that in the end no stock investor lost as a result of the financial difficulties of his broker. However, many were greatly inconvenienced by having their accounts frozen for extended periods, so that they were unable to engage in normal market protective actions.

The NYSE found member-firm earnings inadequate, and the brokerage commissions were increased. Although it cannot be said the low commission income precipitated the financial crisis among commission brokerage firms, it was true that with low income they would not have been able to restore capital from earnings, nor could they hope to attract new outside capital with the prospect of such earnings. Thus in 1970 a $15 surcharge was imposed on orders of 1,000 shares or less (subject to a 50 percent limit). In late 1971 a more permanent change was introduced. These changes were also accompanied by changes in rules for very large orders, so that competitive negotiation could try to attract business from the "third market."

The financial crisis for the commission brokerage business is now past and a new development has taken place: Many of commission brokerage firms have "gone public." Some are even themselves listed on the NYSE. Investors apparently expect them to be profitable enterprises.

THIRD MARKET AND BLOCK TRADING

The increased importance of institutions in the stock market has led to an increase in the number of large transactions. (The NYSE defines a large block as one of 10,000 shares or more.) These large block transactions have taken two forms: transactions on the NYSE and transactions of listed stocks in a special OTC market called the "third market." In 1965 the third market accounted for more volume than big block trading on the NYSE. Each one, however, had only about 2 percent of total volume. Both have since grown, but block trading on the NYSE has grown even faster than third market trading. Since 1967 the growth has been particularly rapid, and in 1971 big block trading accounted for almost 18 percent of NYSE volume. In the same year third market trading had grown to 6 1/2 percent of NYSE volume, but this is obviously a slower growth than that of listed trading. Thus the combination of these two forms of trading now account for about one-fourth of total stock market activity. Some institutional trading, of course, does not involve large blocks. Commercial banks, as was noted above, are the most important of the institutional traders, mainly for their trust accounts. In the case of individual trusts, the size of transaction is not necessarily large and so, although the number of trades originated by commercial banks is substantial, the average size is less than that for other institutions. The allowance for negotiated commissions on large trades doubtless accounts for the fact that the NYSE retained this type of business, which otherwise might have gone to the third market.

The NYSE developed an information system to facilitate big block trading. The Block Automation System (BAS) has computer terminals in twenty-two metropolitan areas with over 180 subscribers. Each subscriber can enter offers or bids for blocks of a thousand or more shares in any listed stock with protection of anonymity. Brokerage firms use this information to bring together buyers and sellers.

THE OVER-THE-COUNTER (OTC) MARKET

At present the OTC market is in such flux that no more than an interim report can be given. The automation of the quotation system in this market has given it new life, and it might be in the forefront of market reorganization in the future. The nature of the automated system of quotations will be examined later in this chapter. Here we shall concentrate on matters of size and significance.

About half a million corporations in the United States are active enough to file a tax return. About nine-tenths of these corporations are so closely held that their stocks never "trade" in any public sense. Thus there are about 50,000 corporations with possible public trades. Most of them, however, do not trade regularly and so are not really within the framework of the OTC or any other securities market.

The NYSE and the AMEX between them list 3,300 corporations. A few more are listed on regional exchanges. There are 1,500 OTC stocks with enough activity to justify daily quotation in *The Wall Street Journal* and *The New York Times*. However, another 1,000 stocks trade actively enough to justify inclusion in the automatic quotation system of the National Association of Security Dealers (NASD). In addition, a number of other stocks get quoted weekly in the pink sheets of the National Quotation Service. Thus it can be said that about 10,000 stocks are "publicly

MARKETS FOR CORPORATE EQUITIES 341

traded." Of these, the OTC concentrates on about 2,500 and can give service to the securities of about 4,000 other companies.

The OTC market is made by dealers. A dealer differs from a broker in that he acts as a principal to a trade. He is similar to the specialist who has already been described or the dealers in other security markets which have already been described. The NASD has 4,600 members but not all of them act as dealers. A small securities firm may be nothing more than a sales agent. However, if they have sponsored the public sale of stock of a local company, they will very likely "make a market" in it. The number of true market makers is not clear, but the bulk of the business is done by a few hundred firms.

Some very big companies still have their stocks traded in the OTC market. Traditionally both banks and insurance companies avoided listing and so were traded in these markets. However, the development of one-bank holding companies and the financial conglomerates which owned insurance companies led to the listing of many leading banks and insurance companies. Nevertheless, the Bank America Corporation and the Conneticut General Life Insurance Company are still OTC-traded. A big company, such as those mentioned above, may attract as many as twenty or more market makers. The NASD likes to have at least two market makers for any company which it includes in its automatic quotation system (NASDAQ).

The new NASDAQ system has given rise to the first volume figures for the OTC market. They are still too truncated to allow much comparison, but on some days the OTC has had twice the share volume of the AMEX and half the share volume of the NYSE. Average price of shares on the OTC is apparently below that of the NYSE but about equal to that of the AMEX.

The NASDAQ system now lists and quotes about fifty listed third market stocks. It is possible that if the service of this market proves to be more efficient than block trading on the NYSE, the reversal of volume, elsewhere described in this chapter, will be rereversed at some later time.

The major change produced by the new system has been to narrow spreads for investors. Formerly, many prudent investors avoided the OTC market because of the wide bid-and-ask spreads. This relative position has been changed. While turnover margins for listed trading have probably widened in recent years, at least for the smaller investor, they have narrowed in the OTC market.

SPECULATION IN EQUITY CAPITAL MARKETS

The popular image of the stock market as a speculative arena needs brief examination. Speculation in securities in contrast with investment is often thought of as an effort to realize capital gains quickly. The element of "quickness" is a legitimate distinction, since investment is clearly a long-range process. But capital gains are common to both types of operations; indeed, capital gains rather than current income have become the goal of a great deal of equity investment.

Even the time distinction is not altogether relevant. It is true that the investor may hold what he buys for long periods of time, but prudence may sometimes require him to sell rather quickly if new circumstances arise. The common canons of investment urge the readjustment of portfolios whenever new conditions would seem to favor the move.

The fact that trading in equities becomes brisk whenever price movements are wide and falls off when prices are lethargic (even at fairly high levels) suggests that there is a fair amount of speculative volume in the market. Speculation, of course, should be viewed as a constructive force in the equity market *if it is based on good information*. The capital markets allocate capital, as we said in Chapter 1. If the bidding for equity securities is based on valid projections of the future, this can encourage the flow of capital into productive uses and discourage it from those that are of flagging value. Since equity returns are based on hope and expectations rather than promises, as is true of debt securities, the art of security selection is based on accuracy of anticipation. If security investors anticipate where future growth will be, they make capital available for the productive segments of the economy. The computer industry has been able to tap the capital markets on good terms because security investors foresaw the growth and were willing to put up the money for the expansion of this vast industry. On the other hand, a declining industry cannot raise new capital, and therefore new capital is not wasted on it by investors. Speculation discriminates not only among industries but also among companies. A good management will be rewarded by good stock prices; a poor one will be disciplined by the retreat of investors.

The National Bureau of Economic Research found that stock prices were a leading indicator, of a fair degree of accuracy, of general economic activity. Thus the stock market speculation also has the merit of giving some guidance to general public economy policy.

If speculation is based on false information, the process tends to be destructive. Much of the speculation of the bad old days was so based. As later segments of this chapter will make clear, the leading regulatory effort with respect to the equity markets has been to assure the honesty and, as far as is possible, the accuracy of information available to investors.

A sober view of the facts, moreover, demonstrates that the speculative content of equity markets is much reduced from former days.

The enforced reduction due to the limitation of credit in equity purchases has already been mentioned. Perhaps the most important point, however, is that the securities exchanges and many other elements in this market, including the leading commission brokerage houses, have attempted to discourage uninformed speculation. Professional speculation is still practiced and stock exchange members engage in it themselves. But the stock market gambler, characterized more by cupidity and stupidity than by acuity, is not given much encouragement except by marginal members of the securities business.

One statistical measure of the great reduction in speculation is afforded by the rate of turnover of corporate equities. This is shown in the following table:

Turnover Ratio for Shares* Listed on the NYSE

Period	Percent per annum
1900–1909	202
1910–1919	97
1920–1929	89
1930–1939	35
1940–1949	16
1950–1959	16
1960–1969	19
1970–1971	21

* A better measure would be provided if turnover were measured in terms of dollar volume, but unfortunately such data are not available.
Source: NYSE, Fact Book, 1971, p. 72.

A 19 percent ratio for the most recent decade suggests that the amount of speculative froth in the equities market is fairly low. If there were none, the rate of turnover of legitimate investors would suggest average holdings of six to seven years. If half of the volume of market trading, which appears to be a generous estimate, is purely speculative and the average holding is just over six months (to put capital gains on a long-term basis), the average holding period of investors appears to be about ten years.

Speculators operating no more actively than this cannot dominate the stock market nor throw it badly off the course indicated by real economic factors. The large amount of true investment funds keeps the market from deviating disastrously from course.

Short selling is sometimes criticized as a form of destructive speculation. Short selling is selling what the seller does not then own and making delivery on this sale by borrowing the security. The completion or the closing of a short position requires that the security borrowed be replaced by a later purchase. The short seller's hope is that he can make this later purchase materially under the price at which he initially sold.

The rules of all organized exchanges regulate short selling rather closely, and short selling on the over-the-counter market is very risky—except for insiders. On the NYSE, the size of the short interest has averaged less than $1/10$ of 1 percent of listed shares and it has almost never gone much above this level since 1934. If the short seller anticipates economic developments correctly, he hastens but does not amplify inevitable price movements. If he is wrong, he loses his capital.

INFORMAL EQUITIES MARKET

If one wishes to stretch the concept of markets just a bit further, still one more equities market should be mentioned: a purely local, informal, and rather confidential market.

All across the United States local businessmen, doctors, dentists, bankers, and others own small interests in local enterprises. Sometimes these enterprises are operated as partnerships, but more often they are incorporated. These owners are mortal men and sometimes must sell their shares in such small local corporations. They may sell because health or nature requires them to do so, for capital gains, or because even newer ventures have become more attractive. The local "capitalist" still exists, even if he has tended to make himself less conspicuous in recent years.

The buying and selling of equities in such local enterprises is sometimes done through business brokers and therefore handled rather impersonally as a market process. These business brokers may even act as financial agents, hunting up capital loans for buyers as well as buyers for sellers. Motels, stores, laundromats, gas stations, frequently pass through their hands, but less well-standardized businesses are also bought and sold. This market is one in which some measure of uniformity exists by virtue of the valuation process. Motels may tend to sell for certain multiples of gross or net earnings. No one knows how large this market really is or how well it fits into the other capital markets. But if one has faith in the process of market leveling, it would seem reasonable to think that some sort of tie probably exists.

The market for small, locally owned banks is also very much like this. Local bank presidents often operate a market in the shares of their banks as a service to shareholders. These presidents keep track of those who have expressed an interest in buying some bank shares; when some shares become available, they call up to find out if the inquiries are backed by money. Often the price is largely set by the president with very little haggling—unless the amounts be large. (Many bank-share deals regularly take place at book value.) There is some evidence that prices in this bank-share market are loosely tied to the more open and urban markets for bank shares.

REGULATION OF THE STOCK MARKET

Capital markets in the United States are regulated, but the character of the regulation differs materially from that applied in other areas. A majority of capital market institutions are not monopolies and therefore the regulation in force is not similar to that governing public utility enterprises which are given an exclusive franchise but then limited in prices and earnings. Nevertheless, there are some near monopolies: for example, the NYSE dominates the organized equity market by accounting for four-fifths of such activity. Furthermore, the stock market lives with a blend of public and self-regulation for which parallels are hard to find except possibly in professions such as law and medicine. Stock market regulation of a limited kind has existed for a long time, but the most important (and controversial) elements of it date back to the mid-1930s. Much of this regulation was a product of vast disillusionment produced by the Great Depression. The philosophy governing the regulation of stock markets may be changing in the opposite direction. During the 1968 presidential campaign, Richard Nixon, then a candidate, sent a letter to the securities industry assuring them that if elected, he would use a lighter regulatory hand. He did not, however, promise to abandon regulation. In fact, it has been hard to detect a material change in the character or direction of current regulation.

Because regulation of the stock markets is marked by a number of strands of intent and guided by several laws and agencies, this chapter will be forced to use fairly rigid expositor devices to avoid confusion. The first section will discuss the basic objectives of this regulation. The second section will outline the specific problems that have led to regulation. Then, and only then, will the legal basis of regulation be introduced. With this background, it will then be possible to enumerate and describe the agencies involved in the regulatory process. Finally, a brief summary evaluation of the results of regulation will be undertaken.

OBJECTIVES OF REGULATION

The story of public regulation has usually been a simple one: Some catastrophic event discloses a problem and public pressure forces the lawmakers to "do something about it." Post hoc analysis with hearings, investigations, and debates among the various parties at interest follow, and then compromises, which always accompany the legislative process, are made. No one is fully satisfied but "something has been done." One of the strange parts of the process is that the objectives of such regulation are often not very much discussed. Lawyers, in drafting these acts, put some lofty language in the preambles, but as often as not it is more windy than meaningful. But with the advantage of hindsight, what were the basic objectives that capital market regulation was expected to accomplish?

Fair and Equitable Treatment of Investors

Prosperity and a more egalitarian distribution of income has created a large number of persons who have the means to be security investors. A large proportion of them have little skill or background for such a function; thus a prevailing ethic is that such persons should be protected. This ethic is similar to the ideas back of pure food and drug laws or laws requiring weights and measures to be shown on packages.

Security selling in the past was sometimes very close to outright fraud. At one time in this country, securities were sold for enterprises that did not exist and for purposes that are describable only as fantastic. But the major problems were of a kind more at the margin of ethics. Railroads were very legitimate and important business enterprises, but in the nineteenth century the stocks of railroads were often grossly manipulated on the NYSE. Investors were not given adequate information by many corporations, so that they were unable to estimate the true value of the securities to be purchased or which they already owned; they were at a disadvantage relative to the better informed "insiders."

It is notable that emphasis was put on the protection of the investor and not on the borrower or raiser of capital. It was thought that corporations were presumably able to protect their interest without help. One possible exception is a small business, where special kinds of financial aid have received a great deal of political support. However, this is not really a part of stock market regulation; it is, rather, a form of special interest legislation.

While the protection of investors was originally considered mainly a matter of equity and ethics, the whole movement probably has had far more sweeping consequences. Participation in the stock markets is now very widespread; the number of persons owning common stock was almost 31 million in 1970; over 18 million owned shares listed on the NYSE. While this may not have raised much new capital for corporations, it certainly has created a very large body of support for the corporate system that would not have existed with narrower common stock ownership.[3]

---

[3] A very interesting and readable account of regulation of equity trading markets may be found in Sidney Robbins, *The Security Markets,* Free Press, New York, 1966.

In spite of its very broad title, this book deals almost solely with the equity market and particularly the NYSE. Robbins was chief economist for the 1963 special study of securities markets sponsored by the Securities Exchange Commission (SEC).

Promotion of Market Efficiency

Better information has been one of the chief means used to promote market efficiency. The publicity that has been required for the process of raising capital has exposed the margins or "markups" taken by the securities industry both in new issue sales and in secondary market transactions. Both sides of the market—investors and borrowers—have become more aware of these margins and more disposed to bargain for narrower spreads. Better information in the OTC market has probably reduced the bid-and-ask spreads and improved executions for investors on both sides of the market. But most important of all, the improved information about the operations of business which have been required for security selling and listing on exchanges has clearly given investors a more accurate view of prospective rewards. By making more correct investment decisions, the whole process of capital allocation is thereby improved.

One of the important feedbacks has been from the more aggressive investors to the management of corporations. In times past, many giant corporations doubtless became complacent and self-satisfied and did not press as aggressively as might have been possible. However, the exposure of such policies in the actions of aggressive investors who dump the shares of such companies if they do not perform has doubtless been a spur to more active search for growth in what might otherwise have been complacent giants.

PROBLEM AREAS WHICH HAVE RECEIVED REGULATORY ATTENTION

Public regulation tends to be pragmatic; it concentrates on problems exposed in past distressful episodes. The objectives we have just finished enumerating may have a general philosophical consistency, but actual regulatory law and action tends to be more specific. This section gets down to specifics; it enumerates the itches that regulatory legislation tried to scratch.

New-Issue Market: "Telling the Truth"

One of the earliest forms of public regulation of security markets was the requirement that those selling securities should tell buyers the truth. State "blue sky" laws long precede federal government entry to this field. (One exception was the application of postal regulations to prosecute security sale frauds that made use of the mails.) The Securities Act of 1933 was the major federal effort in this area. The major impact of this act was to require those selling new issues of securities to provide enough information to permit investors to make a valid investment judgment. The law did not prohibit highly speculative ventures as long as they were honestly and forthrightly described. Not only must the truth be told, material facts could not be withheld; the story had to be the "whole" truth.

The intent is valid; the result less certain. With certain exceptions, whenever a concern sells securities publicly (that is, a large number of buyers), it must issue a prospectus with detailed relevant information. Except for a few students—dragooned in the academic processes—and a few security analysts, these long and dull documents have become among the most unread compilations in an age when the printing press is inundating us all. However, at least a few points have been read and widely understood. Underwriters were required to tell the size of their own margins; this exposure has undoubtedly led to smaller margins (although other forces have helped in this process too).

Security Markets: Organized Exchanges

The central focus of financial market regulation has been on the organized exchanges, which are primarily, as we have seen, secondary markets. Even more specifically, the focus has been on the stock market and particularly the NYSE. The Securities Exchange Act of 1934 was concerned mainly with this central issue (although it did deal with other problems). After a period of preliminary struggle, the major impact of this regulation was to change the NYSE from what amounted to a private club into a public institution with acknowledged public responsibilities. Later in this chapter we shall deal at more length with the double harness of public regulation and self-regulation, but we must immediately recognize that the NYSE has now become a leading regulatory agency.

Stock market regulation dealt with a rather wide range of specific problems. The NYSE had always had trading rules to govern the conduct of its members. After NYSE reorganization in 1938, the trading rules were revised to provide more protection for investors who used the facilities of commission brokerage houses. Financial requirements for membership were beefed up. The practice of floor trading by members was subject to greater limitation. Trading practices that tended to manipulate or artifically influence prices were prohibited. One of the most significant areas of regulation has been an increase in the amount of information that companies listed on the NYSE must supply to investors. This protection was extended, in a measure, to over-the-counter markets in 1964. The whole art (some new-wave security analysts might want to say "science") of security analysis has been vastly supported by prompter access to information of a more extensive and more accurate nature.

One area in which markets have been greatly changed has been in the nature and intent of trading rules. In the days before the Crash of 1929 but even more in the nineteenth century, the NYSE was often more like a gambling enterprise than a true economic instrument of development. Prices of stocks would be bulled up by excessive activity until a speculative following had been attracted. Then the pool pushing the price up would drop out and let the bubble burst. Sometimes corners would be established; sometimes prices would be driven down by vast short selling. Price manipulation was so common that conservative investors often felt it unsafe to include publicly traded common stocks in their portfolios. The pre-1938 trading rules were mainly for purpose of settling differences among members. Protection of the outside public investor using commission brokerage access was not very extensive. However, the exchanges added trading rules which changed this situation materially. In the first place, the practice of floor trading (when a member buys and sells for his own account) was greatly restricted, which made outside investors more nearly on a par with floor traders. Most members on the exchanges now operate solely as agency traders or specialists. The power both of the NYSE and of the SEC to suspend trading in an individual stock was used far more effectively to avoid unsound speculative bursts in the price of an individual stock. Short selling was restricted. Unusual activity in an individual stock has been given much closer scrutiny both by the NYSE and the SEC. Credit sales were greatly restricted. Most of these changes have been aimed one way or another at making the market a safer one for the ordinary outside security investor.

The Specialist

One of the most interesting developments has been the increased role of the specialist and the consequent regulation of his function. Even though a large number of buy and sell orders flow into the floor of the NYSE, matching buy and sell orders may fail to appear within the very few seconds in which a floor broker may try to execute an order. The goal of a floor broker is to do as much business as possible. Some floor members assumed the role of taking the other side of these orders for their own account: They would buy at a price somewhat below the one at which they would sell. They became, in effect, dealers. Soon, they began to "specialize" in this function. Specialists also kept limit orders on their books which were to be executed at preset prices which were at various intervals away from the prevailing market. With the course of time, the specialists' operations became much more formalized—and at the same time more regulated. At the present time specialists are expected to "make markets" in the stock or stocks assigned to them. They are encouraged to quote a narrow bid-and-ask spread and are expected, under some circumstances, to absorb a flow of selling or to accommodate a surge of buying from their own positions. So far as possible, they attempt to make price changes continuous: that is, by steps of one-eighth. This matter becomes of the greatest significance when some momentous news suddenly becomes known. For example, a company unexpectedly announces reduced earnings or cuts its dividend; a surge of selling may develop. The specialist is expected to preside over an orderly retreat in price. (Economists may legitimately ask if important change in investment information may not justify price discontinuity.) The question that really hurts is this: How much of the selling wave should the specialist be required to take into his own position in the process of presiding over the "orderly" retreat? The specialist's book with its sequence of limit orders presumably gives him privileged knowledge, but where should his primary responsibility be: to the continuity of the market or to his own capital gains and losses?

Listing

For the market in a listed stock to be "reasonably good," enough stock must be in the hands of enough shareholders to generate a fair volume of trading. If too few buy and sell orders enter the market, it is too "thin" and trades are too infrequent. Therefore, exchanges have generally enforced listing requirements based on both number of shares outstanding and number of shareholders. The requirements for initial listing tend to be rather more exacting than those for continued listing. The initial listing requirements adopted by the NYSE in the spring of 1968 were:

> 1   Demonstrated earning power under competitive conditions of $2.5 million before federal income taxes for the most recent year and $2 million pretax for the preceding two years
>
> 2   Net tangible assets of $14 million, but greater emphasis will be placed on the aggregate market value of the common stock
>
> 3   A total of $14 million in market value of publicly held common stock
>
> 4   A total of 800,000 common shares publicly held out of 1,000,000 shares outstanding
>
> 5   Round-lot shareholders numbering 1,800 out of a total of 2,000 shareholders[4]

[4]*NYSE Fact Book*, 1971, p. 28.

MARKETS FOR CORPORATE EQUITIES   351

To allow for the fact that a company may experience a period of adversity but still recover from it, the requirements for continued listing are not quite as great as those for initial listing. The NYSE says:

> ... The Exchange may at any time suspend or delist a security where the Board considers that continued dealings in the security are not advisable, even though a security meets or fails to meet any specified criteria. For example, the Exchange would normally give consideration to suspending or removing from the list a common stock of a company when there are:
>
> 1   900 round-lot holders or less, with 1,000 shareholders of record or less.
>
> 2   400,000 shares or less in public hands.
>
> 3 $4,000,000 or less aggregate market value of publicly held shares
>
> 4 $7,000,000 or less in aggregate market value of all outstanding common stock or net tangible assets applicable thereto, combined with an earnings record of less than an average of $600,000 after taxes for the past three years.[5]

Information

One of the interesting by-products of listing requirements has been the agreement by listed corporations that they will supply shareholders with such information as may be required for intelligent evaluation of share prices. Specifically:

> The listing agreement between the company and the Exchange is designed to provide timely disclosure to the public of earnings statements, dividend notices, and other information which may affect security values or influence investment decisions. The Exchange requires actively operating companies to agree to solicit proxies for all meetings of stockholders.[6]

Although the initial requirement came from the NYSE, the SEC has taken continued interest in the matter of public information. Among other things, the SEC has conducted a continuous inquiry into the accounting methods used by listed corporations in reporting to shareholders. They have also pressed for early disclosure of relevant information. An important case illustrative of this issue was one in which Texas Gulf Sulphur made an important mineral discovery which led some insiders to make purchases in the company's stock before the news was released to the public. When rumors became widespread and the stock

[5] Ibid.
[6] Ibid.

price moved up rapidly, the NYSE finally forced Texas Gulf Sulphur to make a formal news release acknowledging the discovery. The SEC later initiated (and won) a suit against the officers of the company and the company itself on the basis of the responsibility to correctly and promptly inform stockholders of important developments that had a bearing on the price of company shares.

Another example involved the large securities firm of Merrill Lynch, Pierce, Fenner & Smith. According to SEC charges, this firm, as an underwriter, found out about still undisclosed large losses that Douglas Aircraft was to announce shortly. This information was relayed to a few important institutional investors who sold out before the news became public. The firm and some of its leading officers were disciplined by the SEC and the firm did not see fit to challenge the disciplining action.

Still another example was the relationship of Walston & Co., a large investment banking and commission brokerage firm, the Four Seasons Nursing Centers of America, and the investors in the stock of this former high flyer. As an investment banker, Walston & Co. aided in the early financing and public offerings of shares in this enterprise. Members of the firm and institutional investors it had as customers were heavy investors in the late 1960s while the stock was going up. At one time the stock hit $181.50 a share. However, affairs of the Four Seasons Nursing Centers turned down and ultimately it went into bankruptcy. The stock is now quoted in pennies. Before the bad news became public and before the price declined greatly, it is alleged that members of the Walston firm and a number of their institutional investor customers sold their holdings out or down. Officers of Walston & Co. accepted disciplinary action on the charge of having used the advance information they had (of the firm's early success and later failure) because of their investment banking role. Publicly, however, they deny wrongdoing. Since turnover of this stock was unusually heavy, the brokerage arm of Walston & Co. also gained by the large volume of transactions it handled in this security.

Advance information is at the heart of the matter. What is the ethical relationship of an investment banker to a customer firm? Should the business of investment banking and brokerage be combined if brokerage volume depends on the ability to feed advance confidential information to institutional investors? Is public protection needed?

Odd-Lot Transactions

One other area potentially subject to regulation, though not much touched as yet, is that of odd-lot purchases and sales. More than 99 percent of NYSE transactions involving less than 100 shares are directed to two large firms. Specialists generally handle such transactions on the regional exchanges. NYSE rules require that such transactions be priced at the price on the *next* round-lot transactions plus a fixed differential on purchases or minus the same differential on sales. Odd-lot dealing is very profitable, and the two firms on the NYSE compensate brokers directing odd-lot business to them by a variety of informal means.

With more widespread share ownership, odd-lot costs have become a matter of increased significance. Furthermore, the frequent use of small stock dividends has created odd-lot shareholding by initial round-lot investors. It is quite likely that the whole process of odd-lot trading could be computerized and made much more efficient, and with the differentials considerably reduced.

Insider Trading

The managers and directors of publicly owned corporations constantly face a serious ethical dilemma: Their position gives them far better knowledge of the future prospects of a firm than outside investors can possibly have. To what extent are they entitled to make use of this superior knowledge in stock market trading? For incentive reasons these managers are usually urged to be substantial stockholders; stock option plans for promoting this are widespread.

In the "bad old days" there was undoubtedly a lot of rather unscrupulous insider trading. Insiders bought on good news before the news became widely known or understood (as in the Texas Gulf Sulphur case). If unfavorable developments were pending, insiders might sell the stocks of their companies. In a few extreme cases, unscrupulous traders would get control of a corporation with no goal other than manipulation. These pirates would sell short the stocks of their own companies and then issue *false* bad news. They would then cover their short sales at lower prices and subsequently correct the false news reports so as to allow them to cover their short sales at a profit. The opposite ploy was also practiced. Misinformation was used as a kind of market strategy. However, this picture of past horrors could be overstated. Many publicly owned corporations conducted their affairs with scrupulous regard for the rights of shareholders and did not allow insiders to engage in any such shenanigans.

The Securities Exchange Act (Sec. 16) provides the following limitations on insider trading:

1 Each officer, director, and beneficial owner of more than 10 percent of any listed class of stock (the legal definition of an "insider") must file with the SEC and the exchange on which it is listed an initial statement of holdings and thereafter monthly reports that reflect changes in holdings.

2   Profits obtained by insiders (as defined above) from purchases and sales of the company's stock with less than a six-month holding period may be recovered by the company or by any security holder on its behalf.

3   Insiders (as defined above) cannot sell short.

It should be noted that long-term capital gains derived from insider purchases are not prohibited by these rules. The impact of the SEC pressure tends to shorten the period that such information is considered insider information. Court decisions have tended to broaden the statutory definition of "insider." Families of the persons named or their agents to whom confidential disclosure might be made (such as brokers) have been found to be covered by the law. The Texas Gulf Sulphur case and the Merrill Lynch, Pierce, Fenner & Smith case both worked in this broadening direction.

In spite of the limitation on insider trading, there is a feeling that insiders still have some trading advantage. A number of stock market advisory services are avid readers of the SEC monthly reports of insider transactions. Insider buying is taken as a good omen for investment in a company and insider selling as a bad omen or a reason for retreat. However, the research studies that have attempted to correlate subsequent price movements with insider trading have failed to prove conclusively that any such relationship exists.

Stock Market Credit

Some aggressive investors attempt to increase their market profits by the use of leverage: They finance a portion of their market purchases with borrowed money. Such "margin trading" has a very long history. Perhaps the most dramatic episode in this history, however, came in the stock market collapse of 1929. In the two years preceding September 1929, brokers' loans grew from $4 billion to $9 billion. Since some direct loans by banks to individuals for stock market purposes are not included in these figures, the total growth of stock market credit is unknown. However, in the last three months of 1929, brokers' loans were reduced from the $9 billion back to $4 billion. In the next 2 1/2 years, brokers' loans all but disappeared.

Exactly what part this rapid and unpremediated liquidation of stock market credit had to do with the ensuing depression is unclear. The relationship of stock prices and business activity, as we have already noted

MARKETS FOR CORPORATE EQUITIES 355

in this chapter, is not wholly clear. But it is clear that the rapid liquidation of that amount of credit was a serious depressant on stock market prices. Many security purchases were margined very thinly; some by as little as 10 percent. Thus a modest drop in prices reduced the coverage of other margined positions. If margin owners were unable to raise more margin, they were then sold out. The selling out of margined positions of owners who could not come up with more margin thus put added pressure on the market. The whole process became self-reinforcing. When regulation of the securities markets was adopted, regulation of stock market credit was one of its principal features.

The Federal Reserve rather than the SEC was directed to regulate stock market credit. The regulation imposed by the Federal Reserve covered, until recently, only listed stocks. Federal Reserve Regulations T and U require the buyer to supply a specified part of the purchase price at time of purchase.

In practice the Federal Reserve has varied the minimum margin to be supplied by purchasers at time of purchase fairly frequently: It was changed eighteen times in the thirty-four years during which stock market credit has been regulated. Since 1945 the required margin has never been less than 50 percent, and for one brief period it was 100 percent.

Since the margin requirement applies to the time of purchase, requests for added margin if security prices go down are a private and not a regulatory matter. Brokers ask for added margin only to protect the security of a credit and not for regulatory reasons. However, if security prices go up, then the security profits, whether realized or not, supplying added margin for further trading. The purchase of stock as the result of a rights offerings is subject to a lower (25 percent) margin, and security brokers in their normal operations (but not for personal speculation) are also subject to lower margins.

The amount of stock market credit outstanding has drifted upward and recently reached a level not far short of $10 billion. However, this is only a little more than 1 percent of total stock market value, whereas in 1929 the $9 billion was closer to 10 percent of the total value of stock. In terms of floating supplies of stock, the contrast between margined holdings and outright holdings is even more striking.

AGENCIES OF SECURITIES MARKET REGULATION

Before undertaking to review the specific agencies involved in securities market regulation, it will be helpful to review briefly the unique principle of regulation widely described as that of "self-regulation." This phrase, by itself, fails to convey the rather subtle combination of forces at work.

Self-regulation, as practiced in the securities markets, means that a large part of the day-to-day rules and standards by which the markets operate are those adopted by private agencies organized by the firms and individuals doing business in these markets—but always subject to the overview of a government agency with strong powers of intervention. The NYSE makes the rules and, strictly speaking, does not have to get approval of the SEC before putting them into effect. But the SEC has large reserve powers granted by the Securities Exchange Act of 1934, and if the NYSE adopted rules that it considered against the public interest or *failed* to adopt rules it considered necessary in the public interest, the SEC could then intervene with its own requirements. The SEC can also initiate civil or criminal suits against firms or individuals. All legal actions of the SEC, of course, are ultimately subject to full judicial review. So far, the courts have tended to support the SEC. The NYSE thus knows that, in the end, it probably would lose if there were a test of wills. For this reason, the degree of public interest self-regulation the NYSE undertakes is probably greater than it would be without prodding. At the same time, the character of regulation is probably better adapted and shaped to the operational problems of business firms operating in the market than if the regulatory harness were one imposed directly by the SEC or any other government agency.

The Self-Regulators: the NYSE and the NASD

Since we have already described the functional organization of the NYSE and other organized exchanges, at this point we need only recount the circumstances in which self-regulation arose and to outline some of its subsequent developments. The original Securities Exchange Act of 1934 gave the SEC broad powers but not very explicit mandates as to how they were to be carried out. Badly shocked by the Great Depression, the securities industry in general and the NYSE specifically were not able to thwart the passage of the legislation. They attempted, however, to resist the implementation of the law. This tactic was dropped in 1938, when the NYSE suffered a devastating publicity blow: Richard Whitney, its president, who had led the fight against the SEC, was found to have been embezzling trust funds. Under the shock of this disclosure, internal NYSE opposition to reform collapsed and a reform administration was put in office. William McChesney Martin, later to achieve even greater fame as the chairman of the Federal Reserve Board, was made president of the NYSE at thirty years of age. Change was prompt and drastic.

Since that time the NYSE has become very conscious of its public role (and of its public image). The membership of the NYSE is subject to disciplining, and the number of publicly exposed cases of discipline underindicates the degree of quiet pressure for living by the rules. The relationship of the NYSE and the SEC has not been exactly friendly, but they have learned to work together in this rather unusual relationship.

The Martin Report

In 1970, after William McChesney Martin had left the Federal Reserve, he returned to the NYSE (which he had left in 1941) and was retained by them to study its operations and to make recommendations for change. Although the report, submitted in 1971, has fourteen recommendations, it can be boiled down to three principal points:

1. That the public representation in the governing of the NYSE be increased and strengthened by more power to control exchange practices.
2. That institutional investors continue to be denied membership on the NYSE, but, at the same time, that NYSE member firms be prohibited from the management of mutual funds.
3. That technology be pushed to permit a national unified securities market.

The first of the Martin recommendations is already being acted upon. The second requires no action—but progress on the third is far from clear.

Governance of the NYSE

Perhaps the long-time description of the NYSE as a "private club" was a bit exaggerated, but it was not far from the truth. The NYSE was organized as a nonprofit association, just like a club. Social pressures were very much like those in any similar group. Moreover, William McChesney Martin, the first paid full-time president, came from inside the exchange. As to organization power, however, the chairman of the exchange was more powerful, and the chairmanship was, until 1972, a part-time job held by an active exchange member. Now that post has also been made a full-time one and the first person to hold it comes from outside the NYSE. Not only that, but public members of the Board of Governors of the Exchange have been nominated, including one female economist.

The regional exchanges faced problems of survival as well as regulation. Most of them had to be reorganized after being registered to effect the changes needed. Full-time professional presidents with considerable regulatory power were often brought in to replace part-time officers drawn from the member firms and individuals. The American Stock Exchange was rather considerably reformed within the past decade as the result of a series of misdealings exposed and prosecuted by the SEC.

Prior to 1938, the over-the-counter market was almost wholly unregulated. In 1933 the Investment Bankers Association had been formed, and later it created a "code" for industry operation under the aegis of the National Industrial Recovery Act (which was declared unconstitutional in 1935). After some negotiation, the Maloney Amendment to the Securities Exchange Act was passed in 1938, and under this act the National Association of Securities Dealers (NASD) was formed. This organization was given powers of self-regulation but—even more important—it was given a power which made it necessary for virtually every securities firm to be an NASD member. Cooperative selling of securities is traditional, and the actual seller is customarily given a "concession" by the underwriters. The NASD was given power to require its members to give such concessions *only to other NASD members*. This made membership virtually mandatory for any firm wishing to join the community of security salesmanship.

The NASD has functioned in a variety of ways, but its effects on the over-the-counter market were most notable. It has narrowed the bid-and-ask spread, generally to not exceed 5 percent. Disclosure of the role of the seller as a dealer or broker has also been required. In general, trading standards have been improved to the point where ordinary private investors can venture into this market without losing too much fleece.

The Governmental Regulators: Mainly the SEC

It has been necessary to mention the Securities and Exchange Commission (SEC) at many previous points. The SEC is an independent federal agency headed by a commission of five members, each serving for a five-year term. They are appointed (and the chairman is also designated) by the President subject to Senate confirmation. The SEC staff has been small as federal agencies go: it has averaged less than 1,500 persons. Every one of the laws mentioned at earlier points in this chapter in some way affects the work of the SEC. (In addition, the SEC has some marginal duties imposed by laws *not* mentioned here, such as those dealing with bankruptcy and corporate reorganization.) As already indicated, a central part of the SEC's work is regulatory. The chairmen of the SEC have usually been lawyers; law school professors have been frequent appointees. The SEC collects and publishes a number of leading statistical series; but apart from this activity, its work in economic analysis has been sporadic and Congress has tended to starve this segment of the SEC's function.

MARKETS FOR CORPORATE EQUITIES 359

The regulatory powers of the SEC are great, but an almost equally powerful impact has resulted from its investigative powers. This power has shown itself in two ways. First, the SEC has often been more diligent than the NYSE or the NASD in digging up cases of market shenanigans; the resulting exposure has sometimes left these agencies with rather red faces. Second, the SEC has several times undertaken detailed investigations of various market practices without the objective of civil or criminal prosecution but to open up industry practices to public scrutiny. Such inquiries have covered commission charges, floor trading, the specialists' function, odd-lot dealing, the influence of institutional investment on the markets, management of investment companies, and other subjects. The publicity resulting from these studies has often resulted in legislation; but even without legislation it has often had marked impact on market practices and on the standards of self-regulation.

Several other government agencies have, in various ways, been involved with the regulation of the financial markets. The Anti-Trust Division of the Department of Justice brought a monopoly suit against a number of investment bankers at one time. The suit was lost, but the decision of the presiding judge has become a classic description of the underwriting process. The Federal Reserve, as already noted, has control of margins required for security purchases. In addition, the Federal Reserve takes a paternal if not regulatory view of the money markets, particularly the market for Treasury securities. The open-market function of the Federal Reserve gives it great power of moral suasion. Trading rules and standards of professional performance in this market have certainly been strongly influenced even if not directly regulated by the Federal Reserve.

Finally, it should not be forgotten that regulation of outright securities frauds was undertaken by most state governments, long before the federal government got into this business, by so-called "blue sky" regulation. In most states this regulatory function still exists, even if it is overshadowed by federal operations.

IS SECURITIES MARKET REGULATION EXCESSIVELY BURDENSOME?

In the fall of 1968 when President Nixon, then a candidate for the office, sent the abovementioned letter to the securities industry promising less strict regulatory policies, the Texas Gulf Sulphur case had only recently been settled and the Merrill Lynch, Pierce, Fenner & Smith—Douglas Aircraft case was still in the process of settlement. Later, when MLPF&S accepted the SEC penalties without further legal challenge, their letter to customers painted the picture of oppressive public regulation. The purpose of this section is not to supply any kind of answer to the question raised but to supply the considerations that each person should recognize in deciding whether or not securities market regulation has been too oppressive.

The standards by which we judge what is fair and equitable constantly change. Behavior that would have been considered normal and acceptable long ago may come to be regarded as unacceptable now. At any time, furthermore, views of what is acceptable behavior differ among persons. There are no absolutes by which behavior can be judged. A very honorable man in a position of corporate responsibility two generations ago would have used his insider knowledge for personal trading profit without twinge of conscience; the same behavior today would make his profits subject to recovery. In order to make some progress in trying to understand the questions involved here, we can only raise some other questions.

Who Should Be a Securities Investor?

If the securities markets were limited to institutional investors who had the same degree of financial sophistication as the financial managements of corporations, it is possible that no regulation at all would be needed. With an equivalence of market power and knowledge, they could fend for themselves without protection. However, if a large number of investors with little market power and less knowledge are involved, they could be fleeced unless protected. Under the shelter of regulatory protection, 25 million citizens have become corporate shareholders. Could it have happened without regulation, or would this growth have been desirable? It is possible that for reasons of long-run interests in business promotion, commission brokerage houses would have supplied some such protection even without public regulation. But can we be sure? In fact, the nature of competition in the securities business deserves some very concentrated attention.

How Competitive Is the Securities Business?

The presence of a large number of firms in the commission brokerage business results in some kinds of competition. However, since the principal price charged by these firms—the commissions for executing market orders—is fixed by the NYSE for all listed stocks (and this has then tended to set the standard for brokerage charges in OTC stocks), it is not competition with respect to price but rather with respect to service. And since the commission structure has not, until recently, contained any element of quantity discount, there has been a strong incentive to concentrate the supply of service on the large, profitable institutional investors.

The NYSE is not an inherent monopoly, but by long standing it is a de facto position of monopoly in the organized trading of the shares of the great nonfinancial corporations. Thus its trading rules can have the effect of limiting market participation. An interesting example can be found in the matter of Rule 394. This rule provides that a member of the NYSE may not trade a listed stock in the OTC market. When the disclosure requirements imposed by the 1964 SEA amendments persuaded the Chase Manhattan Bank to seek NYSE listing, this put a gap in the business of the OTC bank stock trading firms. Later, when the one-bank holdings companies were listed, this increased the transfer of business to the NYSE. This development raises an important question of market efficiency; it can be argued that in this largely institutional market the OTC is more efficient than the listed market. Should the NYSE be able to bar its members from doing business with firms that are not members of the NYSE?

For small but publicly held corporations, a still different problem exists. The presence of a large number of firms in the OTC market suggests strong competition. And to a considerable extent this is true; in the marketing of securities having a broad regional or national appeal, the number of firms assures competition. But in the markets for securities having a rather limited appeal, this will not be true. Only one OTC firm may make markets in the stock of a moderate-sized, publicly owned, but not well-known company. Can competition work in a case such as this? One bit of evidence suggests that it can: The number of bidders for small issues of state and local government obligations is often quite large, suggesting a high level of competition.

The growth of the third market is also an illustration that where a need of any great size exists, financial innovation will increase the amount of competition. At the same time, efforts of the NYSE to keep business from going to the third market may have imposed limitations on its members that some would not view as consistent with the existence of free competition.

Next Steps in Regulation

Technology may well account for some of the most interesting new securities market developments. For example, the computer may make possible a far more efficient national OTC market (but it may also threaten the viability of the small local securities firm that cannot afford this overhead). As already mentioned, it is quite likely that odd-lot trading will be changed by the computer. The punch-card stock certificate may spur more use of stock dividends. Regional exchanges may be linked to the NYSE more closely—and some sort of consolidation of the exchanges is not unthinkable.

One of the most interesting recent developments has been the introduction of a quotation system in the OTC market, the NASDAQ (National Association of Security Dealers Automated Quotation). This new system covers not only OTC stocks but has also included a number of listed stocks. The system is still developing, but it might prove to be more efficient than the organized stock exchange system. If the NASDAQ system should reach such a level of efficiency, there might be resistance on the part of the NYSE, since no institution likes to face its own demise. But electronic communications might make the old verbal auction system obsolete—and too costly.

UNRESOLVED PROBLEMS OF THE EQUITY MARKETS

As this text leaves the authors' hands and starts through the process of publication, the Congress has before it a series of proposals for change that could have far-ranging effects on the equity markets. Much change has taken place, but more could come within the near-term future. The NYSE has already adopted some of the recommendations of the Martin Report. It now has public members on its Board of Directors. It has a full-time paid chairman. And, as indicated earlier, commission rates above $300,000 are now negotiable, and this limit may soon be reduced to $100,000. And some institutional investors are now members of regional exchanges and are thereby getting some reduction in the cost of brokerage.

But the unresolved problems outnumber those that might be considered "solved" or at least made less pressing. The NYSE has mounted a campaign to do away with the third market. It is based on the appeal that a company should be able to control where its securities are to be traded (which, however, would abrogate the right of the investor to determine in which market he should do business.) The conflict of interest between those brokerage firms that have gone into money management remains unresolved. The fear that managed portfolios might be "churned" excessively simply for the sake of brokerage commission has not been allayed. Perhaps the greatest unresolved problem is that of the relationship between our public regulators—the SEC—and the self-regulatory systems. It has become increasingly evident that many important decisions are being hammered out between these two groups in private bargaining sessions to which the public is not invited or about which it is not informed. The complexity of the business may require some continued degree of self-regulation, but it seems likely that the public's "right to know" needs greater respect.

Possibly the greatest of the unresolved problems of the equity markets concerns the new technology that lies just over the horizon. Just as our monetary system may be due for drastic change as a result of computer and credit (or money?) card technology, the system of markets may be changing faster than the institutions involved realize. The need for a physical face-to-face auction market could dwindle as the technology of the dealer market with electronic communications became more efficient.

These unresolved issues may be not only the most important but also the most interesting ones on which the student can focus as he moves beyond the textbook into the affairs of the real world.

Part Four

Evaluation of Financial Market Performance

Chapter 19

Financial Markets and Economic Stability

Economic stability is such an important criterion of our economy's performance that many regard it as our number-one economic goal. Government expresses its concern about economic instability through its monetary and fiscal policies. Such concern is derived from the needs of individuals for security of employment and real income. The United States has had a long history of economic ups and downs (general business cycles) which have deprived people of work and income during the downs (depressions, recessions) and redistributed income and wealth during the ups (inflationary boom periods). In 1933, in the trough of the Great Depression, more than one-quarter of the labor force was totally unemployed and a large proportion of those who were employed worked only part-time. When, during World War II, the economy went through a "guns and butter" recovery, inflation, despite price controls, eroded the real value of the financial savings of millions of individuals. The fear of postwar depression and the obvious need for a more stable economy pushed Congress into passing the Employment Act of 1946. This act made the goal of full employment and maximum purchasing power a matter of public policy. The notion of a self-stabilizing market system was abandoned.

Business cycles have been less pronounced since the passage of the Employment Act than they were before. The economy has had its ups and downs, but the peaks and troughs have been less severe in duration and magnitude. The recessions of 1949, 1954, 1958, 1961, 1967, and 1970 were minor compared to the Great Depression of the 1930s. Nevertheless, instability is still a cause for concern. Monetary and fiscal policies have not been successful in simultaneously keeping the unemployment rate below 5 percent and the inflation rate below 3 percent. Unemployment was low but inflation much too high during the overheated economy of the latter 1960s. Since then, the inflation rate has moderated, but the unemployment rate has increased and lingered around the 5 percent level. As of this writing (summer of 1972) there is some indication of a small decrease in unemployment—but probably at the cost of greater inflation. The business cycle, though diminished, is still with us. The economy is more stable than it was a couple of generations ago but not as stable as most people would like it to be.

Full employment and stable prices are the ultimate targets of stabilization policy, but their stability (or lack of it) is tied to fluctuations in other economic variables, including movements in the financial markets. There is no question that fluctuations in general economic activity and movements in the financial markets are related. There are questions, however, whether financial movements are the causes or the effects of real fluctuations and whether the existence of financial markets contributes to greater or less stability in other markets.

To a large extent, financial movements are the effects of fluctuation in general economic activity. Financial markets are unusually sensitive to the health of the economy. An excellent example may be found in business capital expenditures, which are important factors in the level of business activity. The timing of such expenditures can be adjusted to meet the needs and expectations of business management. The markets for the raising of business capital are early reflectors of variations in the demands for such funds.

A closely related variable is business profits. In the long run, the return on capital as well as the existence of capital itself depends on the level of business profits. Business profits, in turn, influence capital expenditure decisions. Financial markets are swayed by the actions of those in a strategic position to know something about future profits. If the promise of future profits and business prosperity looks bright, stock market trading often leads to rising stock prices well in advance of an actual upturn in economic activity.

FINANCIAL MARKETS AND ECONOMIC STABILITY

While financial markets are affected by economic events originating in other sectors of the economy, reverse causality also exists. Developments in the financial markets influence business, government, and consumer expenditure to a considerable extent. Fluctuations in the cost and availability of credit usually lead to fluctuations in the demand for real goods and services. So do movements in the money supply. Sometimes these effects are merely feedback effects from movements originating in the real side of the economy. Other times these effects originate in the financial markets themselves.

In general equilibrium analysis, everything depends upon everything else. This principle applies to the interrelations between the financial markets and the markets for real goods and services. Fluctuations in financial market activity are both cause and effect of fluctuations in general economic activity. Cyclical impulses can originate anywhere in the economy, including the financial markets. First-round effects and feedback effects can work in any direction.

This leaves us with the question of whether the real side of the economy would be more stable or less so if financial markets did not exist. One might argue that the economy would be more stable in the absence of financial markets because it is these markets which make it possible to separate the acts of saving and investment. Discoordination of investment decisions from saving decisions is a source of instability. If investors want to invest more than savers want to save, an economic expansion is set in motion. On the other hand, if savers want to save more than investors want to invest, the economy contracts. Without financial markets, desired saving and desired investment would always be equal. The economy might still fluctuate, but it would not be due to disparity between ex ante saving and investment. However, such an economy would be characterized by permanent stagnation. Without financial markets, resources would be grossly misallocated; consumer welfare would drop and economic growth would be stifled.

One can also make the opposite case: that is, that the economy is more stable because of financial markets. One line of argument in this case is that the financial markets absorb pressures from other markets in the economy. In this view, swings in financial market activity provide relief from swings which might otherwise occur in the markets for real goods and services. For example, many businesses extend credit to customers in the face of declining income in order to stabilize sales. Such credit often runs counter-cyclically to general economic activity, thereby dampening the general business cycle. Another argument in this case is that the financial markets play an originating causal role in the economy, and that by controlling financial market activity through official monetary and credit policies, one can indirectly control the overall business cycle.

This chapter does not take the position that financial markets are, on balance, either inherently stabilizing or destabilizing in terms of the overall economy. Rather, it recognizes that both the real and financial sides of the economy do in fact fluctuate and that these fluctuations are interconnected, with cause and effect patterns working in both directions. The general theme of this chapter is to examine some of the major patterns of cyclical influence and causality which touch on the financial system.

One problem with discussing fluctuations in financial market activity is that there is no single aggregate measure of the volume of this activity. Unlike the concept of GNP, aggregate measures of credit involve considerable doublecounting because of the layering of credit by financial intermediaries. Thus, in the sections to follow, we shall be looking at movements in specific quantities such as the supply of money. But quantities do not tell the whole story. Interest rates—the prices in financial markets—are logical indicators of economic instability, financial and real. We must pay attention to interest rates and also to stock market prices, since it has long been fashionable for observers to tie the stock market and the business cycle together.

CYCLICAL MOVEMENTS IN MONEY, INTEREST RATES, AND GENERAL ECONOMIC ACTIVITY

The historical record shows that money, interest rates, and general economic activity tend to move together in the same direction. Economic upswings are generally characterized by rising rates of interest and inflation as well as rising rates of growth in money and production. During downswings, rates of interest and inflation as well as growth rates in money and production tend to drop.

These parallel movements are usually but not always visible to the naked eye. Some variables lead while others lag, so at any given point in time a movement in one variable may be nearing completion while another is still picking up steam. The 1970 to 1971 recession was a good example of this. The decline in the rate of growth of the money supply actually began in 1969, several months before production, employment, and interest rates started their downward course. When production hit bottom, the rate of inflation had yet to show any sign of subsiding.

The discussion thus far raises two important questions: Why do money, interest rates, and general economic activity tend to move in parallel fashion? Why do the parallel movements fail to correspond exactly at any point in time? To answer these questions we must analyze the interrelations between the principal variables.

The foundation for a positive relation between the money supply and nominal income (GNP measured at current prices) can be traced to the "quantity theory of money," now commonly called "monetarism." This theory holds that the growth rate of nominal income is tied to the growth rate of the money supply. According to this theory an increase in the growth rate of money will bring about an increase in the growth rate of production after a lag averaging some six to nine months, and it will also bring about an increase in the rate of inflation after an additional lag again averaging about six to nine months. Thus money grows first, then production, and finally prices. Lag time is thought to be long and variable, but apart from this, nominal income cannot expand appreciably without an expansion of the money supply, nor can nominal income fail to contract if the money supply is appreciably contracted.

Economists in the "neo-Keynesian" camp agree that there is a positive relation between money and income, but they do not see a necessary relation. In their view, the level of production and prices can expand or contract without a corresponding expansion or contraction of the money supply. Neo-Keynesians consider "autonomous demand" to be the prime mover of change in general economic activity. An increase in autonomous demand is thought to lead to an increase in production and prices. With nominal income rising, the demand for money also rises, which creates a shortage of money. This shortage may be eliminated by increasing the money supply, so that money rises with production and prices. Alternatively, the shortage may be corrected by a rising level of interest rates which reduces the demand for money. In this alternative case, an expansion in production and prices is accompanied by higher interest rates rather than a growing money supply. The money supply may grow, but it does not have to grow.

Those who hold to the quantity theory position admit that interest rates do tend to rise and fall with general economic expansion and contraction, but not necessarily for the reasons given by the neo-Keynesians. According to the quantity theory, observed interest rates largely reflect expectations regarding inflation. Lenders who want a 4 percent constant-dollar return on their investment and expect a 3 percent rate of inflation must charge a nominal interest rate of 7 percent to obtain a "real" return of 4 percent. If lenders expect inflation to be at a 5 percent rate, they must then charge a nominal interest rate of 9 percent to get a 4 percent "real" return. Thus interest rates vary positively with the rate of inflation, which in turn varies positively with the growth rate of the money supply.

This book is not the appropriate place to go deeply into the various nuances of rival monetary theories, but one key difference between the quantity theory (monetarism) and neo-Keynesianism is worth pointing out, and that has to do with the effect of changes in interest rates. In the quantity theory view, interest rates affect spending decisions more than they do decisions about holding money. If "autonomous demand" but not the money supply is increased, interest rates will rise; but this increase will do more to discourage spending than to directly decrease the demand for money. Reduced spending due to higher interest rates thus works to offset the increase in autonomous demand. On balance, nominal income and the supply of and demand for money are very nearly restored to their original levels. A change in autonomous demand may initiate a change in nominal income, but only a change in the money supply can sustain a change in nominal income.

In the neo-Keynesian view, interest rates affect decisions about holding money more than they do spending decisions. In this view, a change in autonomous demand is sufficient to sustain a change in nominal income. Monetary change is not a necessary condition. If autonomous demand but not the money supply is increased, income and interest rates will rise. The increase in income will increase the demand for money. But the increase in interest rates will decrease the demand for money. On balance, the demand for money will be little affected and will therefore remain in equilibrium with the unchanging money supply.

A synthesis of monetarism and neo-Keynesianism recognizes that interest rates affect both spending decisions and decisions about holding money. Whether one effect is stronger than the other is an empirical question. The facts do reveal that money, interest, and income move up and down together in a systematic fashion. These facts are consistent with a synthetic approach to monetary theory.

The Federal Reserve has generally taken a synthetic or eclectic approach in conducting its monetary policies. Unbound by economic ideology, it has gauged the thrust of its actions by keeping one eye on the money supply and the other on interest rates. However, as we saw in Chapters 10 and 11, the Fed began in the early 1970s to give more weight to monetary aggregates than to interest rates in conducting and monitoring its operations. It is probably too soon to say whether or not this new emphasis will last. As of this writing (1972), there is already some indication that the Fed may not allow interest rates to get too high even if it means that the money supply will have to grow at a faster rate than otherwise desired.

CYCLICAL EFFECT OF NONBANK FINANCIAL INTERMEDIATION

We have seen that monetary policy works through Federal Reserve management of bank reserves and the money supply. Most of the money supply is in the form of demand deposit debt of commercial banks. The commercial banking system, however, is but one part of a larger system of financial intermediaries which borrows from ultimate savers and lends to ultimate investors. Monetary policy therefore works through controlling the liabilities (demand deposits) of one type of financial intermediary (commercial banks). When the economy is overheated, the Fed may attempt to cool it off by contracting the growth of the liabilities of commercial banks. When the economy is depressed, the Fed may try to promote recovery by expanding the liabilities of commercial banks. The idea of discretionary monetary policy is to get the growth rate of these liabilities to move somewhat counter-cyclically to the growth rate of general economic activity.

One might reasonably ask what happens to the liabilities of financial intermediaries other than commercial banks. Do these uncontrolled liabilities follow a cyclical pattern? If so, do they move pro- or counter-cyclically? If pro-cyclically, do they undermine the intent and effect of monetary policy? If counter-cyclically, do they have a general effect on interest rates and capital expenditures, or do they affect certain markets and sectors more than others? These issues have puzzled economists and policy makers for a number of years.

The idea that the liabilities of nonbank financial intermediaries move pro-cyclically with the economy, offsetting the effect of monetary policy in the process, was promoted some fifteen or so years ago by Professors Gurley and Shaw (92). The reasoning went something like this: Suppose the Fed decreases the money supply with the intent of raising open-market interest rates and lowering capital expenditures. In the face of higher open-market rates, nonbank intermediaries will be induced to raise the interest rates which they pay on savings accounts and other liabilities in order to attract more funds. The higher rates paid on these liabilities will increase the demand for them and decrease the demand for non-interest-bearing money. The decreased demand for money, in turn, will decrease open-market interest rates, thereby offsetting the attempt of the contractionary policy to raise open-market rates. In other words, if the monetary contraction is initially successful in increasing open-market rates, it is probable that nonbank intermediaries will raise their rates in order to attract funds for investment. When the intermediaries use these attracted funds to purchase open-market instruments, the effect is to decrease open-market rates. In the end, the open-market rates may fall back nearly to where they began, thereby undermining the intent of the policy.

In a similar vein, an increase in the liabilities of nonbank intermediaries at a time when the liabilities of banks are decreasing will leave the total supply of liquid assets largely unaffected. For those who believe that the economy is related more to "stores of value" than it is to "means of payment," control of only one store of value—demand deposits—is insufficient to control the economy. In this view, monetary control should be extended to the liabilities of all financial intermediaries, not just the liabilities of commercial banks.

These ideas have been criticized both on theoretical and empirical grounds. Even if one accepts the theory, the evidence shows that nonbank financial intermediation has had only a minor pro-cyclical effect at worst. In fact, during the tight credit period of 1966 to 1970, the liabilities of nonbank intermediaries not only failed to expand but actually shrank, and they shrank considerably.

Several reasons account for the disintermediation during this period. Open-market interest rates climbed dramatically, reaching near-historic highs. Rates paid by intermediaries on savings accounts did not increase relatively. They were held back by legal ceilings and by the fact that savings and loan associations and mutual savings banks were carrying a large volume of low-yielding and slow-moving mortgages and therefore could not have raised the rates which they pay by very much, even if they had been allowed to. The demand for money did decrease, but not because people wanted to put it into savings accounts. In fact, the demand for savings accounts also decreased. Many people switched out of demand deposits, savings accounts, and life insurance policy reserves and put their funds directly into the open market to take advantage of extra-good yields. Others liquidated their accounts to finance consumption and other expenditures.

HOUSING CYCLES AND THE MORTGAGE MARKET

One of the more striking features of the postwar period has been the tendency for housing starts to move counter-cyclically with general business conditions. Residential construction has typically risen sharply when general activity was reaching a trough. Declines in building activity have tended to take hold well in advance of peaks in the general business cycle.

Most housing market economists have linked this counter-cyclical behavior to counter-cyclical movements in the supply of mortgage credit. In an expanding economy, the total demand for credit tends to run ahead of the total supply of credit. Credit becomes "tight" and interest rates rise. The feedback effects of tight credit conditions on general expenditures is to dampen economic activity somewhat, but not by enough to reverse its generally upward course. Housing, however, is an exception. The supply of mortgage credit has typically become so short during general expansion that housing starts have actually fallen while other kinds of production have continued to rise. For various reasons, tight credit has a tendency to become concentrated and compounded in the mortgage market.

One reason for this is the "disintermediation" process described in the preceding section. The inability of savings institutions to raise their rates on savings deposits when open-market interest rates are rising serves to facilitate a flow of funds out of these intermediaries and into the open market. This would have little effect on the mortgage market were it not for the fact that savings and loan associations and mutual savings banks, and to a lesser extent life insurance companies and commercial banks, invest heavily and disproportionately in the mortgage market. Consequently, a dollar of savings taken out of one of these intermediaries is apt to be a dollar taken out of the mortgage market. When it is reinvested in the open market, it is unlikely to go back into the mortgage market. The supply of mortgage credit is therefore reduced.

But this is not the end of the story. Financial intermediaries are apt to reduce their investments in mortgages by more than the funds lost through disintermediation. Mortgage rates of interest do not rise or fall as far or as fast as other rates of interest. When interest rates are rising, mortgage rates tend to lag behind. Profit-motivated commercial banks and other intermediaries can therefore increase return by switching out of mortgages and into other forms of investment. The supply of mortgage credit is thus further reduced.

Why do mortgage rates lag behind other interest rates? There are two views. One explains "sticky" mortgage rates as the result of market interferences such as legal rate ceilings on insured and guaranteed mortgage loans. The other view argues that mortgage borrowers are more responsive and sensitive to mortgage rates than other borrowers are to other rates. With an "elastic" demand curve for mortgage funds, mortgage rates may change little even if there is a large shift in demand. There is probably some truth to both of these views.

A different approach to explaining the counter-cyclical behavior of housing starts emphasizes the effect of credit conditions on the supply side of the housing market. In this approach, home building is seen as an inventory problem. Tight credit conditions are thought to reduce the demand for builders' inventories of houses under construction and therefore to reduce the supply of new housing starts. Easy credit is thought to increase the willingness of builders to expand their inventories under construction.

FLUCTUATIONS IN THE BOND MARKET

Movements in business activity clearly have an influence on the bond market. This influence is effective both upon yields and upon the volume of business. The significant point, however, seems to be that although the influence on yields is an early and prompt reflection of movements in business activity, changes in the volume of bonds issued and sold seem to lag. An important question arises: How much is the volume of business influenced by yield changes?

Bond yields show a clear cyclical pattern. They go up as business activity advances; they recede as business activity slackens. The timing of this movement is roughly synchronous, although the yields may have some element of lead in them. If a lead exists, it is probably due to the strong link between the money markets and the bond markets. If the money markets show any tendency to lead, then it is quite natural that the bond markets should reflect a similar pattern.

Within bond yields, the movements are so nearly parallel that one can almost use any one of the yield series as reflective of events in the market as a whole; but some deviations do occur. For example, the yields on tax-exempt state and local government obligations sometimes depart from other yield series by material amounts. A large part of the reason for this is that the demand for state and local government bonds is tied more closely to stock market prices and money market rates than it is to yields on corporate and Treasury bonds. During economic expansion, when stock market prices and money market yields are on the rise, wealthy individuals tend to switch out of state and local obligations and into stocks while commercial banks tend to switch into short-term loans and investments. Often this behavior lowers the prices and raises the yields on state and local government bonds much more dramatically than is the case in other parts of the bond market.

The movements of yields on corporate bonds and on bonds of the U.S. Treasury are parallel. Interest on both types of bonds is now fully exposed to income taxation. The quality of corporate bonds has also become so good that the differential between these yields is deservedly small.

Movements in the volume of bond financing are clearly rather laggard of general business conditions. One of the probable reasons is that bond financing takes a lot of time to put into effect after the decision to finance has been made. This lag is equally true of other business cycle series, such as capital expenditures. Bond financing may lag during the later phases of an upturn since profits are high and because of hope for a slightly better market. When the market does start to change and yields decline, volume picks up while borrowers are taking advantage of the situation. But if lower borrowing costs persist for long enough to indicate a general weakening in business conditions, then overall financing plans probably are changed.

One interesting but unexplained fact is that the yields on lower-grade bonds seem to lag behind changes in the yields on higher-grade bonds. The volume of financing is not classified on a quality basis by months, so the length of this lag cannot be measured. It seems likely, however, that the lower-grade market may be subordinate to the market for top-grade issues and follows it.

One of the problems involved in using bond market data currently in financial analysis is that both yields and volume are subject to short-term variability. Differences in the behavior of new-issue and secondary markets may account for some of this randomness. The new-issue market for both corporate and U.S. government bonds is so sporadic that one cannot secure wholly satisfactory new-issue yields from these markets. For this reason much of the judgment of these markets is drawn from yields taken from secondary markets. These markets produce a steady stream of bid-and-ask quotations from which the published and most widely used statistical series are drawn. Some business is done at these levels, but secondary market yields often depart materially from new-issue market yields, particularly under conditions of stress. It even appears that this differential has a business-cycle character that as yet is not fully understood.

Conditions in the bond markets appear to have a feedback effect on capital expenditure decisions; but aside from this one influence, it seems unlikely that they have any profound effects on business conditions. The market is not very well publicized and its practitioners are skilled professionals, not given to panicking. Most markets produce some feedback influence since that is the very nature of a price system. Prices serve the function of influencing market supplies and demands in an economizing way. Nevertheless, the feedback effect of bond yields on capital expenditure is apt to be small to the extent that decision makers are able to untie their capital expenditure plans from the cost and availability of long-term debt. One such method of "time financing" is to borrow short-term when interest rates are high and long-term when rates are low. However, if interest rates are high over a long period of time, this strategy may not work and decision makers may be forced to abandon certain capital expenditure plans. Studies show that the tight credit conditions of the latter years of the 1960s did in fact lead to cutbacks in planned capital expenditures.

BUSINESS CYCLES AND THE STOCK MARKET

Even the most casual observer of the stock market is aware of the great extent to which the prices of common stocks fluctuate. The conclusion that these fluctuations are related to the ups and downs in general business conditions seems almost equally evident. The purpose of this section is to examine a little more closely the nature of this relationship and to consider the matter of causality.

Stock market prices are used as one of the leading indicators of changes in business conditions by the National Bureau of Economic Research and by other business-cycle analysts. This selection is supported by very widespread popular interest in the stock market. Many businessmen believe it to be a reliable guide as to future economic events and follow the market closely even if they are not themselves much involved in it as investors or speculators. Millions of ordinary citizens are given the impression that stock prices are important economic indicators as the averages are quoted every evening in television news programs.

There is undoubtedly a widespread impression that the stock market has some kind of causal effect on general economic activity. This notion was fostered by the Crash of October 1929, which preceded the 1932 to 1933 trough of the Great Depression But most people do not know that the decline of general economic activity actually began in the summer of 1929, several months before the crash of October. Economic historians now regard the Crash as more of an effect of the deepening Depression than as its cause.

Most of the time the stock market does turn in advance of turns in general economic activity. Figures from the National Bureau of Economic Research show that cycles in stock prices tend to lead general business cycles by an average of four months. Upturns in stock prices are frequently followed by upturns in business conditions, and market downturns are often followed by business downturns. But this is only a general tendency. Sometimes the lead and lag positions are reversed, as they were in 1929. What is more important, sometimes the stock market moves at crosscurrents with general business conditions. Bull markets have occasionally transpired during recessions and bear markets during economic recovery. In 1962, the stock market declined even though the economy was on the road to recovery. More recently, in the 1966 to 1971 period, there seemed to be little relation between stock market movements and movements in general economic activity.

The discussion to this point raises two questions: Why do the stock market and general economic activity sometimes move in opposite directions? Is the stock market a cause or an effect of the business cycle?

There are at least three ways in which a turn in the stock market might cause economic activity to change. One way is through a wealth effect. A sharp fall of stock prices reduces the market value of investors' financial wealth. Feeling poorer, investors may feel compelled to reduce their consumption expenditures for such luxury items as eating out, fancy automobiles, extended vacations, and luxury housing.

Another way is through a financing effect. Business corporations are prone to issue new stock when stock prices are high and terms are favorable. Selling stock when prices are abnormally depressed can have an adverse dilution effect on existing stockholders. To the extent that corporations rely on external equity to finance capital expenditures, an unfavorable stock market can lead to a postponement of business investment and initiate a downturn in economic activity. The fact is, however, that most corporations raise considerably more new capital through retained earnings and by borrowing in the credit markets than by selling new stock. Thus a stock market decline cannot be said to make funds much less available for business capital expenditures.

Still another way is through an expectations effect. A declining stock market may cause businessmen to develop pessimistic expectations of future business conditions. It may make them more cautious and conservative. The thing about expectations is that they have a way of becoming self-fulfilling: Business expects an economic downturn, so it does not invest and a downturn materializes. The Great Depression of the 1930s would have happened anyway, but it probably would not have been as severe as it was had there not been a shattering of business confidence following the Crash.

The fact that declining stock prices are not always followed by declining business conditions lends credence to the idea that the stock market is not the primary mover of economic activity. Even when stock prices and economic activity do move together, stock market causation is questionable. Other, more fundamental causes may be at work. These causes include such factors as changes in the quantity and quality of natural and human resources, innovations and technological change, monetary and fiscal policies, changes in tastes and preferences, war and peace, the weather, etc. The stock market may have some vague effect on general economic activity, but no serious economist would put it at the top of the list of causal factors.

Most economists view stock prices as being more reflective than effective. The main channel of causation is thought to flow from general business conditions to stock market conditions. There is ample theoretical reason to accept this view. Theoretically, stock prices are the capitalized values of future profits. If business conditions and profits improve, so should stock prices.

If stock prices reflect business conditions, why then does the stock price cycle tend to lead the general business cycle? The answer rests in the future profits which investors capitalize. Investors do not know in advance what actual future profits will be, but they can (and do) form expectations of future profits. Current stock prices are, therefore, capitalized values of *expected* future profits. If these expectations come close to the mark, future business conditions will bear a close relation to current stock prices. For this reason stock prices are considered a leading indicator of the course of the economy.

When the stock market runs counter to the general business cycle, incorrect profit expectations are not always the reason. As important as expected profits are in determining stock prices, they are not the only factors affecting the market. Other factors are also important. One such factor is the discount rate by which investors capitalize expected profits. The discount rate has a time value of money component plus a premium for risk and uncertainty. The time value of money is indicated by the level of interest rates. If individuals prefer to trade future consumption for present consumption, they will save less and interest rates will rise. In terms of the stock market, expected profits will be discounted at a higher rate and stock prices will fall. An increase in the uncertainty of the future also raises the rate of discount, thereby lowering stock prices. When interest rates and uncertainty are both increasing, the stock market is apt to be depressed. Such was the case in 1969 to 1970. Interest rates were higher than most people could remember. Vietnam, pollution, student revolt, and general social unrest were dividing the nation and increasing the uncertainty of its future. And the stock market? It was in a terribly depressed condition.

Chapter 20

Financial Markets and Economic Progress

An important criterion of market performance is economic progress. Progress measures the ability of the market system to adapt, adjust, and respond to changing economic needs. The financial system is subject to this pressure. It is expected to perform by raising the quality and variety of financial services which it offers and by improving the techniques used to produce these services, all at an adequate rate of accommodation over time.

Progress is something that everyone is for, but few can agree as to its nature. However, at the heart of progress is change. We may disagree whether the rate of change represents too much or not enough progress, or whether or not all changes are progressive, but the fact remains that in a dynamic world there can be no progress without change. Change is, therefore, a requisite of financial market progress.

An intensive study of money and capital markets during a quarter or a semester might lead the student to believe that these markets are enduring institutions. Change is not at all evident in such a short period of time. In fact, these markets have changed greatly under the influence of events and doubtless will continue to change. Change is caused by the need to adapt to new external influences. Change has almost always been evolutionary rather than revolutionary, but the pace of change is frequently rather brisk. Sometimes change has been forced on these markets by such events as legislation, but the more common force is that of evident economic need.

Rather than elaborate philosophically on the matter of change, a more effective demonstration will be that of reviewing some of the changes during recent years and following them back to their origins. Since these changes during recent years have not been altogether unnoticed in earlier chapters, some sections of this chapter will seem to contain elements of repetition. The student is asked to be patient: The significance of these examples will become clearer and more convincing after several of them have been considered.

The sections of this chapter—except for the concluding one—will consist of such examples. The factors accounting for change will be reviewed in each case, but no effort will be made within the individual sections to dilate on the social, economic, and political significance of the change described. That element will be reserved for the concluding section.

WIDER PARTICIPATION IN EQUITY INVESTMENT

One change of material importance has been the great increase in the number of stock investors. At one time investment in corporate bonds by individuals was fairly widespread, but the ownership of stock was limited to relatively few investors. Now these proportions have been reversed. Corporate bonds are owned by relatively few individuals, but corporate stock ownership is quite widespread.

One moving factor broadening the range of equity investment has doubtless been an improvement in the quality and dependability of the institutions marketing equity securities. Two generations ago (and to some extent during even more recent periods), frauds in the sale of stocks were far from uncommon. Unsophisticated people did not trust common stock investment. Furthermore, shysters invaded the domain of business and used the guise of the corporation to bilk stockholders rather than to earn profits for them. Corporate piracy in the post-Civil War period was less frequent than the muckrakers might lead us to think but more common than is comfortable to recollect. It was one of the less happy episodes of our business history.

That picture has changed greatly. Corporations do not have uniformly inspired and dedicated leadership, but a large portion of the big publicly held corporations are led by men deeply and sincerely aware of their responsibilities to stockholders. In any event their positions are so open and conspicuous that any other attitude would not long be tolerated. Investors can confidently invest in the equity securities of such corporations without real fear of gouging or fraud. The fortunes of various companies and of various industries are not all equally good, but the hazards of common stock investment are more economic risks than moral risks. Exceptions exist, as the business news sometimes reveals, but the significant point is that these defections are exceptions and not the rule.

The business of commission brokerage has also changed its character. The successful firms are not only honest but provide a quality of investment information for investors that is far superior to anything available in earlier periods. It is significant that Merrill Lynch, one of the leaders in changing the character of the commission brokerage business, from its beginning has had a great interest in chain-store merchandising. Other commission brokerage firms now service the small investor. It would be wrong, however, to infer that such service has reached perfection. Some brokers give preferential treatment to the large institutional investors, where large commissions can be earned with less effort. Cries from small investors as being the forgotten men of Wall Street are still heard too frequently. Another problem is the paper-work crunch which faces commission brokerage firms in processing and exchanging stock certificates. High-volume trading has led to interminable delays in stock transfers and to mislocation and occasional theft of the stock certificates themselves. In this regard, a future change may be to get rid of the certificate system by switching to a book-entry computer system. Still, all problems considered, the commission brokerage system is oriented more toward consumer service than it was a few generations ago.

The change in corporations themselves and in the commission brokerage business, however, would not have served to widen equity investment if it had not been for a great change in the level and distribution of income. The increase in per capita national income has been widely distributed. A much larger and more prosperous middle class finds equity investment feasible and even attractive. A large number of investors are in income levels not far from $15,000 a year. At this level of income, saving is possible, and the amount saved can exceed bare liquidity needs. Most personal finance advisers believe that families should have some basic cash savings and adequate life insurance before embarking on equity investment. But once these needs are met, then equity investment is considered appropriate.

While governmental regulation of both corporate practices and the operation of the markets is often viewed by business as unfriendly intervention, the existence of such regulation has probably increased general confidence in corporate responsibility and in the markets for their securities, and it has encouraged wider equity ownership.

Evolutionary changes in the financial system cause disappearances as well as additions. One example of a stock market device that failed to survive is the fixed investment trust. During the stock market boom of the later 1920s, some investment companies or "trusts" were organized on a fixed basis: A buyer was able to get a fixed selection of stocks by buying the shares of such trusts. Amazingly, investors seemed to be willing to pay a premium for this privilege. Like a bon voyage fruit basket, the customer was willing to pay more for the complete bundle than for its parts.

Such foolishness did not survive—it perished with the stock market decline and the Great Depression. If any moral is to be drawn from this story, it is that a financial innovation, to survive, must furnish some real and enduring service. A glossy package may prove to be a good merchandising device for a while, but the contents had better prove to be useful in practice.

The mutual fund, of course, is a relatively new financial innovation which has caught on with the public. Between 1952 and 1972, the assets of mutual funds grew from $4 billion to $60 billion, a multiple growth of some fifteen times, far exceeding the growth of the overall economy. Many small investors have looked to the mutual funds as an indirect way of buying into the "right number" of "right stocks." The mutual funds have given the small investor a degree of diversification that he could not get directly on his own, but they have not outperformed the market. This lack of superior performance, along with loading charges, has diminished the growth rate of the funds in very recent times. Still, the mutual fund does provide the very real service of built-in diversification for the growing populace of small investors.

GROWTH OF PENSION FUNDS

For sheer rapidity of growth, few financial institutions can equal the pension funds. These funds (public and private) had assets of $270 billion at the end of 1971, a growth of almost nineteen times since 1947. These funds have become major demand factors in the capital markets, particularly the stock market. The types of securities bought vary with the nature of the funds and also with circumstances, but the dollar amounts are large and the influence is pervasive.

Why did these funds become such powerful influences in the capital markets? Many reasons can be advanced, but most of them probably grow out of the nature of our employment markets. Some pension funds have been operating for many years. In the postwar years, however, the demand for old-age income beyond social security benefits has become so great that major employers cannot afford to be without pension systems to support their employee and executive officer recruitment programs. This is a matter of widespread social demand, partly induced, no doubt, by adverse experiences during the 1930s. Major employers tended to establish their own funds and smaller ones used ready-made plans such as those sold by life insurance companies. Some established funds increased their benefits, so that they became relatively larger capital market factors as a result of such revisions.

It would be useful if we could carry our observations one step further and find out the impact of the growth of pension funds on the capital markets. It is almost certain that the existence of these funds has influenced the character of the securities offered on the markets. Investment bankers, as merchandisers, are acutely aware of who buy their offerings and what the investment standards of these buyers tend to be. When security offering plans are being formulated, the influence of "what will sell" is overwhelming.

As is generally true in an evolutionary process, some interactions within the area of pension funds have occurred. The rate of earnings is a material factor in the final cost of a pension. If the rate of return can be increased, demands for improved benefits can be met in part by this means rather than by larger assessments. Many private funds have attempted to improve their earnings and have used rather aggressive investment tactics in doing so. Their example has doubtlessly been a factor inducing other funds to change their investment practices. Some governmental pension funds formerly restricted their investment operations wholly to governmental securities. (The civil service fund of the federal government and the social security accounts still do so.) This rather narrow investment policy, however, has frequently been greatly liberalized, as in the case of state and local government funds. Examples of successful increases in earning rates by private pension funds have induced some of these changes.

The pension funds have also set an example for the life insurance companies. The latter used to promote the fixed-value annuity as an excellent device for providing for retirement. However, inflation has taught us that a fixed dollar value of benefits has diminished purchasing power. And the pension funds have proved that investment in equities can provide a variable annuity which hedges against inflation. As a result, the life insurance companies have been moving more in the direction of variable annuities. They have moved into the pension planning field, particularly individual plans. Their policies are much more flexible, thanks to the expanded needs of the public and the increased competition from noninsured pension funds.

Mutual funds, too, have set an example for the life insurance companies. Up until a few years ago, the typical insurance salesman invariably pushed a single product: the ordinary life policy. Such policies provide good insurance protection but are rather "ordinary" investments. As the public became educated to this fact, the life insurance industry adapted. The more progressive companies have expanded into the mutual fund business. Some salesmen are now pushing package plans of term insurance and mutual funds. Under these plans, the policyholder pays the same money and gets the same insurance protection, but the expected return on his investment is higher.

The growth of pension funds, together with that of the mutual funds, has reflected a real need of the middle class to provide for a secure financial future. However, such growth may not be a completely unmixed blessing. Control of these funds has tended to be concentrated in the hands of a relatively small number of large institutional investors. These institutions are expected to hold a majority of publicly traded stocks in the fairly near future. What will this do to competiton in the stock market? How will it affect the behavior of corporate enterprise? What will happen to the vested interests of ordinary workingmen whose savings go into these funds? These are the hard but important issues which will likely guide the future development of our capital markets and institutions.

CHANGES IN REAL ESTATE FINANCING

The evolution of pension funds described in the preceding section was stimulated largely by very general social and economic forces. The influence of governmental actions was rather minor in importance. In the case of real estate finance, however, the federal government has a quite clear and important role. In this case, the role has been a stimulative one, however, and the regulatory or restrictive effects of governmental policy have been small.

Changes in real estate financing came about largely because the pre-Great Depression system of financing worked rather badly. Before the Depression, most mortgages except those made by building and loan associations were five-year instruments without any regular payments in advance of the terminal maturity. The common expectation was that such mortgages could and probably would be renewed when they matured. The portion loaned was "conservative" with respect to appraised value. Niggardly first-mortgage terms meant that second mortgages or other forms of junior financing were frequently employed.

This system worked tolerably well during good times, but it broke down badly during times of stress and difficulty. If lenders were under pressure themselves, they would try to collect from borrowers rather than renew mortgage loans. The junior mortgage system also proved to be a headache for lenders of all kinds. While first mortgages had legal priority, if homeowners or other property owners got into difficulties trying to pay off second mortgages, this had adverse effects on the position of the first-mortgage lenders. In the Great Depression, many mortgages were in default. Many houses with complex liens on them (debts to several levels of mortgage lenders) were for sale but lacked buyers. Because of the confused situation, new construction was almost at a standstill.

The policy of conservatism implicit in the low ratios of loans to assessed value of property failed to be protective when the market values of real estate properties dropped greatly under pressure. Although ultimate losses were considerably less than appeared to be likely at the time of crisis and difficulty, the prevailing mortgage system proved to be quite inadequate.

Governmental insurance of mortgages was the answer. The rules of appraisal for insured mortgage loans are elaborate (and generally more restrictive than the older rules), but the allowable ratios of loans to assessed value were made much higher. The use of second or junior mortgages in conjunction with governmentally insured mortgages was ruled out. Most important of all, the mortgage was made a fully amortized instrument with monthly payments that would retire it by final maturity. The remoteness of the final maturities first permitted seemed very great at that time, but maturities have subsequently been extended even further. The important point, however, was that without any large terminal debt, the renewal problem was eradicated.

This new system made the mortgage a reasonably homogeneous financial instrument. An insured mortgage on a home in California became financially similar to an insured mortgage on a home on Long Island. The great geographical differences in interest rates that had existed before were greatly reduced. (Logic might argue that they should have diappeared, but this goal has not yet been achieved.) More important, however, this new instrument made it possible for mortgage investors to put funds to work not just in their home communities but over wide areas of the United States. Savings bankers in New England could lend on the Pacific Coast. Thus the creation of a new financial instrument of superior but also homogeneous quality became the required first step in the process of turning a series of local markets into a true national market (which is still to be achieved).

This recital of results does not argue that the system has been an unqualified success. The first governmental step was doubtless a very beneficial one. Once started, however, the system has taken on some other aspects that are of less certain social benefit. Congress jealously controls the terms on which insured mortgages are made. The government also used a similar system of mortgage guarantees to promote housing for special groups such as veterans. In the process of fixing the terms for such guarantees, group interests have been represented more often than national interests. For one thing, some members of Congress still delude themselves into thinking that they can legislate market prices. This can be done in some limited circumstances, but the history of price control in a free economy is more often than not one of disruption and failure. In a misguided effort to protect home buyers, Congress has often kept the rate of interest permissible on insured and guaranteed mortgages below market levels of interest rates. As long as investors do not have to buy mortgages and if discounts are not workable in mortgage financing (as is partly true), this system of interest-rate control results mainly in curbing the supply of funds available.

The other side is that this system has also been used to stimulate house construction when building activity lagged. The home builders operate one of the most powerful lobbies in the nation's capital; several times they have pressured Congress into liberalizing terms when a stimulus to housing construction seemed to be needed. Downpayments have been reduced, particularly on very small houses, and maturities have been stretched out in an effort to reduce monthly payments for any given level of mortgage debt and thereby to widen the number of qualifying and potential home buyers. The "no downpayment" standard has become almost a reality in some sectors of housing. Mortgage maturities are occasionally longer than the probable lives of the little jerry-built houses they finance. Thus the potential of new kinds of housing difficulties may have been created by the very system that was intended to increase the security of the mortgage market.

Through the mid-1960s, the principal thrust of government involvement in real estate finance was in the form of guarantees and insurance. These efforts were conducted through the Federal Housing Adminstration (FHA) and the Veterans Administration (VA). Since the latter half of the 1960s, government involvement has extended toward supplying funds to the mortgage credit market. Federally sponsored mortgage credit agencies were reorganized and revitalized to facilitate an orderly flow of funds from saving into mortgage loans.

The late 1960s was a very critical period for housing finance. Rapid economic expansion greatly increased the demand for housing. At the same time, the supply of credit to finance the increased demand was decreasing. Open-market interest rates were climbing to record highs in modern experience. Rates on savings accounts, on the other hand, were held back by, among other things, legal rate ceilings imposed on thrift institutions. Many savers quite naturally shifted their savings out of thrift institutions into more lucrative outlets. Since most mortgage credit is supplied by thrift institutions such as savings and loan associations and mutual savings banks, the supply of mortgage credit quickly dried up. Housing starts fell dramatically.

The mortgage credit crunch of the late 1960s was partially alleviated by the growth of federally sponsored mortgage credit institutions. The Federal National Mortgage Association (FNMA or "Fannie Mae") was reorganized in 1968 to give it much more freedom to borrow in the money and capital markets and to purchase mortgages. Between 1968 and 1971, the FNMA channeled nearly $11 billion into the mortgage market. The Government National Mortgage Association (GNMA or "Ginnie Mae") was created in 1968 to underwrite and service federal housing programs. The Federal Home Loan Mortgage Corporation (FHLMC or "Freddie Mac") was created in 1970 to purchase mortgages from savings and loan associations so that the latter could use the proceeds to originate new mortgages. The FHLMC's parent organization, the Federal Home Loan Bank System, was also active in extending credit to savings and loan associations for use in mortgage lending.

Even more recently, completely private enterprise has gotten into the act of insuring mortgages and of trading them in the secondary market. The leader in the field, MGIC Mortgage Corporation, started doing business in 1972. Its success has been nothing less then phenomenal. Private insurance of conventional mortgages has already outstripped government insurance of FHA mortgages. Moreover, private dealings in the secondary market have not only helped to stabilize the flow of mortgage credit but have also turned out to be profitable.

Another institutional innovation in real estate finance coming out of the tight money experience of the late 1960s was the development of real estate investment trusts (REITs). These institutions have grown substantially since 1968. They have been able to compete effectively for funds because they are not subject to ceilings on interest rates paid to creditors, and furthermore they provide their owners with tax advantages similar to those for mutual funds. However, unlike mutual funds, the REITs invest in real estate and mortgages on real estate. It is probably too soon to evaluate the ultimate effect which the REITs will have on real estate finance.

Still another recent innovation in real estate finance, which is more in the talking stages than actually practiced, is the variable-rate mortgage (VRM). The idea of the VRM is to allow rates on mortgages already outstanding to vary with rates in the open market. During periods of rising interest rates, thrift institutions cannot raise their rates on savings accounts because rates on the mortgages they already hold remain unchanged. Thus, in such periods, the thrift institutions cannot compete effectively for savings and satisfy the demand for mortgage credit. Variable-rate mortgages, in conjunction with a lifting of the legal rate ceilings on savings accounts, might help solve this problem and stabilize the flow of mortgage credit. Although a number of thrift institutions in New England incorporate variable mortgage rates, the practice is not yet widespread.

MEETING THE NEED FOR CONSUMER CREDIT

Not too many generations ago it was considered financially improper for individuals to finance consumption through borrowing or for lending institutions to accommodate such loans. Correct behavior meant that consumers should spend only out of income. Bankers did not particularly welcome the appearance of consumers at the loan desk.

The introduction of automobiles and electrical appliances helped to change this attitude. Consumers were quite willing to buy now, save later. Lenders found this new demand for credit too attractive to pass up; interest rates were good and the loans could be secured by shiny new cars and refrigerators. Consumer loans, at least for financing durables, became an accepted form of credit.

It took some time for this attitude to spread to the financing of nondurables and services. Banks were not quick to make loans without suitable collateral. Small loan companies would make loans for such purposes, but only at very high interest rates. Retail stores sold on credit, but only to reputable customers. However, as the economy expanded and as the middle class grew in size and affluence, human capital became substitutable for tangible property as security for credit. Banks, finance companies, and retail trade began to recognize the profitability and safety of consumer credit for whatever purpose. (Economists had known all along that lifetime income is a constraint on lifetime consumption but not on its timing.) To make a long story short, consumer credit has become one of the fastest-growing segments of the financial system.

Commercial banking, once a reluctant lender, is now among the most aggressive in the consumer credit field. Nowhere is this more evident than in the amazing emergence and growth of bank credit cards. Two national systems—BankAmericard and MasterCharge—had more than 20 million active card holders at the end of 1971. These cards were used to buy goods and services on credit at more than a million business establishments. Outstandings on bank credit cards at the end of 1971 were only a little more than 3 percent of all consumer credit outstanding, but this was up from less than 1 percent just four years earlier and, in the opinion of some observers, it represents only a beginning of the role of the cards in the consumer credit field.

Concurrent with the rapid growth of consumer credit has been a movement by concerned citizens and politicians to educate and inform consumers of the cost of credit. In 1969, the Truth-in-Lending Act was passed by Congress to protect borrowers from deceptive credit practices and to inform them of the true cost of borrowing. This act has probably not succeeded in making the average consumer a careful shopper of credit. On the other hand, it probably has succeeded in making the supply of consumer credit more competitive. Thus many consumer-borrowers are probably receiving better treatment than before without knowing it. Many lenders were opposed to the Truth-in-Lending Act, but in the few years since its passage they have appeared to adapt to it without too much trouble.

OPEN MARKET VERSUS NEGOTIATED FINANCING

Sometimes the financial markets experience changes that are not really evolutionary and do not seem to reflect clear trends. For example, during some periods the open market seems to increase in relative significance, and during others the negotiated market seems to win more participation. In the latter part of the nineteenth century the growth of commercial paper financing was viewed as a great advance in our money markets. This system drew funds from wider areas and was thought to unify our markets. In spite of this, the commercial paper market went through a long period of attrition when negotiated bank lending almost wholly displaced it. Recently there has been a considerable revival of commercial paper financing. Finance companies were first to reactivate it; but during the 1960s and into the 1970s, nonfinancial business corporations have also been heavy users of commercial paper financing.

Another kind of reversal has been that of bond financing. During the 1920s, this was done almost wholly in the open market, at least by the very large corporations. More recently the direct or private placement has tended to short-circuit the investment banking community, even in the case of some very large sales. Term loans by commercial banks have also increased the amount of negotiated financing. However, this shift may have been completed; for a number of years the division between the two channels appears to have become more stabilized.

Another shift in financing has been in the area of trade credit. In the 1950s, many businesses found that they could increase sales and profits by selling to customers on easy credit. Credit terms and credit granting standards were greatly relaxed. Accounts receivable and accounts payable on the books of the business community grew at a faster rate than the economy. Customers found that credit offered by suppliers was often more liberal than credit offered in the open market. Suppliers discovered that loans to customers often had a greater long-run payoff, in increased sales and profit on sales, than investment in money-market instruments. Negotiated trade credit infringed on open-market credit and on negotiated bank lending. Of course, there has to be a limit to trade credit liberalization. In the 1960s, the limit may have been reached as the growth of trade credit slowed down to the growth rate of the overall economy.

EXTERNAL VERSUS INTERNAL FINANCING

In less mature countries, it is commonly found that most businesses have access only to such capital as their owners can save, usually out of the conduct of the business. In other words, financing is mainly from internal sources. One of the signs of a developing country is an increase in the amount of external or market financing. Money and capital markets provide the means by which such financing is possible and available on reasonable terms.

It might be expected, therefore, that as a country becomes more mature and developed, even greater recourse to external financing would characteristically develop. In reality, such may not be the case. Perhaps external financing is characteristic of a growing economy, but it appears to be less so of a slower-growing, mature economy.

A glance at the American economy lends suggestive support to this hypothesis. Coming out of World War II, the United States had reached a stage of economic development and maturity which surpassed other countries. America's economic growth rate during the 1950s and early 1960s was relatively slow if not downright sluggish. During this period of slow growth, the proportion of external financing to total financing gradually diminished. It was not until the late 1960s, a period of war-induced expansion, that external financing increased its position relative to internal financing. The question is, if and when a period of normalcy is restored, will external financing again resume a path of diminishing importance? Is the current boom in external financing only a short-run phase running counter to a long-run trend in the opposite direction?

If this hypothesis has merit, is it at all likely that the market institutions which we have been studying will tend to be of dwindling importance? Questions of this sort are speculative, but it can be averred that many types of financial institutions have been forced to diversify their services in order to earn decent incomes. Investment banking would starve if it were confined to the kind of business it used to do. New functions have been developed to replace the income lost in dwindling functions. New clients have been cultivated. For example, investment banking now arranges much of the financing for the fast-growing state and local government sector. Commercial banks have been forced to enter new areas of finance; those banks that fail to follow such developments aggressively shrink in relative importance. Consumer credit has been one of the "replacement" types of business that has been aggressively developed in recent years. However, an interesting question can be raised: What would happen if all sectors in the economy should become more nearly self-financing, as is becoming increasingly characteristic of mature corporations?

THE EVOLVING MONEY MARKET

Some of the most striking changes in financial arrangements have occurred in the money markets. These markets have had to adapt to changes in short-term borrowing and lending patterns by different economic sectors and to the introduction of new money-market instruments.

In the 1920s the principal way in which short-term money could be invested in an almost wholly liquid way was in call loans on stock exchange collateral. The call loan was used by banks, both in New York City and outside, and by nonfinancial corporations. The economic and financial Depression of the 1930s led to such stringent curbs on stock market credit that the call loan is far less important than it used to be. Brokerage houses often have large credit balances from some customers. In quiet periods they can meet the legal and regulated borrowing demands of debit balance customers with little recourse to bank credit. When securities credit is sought, it is now more nearly a negotiated than an open-market kind of credit.

The Treasury bill has replaced the call loan as the principal money-market vehicle for liquidity investment. This instrument grew out of deficit financing and debt management by the federal government. The federal government has added most to its indebtedness during wartime and recessions, but deficits are often the rule even during normal times. Debt management policy for the refinancing of the federal debt has been in the direction of issuing and reissuing large quantities of Treasury bills. This has partly been in response to a large and growing demand for liquidity. For more than a generation, the Treasury bill market has been large and continuous. The Treasury bill is an instrument of such significance in the money markets that, if by some quite unlikely magic, the federal debt should be greatly reduced or paid off, the markets would be seriously discommoded—for a while. However, faith in the evolutionary process requires us to concede that by some inventive arrangement not now fully foreseeable, the gap probably would be filled in due course.

Many investors already regard the short-term obligations of federally sponsored credit agencies as good substitutes for Treasury bills. Agency obligations pay higher interest rates than Treasury bills, and they are almost as safe. Reception by lenders has been good. Agency issues have grown dramatically since 1968. Proceeds of the issues have gone into the secondary mortgage market and other designated sectors of the economy.

Changes in the character of monetary policy—the prevalence of ease or tightness—also induce structural changes in the money markets. Some of these changes might seem more cyclical than evolutionary, but those mentioned below represent very slow swings in institutional arrangements. For example, the market in federal funds was quite active in the 1920s. However, the federal funds market almost wholly disappeared during the Great Depression and did not really revive until after the Treasury–Federal Reserve "Accord" in 1951. When it did revive, it became an even larger element in money-market affairs than it had been in the 1920s. What is more, the market has been extended to a greater number of banks than formerly used it by virtue of improved communications. It is a large and continuous market.

Another illustration of money market evolution can be drawn from experience with so-called commercial paper. In its origins this paper was truly commercial in that it facilitated the business process of commerce. Entry of sales finance concerns into this market has led to a large part of the paper being based on consumer credit or consumer transactions—something that is quite contrary to the philosophy that formerly prevailed in the money markets. But when philosophy and need conflict, the latter is likely to prevail, and did. "Commercial" paper based on consumer credit has achieved the dominant place in this market and seems to suffer no disadvantage because it really is not all that commercial anymore.

Money markets in the broad sense have shown a parallel shift. It was once thought that commercial bank credit should be based on some self-liquidating transaction—a theory that is sometimes labeled the "real bills" doctrine. This was thought to be the foundation of both safety in credit and monetary appropriateness. It was thought that if all bank credit expansion were for "commercial" purposes, it could not be inflationary.

FINANCIAL MARKETS AND ECONOMIC PROGRESS 395

The theory lasted well into the 1930s, but when true commercial credit became scarce, commercial banks in search of earnings were not much restrained by philosophy: They did what was needed to survive and entered enthusiastically into such ventures as consumer lending.

Money markets have increasingly become world markets. With the trend toward internationalism—economic and political—there is no longer such great fear about lending and borrowing abroad. Many foreign corporations, particularly the Japanese, make extensive use of bankers' acceptances for financing purchases of American goods. Americans have become willing lenders in this important money market. But we are also borrowers. American banks have turned to the Eurodollar market as a major alternative source of short-term credit.

The rapid development, since 1961, of the negotiable certificate of time deposit represents another evolutionary development of the money markets precipitated by the pressure of economic events. Because of curbs on demand deposit expansion by monetary policy, commercial banks had found that they were not able to supply customers with funds as adequately as some other financial intermediaries, nor were they growing as rapidly. Convinced that demand deposit growth would continue to be curbed, they set about competing more actively for time deposit funds. The higher rates on time deposits permitted by the Federal Reserve beginning in 1962 spurred this movement. Increased competition occurred for all forms of time deposits, from savings accounts to certificates of deposit. The negotiable certificates of deposit (created in large round-number units of $100,000, $500,000, and on up to $1 million), their exemption from rate regulation, and the arrangement for a secondary market facility for them was the more evident change of financial practices in response to a need. Events subsequently showed that these certificates commanded a good rate in the market and traded at yields from 2/10 to 4/10 of 1 percent above Treasury bill yields. This financial innovation was a considerable success almost from the very beginning.

While commercial banks have been moving toward time deposits in general and negotiable certificates of deposit in particular as a principal source of funds, nonbank thrift institutions have been looking in the opposite direction toward demand deposits as a possible source of funds. Demand deposits are still largely in the domain of commercial banks, but it is significant that the thrift institutions have already made some inroads. For example, credit unions chartered in Rhode Island are now legally empowered to issue demand deposits, and mutual savings banks in Massachusetts and New Hampshire offer "negotiable order of withdrawal" accounts which, in effect, are checking accounts that pay interest. Clearly, the old lines of demarcation between checking accounts and savings accounts and between commercial banks and nonbank thrift institutions are beginning to crumble. However, it is probably too soon to say whether these developments will go all the way. The Hunt Commission (36) has recently recommended that specialized thrift institutions be allowed to broaden their investment and financing opportunities, but at a price of equality with commercial banks with respect to taxation and reserve requirements. No doubt the specialized institutions are interested in broader powers, but are they willing to pay the price of foregoing their favored tax positions and their exemption from reserve requirements? Time will tell.

MOVING CAUSES OF CHANGE

The rather scattered elements of evolutionary change listed in this chapter have been caused by many factors. In some cases governmental regulation has been an initiating force, but in a great portion of the cases the change has been induced by basic market forces. In other words, much of the progress in the evolution of financial services can be traced to public pressure on the demand side of the market and to competition on the supply side.

A dynamic society changes more, and more rapidly, than we often realize, and its various institutional arrangements must change along with society. The financial markets known to our grandparents had changed greatly by the time our parents entered these markets. They have continued to change even as we describe them. The markets described here will change before present-day students achieve positions of economic responsibility.

Change is usually resisted at the time it takes place; change is almost always uncomfortable. Yet in retrospect, has change been adverse? Without attempting a defense of every change that has taken place, it can be argued that existing markets are far better than those that existed in earlier days. We do not have efficiency tests for markets similar to those applied to physical production, but markets are becoming far more efficient in the sense that they accomplish the same function at lower cost. In one area—that of the raising of corporate debt capital—the increase in efficiency has been demonstrated statistically. It can also be argued that the quality of financial services has been improved. Certainly it is true that in such areas as individual and trust investment, the quality of performance, though still leaving much to be desired, is far better than it was formerly.

When change has been induced by catastrophes (such as the Great Depression, which led to various kinds of governmental regulation), the changes were grudgingly accepted for a considerable period of time. Nonetheless, subsequent developments have suggested that these changes helped markets not only to survive but to increase their effectiveness.

What will be the character of the future change? Clearly, change will come; that is one lesson that history teaches. Most of the changes will come slowly and will be of an evolutionary nature. However, if episodes of traumatic disaster should occur, then rapid and revolutionary changes will be enforced from the outside, as has been true in the past.

Chapter 21

Efficiency, Equity, and Safety

Efficient and equitable financial markets are vital. Nations that do not have such markets tend to be retarded in their economic development. While our opening proposition is so axiomatic as to be beyond dispute, it suffers from two ambiguities: First, how are efficiency and equity measured? Second, what type of public policy is most effective in attaining efficiency and equity?

The concept of efficiency is usually broken into two types: operational and allocational. Operational efficiency is measured by the costs involved in the financial process relative to results. If the going rate on mortgages is 7 percent, the rate that a financial intermediary could return to savers after covering its costs would be a measure of operational efficiency. If one institution could return 5 percent and still make a satisfactory profit but another only 4 percent, the first is obviously more efficient. Transaction costs in the stock market or in the foreign exchange market can also be considered tests of operational efficiency. A low-friction financial machine is an efficient one.

"Allocational efficiency" means effectiveness in channeling the flow of saving into productive use. A capital market that invested funds in low-return companies and industries or uses of capital that had little social utility would be allocationally inefficient. One that channeled funds into highly productive use would be efficient. But how is this to be measured?

The concept of equity seems to be simple and easily grasped on an intuitive level, but in fact it turns out to be highly elusive. The ethical norms of society give us a starting point, but this can lead to conflicting judgments. For example, the principle of egalitarian wealth and income distribution has gained a great deal of support. This principle could be interpreted to mean that all persons should have equal access to financial markets. But if this were the case, the financial markets might not concentrate resources in the hands of those who could make the most efficient use of them. The goals of efficiency and equity might, under an egalitarian system of ethical behavior, come into serious conflict.

Safety differs from the concept of stability developed in Chapter 19 in that it focuses on the losses that usually result from credit defaults. These defaults tend to shake confidence and impede the investment process. Some economic risk is unavoidable. Furthermore, to facilitate the progress, the encouragement of which was evaluated in Chapter 20, it would be unwise to try excessively to avoid risk. But if episodes of random credit losses occur too often, the whole process of financial investment tends to be inhibited.

It is true, of course, that the more dramatic episodes of unsafe financial investment have been concentrated in periods of downside instability. Furthermore, unsafe financial investment has an aspect of equity, since those damaged by such events have tended to be the less well-informed investors and often those with smaller means. As a result, the insurance devices that have been devised to make the financial system safer have tended to concentrate their protection on smaller investors.

As old problems are solved, new ones emerge. For many years the problem of safety in financial markets was viewed mainly as a matter of contract performance. A "safe" credit instrument was one that would be paid as promised in the contract by the debtor. A "safe" broker and dealer in a financial market was one who performed his function according to the terms of the implied or explicit contracts that govern such relationships. Safety was something that could be comprehended within our existing legal and judicial system.

New risks—new at least to the United States—have become more important. The gravest of emerging hazards has been the threat of unending secular inflation. Changes in the value of money tilt greatly the safety of financial contracts that are expressed in terms of money. This risk is one for which our financial markets are not well prepared. Other countries with longer and more severe experience with inflation have invented practical and sometimes legal systems for dealing with the problem. Some countries, particularly those in South America, have adopted systems for the revaluation of financial contracts when the value of money changes drastically. So far, that has not been necessary in this country. However, financial markets have been greatly influenced by the individual efforts of investors to protect themselves against this form of risk.

MEANS FOR ATTAINING EFFICIENCY, EQUITY, AND SAFETY: COMPETITION, REGULATION, AND INSURANCE

In a free economic system, competition is presumed not only to guide the allocation of resources in the most efficient manner but also to ensure that the allocation process is reasonably equitable and safe. Modern capital market theory has been tested, and the results suggest that financial markets are reasonably efficient. However more traditional qualitative tests of competition suggest that the results have often been both inequitable and unsafe. Regulation came into existence in an effort to cure some of these failings. However, regulation itself often seems to be more a shelter for monopolistic practices than a safeguard of public welfare. The problem is that modern and traditional financial theory have somewhat different ways of defining efficiency.

Insurance has become a widespread device for improving financial safety. A large number of financial claims are now insured in governmentally sponsored programs: bank deposits, savings and loan accounts, mortgages, and now even brokerage accounts. Inevitably, some measure of regulation has accompanied the insurance process. As a result of these factors, it is often difficult for the analyst to untangle the influence of competition, regulation, and insurance.

The plan of this chapter, therefore, will be to present some tests of modern capital market theory. They use a somewhat different concept of "efficiency" than the one described in the opening pages of this chapter. We will then return to a somewhat more traditional examination of the qualitative nature of competition in financial markets. Also, the general nature of financial regulation and some critical comments will be presented. Finally, we shall inspect financial insurance in brief and general terms.

TESTS OF FINANCIAL MARKET EFFICIENCY

A branch of economics known as "welfare economics" provides proof that markets are efficient in both an operational and allocational sense when market prices (and quantities) are in a state of competitive equilibrium. In order to test the efficiency of financial markets we need a testable proposition of the price (or expected return) relationships among financial assets when the markets for these assets are in competitive equilibrium. Fortunately, a recent body of theory known as "capital market theory," "asset pricing theory," or "security pricing theory" (as we called it in Chapter 5) provides such a testable proposition. According to this theory, the competitive equilibrium pattern of expected returns should be a simple linear function of risk.

The results of empirical tests of this equilibrium relation have strong implications for judging both the validity of the theory and the efficiency of financial markets. If the results are affirmative, we can infer that the theory does a good job of predicting actual security prices and that these prices are efficient. Even if the results are negative, we cannot infer that financial markets are inefficient. The problem may rest in the inadequacy of the theory to predict an efficient pricing mechanism. Indeed, much of the recent work in capital market theory has been in the direction of perfecting the theory so that it can do a better job of explaining the facts. The presumption is that financial markets are in fact efficient and that it is only a matter of time until a workable hypothesis will be able to verify this fact. Little attention has been given by academicians to the possibility that financial markets may in fact be inefficient.

But enough speculation. A sufficient amount of theoretical and empirical work has already been done in recent years to yield tentative conclusions about the efficiency of financial markets. Jensen (113) has reviewed and summarized this work. His conclusion is that financial markets are efficient insofar as the evidence is consistent with some (but not all) of the equilibrium conditions posited by capital market theory. He suggests that lack of substantiation of all the conditions is more a problem of developing adequate hypotheses than an indication of inefficient financial markets.

Which equilibrium conditions are met and which are not? For this we need to take a closer look at the theoretical relations between risk and expected return and the equilibrium conditions which the theory implies. The reader might recall from Chapter 5 that the theoretical equilibrium relation between risk and return for any asset or any portfolio of assets is given by:

$$\text{Expected return of asset J} = a + b \left\{ \begin{array}{l} \text{systematic risk or volatility of} \\ \text{return of asset J relative to the} \\ \text{return of the market portfolio M} \end{array} \right\}$$

Systematic risk is measured by the covariance of return between asset J and market portfolio M divided by the market portfolio's variance of return. Since the theoretical relation is linear, one should expect to find the same linear relation in the real world provided that the theory is good and that financial markets are really efficient. On this score there seems to be no problem. Jensen (113, p. 368) demonstrates that the relationship using cross-sectional data is "amazingly linear."

But linearity is only one equilibrium condition. The parameters a and b in the relation are carefully defined by capital market theory. The intercept a must equal the risk-free rate of return, and the slope b must be the difference between the expected rate of return on the market portfolio and the risk-free rate of return. (This follows from the geometry of the *SML*, or security market line, graphed in Chapter 5.) Unfortunately, the empirical estimates of the parameters are not equal to their theoretical values. According to Jensen, the statistical value of the intercept is higher and the slope is less than theory predicts. Apparently, the simple asset pricing model provides an inadequate description of the real world.

Again, this does not mean that financial markets are inefficient. The model itself has been criticized for some of the "unreal" assumptions which it makes, among these being that (1) all investors have identical estimates of expected return and risk and (2) all investors can borrow and lend as much as they want at the risk-free rate of return. Clearly, these assumptions and others could have an effect on the adequacy of the theory's power to predict.

A simpler test of the degree of financial market efficiency can be found by examining the pattern of residuals or stochastic terms in regression models of security pricing behavior. If these terms are randomly distributed with an expected value of zero, then playing the securities market is a "fair game" providing no reasonable expectation of outperforming the market. In this case, security prices move *efficiently* along their equilibrium time paths. Deviations from equilibrium occur, but these deviations are random with an expected value of zero.

Such behavior is just the opposite of that assumed by market chartists and technical analysts. In their view, price changes follow a predictable pattern, offering the prospect of knowing better than the market what the market is going to do.

The evidence clearly supports the efficient market model. Without exception, statistical studies reveal that short-run price changes are random deviations from true equilibrium values and as such are unpredictable. (The interested reader may want to refer to Fama (55) for a good review of this literature.)

In sum, the evidence supports the notion that financial markets are efficient. This may not please those who expect to make a fast buck by beating the market, but it is comforting to those of us who are concerned about resource allocation.

COMPETITION AS A SPUR TO EFFICIENCY AND EQUITY

Although financial markets are subject to various forms of regulation, we depend mainly on competition to spur efficiency and equity. However, competition in the financial markets differs in a variety of ways from that in other sectors of the economy. Perhaps the most significant difference is that quality of financial service is very important; so important that price competition is often muted. In order to appreciate fully the nature of financial competition, the next part of this chapter will deal with qualitative elements in competition.

The nature of competition has been changing. Chapter 17 described the competition between negotiated underwriting, competitive bidding, and direct placement as an innovative response to regulation. As Chapter 20 indicated, progress and innovation in the financial markets have shifted the focus of financial competition. Another example came to attention in Chapter 18, where it was shown that NASDAQ terminals have made the OTC market competitive with the organized exchanges—and might ultimately displace them by virtue of superior efficiency.

In finance, information has both cost and value. One of the major thrusts of financial regulation has been to require the publication of a greater amount of more dependable information.

Qualitative Nature of Competition in Financial Markets

Competition among financial businesses is a somewhat more complex economic phenomenon than competition among ordinary industrial or commercial enterprises. Public interest in the level of competition is more complex and characterized by more seeming contradiction than is true of public policy with respect to most other types of business. In the first place, a great many financial institutions cannot start business unless they secure a charter or license: "free entry" is not present. The granting of charters is restricted to those applicants that have adequate capital and have arranged a location in a market area adequate to earn a fair income. When charters are granted in such a restrictive way, the quality of newly formed institutions is improved, but competitive pressures are less than they would be with free entry. The trouble is that the public interest is involved in the solvency as well as the competitiveness of financial institutions. We allow restaurants and grocery stores to fail freely, believing that free entry assures competition. The burden of their failure falls mainly on the owners of such enterprises. But the losses that result from the insolvency of financial institutions, particularly those that handle the money of the relatively unsophisticated public, are thought to be socially if not economically intolerable.

Do Enduring Customer Relationships Minimize Competition?

One of the problems of determining the degree and character of competition in financial markets is that some of the customer-institution relationships in these markets tend to be of a long-standing nature. Just as people cling to a known and trusted doctor, so the relationship of businesses and individuals to commercial and investment banks tends to be personal and enduring. This tendency is common among financial institutions but particularly among commercial banks and investment banks. The financial aid and support together with advice and related aid make the relationship one that considerably transcends matters of price.

This does not mean that price is an unimportant element in such relationships. The financial institution that consistently charged prices that exceeded those prevailing elsewhere would lose business. The concept of the fair price seems to prevail and be accepted widely. Customers bargain with financial institutions about price under some circumstances; under others, they accept the prices quoted without haggling.

The unmeasurable quality, however, is that of service. A financial institution does more than lend money or act as an intermediary in its employment. Particularly in the lending of money, the certain availability of funds may be much more important to borrowers than price. The advisory role is often important. Furthermore, in the reciprocity of favors in the business community, the support of a strong banker who has widespread contacts may be far more important than can be demonstrated by quantitative means.

Competitive Tactics

Financial institutions use many of the devices employed by other businesses in the competitive struggle. Advertising was once frowned on in the financial community and institutions ran only chilly little "tombstone" ads that announced their continued existence. This feeling has changed greatly. The advertising of banks and other financial institutions has become informal, breezy, and often revealing. Many financial institutions have also established public relations departments and concern themselves about their corporate image.

Much of this, however, is applicable mainly to the retail or mass marketing sector of finance. The business of attracting funds from many small savers is a valid use of such mass media devices. Those institutions making small personal or business loans are also inclined to employ such devices. Commission brokerage houses that solicit small accounts and those selling investment company shares are mass merchandisers.

At the same time an important group of businesses—the really large accounts—probably are more successfully approached by other means. It is significant that the few banks that are mainly money wholesalers and a large part of the investment banking community still have not resorted very much to informal advertising.

The answer seems to be that in this sector of finance, close working relationships are achieved by rather different means. As was discussed in the preceding section, the customer relationship in many cases is close and enduring. Furthermore, the matter of the choice of a financial connection is probably made at the very top level of business management. Many purchasing and marketing decisions are made at intermediate levels of management. But the banking connection is changed (or made) only at the top, usually in full consultation with the board of directors. Personal contacts between financial institutions and the top levels of business management are of the greatest importance. This is the reason so much emphasis has been put on the interlocking directorates between banks and nonfinancial corporations by the antitrust investigations. Trusteeship of the Committee for Economic Development or participation in broad spectrum activities of business may provide important contacts where financial-business relationships are initiated or cemented.

Thus the quality of top personnel in financial institutions and their acceptability and personability in dealing with the top levels of business management are of the greatest importance. At one time the personnel of investment banking was drawn to a considerable extent from the great moneyed families; this assured entry into many places denied those of more humble birth. Business management of all types has probably become more fluid in recent years. Most posts are now accessible to the ambitious person with ability and personal charm. But at the same time it cannot be denied that the person fully at home at the city or country club has some advantage over the person who has risen to the top by the Horatio Alger path of the paper route and the night class.

Competitive tactics include a variety of elements. In the first place, financial institutions are still much concerned with projecting an image of wisdom, sagacity, and integrity as well as one of dignity. But they encourage the belief that they are active and aggressive businessmen. They also try to convey this image to much wider audiences. Another change in practice that reflects the new emphasis on aggressiveness is the willingness to visit customers. At one time, most banks waited for business to come in the front door; they did not go out and solicit it. This was particularly true of investment bankers. They did not hesitate to use intermediaries or "finders" to encourage business to come to them, but they felt it beneath their dignity to go out soliciting business. This has changed; the old inhibitions are virtually dead. Both commercial and investment banks have new-business development men constantly traveling and visiting potential customers.

Still another change is in the matter of business size. Leading bankers once rather discouraged the business of small concerns; they had an attitude of polite snobbery about size. Some of this feeling persists, but too many bankers have found that the small boy becomes big and the big may become old and financially feeble. The small businessman with growth potential is often surprised at the welcome he gets from the giants of the financial community.

Competition within Homogeneous Types of Financial Institutions

The usual concept of competition has to do with business concerns that offer similar or identical goods or services to the markets. Among similar financial institutions such competition is the normal order of business. Examples would be competition of commercial banks with other commercial banks, of savings and loan associations with other savings and loan associations, or of investment banking houses with other investment banking houses. Different types of financial institutions, of course, offer similar services, so that the range of competition is somewhat broader than it would be if it were merely within homogeneous types of financial institutions. This broader concept will be considered in a later section of this chapter.

Competition between similar institutions is partly a matter of the quality of the services they offer, but differences in quality may be hard to demonstrate, particularly for rather simple financial services such as those of handling savings accounts. The widespread presence of deposit insurance, for example, has tended to make all savings accounts under the insured limit of $20,000 similar to other savings accounts. The principal variable in such relationships subject to competitive differentiation is price.

Here, however, is an example in which price competition has been more than discouraged, it has been virtually prohibited by regulation. Chapter 9, which dealt with commercial banking, mentioned the influence of Federal Reserve Regulation Q. In the beginning, Regulation Q was an effort to keep banks "safe" by avoiding price competition which might have led first to excessive rates paid on savings deposits and then to unsafe investment practices in the effort to earn enough to cover the higher rates. This was a view held over from the bank failures of the Great Depression. However, recent experience has not revealed much valid evidence that bank failures are any longer a serious threat.

In the mid-1960s, the use of Regulation Q was given a still different focus. In the early 1960s, banks became much more aggressive in their competitive tactics; they put much more reliance on time deposits in getting funds with which to operate. Rates of interest paid on time deposits came to be used more aggressively as a competitive device. Savings and loan associations had before been able to attract money with rates moderately above the time deposit rates of commercial banks. By the mid-1960s, this advantage had dwindled greatly. When the commercial banks started to win this competitive race, it was feared that the loss of funds from savings and loan associations would result in financial problems and possibly even failures among them. Regulation Q (and a parallel nonmember bank FDIC regulation) were then used to hold bank time deposit rates below savings and loan association rates. At the same time, savings and loan associations were put under regulation with respect to the rates they could pay on savings accounts and shares.

The third step in the evolution of Regulation Q came in the late 1960s. The Federal Reserve, anxious to avoid credit expansion, used Regulation Q to hold down the amount banks could pay on NCDs. (This story was related in Chapter 9.) At the present time, it appears possible that Regulation Q will be phased out. The Hunt Commission has so recommended, and finally the Federal Reserve itself appears to share this view.

Price competition in lending rates is less openly displayed by financial institutions, but such competition undoubtedly exists. Among big commercial banks, the prime loan rate (discussed in Chapter 9) applies to a large part of the lending. By and large, the prime loan rate is adhered to. It can be considered a form of price leadership which is generally viewed by economists as involving some restraint on true competition. The significant question, however, is whether other dimensions of credit arrangement are used to express competitive activity. At least one such outlet probably exists. Most customer loans are accompanied by a general understanding that the borrower will also maintain a "satisfactory" depository relationship. The size and character of a satisfactory deposit balance is sometimes left to informal and even vague understandings. Quite often, however, it is formalized in a specific compensatory balance agreement. These arrangements are not uniform, and the sizes of these balances can be and are bargained.

Among commercial banks outside the money market center, loan rates are less uniform. While a given area is usually fairly homogeneous with respect to rates, variations exist and these differences are used competitively. Variations exist even within a given institution, so that good and desirable customers may be given fairly good rates and less desirable customers are charged higher rates. The competition is for good customers, not for a particular bit of business, and good customers are rewarded with more favorable treatment than they can probably expect if they should switch their banking connections.

Competition among life insurance companies as lenders does not appear to take the form of rates as much as of credit selectivity. For administrative reasons a life insurance company may post a uniform rate for mortgage lending. The rate has to be in line with general market conditions, but variations from this rate tend to be infrequent. The significant differences, then, are in the character and quality of credit tolerated within this announced rate. Mortgage bankers, in negotiating sales of mortgages to life insurance companies, know the standards and rules of the various companies and try to tailor the mortgages offered to the requirements of the companies that have funds.

When life insurance companies lend to business in the form of direct placements, rates are not uniform. On all large contracts, the rates are individually negotiated and are influenced mostly by prevailing yields in the corporate bond market. On the smaller placements, rates are likely to be somewhat more uniform and to be changed less frequently. Even in such cases, however, these rates are usually subject to some margin of negotiation. In the end, these rates have to be "competitive."

Investment bankers compete almost solely on the basis of service and not price except in competitive bidding financing. The borrower has a large interest in financing in an acceptable way and of getting good timing in such financing. The fees or margins taken by investment bankers are small in comparison with the savings in cost that can be effected by expert management or the increases in cost due to clumsy handling. Even so, the margins taken by investment bankers have been greatly influenced by examples of narrow margins displayed publicly in competitive bidding. The margins now prevailing are far less than those that used to be charged, and the example of public bidding doubtlessly helped borrowers who have used negotiated financing.

Market Areas

One of the problems of judging the degree and range of competition is the size of the normal market area. The normal market area for a grocery store is bounded by the distance that buyers will drive (or walk) to buy their groceries. The physical representation of market areas might be thought of as a map with a dot shown for each customer's location with respect to the store or financial institution he patronizes.

Market areas vary widely in types of business. The market area of investment bankers tends to be nationwide and even worldwide. Large borrowers are not deterred by distance in going to the investment banker who promises the best service. Most of them are located in the central capital markets anyway, so location is not a critical factor in choice of an investment banker. A saver, in choosing the institution at which he keeps his account, however, may be considerably influenced by convenience and location. A few institutions have successfully attracted funds from great distances by advertising, but these examples are exceptions.

Market area is also influenced by the modes of transportation. On the island of Manhattan, where few residents use automobiles for city travel, the market areas of savings institutions tend to be bounded by modes of travel; an important subway stop may be a locational factor. The distances between savings institutions can be smaller without an overlap of market areas. On the other hand, in thinly populated areas where automobile travel for longer distances is quite common, the market area of a savings institution may be rather large. The number of persons and the wealth in such a large physical area may not be very great, but the distance spread will be considerable.

It seems likely, although no facts are available to support the view, that the sizes of market areas have changed greatly and may be subject to even more change in the future. For example, the greater use of "bank-by-mail" service has been promoted as a modest convenience to customers. With time, however, it could produce very large changes. If one can bank by mail with an institution inconveniently located for a visit by car, why cannot one bank by mail with an institution clear across the country? Why couldn't credit be arranged by mail? Sales finance concerns have operated widely through relatively thin systems of branch location; why is this not possible for other forms of consumer credit? It is true that one cannot cash a check by mail, but chain stores have developed simple systems of check cashing for established customers; therefore why should a customer visit his bank at all? One of the reasons that financial institutions might smile on such developments is that, as personal service institutions, they find personnel costs one of their greatest drains on earnings. Any sort of mechanization that will reduce personnel costs would be a great boon to financial institutions.

The concept of market area has been most important in the decisions of the supervisory authorities for the establishment and merger of existing financial institutions. The crowding together of too many institutions within a natural market area is considered unwise for reasons of solvency protection. The reduction of the number of competing institutions within a market area by merger, however, may reach proportions that are thought to be contrary to the public interest. Unfortunately very little is known about the size of areas served by various financial institutions. The circumstances described above are based on casual observation and intuition rather than on formal and dependable information.

Competition between Various Types of Financial Institutions

The day-to-day competition of financial institutions tends to be among the homogeneous types. There is, however, some overlapping of competition at this level, particularly among savings institutions, in seeking funds. But each type of financial institution tends to evolve as it tries to improve its market position, and this effort generally leads to competition with other types of financial institutions. In the beginning, a bold or innovating institution may devise a way in which it can increase its business by seeking out a type of business not done before or done by some other type of financial institution. Individual commercial banks did this when they invaded the market for consumer credit. If the early innovators are successful, others soon copy them.

Counterinvasions of each other's traditional type of business can also occur. At one time, investment bankers maintained a depository relationship with some customers and so ran what were really private commercial banks. This was forbidden by the Banking Act of 1933, but before this prohibition commercial banks had invaded investment banking territory by going into the securities merchandising business, directly or through affiliates. This countercompetition was likewise outlawed by the same act, but these excursions into each other's type of business still exist in the competition between commercial banks and investment bankers for marketing state and local government obligations.

A more current illustration of interindustry competition is that between self-administered or trusteed pension funds and life insurance pension plans. Life insurance companies have developed pension plans which furnish all technical and financial services and also guarantee the payment of pensions according to the contractual terms. However, some companies believe themselves able to better the terms offered and so have organized do-it-yourself pension plans. Owing to the willingness to engage in somewhat more aggressive investment policies than the life insurance companies like (or can legally undertake), they have generally succeeded in bettering the terms (or at least they did as long as equity prices were rising briskly).

This competition has also led to some very interesting financial innovations. The increases in the price level and talk of secular inflation had led many savers and investors to seek protection against loss of purchasing power. One such form of protection (devised first for college teachers) was a pension annuity invested in common stocks and payable not in fixed dollar terms but in units that varied in price with the prices of equities. This was initiated just before the great boom in the stock market of the last decade. The success of this variable annuity plan (CREF) led to efforts to copy it on a commercial scale. This effort was resisted by various segments of the financial community: the investment companies, because they foresaw a threat from this new invention, and the more conservative insurance companies. Of the two largest life insurance companies, one opposed the idea while the other favored it. Initiation of the new ventures was delayed by legal actions, but they were ultimately allowed to get started, mainly after the larger part of a stock market boom had taken place. This is an unfinished story, but it illustrates the way in which competition sometimes arises—and also the way in which it is often resisted.

Competition can also take the form of lobbying and efforts to influence government action as well as price competition. Legal chartering of the new ventures by public authorities, which was instituted to protect the public against fraud, has also served to hold back innovations of genuinely important purpose. The same system covers both; the question is how to distinguish between good competition and destructive overexpansion.

Bank Chartering and Branching

All corporations must meet some minimum legal requirements in order to obtain a charter. Banks, however, have generally been subject to rather more restrictive requirements than nonfinancial corporations. Prior to World War I, most states were reasonably generous about granting charters for new banks, as was the federal government through the Comptroller of the Currency. By 1920 there were 30,000 banks in the United States. Thirteen years later the number had been reduced to 13,000, mostly by failure. Although a large part of these failures came during the Great Depression, there was a steady stream of bank failures in the otherwise prosperous 1920s.

Branch operation by banks was, on the other hand, almost universally prohibited or closely restricted prior to World War I. There was a moderate degree of liberalization during the 1920s, but branching developed materially only in California, New York State, and a few other states which had fairly liberal branch laws.

The shock of the Great Depression led to supervisory policies that almost completely inhibited the chartering of new banks for thirty years. Branching was allowed to a limited extent, but the number of banking offices lagged behind general economic growth. The excuse for this restrictive regulatory policy was the avoidance of bank failures. In practice, however, the policy was supported by operating bankers who wished to avoid facing the competition of new banks or branches. In addition, a considerable number of mergers of banks took place during the late 1950s and early 1960s, which further reduced the amount of interbank competition.

In 1962, the late President Kennedy appointed James Saxon, an innovative and quite controversial banker, to the post of Comptroller of the Currency. He immediately took a variety of steps which reduced regulatory restrictions and opened up competitive possibilities. He chartered new banks and approved new branches much more freely. He broadened the areas of operation which were permissible by a revision of his own regulations and by a more liberal interpretation of law. At the same time, the Department of Justice started to take a more active interest in bank mergers and reduced greatly the number of bank mergers by a variety of measures.

This greater freedom coincided with a new drive toward innovative practices within commercial banking. The competitive posture of not only commercial banks but also other financial institutions was changed greatly. Prior to the 1960s, other financial institutions had been growing more rapidly than commercial banks. Since that time, commercial banks have been at the forefront of financial growth. One of the most significant efforts to loosen regulatory restrictions is described in the next section.

One-Bank Holding Companies

In areas where branch restrictions inhibited multiple bank office operations, bank holding companies and banking chains were a device of avoidance. However, bank holding companies were involved in some bank failures in the early 1930s (most notably in Detroit). As a result, bank holding companies were put under regulation at the federal level. However, a holding company, usually mainly in some other type of business, which owned only one bank was exempted from such regulation. In the 1960s a majority of the big money-market commercial banks, and a great many others as well, took advantage of this exception and formed holding companies which, in the beginning, owned almost nothing but the bank itself. Shareholders exchanged their bank stock for stock in the holding company. This move could be considered a competitive action to escape regulatory restraint. A great many of these one-bank holding companies shifted policy and listed their stocks on the NYSE rather than depending on OTC trading. (The influence of the disclosure rules of 1964, mentioned in Chapter 18, also stimulated NYSE listing.)

The purpose of these one-bank holding companies was to engage in a wider variety of business than permitted by their basic bank charters. As they expanded, one-bank holding companies bought mortgage banking firms, leasing firms, and other types of financial services. As would be expected, this loophole in the law was closed and they were put under regulation. However, even under regulation, they have more and broader powers than they had as unit banks.

Mutual Funds and Pension Funds

These two classes of financial institutions offer an interesting contrast. Mutual funds are a closely regulated type of financial institution. Pension funds are virtually free of regulation—so far. It appears, however, that both have been about equally effective in serving the needs of their respective customers. Research on the performance of mutual funds is far more extensive than that on pension funds. From such evidence as exists, however, they appear to have achieved about the same level of investment performance. Neither one has been able to do much better than the market as a whole, but the two have run about an even race.

Although regulation sets the standards by which mutual funds must operate, they face intense competition in the sale of their shares to the public. Most private pension funds are managed by investment advisers, of which the trust departments of commercial banks are leading competitors. Thus there is also a great deal of competition for this business. In fact, some corporations divide their pension funds among several banks and then reward the banks with the best investment performance with more business and penalize those who trail, by less business or none at all.

Less Regulation and More Competition for Savings Intermediaries?

The Hunt Commission (HC) report recommended that savings intermediaries be given a much broader opportunity both in attracting funds and then in investing them. At the same time the HC recommended changes that would have more nearly equalized the competitive scales—such changes as in tax laws and reserve requirements.

At one time, most savings intermediaries really offered only one type of investment vehicle to savers: a savings account usually evidenced by a passbook. Commercial banks varied this offering slightly by also offering nonnegotiable certificates of deposit maturing at fixed dates. Recently both types of institutions have innovated by expanding the types of deposit accounts considerably. Some are aimed at small savers; others at substantial investors. The HC would have gone further and allowed savings intermediaries to invade the area formerly available only to commercial banks and to offer the equivalent of checking accounts—"third-party payment services"—to their customers. In addition they recommend broadening the type of savings instruments very materially. However, the HC also recommended that savings intermediaries be subject to the reserve requirements and the tax provisions that apply to commercial banks and other types of financial institutions.

The broadening recommended by the HC also included the permission to invest funds in a wider variety of outlets. In effect, the recommendations attempted to make savings intermediaries full-service financial institutions for individuals, just as commercial banks are full-service institutions for corporations as well as individuals.

Price Competition for Small Brokerage Transactions?

The account of regulation of commission brokerage rates given previously, in Chapter 18, raises some interesting questions. Although competition for the setting of all brokerage commissions has never been seriously advanced, the idea is worth reflection. At present the handling of small accounts still requires the services of account representatives and usually some research. It is possible that even small investors, if they were willing to ask only for straight brokerage service, could get this at rates lower than present commissions. In other words, is the fixed commission rate resulting in the supplying of services that customers do not want or cannot use very well and therefore making the market less efficient?

In dealing with the odd-lot market, it was pointed out that this function almost certainly could be completely computerized. It is quite possible that, in addition, the paper work of the stock certificate could be eliminated and replaced with a punch card system. If this were done, rates for the small investor could be reduced. In order to get a lower price, the small investor would have to dispense with the services of his account representative. He would have to enter his order, perhaps impersonally by a punch card or some similar means. He would have no one to "hold his hand" and comfort him when the market took a quick down move, but the cost would be lower. Is it regulation (whether "self" or public) that is holding back such developments?

Information as a Guide to Competition

One of the assumptions of perfect competition is the complete and instantaneous availability of pertinent market information to all participants. Obviously, this assumption can never be more than partly true. However, the amount of information in financial markets has been greatly expanded and the quality improved. To the extent that regulation has caused the greater and better information, it can be said that regulation here was tending to make competition more nearly perfect.

Examples of greater information are legion. For a long time the NYSE has required listed corporations to make public their financial statements. They also required the statements to be audited periodically. The quality of this information has been improved, partly by the action of the SEC but also by self-imposed standards of the accounting profession. The regulation of new security issues has required the release of detailed financial information (called 10K reports) to the public via the SEC. "Insiders" (managers, directors) are required to report buy or sell transactions in the stock of their companies.

Until about two decades ago, banks very seldom published any earnings figures.[1] After World War II a few banks started publishing such figures, but the number was not large. However, in 1964 larger banks and other companies with OTC-traded stocks were required to publish financial information much like listed companies. Banks now publish reports with full disclosure of earnings. The quality of these earnings has also been more fully disclosed as a result of an opinion of the accounting principles board.

Information, however, is not without cost. As was related in Chapter 17, many corporations have chosen to seek new money via direct placements, with its slightly higher costs, rather than prepare the re-

[1] The author of this chapter had the following experience in 1962. The father of one of the boys in his class, an officer in a fairly large Michigan bank, died, leaving his son a block of shares in this bank as his principal legacy. One of the directors of the bank immediately offered to purchase the shares. The boy asked me if the price seemed reasonable; superficially it seemed rather low. I armed the boy with several questions about earnings and suggested he ask them of the director or such officer as the director should designate. To these questions the boy got an angry and profane response, the burden of which was that it was none of his business. Such treatment of a stockholder currently would be unthinkable. The story has a happy ending, however. From published condition reports it was possible to deduce rough earnings estimates, which suggested a higher price. Furthermore, the legislation of 1964 was then in prospect, and with it the expectation of better information. The advice to the boy to hold the stock (and borrow on it from some other bank if necessary) proved to be sound.

quired 10K (and bear other expenses involved in a public offering). Legal and accounting costs involved in complying with the public information requirements are material.

More important, questions have been raised as to the extent to which this great information explosion has been of real benefit to investors. Research on the subject is not uniform in its finding, but it cannot be assumed any longer that more information necessarily increases net social benefits (13, 16, 74, 211, 228).

Is the Zeal for Regulation Weakening?

After a generation in which the degree of financial regulation tended to widen and strengthen, there is some evidence of a reversal of this trend. The case for regulation has been attacked and often none too convincingly defended. Self-regulation has sometimes been self-serving; public regulation has sometimes not served the public welfare.

Outright frauds on the public have become relatively rare. But at the same time, those that have been perpetrated have often been carefully located outside the sphere of regulatory influence. Probably the largest and most dramatic financial fraud of modern times was the system of offshore mutual funds, headquartered either in Switzerland or the Bahamas, selling to investors only outside the continental United States (176). The reason for the location, of course, was to avoid the regulatory influence of the SEC.

Perhaps the greatest failure of regulation has been its emphasis on negative rather than positive matters. However, this may be changing. Greater operational efficiency has become a matter of regulatory interest in the securities market; particularly the market for Treasury obligations which apparently will be the first to be completely computerized. Many recent studies sponsored by the SEC have been putting emphasis on the allocational efficiency of institutional investors (73).

It would be a mistake to say that the zeal for regulation is weakening, but the directions being taken by contemporary regulation are changing.

GOVERNMENT-SPONSORED FINANCIAL INSURANCE

The various programs of government-sponsored financial insurance were adopted under circumstances of public mistrust. The insurance of bank deposits and of savings and loan shares was adopted in the 1930s, when public confidence in such institutions had been reduced by many institutional failures. The insurance of mortgages was used as a device to lure institutional investors back into a market which had been shattered by many mortgage defaults. The insurance of brokerage accounts came when brokerage customers added to the crush of paper work by a panic of security withdrawal.

So far we do not have insurance of life insurance liabilities, pension fund liabilities, or of state and local government securities. The reason, no doubt, is that these liabilities have not suffered any appreciable threat of default or failure. If there had been such a threat, it is almost certain that some form of insurance would have been adopted.

The feature common to all forms of government-sponsored financial insurance is some measure of regulation. The Hunt Commission recommended that the regulatory and insurance functions be separated. This recommendation has not seemed to spark very much support so far.

Government-sponsored financial insurance can be counted as a success in two ways. First, the public has received a great deal of protection. Second, at the rates charged, insurance has so far proved to be self-supporting. (So much so that private companies have been attracted into the business of mortgage insurance.)

SUMMARY EVALUATION

The mixed picture of regulation and competition in financial markets does not yield to easy summarization. The mood of general public dissatisfaction with the performance of our society has extended to the financial markets. Much of recent commentary has been critical of its performance. The decline of the dollar from the strongest currency in the world during the 1950s to its much reduced position (at least in terms of prestige) has been a further cause of self-criticism.

Research has filled some of the gaps in our knowledge and has been a healthy restraint on too broad generalization. For example, the inability of professional investment management to demonstrate a clear superiority over chance has been a sobering commentary on the value of information. A reexamination of the pre-SEC period has opened up renewed doubt about the disclosure requirements of that agency. Studies of the banking structure and of the economies of scale in banking have raised grave doubts about the merit of banking regulation.

It would be wrong, however, to downgrade the functioning of financial markets in the United States. The remarkable recovery of some defeated nations of World War II—Japan and Germany—has led to many unfavorable comparisons. It is true that the rate of saving and of productivity increase in both countries has far exceeded that of the United States. But both factors are results of characteristics of the social structure that are outside the financial markets. Allowing for differences in rate of saving and productivity increase, it can be argued that the United States's financial markets have channeled and used our resources fully as well and possibly better than these competitor countries. For all of the possibly inefficient intervention of the federal government in the housing and mortgage markets, it is still true that no other major nation has such a high rate of home ownership. The United States has failed to wipe out poverty, but at the same time it has the largest middle class that is sufficiently prosperous to use the services of financial markets.

Perhaps the most encouraging of all signs is the willingness to accept change and to progress. The very factors that may quickly make this textbook out of date are factors of great strength: rapid evolution and material improvement in performance.

Bibliography

1. Ahearn, L. F., "The Financing of U.S. Government Securities Dealers," unpublished Ph.D. Dissertation, Columbia University, 1965.
2. Alberts, W. W., "Business Cycles, Residential Construction Cycles, and the Mortgage Market," *Journal of Political Economy*, June 1962, pp. 263-281.
3. Allen, J. B., "Factors Determining the Volume of Certificates of Deposit Outstanding: A Case Study of the Drain-Off in 1969," *American Economist*, Fall 1971, pp. 32-38.
4. American Bankers Association, *The Commercial Banking Industry*, Prentice-Hall, Englewood Cliffs, N.J., 1962.
5. American Mutual Insurance Alliance et al., *Property and Casualty Insurance Companies: Their Role as Financial Intermediaries*, Prentice-Hall, Englewood Cliffs, N.J., 1962.
6. Anderson, P. S., and J. P. Hinson, "Variable Rates on Mortgages: Their Impact and Use," *New England Economic Review*, Federal Reserve Bank of Boston, March-April 1970, pp. 3-20.
7. Ando, A., and F. Modigliani, "The 'Life Cycle' Hypothesis of Saving," *American Economic Review*, March 1963, pp. 55-84.

8. Andrews, V. L., "Noninsured Corporate and State and Local Government Retirement Funds in the Financial Structure," in *Private Capital Markets*, Prentice-Hall, Englewood Cliffs, N.J., 1964.
9. Arena, J. J., "Postwar Stock Market Changes and Consumer Spending," *Review of Economics and Statistics*, November 1965, pp. 379-391.
10. Atkinson, T. R., *Trends in Corporate Bond Quality*, National Bureau of Economic Research, New York, 1967.
11. Bagehot, W., *Lombard Street: A Description of the Money Market*, Irwin, Homewood, Ill., 1962 (reprint).
12. Bankers Trust Company, *Investment Outlook* (annual).
13. Baumol, W. J., *The Stock Market and Economic Efficiency*, Fordham, New York, 1965.
14. Baxter, N. D., *The Commercial Paper Market*, Bankers, Boston, 1966.
15. ———, "Marketability, Default Risk, and Yields on Money Market Instruments," *Journal of Financial and Quantitative Analysis*, March 1968, pp. 75-85.
16. Benston, G. J., "The Effectiveness and Effects of the SEC's Accounting Disclosure Requirements," *Proceedings*, Symposium of AEI and National Law Center of George Washington University, 1968, pp. 25-78.
17. ———, "Savings Banking and the Public Interest," *Journal of Money, Credit and Banking*, February 1972, pp. 133-226.
18. Board of Governors of the Federal Reserve System, *Federal Reserve Bulletin* (monthly).
19. ———, *Federal Reserve System: Purposes and Functions*, Washington, D.C., 1963.
20. ———, Division of Research and Statistics, *Flow of Funds* (quarterly) and *Flow of Funds Accounts* (annual).
21. ———, *Joint Treasury-Federal Reserve Study of the U.S. Government Securities Market*, Washington, D.C., 1969, 1970, 1971.
22. Boughton, J. M., *Monetary Policy and the Federal Funds Market*, Duke, Durham, N.C., 1972.
23. Brady, E. A., "A Sectoral Econometric Study of the Postwar Residential Housing Market," *Journal of Political Economy*, April 1967, pp. 147-158.
24. Break, G. F. et al., *Federal Credit Agencies*, Prentice-Hall, Englewood Cliffs, N.J., 1963.
25. Brill, D. H., and A. Ulrey, "The Role of Financial Intermediaries in U.S. Capital Markets," *Federal Reserve Bulletin*, January 1967, pp. 18-31.
26. Brimmer, A. F., *Life Insurance Companies in the Capital Market*, Bureau of Business and Economic Research, Michigan State University, East Lansing, Mich., 1962.
27. Cagan, P., "A Study of Liquidity Premiums on Federal and Municipal Government Securities," in *Essays on Interest Rates*, vol. I, National Bureau of Economic Research, New York, 1969.
28. Carosso, V. P., *Investment Banking in America: A History*, Harvard, Cambridge, Mass., 1970.
29. Chandler, L., *Benjamin Strong: Central Banker*, Brookings, Washington, D.C., 1958.

30. Chown, J. F., *The International Bond Market in the 1960s*, Praeger, New York, 1968.
31. Christy, G. A., "A Rationalization of the Stock-Bond Yield Spread," *Quarterly Review of Economics and Business*, Spring 1967, pp. 63–70.
32. Clendenning, E. W., *The Euro-dollar Market*, Clarendon Press, Oxford, 1970.
33. Cohan, A. B., *Yields on Corporate Debt Directly Placed*, Columbia, New York, 1967.
34. Cohan, S. B., "The Determinants of Supply and Demand for Certificates of Deposit," unpublished Ph.D. dissertation, University of Michigan Press, Ann Arbor, Mich., 1969.
35. Cohen, J., "Copeland's Moneyflows After Twenty-Five Years: A Survey," *Journal of Economic Literature*, March 1972, pp. 1–25.
36. Commission on Financial Structure and Regulation, *Report* (popularly called the Hunt Commission Report), Washington, D.C., 1971.
37. Commission on Money and Credit, *Money and Credit*, Prentice-Hall, Englewood Cliffs, N.J., 1961.
38. Conard, J. W., *The Behavior of Interest Rates*, National Bureau of Economic Research, New York, 1966.
39. ———, *An Introduction to the Theory of Interest*, University of California Press, Berkeley, 1959.
40. Cooper, R. L., "Bankers' Acceptances," *Monthly Review*, Federal Reserve Bank of New York, June 1966, pp. 127–135.
41. Copeland, M. A., *A Study of Moneyflows in the United States*, National Bureau of Economic Research, New York, 1952.
42. Crockett, J., and I. Friend, "Consumer Investment Behavior," in *Determinants of Investment Behavior*, National Bureau of Economic Research, New York, 1967.
43. Croteau, J. T., *The Economics of the Credit Union*, Wayne State University Press, Detroit, 1963.
44. Culbertson, J. M., "The Term Structure of Interest Rates," *Quarterly Journal of Economics*, November 1957, pp. 485–517.
45. Davidson, P. H., "Structure of the Residential Mortgage Market," *Monthly Review*, Federal Reserve Bank of Richmond, September 1972. pp. 2–6.
46. Davis, R. G., and L. Banks, "Interregional Interest Rate Differentials," *Monthly Review*, Federal Reserve Bank of New York, August 1965, pp. 165–174.
47. Dietz, P. D., *Pension Funds: Measuring Investment Performance*, Free Press, New York, 1966.
48. Dougall, H. E., *Capital Markets and Institutions*, 2d ed., Prentice-Hall, Englewood Cliffs, N.J., 1970.
49. Duesenberry, J. S., *Income, Saving, and the Theory of Consumer Behavior*, Harvard, Cambridge, Mass., 1949.
50. Durand, D., *Basic Yields of Corporate Bonds, 1900–1942*, National Bureau of Economic Research, New York, 1942.
51. Einzig, P., *The Euro-Dollar System*, 3d ed., Macmillan, London, 1967.
52. ———, *Parallel Money Markets*, St. Martin's, New York, 1971.
53. Eisner, R., and R. H. Strotz, "Determinants of Business Investment," in

Impacts of Monetary Policy, Prentice-Hall, Englewood Cliffs, N.J., 1963.
54. Fair, R. C., "Disequilibrium in Housing Models," *Journal of Finance*, May 1972, pp. 207-221.
55. Fama, E. F., "Efficient Capital Markets: A Review of Theory and Empirical Work," *Journal of Finance*, May 1970, pp. 383-417.
56. ———, "Risk, Return, and Equilibrium: Some Clarifying Comments," *Journal of Finance*, March 1968, pp. 29-40.
57. ———, and A. B. Laffer, "Information and Capital Markets," *Journal of Business*, July 1971, pp. 289-298.
58. Fand, D., "Financial Regulations and the Allocative Efficiency of Our Capital Markets," *National Banking Review*, September 1965.
59. Federal Home Loan Bank Board, *Study of the Savings and Loan Industry*, Washington, D.C., 1970 (four volumes).
60. Federal Reserve Bank of Cleveland, *Money Market Instruments*, 3d ed., Cleveland, 1970.
61. ———, *Economic Review* (monthly).
62. Federal Reserve Bank of New York, *Monthly Review* (monthly).
63. Federal Reserve Bank of St. Louis, *Review* (monthly).
64. Fisher, L., "Determinants of Risk Premiums on Corporate Bonds," *Journal of Political Economy*, June 1959, pp. 217-237.
65. Fisher, L., and J. H. Lorie, "Rates of Return on Investments in Common Stock: The Year-by-Year Record, 1926-1965," *Journal of Business*, July 1968, pp. 291-316.
66. Fraine, H. G., and R. H. Mills, "Effects of Defaults and Credit Deterioration on Yields of Corporate Bonds," *Journal of Finance*, September 1961, pp. 423-434.
67. Francis, J. C., and S. H. Archer, *Portfolio Analysis*, Prentice-Hall, Englewood Cliffs, N.J., 1971.
68. Frankena, M. W., "The Influence of Call Provisions and Coupon Rate on the Yields of Corporate Bonds," in *Essays on Interest Rates*, vol. II, National Bureau of Economic Research, New York, 1971.
69. Frederickson, E. B., "The Geographic Structure of Residential Mortgage Yields," in *Essays on Interest Rates*, vol. II, National Bureau of Economic Research, New York, 1971.
70. Friedrich, K., "The Euro-Dollar System and International Liquidity." *Journal of Money, Credit and Banking*, August 1970, pp. 337-347.
71. Friend, I., "Determinants of the Volume and Composition of Saving with Special Reference to the Influence of Monetary Policy," in *Impacts of Monetary Policy*, Prentice-Hall, Englewood Cliffs, N.J., 1963.
72. ———, and M. Blume, "Measurement of Portfolio Performance under Uncertainty," *American Economic Review*, September 1970, pp. 561-575.
73. ———, ———, and J. Crockett, *Mutual Funds and Other Institutional Investors: A New Perspective*, McGraw-Hill, New York, 1970.
74. ———, and E. S. Herman, "The SEC through a Glass Darkly," *Journal of Business*, October 1964, pp. 382-405.

75. ———, C. W. Hoffman, and W. J. Winn, *Over-the-Counter Securities Markets*, McGraw-Hill, New York, 1958.
76. ———, et al., *Investment Banking and the New Issues Market*, World, Cleveland, 1967.
77. Friedman, M., *A Theory of the Consumption Function*, Princeton, Princeton, N.J., 1957.
78. Ganoe, C. S., "Working Capital Acceptances," *Journal of Commercial Bank Lending*, January 1970, pp. 50–53.
79. Gardner, E. B. (ed.), *Pension Fund Investment Management*, Irwin, Homewood, Ill., 1969.
80. Gentry, J. A., "Do Institutional Investors Buy and Sell Common Stocks With Similar Characteristics?" *Quarterly Review of Economics and Business*, Winter 1968, pp. 21–29.
81. Goldfeld, S. M., *Commercial Bank Behavior and Economic Activity: A Structural Study of Monetary Policy in the Postwar United States*, North-Holland, Amsterdam, 1966.
82. ———, "Savings and Loan Associations and the Market for Savings: Aspects of Allocational Efficiency," in *Study of the Savings and Loan Industry*, vol. II, Federal Home Loan Bank Board, Washington, D.C., 1969.
83. Goldsmith, R. W., *The Flow of Capital Funds in the Postwar Economy*, National Bureau of Economic Research, New York, 1965.
84. ———, *Financial Institutions*, Random House, New York, 1968.
85. ———, *Financial Intermediaries in the American Economy Since 1900*, Princeton, Princeton, N.J., 1958.
86. ———, *A Study of Saving in the United States*, Princeton, Princeton, N.J., 1955 and 1956 (three volumes).
87. Goudzwaard, M. B., "Rate Ceilings, Loan Turn-Downs, and Credit Opportunity," *Western Economic Journal*, December 1968, pp. 404–412.
88. Gramlich, E. N., "State and Local Governments and Their Budget Constraint," *International Economic Review*, June 1969, pp. 163–182.
89. Grebler, L., *The Future of Thrift Institutions*, Joint Savings and Mutual Savings Banks Exchange Groups, Danville, Ill., 1969.
90. ———, D. M. Blank, and L. Winnick, *Capital Formation in Residential Real Estate: Trends and Prospects*, Princeton, Princeton, N.J., 1956.
91. ———, and S. J. Maisel, "Determinants of Residential Construction: A Review of Present Knowledge," in *Impacts of Monetary Policy*, Prentice-Hall, Englewood Cliffs, N.J., 1963.
92. Gurley, J. G., and E. S. Shaw, *Money in a Theory of Finance*, Brookings, Washington, D. C., 1960.
93. Guttentag, J. M., "The Short Cycle in Residential Construction, 1946–1959," *American Economic Review*, June 1961, pp. 275–298.
94. ———, and M. Beck, *New Series on Home Mortgage Yields Since 1951*, Columbia, New York, 1970.
95. Hamburger, M. J., "Household Demand for Financial Assets," *Econometrica*, January 1968, pp. 97–118.

96. ———, *The Impact of Monetary Variables: A Selected Survey of the Recent Empirical Literature*, Staff Economic Study 34, Board of Governors of the Federal Reserve System, 1967.
97. Heebner, A. G., *Negotiable Certificates of Deposits: The Development of a Money Market Instrument*, New York University Press, New York, 1969.
98. Hempel, G. H., *Municipal Bonds*, Bureau of Business Research, University of Michigan, Ann Arbor, Mich., 1967.
99. ———, *The Postwar Quality of State and Local Debt*. National Bureau of Economic Research, New York, 1971.
100. Hess, A. P., Jr., and W. J. Winn, *The Value of the Call Privilege*, University of Pennsylvania Press, Philadelphia, 1962.
101. Hickman, W. B., *Corporate Bond Quality and Investor Experience*, Princeton, Princeton, N.J., 1958.
102. Hoagland, H. E., and L. D. Stone, *Real Estate Finance*, 5th ed., Irwin, Homewood, Ill., 1972.
103. Hodgman, D. R., *Commercial Bank Loan and Investment Policy*, Bureau of Business Research, University of Illinois, Champaign, Ill., 1963.
104. Holmes, A. R., and F. H. Schott, *The New York Foreign Exchange Market*, Federal Reserve Bank of New York, New York, 1965.
105. Homer, S., and R. I. Johannesen, *The Price of Money, 1946 to 1969*, Rutgers University Press, New Brunswick, N.J., 1969.
106. Horvitz, P. M. et al., *Private Financial Institutions*, Prentice-Hall, Englewood Cliffs, N.J., 1963.
107. Investment Company Institute, *Management Investment Companies*, Prentice-Hall, Englewood Cliffs, N.J., 1962.
108. Jacobs, D. P. et al., *Financial Institutions*, 5th ed., Irwin, Homewood, Ill., 1971.
109. Jafee, D. M., *Credit Rationing and the Commercial Loan Market: An Econometric Study of the Structure of the Commercial Loan Market*, Wiley, New York, 1971.
110. Jeffers, J. R., and J. Kevon, "A Portfolio for Government Securities," *Journal of Finance*, December 1969, pp. 905–919.
111. Jen, F. C., and J. E. Wert, "The Deferred Call Provision and Corporate Bond Yields," *Journal of Financial and Quantitative Analysis*, June 1968, pp. 157–169.
112. ———, "The Effect of Call Risk on Corporate Bond Yields," *Journal of Finance*, December 1967, pp. 637–651.
113. Jensen, M. C., "Capital Markets: Theory and Evidence," *Bell Journal of Economics and Management Science*, Autumn 1972, pp. 357–398.
114. ———, "Risk, The Pricing of Capital Assets, and the Evaluation of Investment Portfolios," *Journal of Business*, April 1969, pp. 167–247.
115. Johnson, R. E., "Term Structures of Corporate Bond Yields as a Function of Risk of Default," *Journal of Finance*, May 1967, pp. 313–345.
116. Jones, L. D., *Investment Policies of Life Insurance Companies*, Division of Research, Graduate School of Business, Harvard University, Boston, 1968.

117. Jones, O., "Private Secondary (Mortgage) Market Facilities," *Journal of Finance*, May 1968, pp. 359–366.
118. ———, and L. Grebler, *The Secondary Mortgage Market*, University of California, Los Angeles, 1961.
119. Jorgenson, D. W., "Econometric Studies of Investment Behavior: A Survey," *Journal of Economic Literature*, December 1971, pp. 1111–1147.
120. Kendall, L. T., *The Savings and Loan Business: Its Purposes, Functions, and Economic Justification*, Prentice-Hall, Englewood Cliffs, N.J., 1962.
121. Keran, M. W., "Expectations, Money and the Stock Market," *Review*, Federal Reserve Bank of St. Louis, January 1971, pp. 16–31.
122. Kessel, R. A., *The Cyclical Behavior of the Term Structure of Interest Rates*, National Bureau of Economic Research, New York, 1965.
123. ———, "A Study of the Effects of Competition in the Tax-Exempt Bond Market," *Journal of Political Economy*, July–August 1971, pp. 706–738.
124. Keynes, J. M., *The General Theory of Employment, Interest, and Money*, Harcourt, Brace, New York, 1936.
125. Klaman, S. B., *The Postwar Residential Mortgage Market*, Princeton, Princeton, N.J., 1961.
126. Klopstock, F. H., "Eurodollars in the Liquidity and Reserve Management of United States Banks," *Monthly Review*, Federal Reserve Bank of New York, July 1968.
127. Korobow, L., and R. J. Gelson, "Real Estate Investment Trusts: An Appraisal of Their Impact on Mortgage Credit," *Monthly Review*, Federal Reserve Bank of New York, August 1971, pp. 188–195.
128. Krause, L., "Private International Finance," in *International Organization*, Brookings, Washington, D.C., 1972 (vol. 25).
129. Kuznets, P. W., "Financial Determinants of Manufacturing Inventory Behavior," *Yale Economic Essays*, 1964, pp. 331–369.
130. Kwon, J. K., "Demand for Government Securities by Financial Sectors," *Economic and Business Bulletin*, Winter 1971, pp. 28–36.
131. Lees, F. A., "Interregional Flows of Funds through State and Local Government Securities," *Journal of Regional Science*, April 1969, pp. 79–86.
132. Leffler, G. L., and L. C. Farwell, *The Stock Market*, 3d ed., Ronald, New York, 1963.
133. Life Insurance Association of America, *Life Insurance Companies as Financial Institutions*, Prentice-Hall, Englewood Cliffs, N.J., 1962.
134. Lindow, W., *Inside the Money Market*, Random House, New York, 1972.
135. Lintner, J., "Security Prices, Risk, and Maximal Gains from Diversification," *Journal of Finance*, December 1965, pp. 587–615.
136. ———, "The Valuation of Risk Assets and the Selection of Risky Investments in Stock Portfolios and Capital Budgets," *Review of Economics and Statistics*, February 1965, pp. 394–419.
137. Lovell, M. C., "Determinants of Inventory Investment," in *Models of Income Determination*, Princeton, Princeton, N.J., 1964.

138. Ludtke, J., *The American Financial System: Markets and Institutions,* 2d ed., Allyn and Bacon, Boston, 1967.
139. Lutz, F. A., *The Theory of Interest,* Aldine, Chicago, 1968.
140. Maisel, S. J., *Financing Real Estate,* McGraw-Hill, New York, 1965.
141. ———, "A Theory of Fluctuations in Residential Construction Starts," *American Economic Review,* June 1963, pp. 359–379.
142. Malkiel, B. G., *The Term Structure of Interest Rates: Expectations and Behavior Patterns,* Princeton, Princeton, N.J., 1966.
143. ———, *The Term Structure of Interest Rates: Theory, Empirical Evidence, and Applications,* McCaleb-Seiler, New York, 1970.
144. Markowitz, H. M., "Portfolio Selection," *Journal of Finance,* March 1952, pp. 77–91.
145. ———, *Portfolio Selection: Efficient Diversification of Investments,* Wiley, New York, 1959.
146. McGouldrick, P. F., and J. E. Peterson, "Monetary Restraint and Borrowing and Capital Spending by Large State and Local Governments in 1966," *Federal Reserve Bulletin,* July 1968, pp. 552–581.
147. Meigs, J., *Money Matters,* Harper and Row, New York, 1971.
148. Meiselman, D., *The Term Structure of Interest Rates,* Prentice-Hall, Englewood Cliffs, N.J., 1962.
149. Mendelson, M., "The Eurobond and Capital Market Integration," *Journal of Finance,* March 1972, pp. 110–126.
150. Meyer, J. R., and E. Kuh, *The Investment Decision: An Empirical Study,* Harvard, Cambridge, Mass., 1959.
151. Modigliani, F., and R. Sutch, "Innovations in Interest Rate Policy," *American Economic Review,* May 1966, pp. 178–197.
152. Moore, B. J., *An Introduction to the Theory of Finance,* Free Press, New York, 1968.
153. Morrissey, T. F., "The Demand for Mortgage Loans and the Concomitant Demand for Home Loan Bank Advances by Savings and Loan Associations," *Journal of Finance,* June 1971, pp. 687–698.
154. Morton, J. E., *Urban Mortgage Lending: Comparative Markets and Experience,* Princeton, Princeton, N.J., 1965.
155. Mossin, J., "Equilibrium in a Capital Asset Market," *Econometrica,* October 1966, pp. 768–783.
156. Murray, R., *First Buttonwood Lecture,* NYSE and Columbia University, New York, 1972.
157. Muth, R. E., "The Demand for Non-Farm Housing," in *The Demand for Durable Goods,* The University of Chicago Press, Chicago, 1960.
158. National Association of Mutual Savings Banks, *Mutual Savings Banks: Basic Characteristics and Role in the National Economy,* Prentice-Hall, Englewood Cliffs, N.J., 1962.
159. National Bureau of Economic Research, *The Flow of Funds Approach to Social Accounting,* Princeton, Princeton, N.J., 1962.
160. Nelson, C. R., *The Term Structure of Interest Rates,* Basic Books, New York, 1972.
161. New York Stock Exchange, *Fact Book* (annual).

162. Nichols, D. M., *Trading in Federal Funds: Findings of a Three-Year Study*, Board of Governors of the Federal Reserve System, Washington, D.C., 1965.
163. Ott, D. J., and A. H. Meltzer, *Federal Taxation of State and Local Securities*, Brookings, Washington, D.C., 1963.
164. Phelps, C. D., "The Impact of Monetary Policy on State and Local Government Expenditure in the United States," in *Impacts of Monetary Policy*, Prentice-Hall, Englewood Cliffs, N.J., 1963.
165. ———, "The Impact of Tightening Credit on Municipal Capital Expenditures in the United States," *Yale Economic Essays*, Fall 1961, pp. 275–321.
166. ———, "Real and Monetary Determinants of State and Local Highway Investment, 1951–1961," *American Economic Review*, September 1969, pp. 507–521.
167. Peterson, J. E., "Response of State and Local Governments to Varying Credit Conditions," *Federal Reserve Bulletin*, March 1971, pp. 209–232.
168. ———, and P. F. McGouldrick, "Monetary Restraint, Borrowing, and Capital Spending by Small Local Governments and State Colleges in 1966," *Federal Reserve Bulletin*, December 1968, pp. 953–982.
169. Platt, R. B., "The Interest Rate on Federal Funds: An Empirical Approach," *Journal of Finance*, June 1970, pp. 585–598.
170. Pogue, T., and R. Soldofsky, "What's in a Bond Rating?" *Journal of Financial and Quantitative Analysis*, June 1969, pp. 201–224.
171. Polakoff, M. E. et al., *Financial Institutions and Markets*, Houghton Mifflin, Boston, 1970.
172. Prochnow, H. V. (ed.), *The Eurodollar*, Rand McNally, Skokie, Ill. 1970.
173. Pye, G., "On the Tax Structure of Interest Rates," *Quarterly Journal of Economics*, November 1969, pp. 562–579.
174. ———, "The Value of Call Deferment on a Bond: Some Empirical Results," *Journal of Finance*, December 1967, pp. 623–636.
175. Rabinowitz, A., *Municipal Bond Finance and Administration*, Wiley, New York, 1969.
176. Raw, C., Page, and Hodgsen, *Do You Sincerely Want to Be Rich?*, Penguin, Baltimore, 1972.
177. Ritter, L. S. et al., "The Flow-of-Funds Accounts: A New Approach to Financial Market Analysis," *Journal of Finance*, May 1963, pp. 219–263.
178. Robbins, S. M., "A Plea for a Largely Auction Central Market System," *Money Manager*, January 2, 1973.
179. ———, *The Securities Markets*, Free Press, New York, 1966.
180. Robichek, A. A., "Risk and the Value of Securities," *Journal of Financial and Quantitative Analysis*, December 1969, pp. 513–538.
181. Robinson, R. I., "The Hunt Commission Report: A Search for Politically Feasible Solutions to the Problems of Financial Structure," *Journal of Finance*, September 1972, pp. 765–778.
182. ———, *The Management of Bank Funds*, 2d ed., McGraw-Hill, New York, 1962.

183. ——, *Postwar Market for State and Local Government Securities*, Princeton, Princeton, N.J., 1960.
184. Roll, R., *The Behavior of Interest Rates: Application of the Efficient Market Model to U.S. Treasury Bill Rates*, Basic Books, New York, 1970.
185. Roosa, R. V., *Federal Reserve Operations in the Money and Government Securities Market*, Federal Reserve Bank of New York, New York, 1956.
186. Schaaf, A. H., "Regional Differences in Mortgage Financing Costs," *Journal of Finance*, March 1966, pp. 85–94.
187. Schadrack, F. C., "Demand and Supply in the Commercial Paper Market," *Journal of Finance*, September 1970, pp. 837–852.
188. ——, and F. S. Breimer, "Recent Developments in the Commercial Paper Market," *Monthly Review*, Federal Reserve Bank of New York, December 1970, pp. 280–291.
189. Schneiderman, P., "Planned and Actual Long-Term Borrowing by State and Local Governments," *Federal Reserve Bulletin*, December 1971, pp. 977–987.
190. Schulkin, P. A., "Real Estate Investment Trusts: A New Financial Intermediary," *New England Economic Review*, Federal Reserve Bank of Boston, November-December 1970, pp. 2–14.
191. Scott, I. O. Jr., *The Government Securities Market*, McGraw-Hill, New York, 1965.
192. Securities and Exchange Commission, *Statistical Bulletin* (monthly).
193. Securities Industry Association, *Municipal Statistical Bulletin* (quarterly).
194. Seldon, R. T., *Trends and Cycles in the Commercial Paper Market*, National Bureau of Economic Research, New York, 1963.
195. Shapiro, E., "The Absolute Level of Bond Yields and the Corporate-Municipal Differential," *Nebraska Journal of Economics and Business*, Summer 1970, pp. 3–13.
196. Sharpe, W. F., "Capital Asset Prices: A Theory of Market Equilibrium Under Conditions of Risk," *Journal of Finance*, September 1964, pp. 425–442.
197. ——, "Mutual Fund Performance," *Journal of Business*, January 1966, pp. 119–138.
198. ——, *Portfolio Theory and Capital Markets*, McGraw-Hill, New York, 1970.
199. ——, "Security Prices, Risk, and Maximal Gains from Diversification: Reply," *Journal of Finance*, December 1966, pp. 743–744.
200. ——, "A Simplified Model for Portfolio Analysis," *Management Science*, January 1963, pp. 277–293.
201. Shay, R. P., "Factors Affecting Price, Volume, and Credit Risk in the Consumer Finance Industry," *Journal of Finance*, May 1970, pp. 503–515.
202. Sloane, P. E., "Determinants of Bond Yield Differentials, 1954–1959," in *Financial Markets and Economic Activity*, Wiley, New York, 1967.
203. "Smith, A." (G. J. W. Goodman), *The Money Game*, Random House, New York, 1968.
204. ——, *Super Money*, Random House, New York, 1972.

205. Smith, H. C., "Institutional Aspects of Interregional Mortgage Investment," *Journal of Finance*, May 1968, pp. 349-358.
206. Smith, P. F., *Economics of Financial Institutions and Markets*, Irwin, Homewood, Ill., 1971.
207. ———, "Pricing Policies on Consumer Loans at Commercial Banks," *Journal of Finance*, May 1970, pp. 517-525.
208. Sparks, G., "An Econometric Analysis of the Role of Financial Intermediaries in Postwar Residential Building Cycles," in *Determinants of Investment Behavior*, National Bureau of Economic Research, New York, 1967.
209. Sprinkel, B. W., *Money and Markets: A Monetarist View*, Irwin, Homewood, Ill., 1971.
210. Stigler, G. J., "Imperfections in the Capital Market," *Journal of Political Economy*, June 1967, pp. 287-292.
211. ———, "Public Regulation of the Securities Markets," *Journal of Business*, April 1964, pp. 117-142.
212. Stone, B. K., *Risk, Return, and Equilibrium*, M.I.T., Cambridge, Mass., 1970.
213. Suits, D. B., "The Determinants of Consumer Expenditure: A Review of Present Knowledge," in *Impacts of Monetary Policy*, Prentice-Hall, Englewood Cliffs, N.J., 1963.
214. Tanner, J. E., and L. A. Kochin, "The Determinants of the Difference Between Bid and Ask Prices on Government Bonds," *Journal of Business*, October 1971, pp. 375-379.
215. Teck, A., *Mutual Savings Banks and Savings and Loan Associations: Aspects of Growth*, Columbia, New York, 1968.
216. Telser, L. G., "A Critique of Some Recent Empirical Research on the Explanation of the Term Structure of Interest Rates," *Journal of Political Economy*, August 1967, pp. 546-561.
217. Tobin, J., "Liquidity Preference as Behavior Towards Risk," *Review of Economic Studies*, February 1958, pp. 65-86.
218. Treynor, J. L., "How to Rate Management of Investment Funds," *Harvard Business Review*, January-February 1965, pp. 63-75.
219. United States Savings and Loan League, *Fact Book* (annual).
220. Van Horne, J. C., *The Functions and Analysis of Capital Market Rates*, Prentice-Hall, Englewood Cliffs, N.J., 1970.
221. Vinson, C. E., "Pricing Practices in the Primary Convertible Bond Market," *Quarterly Review of Economics and Business*, Summer 1970, pp. 47-60.
222. Wallace, N., "The Term Structure of Interest Rates and the Maturity Composition of the Federal Debt," *Journal of Finance*, May 1967, pp. 301-312.
223. Weber, G. I., "Interest Rates on Mortgages and Dividend Rates on Savings and Loan Shares," *Journal of Finance*, September 1966, pp. 515-521.
224. Weber, W. E., "The Effect of Interest Rates on Aggregate Consumption," *American Economic Review*, September 1970, pp. 591-600.

225. Welfling, W., *Mutual Savings Banks: The Evolution of a Financial Intermediary*, The Press of Case Western Reserve University, Cleveland, 1968.
226. West, R. R., "Determinants of Underwriters' Spreads on Tax Exempt Bond Issues," *Journal of Financial and Quantitative Analysis*, September 1967, pp. 241–263.
227. ———, and S. M. Tinic, *The Economics of the Stock Market*, Praeger, New York, 1971.
228. Wheat, F. M., "Truth in Securities Three Decades Later," *Howard Law Review*, Winter 1967, pp. 100–107.
229. White, W. H., "The Structure of the Bond Market and the Cyclical Variability of Interest Rates," *IMF Staff Papers*, March 1962.
230. Willis, P. B., *The Federal Funds Market: Its Origin and Development*, 3d ed., Federal Reserve Bank of Boston, Boston, 1968.
231. ———, *The Secondary Market for Negotiable Certificates of Deposit*, Board of Governors of the Federal Reserve System, Washington, D.C., 1967.
232. ———, *A Study of the Market for Federal Funds*, Board of Governors of the Federal Reserve System, Washington, D.C., 1967.
233. Wolf, C. R., "Bank Preferences and Government Security Yields," *Quarterly Journal of Economics*, May 1971, pp. 283–303.
234. Woodworth, G. W., *The Money Market and Monetary Management*, 2d ed., Harper & Row, New York, 1972.
235. Wright, C., "Saving and the Rate of Interest," in *The Taxation of Income from Capital*, Brookings, Washington, D.C., 1969.
236. ———, "Some Evidence on the Interest Elasticity of Consumption," *American Economic Review*, September 1967, pp. 850–854.
237. Wrightsman, D., *An Introduction to Monetary Theory and Policy*, Free Press, New York, 1971.
238. ———, "Pension Funds and Economic Concentration," *Quarterly Review of Economics and Business*, Winter 1967, pp. 29–36.

Index

A Glossary of definitions and a Glossary of acronyms have been incorporated into this index. Glossary terms, in **boldface**, are followed by their definitions and any Subject Index page references, subentries, and/or cross-references.

Accelerated depreciation (*see* Depreciation)
Accord, U.S. Treasury, Federal Reserve, 183, 246
Adjusted credit proxy A preliminary estimate of bank loans and investments derived from the reports of deposit liabilities received by the Federal Reserve more frequently than asset reports.
Agency securities Obligations of credit agencies sponsored by the Federal government such as FHLB, FHLMC, GNMA, FCA, and FICB. Most of these securities are not directly guaranteed by the federal government but the implied support of the sponsorship causes them to sell at yields only moderately above those of Treasury obligations of the same maturity. 148–149
Aggregates (*see* M_1, M_2, and M_3)
Alberts, W. W., 32
AMEX American Stock Exchange, 335
Ando, A., 24
Arbitrage:
 foreign exchange, 218
 securities markets, 335
Atkinson, T. R., 115
Auction sale of U.S. Treasury securities, 248, 255
Automation, securities market, stock market, 363, 414
 U.S. Treasury debt, 257

Balance of payments The social accounting system embracing all of the financial transactions of a nation with the rest of the world for a designated period of time. 214
Bank for Cooperatives (*see* **COOP**)
Bankers' acceptance A credit instrument initiated by a creditor with payment guaranteed by the debtor's bank (i.e. it is "accepted"). Most bankers' acceptances originate in foreign trade but a few are solely for the purpose of borrowing money in this market. Bankers buy their own acceptances sometimes but foreigners account for most of the purchasing in our money markets.
Banking Act of 1933, 410
Banks, L., 121
Basis points A basis point is $1/100$ of a percent. An interest rate of 6.85 percent is ten basis points above a rate of 6.75 percent.
Baxter, N. D., 112*n*.
Beta coefficient A measure of the volatility of the rate of return on a security or portfolio of securities relative to the rate of return on the market portfolio. If the beta coefficient is less than one, the security or portfolio of securities is less risky than the market; if beta is greater than one, the security or portfolio is more risky than the market. The beta coefficient of the market portfolio, itself, is equal to one. 96
BIS Bank for International Settlements.
Blank, D. M., 120
Block trading, 339–340
Blue List (state and local government securities), 270
Blume, M., 55*n*., 92*n*., 99
Brady, E. A., 32
Bretton Woods, 213
Broker One who acts as an intermediary between buyers and sellers but does not himself take a position in the securities for which he acts as broker. (Customers' representatives of commission brokerage firms are not, strictly speaking, themselves brokers but are sales representatives who transmit orders to the professional brokers or traders within the firm who perform the brokerage function.)
Business investment, determinants of, 25–29

Cagan, P., 111
Call feature An option which permits the issuer of corporate bonds to buy back the bonds at a specified call price before the bonds mature.
 call structure of interest rates, 116–118
 corporate bonds, 315

431

Capacity utilization of business plant and equipment, 27
Capital   Cumulated employment of funds in the form of assets, both real and financial. Economists usually use it to mean only real assets such as housing, plant and equipment, inventories, and the present value of the flow of human services. Accountants use it to mean the sources of funds cumulating in the form of liabilities (debt capital) and net worth (equity capital). Still other meanings of this much overused word may be found.
Capital expenditures:
   fixed, 307
   state and local government, 261
Capital market line (*CML*)   Equilibrium relationship between the expected rate of return and the standard deviation of return for efficient portfolios of risky and riskless securities. In graphical terms the *CML* shows that expected rate of return on an efficient portfolio of risky and riskless securities as a positive and straight-line function of risk, as measured by the standard deviation of return. The slope of the line is the extra expected return per unit of risk; the intercept is the risk-free rate of return. 95
Capital markets   Financial markets where securities with maturities of more than one year are bought and sold. The principal capital markets are the corporate stock and bond markets, the mortgage market, and the markets for municipal and Treasury securities.
Ceiling, interest rates, 255
   (*See also* **Regulation Q**)
Central money market   City with a major concentration of large commercial banks which engage in wholesale banking.
CD   Certificate of deposit. Time deposit evidenced by a credit instrument which may be nonnegotiable.
   (*See also* **NCD**)
Chartering of banks, 411–412
CML   Capital market line, 95
Cohan, A., 105
Cohen, Jacob, 79*n*.
Commercial banks:
   as financial intermediaries, 44–47
   in mortgage market, 293
Commercial paper   Negotiable note sold by corporations in the open money market. They may be "directly" sold by the issuer, or "dealer-placed." Maturity ranges from 3 to 270 days but most transactions are from 90 to 180 days.
   evolution, 394
Commission brokerage firms. Partnerships or corporation organized to handle brokerage business for customers. They usually not only execute sales and purchases but also arrange credit for margin transactions and hold securities in custody. Commission brokerage business may be combined with investment banking, money management, commodity as well as securities brokerage, and other financial functions.

   failures, 338
Compensatory balance   Part of a loan agreement, of varying degrees of explicitness, by which a borrowing customer agrees to maintain some minimum balance. The amount is usually computed as a proportion of the maximum loan outstanding. 165, 172
Competition:
   among financial institutions, 403–411
   in securities industry, 360–361
Competitive bidding:
   for corporate bonds, 311, 313–314
   for state and local government bonds, 268
COOP   Bank for Cooperatives, generally dealing with agricultural cooperatives. 256
Copeland, M. A., 58*n*.
Corporate equities:
   informal markets, 344
   leading indicator, 342
   ownership, 331
Correspondent banking, 143, 163–164
Coupon rate   Ratio of annual interest, in dollars, to the par value of the bond. Since the number of dollars of interest promised and the par value of the bond are fixed at time of sale, the coupon rate is fixed for the life of the bond. When a bond is first sold by its issuer, its coupon rate is usually close to then prevailing current market yields.
CP   Commercial paper.
Credit line   Loan limit given by a commercial bank to regular customers. The amount is reviewed annually or oftener and is considered an informal but not legal obligation by the bank for the accommodation of its customers.
Credit rating, state and local government securities, 262–263
Credit risk   Possibility that the borrower will not pay as promised.
Crockett, J., 40, 55*n*., 99
CSDS   Comprehensive Securities Depository System, 338
Culbertson, J. M., 108*n*.

Davis, R. G., 121
Dealer   A man or firm which makes both bids and offers for a designated security or securities. Dealers usually accumulate a "position" or inventory in such security or securities, which may be "long" or "short." A dealer risks his own money in contrast with a broker who acts only as an intermediary in trying to match buyers and sellers, taking a commission "in the middle."
Debt management, U.S. Treasury, 244
Default structure of interest rates, 112–116
Demographic factors in housing, 281
Depreciation, accelerated, 284, 308
Devaluation   The reduction of the command of a currency either on gold or, more recently, on SDRs.
Direct investment   Investment by U.S. corporations in plant and equipment and other business properties in foreign countries.
Direct placement   Negotiation of a credit between a corporate borrower and an

INDEX 433

institutional investor. It is an alternative to an open market sale of securities. 313
Disintermediation (*see* Intermediation)
Diversification, effect on risk, 86–89
Dougall, H. E., 37*n*.
Duesenberry, J. S., 23
Durand, D., 105, 110

Eccles, Marriner, 183, 190
EDP   Electronic data processing.
Efficiency of financial markets, 402
  allocational versus operational, 398
  securities markets generally, 347
  state and local government securities, 271
Efficient market   Market in which the prices reflect fully and immediately all available and pertinent information. It would be impossible to "beat" an efficient market, if such existed, since no one would know anything that is not already known and therefore reflected in market prices. 99, 400–402
Efficient portfolio   Portfolio that offers maximum expected return for given risk, or minimum risk for given expected return. An efficient portfolio is fully diversified to eliminate unsystematic risk. 90–93
Eisner, R., 29
Employment Act of 1946, 192
Equity "kickers" or participation   Contractual arrangements by which an institutional lender exacts, as the price of making a loan, some added return of an equity nature. The amount of this return is dependent on the income earned by the project or company for which the loan is made. It may be a percentage of sales or rentals or a warrant to purchase shares of common stock.
  in mortgage loans, 292
Exchange rates:
  fixed, 213, 219
  flexible, 221
  forward, 217
Expectations theory of term structure of interest rates, 107–108
Expected rate of return   Weighted average of all possible rates of return on a security or portfolio of securities, the weights being probabilities. 83
External versus internal financing, 392
Eurobond   Bonds denominated in a currency other than that of the country in which it is marketed. The currency denomination may be, but does not necessarily have to be, that of the issuer. U.S. corporations have sold bonds denominated in dollars, in Europe. Swedish cities have sold bonds, denominated in D-marks, in Switzerland. 326–327
Eurocurrency   Deposit account denominated in a currency other than that of the host country. A dollar, Deutschemark, or Swiss franc deposit in a London-based bank would be a Eurocurrency. 155–160
Eurodollar   A Eurocurrency denominated in U.S. dollars.

Fair, R. C., 32

Fama, E. F., 99*n*., 402
"Fannie Mae" (*see* **FNMA**)
Farm mortgages, 305
Farwell, L. C., 37*n*.
"Fed"   Informal abbreviation of Federal Reserve; sometimes applied to the whole system, sometimes to the Board of Governors of the Federal Reserve System; sometimes to an individual Federal Reserve bank such as the Federal Reserve Bank of New York.
Fed funds   A collected or available reserve balance at a Federal Reserve bank which is loaned ("sold") by a bank with excess reserves to a borrowing ("purchasing") bank which is in need of reserves. Most transactions are between member banks but a few other financial institutions, mainly dealers in Treasury securities, buy and sell Fed funds. 129, 152–153
  evolution of market, 394
FHA   Federal Housing Administration. May disappear by merger into HUD by the time this index is in print. Also used to indicate the Farmers Home Administration. 285, 297, 298, 388
FHLB   Federal Home Loan Board; sometimes used to apply to the whole system of Board and banks. 256
FHLBS   Federal Home Loan Bank System, 300
FHLMC   Federal Home Loan Mortgage Corporation; under the supervision of the FHLB and for creation of a secondary market in conventional mortgages.
FICB   Federal Intermediate Credit Bank. Federal agency for financing the Production Credit Associations. 256
Financial assets   A claim in money terms on some other economic unit which thus is a liability of the other unit. Since every financial asset is matched by a liability, financial assets net out to zero when all balance sheets are consolidated, leaving only real assets as the basis for wealth. Financial assets are the outgrowth of the separation of the acts of saving and real investment. Savers who do not wish to acquire real assets have the alternative of acquiring financial assets issued by investors who wish to acquire real assets without having to save. Financial assets are traded in financial markets.
Financial institutions   Composite of inter- mediating and marketing institutions operating in the financial markets. Financial intermediaries borrow from savers and lend to ultimate investors at terms which are attractive to all parties. Financial marketing institutions offer facilities by which buyers and sellers of securities can effect purchases and sales.
Financial intermediaries   Institutions which transfer funds from ultimate lenders (savers) to ultimate borrowers (investors in real assets). They include commercial banks, mutual savings banks, savings and loan

associations, credit unions, insurance companies, pension funds, finance companies, and investment companies. The process of intermediation is carried out by borrowing from ultimate lenders and lending to ultimate borrowers at terms attractive to all parties.

Financial investment Acquisition of financial assets over a period of time. Making loans and purchasing securities are acts of financial investment. These acts take place in financial markets.

Financial markets The institutional facilities that link saving and real investment. Individuals who want to save but not invest (in a real sense) can do so only if there are financial markets in which to lend. Anyone who wants to invest, but lacks the savings, can do so only if there is a source of external financing via the financial markets. The instruments traded in financial markets are called financial assets, including loans and securities of all types.

  function, 9
  monetary role, 12-15
  price elasticity, 6

Fire and casualty insurance companies, 52
Fisher, L., 113
Fixed capital expenditures (*see* Capital expenditures)

FLB Federal Land Banks, 256

Flow of funds An interlocking system of accounts which traces the sources and uses of capital funds by different economic sectors in different financial markets.

Flow-of-funds accounting:
  condensed form, 75
  matrix: asset-liability, 61-65
    financial market, 238
    money market, 132-133
    source-use, 59-60, 62-63
  sectors, 60
  transactions, 59-60

FNMA Federal National Mortgage Association; also often known as "Fanny Mae." Now a private corporation listed on the NYSE and making a secondary market in mortgages of all types. 297, 299, 389

FOMC Federal Open Market Committee; part of the "Fed." 138, 197-207
  directive, 200-201

Foreign exchange market:
  commercial bank role, 177-180
  Federal Reserve participation, 205-206

Forward exchange A contract to sell or buy a specified foreign currency at a rate fixed at time of transaction but with delivery at the specified future time.

Fraine, H. G., 116
Frankena, M. W., 117-119
Frederickson, E. B., 121
Friedman, Milton, 24, 194
Friend, I., 40, 55*n.*, 92*n.*, 99

FSLIC Federal Savings and Loan Insurance Corporation. Insures deposit liabilities of savings and loan associations up to specified limits; under the supervision of the FHLB. 256

Gardner, E. B., 53*n.*
Geographic structure of interest rates, 120-121

GNMA Government National Mortgage Association. A Federal government agency to improve the marketability of conventional mortgages; usually by packaging such mortgages into more attractive market securities; some of which "pass through" all cash receipts. 297, 299, 389

GNP Gross national product, 58-59
Gold, as a monetary asset, 213
Goldfeld, S. M., 45
Goldsmith, R. W., 23
Government investment:
  Federal, 32
  state and local, 33-34
Gramlich, E. M., 33
Grebler, L., 32, 120
Ground rents, 284
Growth rates, financial assets, 231
Gurley, J. G., 373
Guttentag, J. M., 32

Hedging-pressure theory of the term structure of interest rates (*see* Segmented-market theory)
Hickman, W. B., 114, 116
Hodgman, D. R., 45

Holding period Period of time an investor plans to hold securities. If holding period is longer than the maturity period of the securities, the investor must reinvest. If shorter, he must liquidate before maturity.

Homer, S., 105
Housing cycle, 374-375

HUD Department of Housing and Urban Development. Principal agency of the Federal government dealing with housing, FHA, so long as it exists, is under HUD. 285, 297, 300-301

Humped yield curve (*see* **Term structure of interest rates**)
Hunt Commission, 396, 407, 414

IMF International Monetary Fund, 213
Income real estate, 283
Insider trading, 353
Institutional membership, organized exchanges, 336
Insurance of financial institutions, 416-417
Interest equalization tax, 220
Interest rates:
  call structure, 116-118
  on corporate bonds, 322-325
  cyclical relation, 376
  default structure, 112-116
  geographic structure, 120-121
  international differentials, 216
  money market, 160-161
  on mortgages, 302-304
  risk structure, 112-116
  on state and local government obligations, 275
  tax structure, 118-120
  term structure, 105-108
    empirical evidence, 109-112
Intermediaries, financial, 39

Internal rate of return (IRR) The rate of

INDEX

discount which makes the present value of the stream of future dollar returns plus the terminal value of the asset equal to the current market price of the asset. If the asset is a security held to maturity, IRR is called yield to maturity. The internal rate of return varies inversely with the current market price of the asset.
International Bank for Reconstruction and Development ("World" Bank), 213
International Monetary Fund (IMF), 213
Interregional flows of funds, 143
Intermediation:
  degree of, 232–234
  by financial institutions, 40–42
Internal versus external financing, 392
Investment   Conversion of money to assets. In economics, the word usually means the acquisition of real assets such as plant and equipment, etc. In finance, the word is often used more broadly to also include the acquisition of financial assets.
  determinants of, 24–34
Investment banker   An individual or firm of individuals (traditionally in partnership form but now increasingly often as corporations) which arranges long-term financial transactions for customers. The traditional transaction is raising capital, which may involve underwriting such sales, but the negotiation of mergers, planning reorganizations, investing pension funds and financial advising are frequent services. Investment bankers also may bid for securities in open competitive sales.
Investment banks:
  as marketers of corporate bonds, 318–321
  as marketers of state and local government obligations. 268–273
Investment companies, 55–56, 332
IRR   Internal rate of return.

Jacobs, D. P., 37n.
Jen, F. C., 117, 118
Jensen, M., 98–100, 401, 402
Jones, L. D., 49n.
Jorgenson, D. W., 29
Junior mortgages, 285

Kessel, R. A., 110, 111
Keyner, J. M., 23
"Kickers" (see Equity "kickers")
Kuznets, P. W., 29

Lags in monetary effects, 371
Life insurance companies, 49–51
  in mortgage market, 291
Linear relationship of risk and return, 93–96
Lintner, J., 81n.
Liquidity management:
  commercial banks, 136–138, 174
  corporations, 131–134
  U.S. Treasury, 134–135
Listing requirements for stocks, 350
Lovell, M. C., 29
Ludlke, J., 37n.

M_1, M_2, and M_3 Definitions of money supply of increasing comprehension.
M_1 Demand deposits and currency owned by nonbanks.
M_2 M_1 + commercial bank time deposits less large NCDs.
M_3 M_2 + deposits of other savings intermediaries.
McGouldrick, P. F., 33
Maisel, S. J., 32
Malkiel, B. G., 109
Market portfolio   All risky securities that actually exist in the market, and in proportions that actually exist. An individual holds the market portfolio when the percentage composition of his portfolio is identical to the percentage composition of all risky securities in the market. In security pricing theory, the market portfolio is the optimum portfolio of risky securities for all investors. 94–96
Markowitz, H. M., 81n.
Martin, William McChesney, 190
Martin report, 357
Matched sale-purchase contracts (see Repurchase agreements)
Matrix:
  financial market, 238
  money market, 132–133
Maturity   The date when repayment of the principal of a debt instrument is due; also refers to the span of time between issue or purchase and ultimate maturity. Original maturity is the period of time between the issuing date and the maturity date. Term or period to maturity is the period of time remaining before an instrument matures. Maturities can range from as short as one day to as long as several decades, depending on the type of instrument.
  debt instruments, 128
  as a factor in interest rates, 102–112
  (See also Term structure of interest rates)
Meiselman, D., 109
Meltzer, A. H., 119
MGIC   Mortgage Guarantee and Insurance Corporation. A private mortgage insurance agency "Maggie Mae." 301, 389
Mills, R. H., 116
Modigliani, F., 24, 109
Monetarism, 371–372
Monetary aggregates (see M_1, M_2, and M_3)
Money   Broadly defined, money is any liquid store of value. Narrowly defined, money is a medium of exchange (or means of payment). Financial assets which satisfy both definitions include currency and demand deposits. Instruments traded in the so-called money markets, while highly liquid, do not satisfy the medium of exchange definition of money (See also M_1, M_2, and M_3)
Money market instruments (see Agency securities; Bankers' acceptance; CD; Commercial paper; Eurodollar; Fed funds; Treasury securities)
Money markets   Financial markets where credit instruments, with maturities of less than one year, are traded. The principal money market

instruments are Treasury bills, securities of U.S. Government agencies, repurchase agreements, federal funds, commercial paper, negotiable certificates of deposit, Eurodollars, and bankers' acceptances.
  foreign participation, 135–136
Money-rate risk   Possibility that an investor will realize a lower yield than indicated when a credit instrument was purchased due to interest rate changes. An investor may receive a smaller return from a sale of a credit instrument before final maturity in the secondary markets than he had originally expected, even if the borrower pays exactly as he promised.
Mortgage banker   A financial intermediary who makes or "originates" mortgages and then sells them to ultimate investors. Mortgage bankers often continue to collect the payments on the mortgage they have originated (i.e., to "service" them). 281, 295–296
Mortgage insurance:
  private, 301–302
  public, 298
Mossin, J., 81n.
Multinational corporations, 215
Multiple expansion (of deposits)   Process by which the commercial banking system is able to expand its loans, securities, and deposits by a multiple of any increase in reserves supplied to it by the central bank. The process of multiple expansion is based on the fractional reserve system. Since the commercial banking system is required to keep only a fraction of its deposits in the form of reserves, the corollary is that deposits will be a multiple of reserves. 14
Municipal bonds (*see* **State and local government securities**), 259
Muth, R. E., 32
Mutual funds, 55–56
  (*See also* Investment companies)
Mutual savings banks, 47–48
  in mortgage market, 290

NASD   National Association of Security Dealers. Includes most investment bankers and other security houses active in the OTC market. 341, 356
NASDAQ   NASD automated quotation system; the computerized system of quotation of OTC securities (and also selected listed securities) sponsored by the NASD. 341, 362, 403
NCD   Negotiable certificates of deposit 395, 407
  (*See also* **CD**)
Neave, E., 37n.
Negotiated markets   Transactions between a single lender and a single borrower who, between them, personally bargain the terms of a loan. A loan transaction between a farmer and his banker is a negotiated transaction. The terms of the loan are usually tailor-made to fit the special circumstances of the case.
Net free or borrowed reserves   The difference between member bank borrowings from the Federal Reserve and excess reserves. If the difference is negative it is "net free reserves."
New issue market, 14, 347–348
New York, Federal Reserve Bank of, 183, 190, 191, 199
Nixon, Richard M., statement on security industry regulation, 345, 359–360
NYSE   New York Stock Exchange.
  as market for corporate bonds, 321
  as market for equities, 328–338
  self-regulation, 356–358
  Odd-lot transactions, 352–353
One-bank holding companies, 412–413
Open-market operations, discovery, 188
Open markets   A market open to all qualified participants. The number of buyers and sellers is large enough that prices are determined impersonally by the forces of supply and demand. The open market involves audible and/or visible price quotations so that uniform securities tend to be traded at uniform prices. Open-market prices and rates are quoted daily in the financial press. 18
Optimum combination of securities (*see* **Efficient portfolio**)
OTC   "Over-the-counter" market for securities which is really over the telephone or teletype. 362, 413, 415
  as market for corporate bonds, 321
  as market for corporate equities, 328, 340–341
Ott, D. J., 119
Paper-work problem, 337
Par value   The stated or face value of a security; usually also the final principal payment of a debt instrument at maturity. It differs from market value as the market rate of interest differs from the coupon rate of interest. Bonds sell below par (at a discount) when the market rate is above the coupon rate, and they sell above par (at a premium) when the market rate is below the coupon rate. Variations of market value from par value are larger the longer the period to maturity. As a bond approaches maturity, market value approaches par value.
Pension funds:
  as buyers of corporate bonds, 317
  government, 54–55
  growth, 384–386
  private, 53
Peterson, J. E., 33, 34
Phelps, C. D., 33
PMIA   Private Mortgage Insurance Agency (*see* **MGIC**)
Polakoff, M. E., 37n.
Pollution control revenue bonds (tax-exempt), 272
Present value   Current worth of future returns, computed by discounting future returns at an appropriate rate of interest. A dollar today is worth more than a dollar in the future; the present value of a dollar in the future is therefore less than a full dollar. The more distant the future return, and the higher the appropriate rate of discount, the less the present value of the return.

INDEX

Primary markets Financial markets in which financial assets and liabilities are created; also called "new issue" markets. A primary market is a market for newly issued securities as opposed to a secondary market which is a market for securities already outstanding. When a corporation goes into debt by issuing bonds it sells them in the primary market. Primary markets, or new-issue markets, add to the flow of saving and investment.

Prime loan rate The rate publicly announced or "posted" by a bank as the one charged to its best customers for short-term credit. 165–166, 407

Public housing obligations, 273
Public Utility Holding Company Act of 1935, 314
Pye, G., 117, 118*n*., 119

Quantity theory (*see* Monetarism)

Real assets The stocks of houses, factories, machines, inventories, etc. which exist at a point in time and which yield real productive services over time. Real assets constitute the wealth of society. 4

Real interest rates, 371

Real investment The acquisition of real assets over a period of time. Real investment includes expenditures for housing, plant and equipment, inventories, and human capital. These expenditures do not take place in financial markets but are often financed with funds secured from financial markets. estimates of, 227

Real saving and investment (*see* specific entries on saving and investment)

Real wealth, 10
(*See also* **Real assets**)

Rediscount A further discounting of a credit obligation that has already been discounted one or more times. Its most common usage referred to transactions in which a Federal Reserve bank rediscounted a loan that had already been discounted by a member bank. Such transactions have become uncommon but the term is still used (loosely) to refer to member bank borrowings from a Federal Reserve bank.

Refunding, U.S. Treasury debt, 245
Regulation:
 corporate equity markets, 345–360
 credit for stock purchases, 354–355
 value of, 416

Regulation ("Reg") Q Limits the rate of interest that may be paid on time and savings deposits by member banks. 149, 170–171, 289, 406–407

REIT Real Estate Investment Trust, 283, 294–295, 389

Repurchase agreements direct and reverse, 154–155
(*See also* **RP**)

Reserve requirements, 188
Reserves, secondary, 250
Residential construction, determinants of, 29–32
"Rest of the World" Used in flow-of-funds accounting to lump into one sector all financial sectors outside continental United States. "Rest of the World" embraces more than just "other nations" since it also includes international financial institutions such as the IMF and the World Bank.

Retail banking Transactions with customers of smaller means: small checking accounts, consumer credit, the holding of savings deposits, or the sale of certificates of deposit in small amounts to individuals.

Revaluation An increase in the command of a currency either on gold or, more recently, on SDRs.

Revenue bonds (state and local government obligations), 271

Risk The possibility of an adverse outcome to an event. Its application in this text is mainly adverse outcomes to investment activities. (*see* **Credit risk**)
 calculation of, 84
 and interest rates, 101–102
 linear relationship, 93–96
 relation to expected return, 83

Risk aversion Attitude that most investors have toward risk, which is: less risk is preferred to more risk, all other things being the same. A risk-averse investor will assume more risk only if other things are not the same, such as if he expects to earn a sufficiently higher rate of return on his investment.

Risk-free rate of return The IRR of a security having what is believed to be a certain or invariate outcome. The best example of a risk-free rate of return is the yield on short-term Treasury securities such as Treasury bills. 91

Risk premium The difference between the rate of return on a risky security and the risk-free rate of return. The risk premium is the reward for incurring risk. The greater the risk, the greater the risk premium.

Risk structure of interest rates (*see* Default structure of interest rates)
Robinson, R. I., 45
Roll, R., 99, 111
Roosa, Robert J., 157*n*., 202

RP Repurchase agreement. A simultaneous sale of securities together with a contract to repurchase them at a fixed date and at a price which provides an agreed rate of interest. "Reverse" RPs or "matched sale and purchase" agreements are the same type of transaction; the initial seller (usually the "Fed") originates the transaction. 139

RPD Reserves to support private deposits. The newest and apparently leading guide to the monetary actions of the Fed. 191, 195, 204

S&Ls Savings and loan associations.
St. Louis, Federal Reserve Bank of, 199
Saving Income not spent on consumption. Saving is a source of capital funds which can

be used to acquire assets, real and financial, or for the repayment of debt. When all accounts are consolidated, saving is the ultimate source of real capital.
 determinants of, 21–24
 employment of, 38
 and investment, equality of, 9
 real, estimates, 227
Savings and loan associations, 48–49
 in mortgage market, 287
 stock, 289
Schaaf, A. H., 121
SDRs Special drawing rights. Issued by the International Monetary Fund. They may be used to settle transactions among members of the IMF in the same way gold may be used; indeed they have been called "paper gold." 220
SEC Securities and Exchange Commission, 358, 416, 417
Securities dealers (*SML*)
 (*see* **Secondary markets**)
Secondary markets Those financial markets in which existing financial assets are sold by one owner to another. A secondary market is a market for securities already outstanding as opposed to a primary market which is a market for newly issued securities. Secondary markets are the "used car lots" of the financial world. Their purpose is to enable portfolio adjustments. The best known secondary market is the New York Stock Exchange. 11–12, 17
 for corporate bonds, 321
 for corporate equities, 328–331
 for mortgages, 299
 for state and local government securities, 273–275
 for U.S. Treasury obligations, 254–255
Securities market line, 96–99
 and mutual fund performance, 99–100
Security dealers, U.S. government, 156–159
 bankers acceptances, 160
 commercial paper, 160
Segmented-market theory of the term structure of interest rates, 108–109
Self-regulation of securities markets, 348–349, 356
Serial bonds:
 rail-equipment obligations, 270, 312–313
 state and local government, 269
Sharpe, W. F., 81*n*., 96, 98, 99
Shaw, E. S., 373
Short position One in which an investor (more often thought of as a speculator) has sold an asset he does not own, has borrowed the asset to make delivery of it, and therefore is obligated to repurchase or otherwise reacquire the asset for ultimate return to the owner from whom he borrowed the asset.
Short sales, 16
Sinking funds, 313
Sloane, P. E., 115
SML Security market line. Equilibrium relationship between the expected rate of return and risk (measured by the beta coefficient) for individual securities and for portfolios, efficient and inefficient. The *SML* is believed by some theorists to be a straight line. The slope of the line is the extra expected return per unit of risk; the intercept is the risk-free rate of return. The *SML* is more general than the *CML* in that it describes risk-return relations for all securities and all portfolios. 97
Smith, Paul F., 37*n*.
SOMA System Open Market Account, 138, 197–207
 manager, 199
Sources and uses of funds, nonfinancial corporations, 308
 (*See also* Flow-of-funds accounting)
Sparks, G., 32
Special Drawing Rights (SDRs), 220
Specialist on organized exchanges, 336, 349–350
Speculation, corporate equities, 341–344
Sprinkel, B. W., 8*n*.
State and local government securities Debt instruments issued by states, cities, school districts or any of the 90,000 governmental units below the federal level. The distinctive feature of these securities is that their coupon income is exempt from the income taxation of the Federal government, and usually of the state in which issued. They are not exempt from capital gains taxation. These securities have sometimes been described as "municipal" bonds. 259–276
Stock market, as a leading indicator, 378
Stone, B. K., 81*n*.
Strong, Ben, 183, 190, 191
Strotz, R. H., 29
Sutch, R., 109
Syndicate A group of investment bankers organized to share in the risk of selling a security to the public. The leader of a syndicate is its manager; most, but not necessarily all, of the members are involved in the selling effort.
 organization, 268–269
Systematic risk Deviation of realized from expected return on an efficient portfolio due to the tendency for rates of return on individual securities and portfolios to move with the rate of return on the market as a whole. A measure of systematic risk is given by the beta coefficient. Movements in rates of return which cannot be explained by movements in the market as a whole fall in the category of unsystematic risk.

TABs Tax anticipation bills mature a few days after one of the quarterly tax payment dates. Since they can be used to pay taxes on the tax payment date they give their holders a slightly better yield when used for this purpose. 253
Tax-exempt obligations:
 in commercial banks, 168–169
 short term, 151–152

INDEX

Tax-exempt securities (*see* **State and local government securities**)
Tax exemptions of interest income, 264
Tax structure of interest rates, 118-120
Term loan A loan of intermediate maturity, mainly made by commercial banks and generally to corporate borrowers.
Term to maturity (or period to maturity) The remaining period of time before a debt instrument comes due. A ten-year bond issued four years ago has a remaining period to maturity of six years.
Term structure of interest rates The functional relation between yield to maturity and term to maturity. Graphically, this relation is called the yield curve. 105-112
 empirical evidence, 109-112
Theories of interest rates, 102-112
Third market, 339-340
Time deposits, 170
T&L Tax and loan accounts kept by the Treasury Department.
 in commercial banks, 243-244, 247
Tobin, J., 81*n*.
Treasury securities, 147-148, 240-258
Treynor, J. L., 99
Trust Indenture Act of 1939, 312
Truth-in-Lending Act, 391

Underwriting Guarantee of the sale of a financial obligation. Formal contracts by investment bankers to corporations selling securities provide that the investment bankers will themselves buy the securities at the selected date of issue if they fail to sell them to others by that time. Informal underwriting also takes place when U.S. government security dealers, by informal understanding but not by contract, bid for large enough a volume of new issues to assure the sale of all of an issue offered by the Treasury Department. 247
U.S. government security dealers, 254-255
Unsystematic risk The tendency for rates of return on individual securities and portfolios to move independently of general price movements in the market. Unsystematic risk can be reduced through diversification. The market portfolio is a fully diversified portfolio and therefore contains no elements of unsystematic risk.
Uses of funds Real or financial investment. In accounting terms, a use of funds is any increase in assets or any decrease in liabilities and net worth.

VA Veterans Administration, which guarantees (not insures) mortgages given by qualifying applicant veterans of the armed forces. 285, 297, 298, 388
Volatility of interest rates, 122*n*.
VRM Variable rate mortgage, 389

Wallace, N., 109
Wealth The assets of an economic unit, real and financial, minus its liabilities. Wealth is synonymous with net worth. The wealth of the world consists of real assets only; financial assets are cancelled out by an equal amount of liabilities. Any smaller economic unit, including a nation, may have a portion of its wealth in net holdings of financial assets.
Weber, W. E., 22*n*.
Welfling, W., 47*n*.
Wert, J. E., 117, 118
Wholesale money markets, 130, 142
Winnick, L., 120
Working capital, 307
World Bank The International Bank for Reconstruction and Development, which together with the International Monetary Fund were the institutions created at the end of World War II to regularize international monetary and credit relationships. Early emphasis was on postwar reconstruction but recent emphasis has been almost wholly on the development of relatively underdeveloped countries. 213
Wright, C., 22*n*.
Wrightsman, D., 53*n*.

Yield The rate of discount which makes the present value of the stream of future dollar returns plus the terminal value of the asset equal to the current market price of the asset. (*see* **Internal rate of return**)
Yield curve Describes graphically the relationship between yield to maturity and term to maturity (or period to maturity). The curve depicts yields as a function of maturity for otherwise homogeneous securities. The slope and shape of a yield curve change as market conditions and expectations about market conditions change.
Yield to maturity The rate of discount which makes the present value of the stream of future interest payments, plus the return of principal at maturity, equal to the current market price of the debt instrument. It is the internal rate of return (IRR) on a debt instrument held to maturity.